THE LIFE

OF

WILLIAM STERNDALE BENNETT

BY HIS SON

J. R. STERNDALE BENNETT

M.A. ST JOHN'S COLLEGE, CAMBRIDGE
FELLOW OF KING'S COLLEGE, LONDON

Travis & Emery Music Bookshop

James Robert Sterndale Bennett

The Life
Of
William Sterndale Bennett

Facsimile of 1907 edition.

First published Cambridge University Press 1907.

Republished Travis & Emery 2010.

Published by
Travis & Emery Music Bookshop
17 Cecil Court, London, WC2N 4EZ, United Kingdom.
(+44) 20 7240 2129
neworders@travis-and-emery.com

ISBN Hardback: 978-1-84955-062-8   Paperback: 978-1-84955-063-5

WILLIAM STERNDALE BENNETT

1816—1875

CAMBRIDGE UNIVERSITY PRESS WAREHOUSE,
C. F. CLAY, Manager.
London: FETTER LANE, E.C.
Glasgow: 50, WELLINGTON STREET.

Leipzig: F. A. BROCKHAUS.
New York: G. P. PUTNAM'S SONS.
Bombay and Calcutta: MACMILLAN AND CO., Ltd.

[All Rights reserved.]

SIR W. STERNDALE BENNETT
AET. LVI

FROM AN ENGRAVING BY T. OLDHAM BARLOW, A.R.A.
OF A PORTRAIT BY SIR JOHN E. MILLAIS, BART., P.R.A.

THE LIFE

OF

WILLIAM STERNDALE BENNETT

BY HIS SON

J. R. STERNDALE BENNETT

M.A. ST JOHN'S COLLEGE, CAMBRIDGE
FELLOW OF KING'S COLLEGE, LONDON

CAMBRIDGE:
AT THE UNIVERSITY PRESS
1907

Cambridge:
PRINTED BY JOHN CLAY, M.A.
AT THE UNIVERSITY PRESS.

TO

ELIZABETH DONN CASE
DAUGHTER OF
WILLIAM STERNDALE BENNETT

November 4, 1907

PREFACE

IN 1881, the seventh year after my father's death, I began to collect the materials with which his biography, if thereafter required, might be constructed. He had died in his 59th year. Many who had known him in youth long survived him, and were, at the time to which I refer, readily accessible. His aunt, Mrs Glasscock, his senior by only thirteen years, was still living and could tell me of his childhood. His early friends, Davison and Macfarren, the one orally, the other in writing, recounted, with loving interest, their reminiscences of his student days. The extent of their aid, and of the aid given by others who have long since passed away, will, I hope, manifest itself in the following pages, wherein, I believe, the sources of these old memories are, in almost all cases, clearly shown.

For much other valuable help rendered at various times and in a variety of ways, I take this chance of recording my great obligations to Mr W. Crowther Alwyn, Mr J. C. Beazley, Mr P. V. M. Benecke, Sir Frederick Bridge, Mr J. S. Bumpus, Miss H. M. Burningham, Mrs Robert Burrows, Mr H. Entwisle Bury, Mr George Case, Mr W. S. Case, Mr A. D. Coleridge, Mr C. H. Couldery, Miss Frances Cox, Dr Eaton Faning, Mr J. A. Fuller Maitland, Dr Gensel, Herr Gustav Jansen, Mr S. B. Kemp, Miss Julia Kennedy, Rev. W. T. Kingsley, Rev. Canon

Kynaston, D.D., Rev. J. R. Luxmoore, Mr Arthur O'Leary, Mr Oliver Notcutt, Mrs Rupert Owen, Mr Louis N. Parker, Mr R. Peyton, Mr D. W. Rootham, Mr W. Shakespeare, Mr C. E. Sparrow, Mr Fred. R. Spark, Mr W. Barclay Squire, Sir Charles V. Stanford, Mr W. C. Stockley, Dr Hans Voigt and Miss Wageman.

By the permission and with the sympathetic assistance of the Mendelssohn Bartholdy family, the letters which passed between my father and his illustrious friend became available. The late Mrs Benecke herself translated those of her father's letters which he wrote in German. For similarly valued permissions I have to thank Miss Rose G. Kingsley, Fraülein Marie Schumann, Lord Tennyson, Herr F. A. Brockhaus and Mr Paul David. I have gratefully received the sanction (1) of Messrs Macmillan and Co. to quote from Miss Bettina Walker's *My Musical Experiences*, (2) of Messrs Kegan Paul, Trench Trubner and Co. to quote from the *Life of Dr Whewell*, by Mrs Stair Douglas, (3) of Mr Wm. Reeves to use F. R. Ritter's translations of Schumann's criticisms, and (4) of Messrs Keene of Derby to reproduce their versions of old pictures which face pp. 29, 158, 209. Mr T. J. Wright, of Westminster, most kindly contributed a photograph, which after long patience he secured, of my father's grave in a dark corner of the Abbey.

Mr W. T. Freemantle, without regard to the interests of his own literary projects, unreservedly placed at my disposal, not only his unique knowledge of Sheffield in the past, but also his valuable collection of musical treasures relating to the period in which my father lived.

Preface

To consult the Minute-books of the Royal Academy of Music, and to use a few extracts therefrom, I obtained the authority of Sir George Macfarren when he was Chairman of the Committee of Management. Mr Kellow J. Pye, Chairman, at an earlier time, of the same Committee, placed interesting correspondence in my hands. Some of my references to the Royal Academy of Music and the Philharmonic Society of London are drawn from Histories of those Institutions written respectively by Cazalet and Hogarth.

When time was given me to write this *Life*, then also came the privilege of discussing it, chapter by chapter, with my revered friend, the late Otto Goldschmidt. His persistent yet gentle pressure never failed to direct my faltering steps. While revising my manuscript for publication, I gained great advantage from the criticisms and suggestions of the President of Corpus Christi College, Oxford.

J. R. S. B.

THE ATHENAEUM,
   PALL MALL,
      November 1907.

CONTENTS

PART I

CHILDHOOD, EDUCATION AND VISITS TO GERMANY
1816–39

CHAP.		PAGE
I	PARENTAGE AND CHILDHOOD, TO 1826	3
II	SCHOOL-DAYS, 1826–33	12
III	ADVANCED STUDENTSHIP, 1833–36	31
IV	LEIPZIG, 1836–37	44
V	LONDON AND, AGAIN, LEIPZIG, 1837–39	63

PART II

A YOUNG MUSICIAN IN LONDON
1839–47

VI	PORTLAND CHAMBERS, 1839–41	83
VII	COMPOSITION IN PORTLAND CHAMBERS, 1839–41	95
VIII	HESSE-CASSEL, LEIPZIG, BERLIN, 1842	115
IX	THE PHILHARMONIC SOCIETY. THE MUSICAL SEASON OF 1842	132
X	CORRESPONDENCE WITH MENDELSSOHN, 1842–43	145
XI	MARRIAGE. CORRESPONDENCE CONTINUED, 1844–46	155
XII	THE UNFORESEEN STROKE. DEATH OF MENDELSSOHN, 1846–47	169

PART III

A HARSH REBUFF. QUIET SPHERES OF ARTISTIC USEFULNESS
1848–55

CHAP.		PAGE
XIII	Rupture with Costa and the Philharmonic Society. Occupations as a Teacher, 1848	183
XIV	The Bach Society. Chamber Concerts, 1849–55	202
XV	Correspondence with the Schumanns. Great Exhibition of 1851. Revival of the Philharmonic Trouble. Conductorship of Gewandhaus Concerts. Production of Bach's 'Passions-Musik,' 1850–55	218

PART IV

CALLED TO THE FRONT
1855–66

XVI	Public Appointments, 1855–56	241
XVII	The Cambridge Professorship	256
XVIII	Difference with the Philharmonic Directors. Bach Society. The Earl of Westmorland and the R.A. of Music, 1856–58	273
XIX	Leeds Festival. 'The May Queen,' 1858	285
XX	The Chorale Book for England, 1859–62	291
XXI	His Position at the Philharmonic assured. Withdrawal of the Society's Orchestra, 1859–61	294
XXII	The International Exhibition of 1862, 1861–62	303
XXIII	A Year of Contrasting Imports. Installation of the Chancellor at Cambridge. Jubilee of the Philharmonic Society. Domestic Bereavement, 1862	318
XXIV	He faces Sorrow. A Symphony in G Minor. Visit to Leipzig. The Professorship of Music at Edinburgh. He resigns the Philharmonic Conductorship, 1862–66	329

Contents xiii

PART V

REPAYMENT OF A DEBT TO ALMA MATER
1866–75

CHAP.		PAGE
XXV	The Royal Academy of Music. Bennett is appointed Principal, 1866–67	347
XXVI	Cambridge Professorship. 'The Woman of Samaria,' 1867	361
XXVII	A Crisis at the R.A. of Music, 1867–68	369
XXVIII	Cambridge Local Examinations. Additions to 'The Woman of Samaria.' Associations with Germany. Uppingham School, 1868	376
XXIX	Government Grant restored to the R.A. of Music. The R.A. of Music and the Society of Arts, 1868–69	384
XXX	Compositions. Some Circumstances of his Private Life, 1869–70	389
XXXI	Bennett with the Academy Students, 1866–74	394
XXXII	Honours and Rewards, 1870–72	407
XXXIII	Compositions. The R.A. of Music and the Albert Hall, 1872–73	417
XXXIV	Some Personal Characteristics	422
XXXV	Last Days, 1873–75	440

APPENDIX

A Notes
   (1) Annals of the Bach Society 451
   (2) Bennett placed among the opponents of Chopin . . 451
   (3) On the order in which Schumann reviewed some of Bennett's works 453
   (4) The production, in 1856, of Schumann's 'Paradise and The Peri' by The Philharmonic Society 454

B List of Published and MSS. Works, according to date of composition—with references to the pages where they are mentioned in this book 455

C List of Published Works, according to their Opus Numbers . 461

D Table of Compositions, showing the amount produced at successive periods of his life 463

Index 465

LIST OF ILLUSTRATIONS

	PAGE
SIR W. STERNDALE BENNETT. In his fifty-seventh year. From a portrait by Sir John E. Millais, Bart. . . . *Frontispiece*	
WILLIAM STERNDALE BENNETT. When (about) sixteen years old. From a water-colour drawing by Child . . . . *to face*	29
PORTLAND CHAMBERS. Great Titchfield Street, London . *to face*	95
THE GEWANDHAUS CONCERT ROOM, LEIPZIG . . . *to face*	131
MRS W. STERNDALE BENNETT. From a water-colour drawing *to face*	158
LETTER, IN FACSIMILE, MENDELSSOHN TO BENNETT . . .	159
LETTER, IN FACSIMILE, BENNETT TO MENDELSSOHN . . .	160
EXTRACT FROM OVERTURE TO 'THE MAY QUEEN' . . *to face*	164
LETTER, IN FACSIMILE, FROM BENNETT TO LUCAS . *between pp.* 190–191	
WILLIAM STERNDALE BENNETT. When (about) thirty-five years old. From a Daguerreotype, said to have been taken in 1851 *to face*	209
PLAY BILL OF PRIVATE THEATRICALS	226
'THE GILBERT ARMS,' EASTBOURNE. From a water-colour drawing by W. Chalmers Masters (musician) . . . . *to face*	287
PAGE OF A LETTER, IN FACSIMILE, WRITTEN BY BENNETT, TO SOUTHAMPTON. Addressee Unknown . . . . *to face*	352
THE NORTH CHOIR AISLE, WESTMINSTER ABBEY . . *to face*	450

PART I

CHILDHOOD, EDUCATION, AND VISITS TO GERMANY

CHAPTER I.

PARENTAGE AND CHILDHOOD.

—1826.
—æt. 9.

WILLIAM STERNDALE BENNETT was born at Sheffield on Easter Eve, April 13, 1816. He came of a musical family. His father, Robert Bennett, was an organist; his grandfather, John Bennett, was a singer and a hautboy-player; moreover, his forefathers, for some generations back, dwelt in a district noted for song.

Their home was at Ashford-in-the-water, a village situate 'in the sweetest and most sylvan part of the Peak of Derbyshire.' The neighbourhood reverberated with music, and that not only of a local or traditional kind; for in the larger churches, such as those of Bakewell and Tideswell, the Services and Anthems of England's church-composers and the Choruses of Handel were, in the latter part of the eighteenth century, well known and sung with enthusiasm. Singers and choir-leaders of exceptional ability were held in high repute, as is shown on the gravestones in many a churchyard. It is related that on a day when the beautiful Duchess of Devonshire was at Court, and was extolling the Derbyshire singing, George III seemed a little sceptical, and hinted at the proverbial partiality which the lady had for the county in which she resided. Thereupon, Her Grace sent off to Tideswell, and one Samuel Slack was brought up to sing before the King. The first sounds of his voice electrified the Royal group, and as the performance went on, the Duchess, radiant at the effect produced and at the success of her experiment, triumphantly waved her handkerchief at the King from across the room. In 1791, this same Slack competed for a lay-clerkship at Cambridge in the one choir which served for the chapels of the three colleges, King's, St John's and Trinity. At the trial, the judges, when they heard him sing, said that it would be waste of time to call up the other candidates. He was elected, but in less than a year had resigned, and another singer of 'The Peak,' in the person of John Bennett (Sterndale Bennett's grandfather), who was also the possessor of an exceptionally fine bass voice, had been chosen to succeed him.

John Bennett left Derbyshire, and entered upon his new duties at Cambridge, early in 1792. He was then thirty-seven years old, but he remained on the active list for another thirty-seven years, retiring, at the age of seventy-four, with a pension from each of the three colleges. Three of his sons had died in infancy; but he brought up five others, four daughters, and, afterwards, three orphan grand-children. The removal to Cambridge gave good opportunity for the sons of a poor man to make the first start on a musical career. His eldest son, William, had already shown aptitude as a performer on all kinds of instruments, and worked on till he became a military bandmaster. His sixth and third surviving son, Robert (baptized at Bakewell, Feb. 8, 1788), was placed at eight years of age in the choir of King's College[1]; another son, Thomas (afterwards lay-clerk and master of the choristers' school at Ely), starting life in the same way. Both brothers became solo-singers in the Chapel, and, on leaving, received the sums of £5. 12s. 6d., and £5. 0s. 8d., as 'box-money' to help them on their way, these amounts being in excess of that given to most of the choristers. At the age of 16, Robert (Sterndale Bennett's father) was placed under Dr Clarke Whitfeld, at that time organist of St John's and Trinity Colleges, and afterwards Professor of Music in the University. With that eminent musician he remained for seven years; first, as an articled pupil; and, later, as a student of composition and assistant at the Trinity organ.

[1] The same *lay-clerks* sang at the three colleges; but King's had a set of choristers and an organist of its own, while St John's and Trinity shared between them a second organist and a second set of choristers.

At the end of the sixth year under Dr Clarke Whitfeld, he competed, in 1810, for the important post of organist at Sheffield parish church. The judges specially commended his performance, but preferred another candidate. The latter resigned within a twelvemonth, and the post was then offered to Robert without further trial, his election taking place on June 10, 1811.

A young man of energy and activity,—words used by nearly all who, in after years, were asked to describe him,— he was not long in securing full occupation. Within a year he was able to take a wife, and on May 28, 1812, married Elizabeth Donn of Cambridge. Her father, James Donn, had been a pupil of William Aulton, the King's gardener at Kew, from which place he, Donn, had gone to Cambridge as Curator of the Botanic Gardens. The issue of printed leaflets, giving lists of plants which he wished members of the University to bring him from different parts of the country, led him, by degrees, to the publication of an elaborate book, which, under the title of *Hortus Cantabrigiensis*, went through six editions in his life-time, and seven more, under various editors, during the thirty-seven years after his death. He was elected a member of the Linnæan Society, and he made a name for himself, as a botanist, which is not entirely forgotten, a little space having been found for him in the *Dictionary of National Biography*. From his maternal grandfather, Sterndale Bennett inherited much of his personal appearance, perhaps also that love of order which distinguished them both alike, and certainly a sum of money the usefulness of which will presently appear.

Robert Bennett, on his marriage with James Donn's daughter, took a house in Howard Street, Sheffield, and in that house his three eldest children were born. His ability and his genial disposition brought him into great favour. As organist of the parish church, 'he discharged the duties of his office in a manner highly satisfactory to the congregation, and creditable to himself..., he successfully cultivated a style of playing, remarkably chaste and graceful, admirably adapted to the sanctity of the temple, and the solemnity of the service. He uniformly displayed a considerable degree of taste; but in pathetically plaintive music there were few who could surpass him[1].' He was not only an organist, but also a busy pianoforte teacher, and his wife wrote to Cambridge that his work left him 'scarcely any time for his meals.' A lady, at whose father's house he dined every week, on one of his country rounds, wrote that he had 'the first course of teaching with private pupils and at the boarding-schools' throughout the Sheffield district. He also taught at Bakewell, whither he rode on horseback across the moors from Sheffield. Then, again, he was to the front in all the music of the town, whether in private society or in the concert room. He was one of a set of good musicians then resident in Sheffield, who combined for the general good. Wageman, a Dutch portrait-painter, has left a highly finished pencil-sketch of the four Sheffield organists, and three or four of the best amateurs, in the enjoyment of a musical meeting. In Madrigal and Glee Societies, Robert found his place, as a trained singer with a beautiful tenor voice. His solo-singing, refined in style and full of intense feeling, was the special gift which remained longest in the memory of his friends, as the writer has been told by their descendants. He was appointed one of the musical Directors of the Yorkshire Choral Concerts, which were held at York, Sheffield, and other important places in the county. The programmes of these concerts are difficult to obtain; but, if the announcement of a single one—at which 'Alexander's Feast' was to be sung, and the instrumental pieces were to be chosen from the works of Haydn, Mozart, and Beethoven—may be taken as a type, it would seem that Yorkshire, in its taste not only for vocal but also for orchestral music, was sound and abreast of the times. As regards Beethoven, there is a tradition in Sheffield musical families that one of his Symphonies was played at these Yorkshire concerts for the first time in England. Robert also gave annual concerts of his own, for the first of which the famous singer, Mrs Salmon, was engaged. Another incident in his life was the directing of a festival performance of 'The Messiah' in Bakewell church, for which occasion his father, John, came from Cambridge to sing the bass solos.

[1] From an obituary notice in *The Sheffield Iris*, a paper edited by James Montgomery, the sacred poet.

Amongst his intimate friends at Sheffield must be mentioned: William Howard, an amateur violinist who later possessed the 'Stradivarius' that had belonged to Salomon; the Rev. Thomas Cotterill, who sought his constant assistance in the compilation of a Psalmody; and John Sterndale, a surgeon, whose wife and sons were well known as artists and authors. One son, William, supplied Robert with words for a set of *Six Songs*, which were published, and dedicated to the Duke of Devonshire. The following note appeared on the copies :—

'The Composer of the annexed Melodies cannot allow this opportunity to pass without expressing his acknowledgments to those Friends who have favoured him with their support; amongst whom he must particularize Mr WILLIAM STERNDALE, to whose kindness he is indebted for the original words that accompany the Melodies.

Sheffield, June 30, 1815.'

So, in the next year, Robert conceived the happy idea of perpetuating the memory of this artistic partnership, by giving to his third child and only son the names of his friend. When William Sterndale Bennett was born, on April 13, 1816, his parents were living in Howard Street; but, soon after, they removed to a house in Norfolk Street, to which was attached an orchard and garden, where Mrs Robert was often seen playing with her children, and tending her flowers, as became the dutiful daughter of the Cambridge botanist. Such happiness, however, was of short duration. Two years passed, and after giving birth to a fourth child, she died, May 7, 1818, and was buried in Ecclesall churchyard, whither her infant daughter followed in a few days.

The child, William Sterndale, was put out to nurse at Darnall, a village a few miles out of the town, and Robert's youngest sister, Sarah, then fifteen years old, was sent from Cambridge to look after the elder children. For some time after her arrival, she did not see the little nephew to whom in later life she showed so much attachment. Of her first remembrance of him, she thus wrote in her eightieth year:

'After I had been at Sheffield a few months he was brought home to stay a day or two. When the evening of the first day came he cried to go home to his mother as he called his nurse; in order to see what he would do, he was dressed in his little coat and cap and he would have gone out in the dark to find his *mother* whom he loved so much. This happened when he was two years and seven months old, and showed the loving disposition which characterized him through life.'

Robert had now been at Sheffield for seven years. About this time he seized a chance of bettering his position by adopting the novel method of piano-teaching which Logier had lately introduced. This method had two striking features: the one, an apparatus called 'chiroplast' designed by Logier and patented by him in 1814; the other, a plan laid down for systematic class-teaching. If twelve or more children could, as was asserted, be taught conjointly not only as well but better than separately, then the pupil, the parent, and the professor might all have a share in the benefit. Robert visited London and Manchester in order to learn the method, and Logier must have been favourably impressed by him, or he would not have entrusted him with the education of his son Henry, who came to Sheffield as an articled pupil. A move was now made from Norfolk Street to Eyre Street, where a house was found with a room in it of sufficient dimensions to hold the pianos on which the pupils simultaneously performed, and also to admit of frequent exhibitions—a subsidiary but no insignificant feature of the system—before admiring parents. The Logierians, and Robert among them, learnt from their chief the art of compiling very alluring prospectuses.

Within a year of his first wife's death, Robert married Miss Harriet Blake of Sheffield. William Sterndale, now three years old, had returned home, and was giving the first signs of a musical bent by the interest which he took in the Logierian proceedings, readily assimilating the tunes which he heard, and probably, if one may judge from something that occurred later, gaining a little acquaintance with the key-board of a pianoforte. He was not, however, destined to be trained by a mechanical process, or to run the risk of exhibition as an infant prodigy. An otherwise sad fatality saved him. A few months after his second marriage, Robert's health broke down. Forced to leave his work in the hands of his partner, Rogers, he retired into the country, and, after an illness only long enough to exhaust his resources, died of consumption, Nov. 3, 1819, in the thirty-second year of his age. He was buried at Ecclesall by the side of his first wife. His possessions were dispersed. His musical manuscripts may have passed into the hands of his partner and were, perhaps, in course of time, not deemed worth preserving. Yet his published songs, though they may not have marked individuality, show grace and refinement, while the accompaniments are conceived with fancy and are the work of a well-trained musician. He sang the songs himself to the great delight of his hearers, but the title-pages of a second edition record that they were sung by more eminent vocalists[1]. His father possessed a fine portrait of him, painted in oils by Wageman, which still remains in the family.

On his death, the orphan children were received into the house of his friends, the Howards, who treated them with the most considerate kindness; but their grandfather, when communicated with, at once offered them a permanent home. They arrived at Cambridge in December, 1819, during a severe snow-storm. Their step-mother, who had accompanied them, returned to her own friends, and did not see them again.

John Bennett, now sixty-five years old, had lost, by the death of Robert, the one son out of many who had made a distinct step forward in the world. He had loved him for the amiability and gaiety of disposition which had endeared him to many friends both in Cambridge and Sheffield. He had been justified in hoping that Robert would become a Cathedral organist, which would have satisfied his highest ambition as a parent. Of musical distinction in the family, where could the hope be now? But for the personal loss some solace was at hand. From the first instant that John set eyes on his grandson, he was observed to be taking a fresh interest in life. It was not much that the little boy could do; but his aunt Sarah, in her old age, would recall the evening on which he arrived with his two sisters, and would try to imitate the child as he moved about the room,

---

[1] Public performances of them can be traced up to 1850, when Mrs John Wood sang one at a chamber concert given by Ernst and Hallé in Manchester.

pointing eagerly at the unfamiliar ornaments and pictures, and making friends with his relations.

That he prattled for some little time about his father, and sang around the house the tunes he had heard in the Logierian schoolroom, putting his own childish words to them, is all that is known of him until a day, in his fifth year, when his grandfather took him to King's College Chapel. There he heard Handel's 'Hallelujah' Chorus for the first time, and on his return home startled his relations by repeating portions of it on the piano with accuracy and precision. John Bennett went off next day to consult Gifford, who kept the chief music-shop in Cambridge, with the result that the boy took his first lessons from Miss Gifford, the music-seller's daughter. He made progress, and was later placed under William Nunn, but from the first he shrank from the notice which his attainments occasioned, giving early signs of a certain reluctance, which never left him, to unfold himself as a musician. At a juvenile party, while still a child, he was placed at the piano to play. A little girl, older than himself, who was present, always remembered the piteous appeal which he made, as he turned round on the revolving music-stool, to be let off, and to be allowed to play 'puss-in-the-corner' with the other children. At another house, as he grew a little older, he would sometimes play 'The Battle of Prague' and other pieces, but notwithstanding the prospect of the half-crown, with which his kind hostess invariably rewarded such performances, he could not always face the ordeal.

In his eighth year, he was admitted, on Feb. 17, 1824, to the choir of King's College, and he remained in it two years. John Pratt, the organist, was not impressed by him, and, according to a tradition in Cambridge, considered him a dull boy. Another officer of the college formed a different opinion. This was the Vice-Provost, the Rev. S. B. Vince, who in earlier days had admitted Robert Bennett to his intimate friendship, and who, after the Sheffield appointment, would seldom pass John Bennett's door without stopping to enquire after his friend or to have a look at Wageman's speaking portrait of him. When the orphans came to Cambridge he extended his interest to them, and, as time passed, watched the development of

William Sterndale's ability. In the spring of 1826, the Rev. Frederick Hamilton, who had recently been appointed resident Superintendent of the Royal Academy of Music, was on a visit to his friends in Cambridge. There he heard of little Bennett's talents from Mr Vince, who even went so far as to call him a 'prodigy.' The boy was summoned to the Vice-Provost's rooms, and Mr Hamilton then advised his being examined at the Royal Academy of Music. He was accordingly sent up to London, consigned to the care of his grandfather's friend, Mrs Taylor, by whom he was taken, on March 7, 1826, to the Academy house in Tenterden Street. Thus, on the point of completing his tenth year, William Sterndale Bennett was launched on his career in London.

CHAPTER II.

SCHOOL-DAYS.

1826—1833.
æt. 9—17.

THE Royal Academy of Music, instituted in 1822, began its work on the evening of Feb. 10, 1823, at No. 4 Tenterden Street, Hanover Square, formerly the town mansion of the Earl of Carnarvon. Lord Burghersh,—afterwards Earl of Westmorland,—the founder of the Institution, had recently gone to Florence, as British Envoy, and was therefore unable to see the firstfruits of his labours; but his colleagues corresponded with him, and no detail of what happened in his absence was too trivial to interest him. On the evening in question, 'the whole of the rooms on the two floors were lighted up, and the place was thoroughly warm, cheerful, and comfortable.' A Committee of Directors were presiding over an examination of candidates for admission on the foundation. The eleven professional examiners, amongst whom were Sir George Smart, Dr Crotch[1] (Principal of the Academy), Greatorex, Horsley, J. B. Cramer, and Shield, 'entered into their work with the greatest good humour, patience, attention, and kindness to the children, who of course were in general extremely alarmed.' After three such evenings, the examiners made their report, and the subscribers, who, as such, were members of the Corporation, gave their votes. Eleven boys and ten girls were elected on the foundation. They were promised residence in the house, and a musical education under the first Professors of the day, at the small cost of twenty guineas and in some cases fifteen guineas a year. The

---

[1] Dr Crotch was absent on the *first* evening of the examination.

name of W. H. Holmes, a Derbyshire boy, appeared first on the list, as nominee of the King, but most votes were given to H. A. M. Cooke (afterwards known as Grattan Cooke), who may have been less alarmed at the examination than the rest of the party. Son of the eminent Tom Cooke, he himself, in due course, reached fame as the chief Oboist, but also as the irrepressible wag, of the London orchestras. These two boys, Holmes and Cooke, will be mentioned later. The unsuccessful candidates were terribly disappointed, and room was shortly found for fifteen of them, who were glad to pay a higher fee of thirty-eight guineas for advantages hitherto unattainable in this country on such terms. The house was then full; but applications for possible vacancies became so numerous, that, in a year's time, when the first contract with parents expired, the Directors raised the fees all round to forty pounds, observing that if any of the first foundationers objected they might withdraw, since others were waiting to fill their places.

Most thoughtful provision was made for the general training of these young boarders. The Directors held the opinion that there existed no profession whose members were more exposed to every species of temptation than the one for which the pupils of the Academy were to be prepared; so that, in selecting a Headmaster or Lady Superior, they felt it 'an imperious duty' to scrutinize the character and abilities of those 'whose mind and manners, precepts and example, must have a material effect upon the future welfare of the children entrusted to their care.' The Rev. John Miles, Lecturer of St Michael's, Cornhill; the Rev. Frederick Hamilton, who had held a commission in the army and had fought at Waterloo, before taking Orders and becoming Chaplain to the Earl of Melbourne; the widow of Colonel Wade, a lady personally well known to some of the Directors; these were the officials appointed to reside in the house and to take charge of the young scholars. Hours—none too many—were apportioned to lessons other than musical; but the paramount idea was, that the children should be brought up under religious and refined influences. The Directors and their Ladies, for some years, made a point of visiting the house and taking notice of their protégés. Nor was it forgotten that childhood should as far as possible be passed amidst bright surroundings. Lord Carnarvon's mansion was described at the time as situate 'in the outskirts of the metropolis.' Its interior was renovated throughout. An annex of the building served as a separate residence for the girls, and the gardens at the back, shaded by high trees which ensured privacy, were divided into two playgrounds. Some forty years later, Bennett told a musical Committee of the Society of Arts that the Academy had been, in his young days, 'really a very pretty place.'

But the maintenance, with the musical and the moral training, of the thirty-six boarders proved very expensive, and fees, even when raised, covered but a small part of the cost. Contributions and subscriptions did not meet expectations, and notwithstanding the concerts, balls, and public dinners, which the Directors, as leaders of Society, were able to organize, the early balance-sheets spelt speedy ruin. In 1825 it was announced that day-students would be taken. Some of the Directors, in view of the 'career beset with dangers,' shrank from the responsibility of dealing with pupils over whom they could not have entire control; but Lord Burghersh, who wished to see the benefits of the Institution more widely enjoyed, was supported by a majority, and early in the year 1826, upwards of sixty out-door students were receiving instruction for which they paid £30 per annum. The gross income was increased, but so still more were the expenses. An extra house was taken, more Professors were engaged, and dangerous encroachments were made upon a small invested endowment.

Bennett arrived on March 7, 1826. As the funds of the Academy were low, while the number of applicants willing to pay fees was increasing, it appears certain that his musical gifts impressed his examiners; for it was promptly decided to accept him as a boarder, free of any expense,—the only known case of such a favour being granted in the early days of the Academy. His relations, expecting that he would return to them before anything was finally settled, had only provided him with his night-things, and a few frills packed in a little dressing-case; but he was now ordered to enter into residence at once, and a request for his clothes was despatched to Cambridge. Mr Hamilton then took him off to the schoolroom, where he introduced him to his school-fellows; and soon after this, John Ella, who was giving lessons that day as a sub-professor, was fetched out of his room by Grattan Cooke to come and see 'the funny little fellow who had just come into the house.' The boys had been holding an extra examination on their own account, and Ella found them striking on a piano confused handfuls of notes, which Bennett, from a distant corner of the room, was naming to their great satisfaction. He was dressed in a brown jacket with two rows of brass buttons on it, and a white frill. Though nearly ten years old, he was in Ella's remembrance 'a wee boy,' and Grattan Cooke, in after-life, wrote of him as 'the smallest boy,' though 'the greatest man' with whom the Academy had had to do. Bennett would himself recall how the older scholars, taking advantage of his size, used to let him down from a window in a basket, so that he might fetch them school-boy luxuries after 'locking-up.' He had one treasured recollection of the time when he first entered the musical world. A day or two before he reached London, Weber had arrived to produce his English Opera 'Oberon,' and the boy now had his first sight of a great musician. Sir George Smart brought Weber, who was staying with him in Great Portland Street, to inspect the Academy, and Bennett also saw him at a concert where he conducted his Overture to 'The Ruler of the Spirits.'

The boys' side of the Academy, at the time of his entrance, mustered between forty and fifty pupils, of whom about half were boarders. The head-boy was Charles Lucas, eighteen years of age and already a sub-professor. The new-comer was placed in his class for theoretical studies. By the express wish of his grandfather, the violin became Bennett's principal instrument, and so it remained, at least in name, for five years or more. Spagnoletti and Oury were in turn his teachers. Oury, in his old age, remembered him as a quick and intelligent pupil. On the piano he had already made progress at Cambridge. He now took it for a second study under W. H. Holmes, a clever lad of fourteen, whose own master, Cipriani Potter, would perhaps supervise this pupil-teaching. Sixty years later Holmes wrote of Bennett, 'He was my first pupil; * * * I always had the opinion of him as from a child that he could look music thro' and thro'; * * * I remember when I first gave him lessons I thought what a delightful thing it was to teach, when you could get any one to do anything with so little trouble; * * * He could always do much more than I could tell him.'

Two years and more passed, and then some of the landmarks in a boy's life appeared. His first prize, Goldsmith's *History of Rome*, was given him, in the summer of 1828, by the Countess St Antonio, for progress in Harmony; he made his debût, when twelve-and-a-half years old, in Dussek's Pfte. Concerto in B♭, at a students' concert; and then made his first essay in composition, as he neared his thirteenth year, when he competed, though unsuccessfully, with older boys for the gold pencil-case which Sir Andrew Barnard offered for the best setting of a Fairy Chorus with orchestral accompaniment. But though his day as a composer had not yet come, he was being gradually prepared for it by the exercises for Lucas, with which, as far as writing was concerned, he now contented himself for two or three years longer. His violin-playing, no doubt, also helped him much. It had already brought him under the influence of Cipriani Potter, who, during Dr Crotch's Principalship, conducted the pupils' orchestra. A feature of the Academy training, and one that distinguished it from the courses of education which musical students had generally followed in this country, was the constant practice of the instrumental works of such masters as Haydn, Mozart, and Beethoven, and the exposition of the 'forms' they used. Potter took an exceptional place among the British composers of his day, by devoting himself chiefly to instrumental composition, and by basing his works on such forms; and he was certainly the first who had the opportunity through his connection with the Academy, of setting any appreciable number of English students on the same track. Concerted instrumental music, whether for the orchestra or the chamber, became the daily study of many Academy boys. Residence in the house, as Bennett would afterwards say, made it easy to arrange meetings. There were at the Academy several clever boys destined to take, before long, leading places as orchestral players in London; Professors assisted them at their more important rehearsals; but Potter did not make proficiency a necessary qualification for his student-band. On the contrary, into it he thrust the boys, as soon as they had learnt to hold their instruments, and could follow their parts if only in their mind; and he would make his practices the occasions for explaining to these young beginners the *plan*—the word he himself used—of the master-works played, and the devices of orchestration. Thus could a boy like Bennett, with quick perception and a retentive memory, begin, at an early age, to store his mind with fine music and with models for future work of his own.

In the spring of 1829, the Academy was carefully inspected by Fétis, the distinguished musical savant and, at the time, Professor of Counterpoint and Fugue at the Paris Conservatoire. He was able to send a most favourable account to Paris of the English Institution. In referring to the students as composers, he wrote:—'These young persons enjoy the inestimable advantage of having their compositions performed by a complete orchestra on the Tuesday and Saturday of every week. This practical instruction seems to me to be the best that is received in the Academy. * * * * The practices are directed by Mr Potter, who resided for a long time in Vienna, and received instruction from Beethoven, whose style he imitates in his compositions. Mr Potter is an excellent musician, and in every respect qualified for the office which he fills. These practices were very interesting. I was present at several of them, and was always satisfied with what I heard.'

In the summer of 1829, at the close of his third academical year, Bennett gained a bronze medal for general progress, and so far all had gone well; but in the following December he had so serious an illness, that he was unable to go home for the holidays. His only companion in the deserted house was Scipione Brizzi, a young Italian, who, by a curious reversal of usual procedure, had come to England to study singing. In the night of Christmas Eve, Bennett was taken so much worse, that Brizzi became seriously alarmed, and, not daring to leave the invalid, in order to fetch servants from a remote part of the house, he nursed him in his arms, till morning brought the help of others. Dr Granville, the eminent physician who gave his services free to the Academy, was so impressed with the circumstance, that he reminded Bennett of it, when they met again towards the close of their lives, at the Athenæum Club. When Bennett lay dying in 1875, Brizzi called at the house, and said at the door: 'I think he will get better, but I wish I could nurse him, for I saved his life once before.' Whether this illness was the result, or the cause, of a failure of strength, it certainly came at a time when a check to his progress is noticeable. Prizes, compositions, solo-playing at concerts, are not heard of for some time. He seems to have lacked the power, or perhaps the desire to keep himself to the front. Still, he remained in the midst of music, and was gathering experience. He had a beautiful alto voice. This happily brought him to the notice of Attwood, who often sent for him to sing in the choir of St Paul's. With another boy, Lovell Phillips, he was in constant request to join in the glee-singing at public entertainments. He played the violin in the orchestra at the series of Operas given by the Academy students at the King's Theatre, and at the end of 1831 took the part of Cherubino in *Figaro*, an event which he liked to speak of in after-life. Sir George Macfarren, who played the trombone in the orchestra on the occasion, remembered Bennett's rendering of the part as interesting and effective, though it is true that the critic of *The Harmonicon* took a different view at the time.

On the piano, unobserved except by his teacher, he was still advancing. One day, probably in the winter of 1830–31, Holmes said to his private pupil, J. W. Davison, 'Come, I must take you to hear my Academy boy, who plays better than I do;' and, from that day, Davison, who afterwards became the leading musical critic in this country, began to watch Bennett with keen interest. He has written, as a recollection of the time, that the boy, at the outset of his Academy life, was 'apparently somewhat apathetic if not to say idle.' The music-book, in which Bennett entered and dated his 'approved' exercises, shows that he was now studying Canon and Fugue with Lucas; and Davison remembered that a Canon on the subject of 'La ci darem' was made to do duty on more than one occasion, when work was called up for examiners' inspection. 'Bunny,' as his school-fellows named him, was so far best known to them as 'a merry-hearted boy in the playground;' as the collector of a museum of doubtful antiquities, which he kept and exhibited in his bed-room; as a promoter of concerts of humorous classical music, for which he would copy the orchestral parts on gigantic pieces of paper; or as a spirited actor in *Bombastes Furioso* and other plays.

When he was just fifteen years old, his grandfather wrote to him, on May 17, 1831:—

MY DEAR WILLIAM,

I write to let you see that I am still alive, and better than ever I expected to be, but I am far from being myself again, but thank God I am no worse. * * *

* * * * * * * * *

Now I must change the subject. Volti!—I wish to know what progress you are making in music. Do you practise much on the violin and do you improve? Is the piano your favorite instrument still? Harmony must not be neglected, and above all your duty to God. I frequently see or hear of your Academical concerts, but never see or hear of any of your performances, therefore conclude you are lazy or negligent, and must or will remain as a cypher or even a blank amongst them. The *Morning Chronicle* spoke last week of your [concert] and mentioned many names, but alas! yours was not there. * * * *

Have you any idea when we may expect to see you again? Let me particularly [hear] how you are proceeding in your different studies, by whom you are taught, and whose and what music you are practising. Persevere and be diligent; mediocrity stands but a poor chance in the science of music in these days. It must be Eminence or nothing. Write to me soon and satisfy my anxiety or curiosity, whatever you please to call it. I hope you are in good health and not in want of anything. If you are let me know.

I remain,
Your affectionate grandfather,
JOHN BENNETT.

The boy had now been five years at the Academy, and his grandfather would surely before this have asked him, in holiday time, for the details of his work; but Bennett, like other school-boys, would avoid such a subject, and his relations could not get much out of him. At Cambridge, he was often asked out to sing or play. On his return he would never satisfy the family curiosity. 'Well, what did they say?' would be asked. 'What *should* they say?' was the only form of reply. His aunt Sarah, when relating this, added, 'We should have kept the letters he wrote from the Academy, if we had had any presentiment that he would become an eminent man, but he never gave us any chance to expect it.' He was, however, on most affectionate terms with his grandparents. His grandfather would laugh at his drolleries till the tears rolled down his face, and would at last burst out with the exclamation, as if it were a term of endearment, 'Thou fool, thou fool!' Early in life the boy learnt to realize the obligation he was under, as an orphan, to these second parents. He would often, in after-life, speak of his grandfather's distress in being obliged to ask him, when he had been some little time at the Academy, not to write home so often, as they could not afford to pay for the letters on their arrival. He preserved two of his grandfather's letters; the one given above, because it contained the words, 'Harmony must not be neglected, and above all your duty to God;' and another because it ended with the words, 'From my little kitchen, I write farewell;' and these two phrases he would often quote, as if they still touched him in a tender place. If he spoke of his grandmother, it was generally to refer to the first night of the holidays, when the old lady, with a certain amount of ceremony, would open a cupboard and reveal a special fruit-pie, which she always made to celebrate the occasion. At the end of the holidays, he would escape to the coach, without the farewells that he dared not face.

By the Academy examiners, in the summer of 1831, he was rebuked for his diffidence with respect to composition. Other pupils in Lucas's class, George Macfarren for one, were already writing elaborate works. Bennett alone held back. 'Here is a boy,' said one of the Professors, 'who could do something if he chose.' To this branch of work, however, it seems to have been as futile to press him then, as it invariably proved later. A promotion, which now took place, to Dr Crotch's class, certainly gave no impetus; for, in lieu of the Fugues written for Lucas, his music-book contains a series of single and double Chants, a form of exercise on which Dr Crotch is said to have set great value.

That Bennett, after the summer of 1831, entered upon a course of unflagging industry, had, at the outset, nothing to do with composition. On the violin, he had reached the stage of playing the Concertos of Rode and Viotti, but the instrument was not his favourite one. His grandfather's letter had given him the opportunity of saying so, and of getting permission to abandon it as his principal study. A change was made, and, to use his own words, he took to the pianoforte 'con amore.' 'Instead of playing about the house,' he once said to the writer, 'I began to practise incessantly.' But great proficiency on what had so far been his second instrument was already acquired, though without attracting notice. In December he made his first important appearance, playing in the Academy room Hummel's Concerto in A flat, a work which Hummel had himself introduced to this country earlier in the year. Bennett's performance took everybody by surprise. He would say in his latter days that he had heard no more beautiful pianoforte-playing than that of Hummel. He may have heard him play this same Concerto, and assimilated something; for Sir George Macfarren has written of 'silly praisers,' who, after this Academy concert, at once styled him 'The English Hummel,' whereas, in Sir George's opinion, he had done quite well enough to deserve the use of his own name. John Field, who had just arrived in England, after thirty years' absence, was present at the concert and on leaving the room said of Bennett to one of the Professors, 'That *little* fellow knows what he's about.'

While writing the Chants for Dr Crotch, he composed his first extended work, a string Quartet in G minor. As he did not intend to show it to his master, he did not trouble to make a score, but wrote straight off the separate parts to try the music with his school-fellows. Fifty years afterwards, his devoted pupil, Thomas Wingham, found these parts, dated October, 1831, in the possession of a former Academy student, and purchased them. He then arranged for one or two performances of the work in London, and asked Mr Joseph Bennett, the eminent musical critic, to write an analytical pamphlet. This was printed and in it the following passage occurs:—

'In hearing the Quartet it is impossible to overlook the composer's youth. This is sufficiently asserted by the intrinsic character of the music, as well as by comparison with more mature productions. Equally clear is the fact, that Bennett's master for composition had trained him in the school of Mozart, whose orderly method, grace, and clearness of expression are here emulated as far as a student's unripe powers allowed.'

It is to the last sentence of this extract, rather than to the Quartet itself or to its discovery, that attention is paid here. Bennett had not written this work, nor as yet any such work, under the eye of a living teacher. Who then had trained him in the school of Mozart? It was no other than Mozart himself. Music, in variety sufficient to draw his attention in many directions, had now for some years been before his receptive and discriminating mind; but he had already determined to turn a deaf ear to vanities, to study exclusively in a school of Great Masters, and even to find still further security, by selecting one great musician as the centre of his thoughts and the first moulder of his taste. There can be no doubt that the placing of himself at the feet of Mozart was a deliberate act of his own. This was clearly shown, if not literally said, by himself, later in life, on an occasion when, though he made no positive personal reference, he was nevertheless obviously recalling his own young days, with their hours of perplexity, and their hour of firm resolve. He was lecturing at Cambridge in 1871, and exhorting musical students to great caution in the selection of models for study. He assumed, for the nonce, that his hearers had passed through the earlier stages of theoretical knowledge, that they could, for the purpose of study, read musical scores like ordinary books, and were wishing to compose.—Here is seen a description of himself in his fifteenth year.—He next spoke of the 'favourite composer' which a young musician would probably have, of whom he would be 'continually thinking;' and whose works would 'continually possess him;' but he feared that the favourite might be admired for some specially fascinating characteristics, which it would be folly to imitate; the beginner was, in his opinion, in a perilous position; music, good, indifferent, and bad, was hovering round; and though experienced teachers might advise, it mainly rested with the student himself 'to choose his own path and shape his own taste.' He went on to say, that the adoption of a chief model must come as the result of 'much self-control and patient study,' and then, after paying tribute to several great musicians, in particular reference to instrumental and operatic music, from the time of Haydn to that of Mendelssohn, he turned to Mozart, speaking of him at great length, and urging his listeners to consider the adoption of that Master as the chief guide of their musical life.—Here, in his mind's eye, stood the rock on which he had himself sought security.—He was careful to explain, that, apart from the immediate purpose of his lecture, viz., to direct attention to an exemplary model, he had nothing to do with placing great men in order of merit; he was not naming Mozart as the greatest man of an epoch; the Great Masters were to him the links of an inseparable chain. Nevertheless, in the history of music as Bennett read it, and in the period which most interested him,—i.e. from the birth of the elder Scarlatti in 1659 to the death of Spohr in 1859,—Mozart, if not in his view standing higher than others, was in any case the *central* figure, occupying the position from which you could, as he put it, 'best review music from the earliest to the latest times.'

His particular devotion to Mozart was known to his school-companions. He told his friend Bowley, who was a non-resident student, that it was his habit to take Mozart's scores to bed with him, and to read them in the early summer mornings. Thus did the seemingly childish or indolent boy work on, and when his first efforts at composition came under the criticism of those around him, a certain 'finish' was noticed in them, which caused surprise, because he seemed to have got over the first stage of a journey without assistance, and without letting any one know that he had started. Sir George Macfarren remembered his boyish 'love for Mozart,' and how 'he proved it once to the delight of a few bystanders by playing many pieces from the score of Don Giovanni, which he so vitalized by distinguishing the characters of different instruments, and contrasting them with the vocal effects, as to fix and to fill the attention of his listeners, though other boys were practising other music on other pianofortes in the same school-room.' Davison, whose personal acquaintance with him, and whose interest in every detail of his work, dated from the very outset of his career as a composer, has drawn attention to his early and continued adherence to Mozart. After Bennett's death, he analyzed, for a concert programme, a Pianoforte Concerto in C minor composed in 1834, the third of six such works, and wrote :—

'In none of his Concertos does Bennett dispense with the old classical *tutti*, although he had the examples set by Beethoven in his G and E flat, and by Mendelssohn in his G minor, which had just burst fresh upon the world of art, to encourage and support him; but no, the young English musician was heart and soul with Mozart; and in that faith he remained unswervingly till the close of his career.'

How far Bennett succeeded in modelling his music on that of Mozart, is a question which the music itself can best answer. The 'orderly method' and the 'clearness of expression' found in his early efforts, and always noticed with commendation in his later works, were probably qualities inherent in him; but their development certainly connects him with his chosen guide. He did not hope to be another Mozart. Such an ideal was only to be reached through avenues along some of which he could not walk far; nor did he think that many had walked the whole way. Thus, he wrote of Mozart as a Master of '*Broad Rhythm*, which so few could manage;' and, again, as the writer of 'the real Adagio, of which no composer with the exception, perhaps, of Beethoven, had left such specimens.' His reverence for Mozart is also shown in the fact, that the existence of that Master's Operas furnished one reason for his not attempting to write such a work himself. But apart from Mozart's, to him inimitable, power, there were other traits, both in Mozart's music and in his character as an artist, which sooner or later were observed by Bennett, which strongly appealed to his own nature, and which helped to confirm the principles that guided his musical life. When upholding Mozart as an example to others, he extolled 'the serious earnestness and deep thought,' and the 'conscience,' as he called it, which pervaded all that composer's works; the 'control' which the 'consummate master' exercised over his 'genius;' the 'modesty and veneration' with which he observed 'the canons of his art,' and 'tempered his great power.' To Bennett's mind, Mozart was the musician 'who never seemed to make a mistake,' unless, perhaps, he at times erred through over-seriousness. Of the man himself, Bennett had, as a boy, learnt something, not from biographies, for there were none at hand, but from 'many interesting conversations' with his 'very dear old friend, Thomas Attwood, about his master Mozart;' and in that way he no doubt inherited the warmth of tone, which was mingled with the reverence of every word he afterwards used in speaking of the great musician. Thus early in life he would be told, as he afterwards liked to tell others, of Mozart's disregard for popularity, and of his flat refusal to lower the standard of his work to gain money, even if starvation must come as the alternative.

Much that Bennett said of Mozart, might, if only the words could be modified to satisfy the sense of proportion, be said of Bennett himself. Serious earnestness, conscience, the control of mastery over impulse, modesty and veneration, disregard of popularity, and resistance of the money-tempter, are to be seen as clearly in the disciple as in the Master. With Mozart as the centre of his thoughts, Bennett extended his studies backwards and forwards along the legitimate line of the musical dynasty. When he reached manhood, he became intimately associated with great musicians of his own time; but they were such as had learnt the same lessons as himself, and could welcome him as one who had worn the same school-colours as themselves. However much he came to be influenced at times of his life by new impressions, his early love for Mozart never left him; and, indeed, his later works breathe more and more the pure Mozartian spirit. 'The young English musician'—to repeat Davison's words—'was heart and soul with Mozart, and in that faith he remained unswervingly to the close of his career.'

To return to the Academy. Though Dr Crotch had had no hand in the little Quartet, he may have heard of it, for Bennett was now allowed to take a sudden leap from Chants to Symphonies, the first of which, in the key of E flat, was finished on April 6, 1832, a week before the composer's sixteenth birthday. This work is not quite dead yet, for the opening subject was used much later for an eight-part Motet, 'In Thee, O Lord, do I put my trust,' a posthumous publication, often heard at the present day in Westminster Abbey and other Cathedral churches. The Symphony was played at the Academy concert in the following June, and the same day, Bennett took part in Mozart's Horn Quintet, playing the viola, the stringed instrument which he had now adopted instead of the violin. The prize-day occurred ten days later, and he then set out for Cambridge, carrying a printed document that would at length allay 'anxiety,' and satisfy 'curiosity.' His grandfather could now read in the Report of the Committee: that 'Bennett had composed a Symphony, performed at the last concert, which had done him the greatest credit;' that 'Bennett and Dorrell had made the greatest progress on the pianoforte;' again, that Bennett had been one of seven 'most regular and attentive to their orchestral duties;' and, finally, that the Committee had adjudged to BENNETT 'a silver medal, for his great proficiency in the past year in composition and the Pianoforte, and for his undeviating good conduct.' Thackeray's Royal Prince did not take home, from the University of Bosforo, a more glowing record of a year's work.

Dr Crotch now resigned his connection with the

Academy. As he had given concerts in London in his sixth year, and had reached his sixtieth, he had passed through a long career of professional work. An active man, he used to walk from his house in the neighbourhood of Campden Hill to Tenterden Street, entering his classroom with his pockets distended by paint-boxes and sketchbooks, and allowing his pupils, to their great delight, to examine any additions he had made on his walk through Kensington Gardens. A musical treat, often enjoyed by his class, was his playing from memory a series of the Choruses of Handel, which he could select with endless variety. A short connection with Dr Crotch, as his pupil in composition for one year, was sufficient to make a great impression on Bennett's mind of the extent of his master's erudition and accomplishments. It was to Taunton, where Dr Crotch lived in retirement to an advanced age, that Bennett would write, in after years, if he required information about music of an earlier period. When Mendelssohn wished to make Handelian researches in England, Bennett told him that, notwithstanding other reputed authorities, Dr Crotch was the only man in this country, who really knew much about Handel's music[1].

Bennett, however, had a special cause for satisfaction at the prospect of studying composition under Cipriani Potter, who now succeeded to the Principalship. His thoughts were centred on his favourite instrument. A little while before, he had said to his friend Dorrell, 'I want to write a Pianoforte Concerto, but it is no use doing it for Dr Crotch.' Before the summer holidays (1832) were over, he must have heard of Potter's appointment; for he set diligently to work, at Cambridge, on the first movement of a Concerto in D minor. After the introduction of the second subject in the *tutti*, he had a difficulty in continuing the music to his liking, and his aged grandfather, hearing him from time to time play up to a certain point and then stop, would tease him and cry out, 'Ah, you can't

---

[1] i.e. had extensive knowledge of the music itself. He was not at the time referring to *performance*. As to the performance of the best-known Oratorios, he recognized in Sir George Smart a high authority, and would say that Smart claimed to have inherited, through his father, the true Handelian 'tempi.' Some of these, which Sir George passed on to Bennett, differed much from those adopted during the long régime of Sir Michael Costa.

get over that!' He did, however, complete the opening *tutti* for his first lesson with Potter; and the pat on the shoulder, and the kind 'Well done, my boy,' were encouragements which he never forgot. The Concerto was finished in October; a second Symphony, in D minor, immediately followed; and three days of the Christmas holiday at Cambridge were spent in writing an Overture to *The Tempest.*

Sir George Macfarren has thus referred to the production of the Concerto in D minor:—

'The first trial with the band at one of the weekly Academy rehearsals excited the boundless admiration of us other boys who had always loved and now began fully to prize him. Many and meritorious had been the compositions of Academy students that had been tried at these periodical practices, not a few of which had been displayed at the public concerts of the institution; but this Concerto seemed to step out of the range of pupil work and show something of the maturity of mastership. A shout of enthusiasm went up from us all, each one proud to acknowledge the rare merit of his school-mate, and it was not the students alone who perceived this merit, but professors were as ready to applaud it.'

Bennett played the Concerto at an orchestral concert, which, with the aid of his Academy friends, he gave at Cambridge, on Nov. 28, 1832; and then, for the first time in London, at an Academy concert in the Hanover Square Rooms, March 30, 1833. A few days later, he was summoned to Windsor, and his visit furnished news, which, though about himself, was of too special a kind to be withheld from his relations. The following letter was thought worth preserving. It bears the date of his seventeenth birthday.

ROYAL ACADEMY OF MUSIC,
April 13, 1833.

MY DEAR AUNT,

I wrote to you last, but not having heard from you I write again to acquaint [you] that I have been spending my Easter holidays at *Windsor*, whither I have been to play on the Pianoforte *before their Majesties.* I received a command to attend from Sir Andrew Barnard

WILLIAM STERNDALE BENNETT
AET. CIRCA XVI
IN THE UNIFORM JACKET OF A STUDENT OF
THE ROYAL ACADEMY OF MUSIC
From a water-colour drawing

soon after I last wrote to you, and have had the honor of playing before the Court *three times*. Now I'm going to give you the particulars. After I had played the first time, Her Majesty did me the honor to rise from her seat (where she was sitting at needlework) and came to me, when the following conversation took place between *Queen Adelaide* and your humble servant. *Queen.*—'I am much obliged to you for playing that Solo.' (*I of course made a very low bow.*) *Queen.*—'Is that your own composition?' I mustered up courage to say 'Yes, your Majesty.' *Queen.*—'Well, if you keep on studying hard you will make something very great.'

Now what do you think of that—Your nephew having a conversation with Queen Adelaide of England. She spoke afterwards to Mr Cramer, the Leader of her Band, about me. I can assure you that I am as conceited as possible—playing three different nights before their Majesties. I played my own Concerto twice, the same that I played at the Hanover Square Rooms. Mr Hamilton called me up the other day to say that it was to be published and that the Committee will take care that I do not lose by the publication. Pray take care of the three newspapers I have sent. I have some other papers which speak very highly of me. I am very well, and having chiefly written to tell you of my trip to Windsor Castle, I must beg to conclude with love to all, not forgetting to be kindly remembered to the Nutters,

Your affectionate nephew,
WILLIAM STERNDALE BENNETT.

Once more the Concerto was played in the Hanover Square Rooms, at the Midsummer concert of the Academy on June 26, 1833, and a critic then wrote of Bennett:—

'His execution is wonderful; and his ease and total absence of affectation, made him a general favourite. * * * The company was charmed with his simple unpretending manners, as well as surprised by his display of genius.'

By the side of Lord Burghersh, at this concert, sat a young foreigner whom the Ambassador, adopting a then usual precaution of British diplomacy, addressed by the title of Count. When Bennett had finished the slow movement of his Concerto, the *Count*, being short of stature, stood up, saying, 'I want to have a good look at him.' Later he asked to be made acquainted with the boy, and was accordingly taken by Lord Burghersh to the green-room. Thus was Bennett introduced to Mendelssohn, the lad of seventeen to the young man of twenty-four. Mendelssohn forthwith invited him to Germany. 'If I come,' said Bennett, 'may I come to be your pupil?' 'No, no,' was the reply, 'you must come to be my friend.'

CHAPTER III.

ADVANCED STUDENTSHIP.

1833—1836.

æt. 17—20.

BENNETT met Mendelssohn again at this time, for he has written of an evening when he took part in Attwood's Glee, 'The Curfew,' and then heard Mendelssohn extemporize on the subject of the music, in the presence, and to the great delight, of its composer. This is but a single glimpse of Attwood, Mendelssohn, and Bennett in one and the same place, nor could the three have often met together, since the chances of their doing so were confined within a few days of the year 1833, and a few days in the autumn of 1837. Yet Attwood, with a strong tie of affection binding him to each, had no little to do with bringing his young friends together. Of the English musicians with whom Mendelssohn became acquainted during his early visits to this country, Attwood was one that he certainly loved; and Bennett, when writing of his 'very dear old friend,' expressed himself certain that 'no more genial musician ever lived.' Attwood, who could look back to four years spent in his youth as a student on the continent, was immediately interested in the proposal that Bennett should sooner or later go to Germany, and continued to keep him in mind as one who would deserve the advantage of foreign intercourse, when the days of pupilage in England were over.

After the summer holidays of 1833, Bennett returned to Tenterden Street, which was to remain his home for another three years. He was now nearly seventeen-and-a-half years old. He had won his boyish laurels, and it may be said that his school-days were over. It was, indeed, only in the early days of the Academy, that the majority of the boarders were young enough to make the term 'school-life' applicable. George Macfarren, three years older than Bennett, worked on by his side under Potter until they, at the same time, completed a course of advanced studentship. In the summer of 1833, Bennett had prepared at Cambridge, as in the previous year, the first movement of a Pianoforte Concerto. Potter's encouragement now took a different form. He did not again pat his pupil on the back, but spurred him instead to increased endeavour, by advising him to re-write the whole movement. This Concerto, No. II in E flat, when finished and played a few weeks later, raised Bennett a step higher in the estimation of the Academy circle, not only as a composer, but also as a pianist. It was a moot point, in which capacity the work showed him to greater advantage. A knot of students gathered round Lucas, when he had finished conducting the rehearsal, and asked him what he thought about the Concerto. 'Ah,' he replied, 'but what about the *playing*?' And now, when after more than seven years under Holmes, a change of pianoforte-master was made, the elder students asked each other, 'What does he want with lessons? What is the use of his going under Potter?'

What Bennett, as a pianist, gained from one teacher or another cannot be determined; but, speaking generally, he was taught his instrument in a place where grand traditions were within reach of those who had the sense to accept them. Fétis, when he inspected the Academy in 1829, noticed how fortunate the Institution was in its pianoforte teachers. Great names can be mentioned in connection with this. England had been the chosen residence of many eminent foreign pianists. The very instrument itself owed much of its development to this country. When the Academy opened, teachers of rare distinction were at hand, whilst others claimed direct descent from illustrious men. Clementi was a constant visitor in Tenterden Street. J. B. Cramer taught there. Potter, who gave the first pianoforte lesson in the house, had studied in London for five years under the celebrated Woelfl, the pupil of Leopold

Mozart. Bennett has written that he made acquaintance at the Academy with an intimate friend of C. P. Emanuel Bach. No one who followed such guides could go astray. Nevertheless, Bennett learnt the piano at a time of some perplexity. During the years of his apprenticeship a new school of playing, with new music to correspond with it, came into vogue on the continent, and a dazzling brilliancy of performance was, or seemed to be, the one object which the majority of rising pianists had in view. The taste of this country was thereby rapidly affected. Academy students who desired to devote themselves to the music of the Great Masters and their legitimate followers found sufficient encouragement, but even in Tenterden Street there was a divergence of interests. Davison found Bennett, towards the end of his Academy life, exerting an active influence, and leading a small party of students who were pledged to what they considered the 'classical' side of pianoforte music.

Potter, from one source or another, had inherited a key without which much of the music of certain masters cannot be fully displayed; and here a debt which his pupil may have owed him can be imagined; for Bennett certainly played the harpsichord Lessons of Handel, or the P.F. Concertos of Mozart in a way that revealed to many hearers unimagined beauties. He would tell a story that gives a clue to another direction in which Potter guided his studies. The master wished to introduce his pupil to a certain composition by Beethoven, now very generally known as Opus 106. The purchase of any Sonata in those days was beset with difficulty. Academy boys had to exercise patience, until the longest ladder in the shop could be found, and until an avalanche of dust and cobwebs had fallen from the topmost shelf. On this occasion, Bennett started with little faith in the success of his errand; for Potter's sole direction had been, 'Go and ask for the Sonata that nobody plays.' That description, however, proved sufficient for the music-seller, and he brought down the work. Sir George Grove has suggested that the appreciation of Beethoven's later works by 'so conservative a musician as Bennett' might have been due to his association with Mendelssohn. It was not so. If persuasion towards Beethoven was needed, which is very improbable, one can look for it nearer home. The pupils of Potter saw in their own master a direct link with Beethoven. They were, indeed, very proud of this, and would not require anyone else to explain the great composer to them. Bennett had gone very far in his understanding of Beethoven long before he left the Academy. When he first went to Leipzig, his playing of that master's works was regarded as one of his best credentials. Mendelssohn's friend, Dr Klengel, would, years afterwards, make special reference to it, when Bennett's name was mentioned in his hearing.

While writing Concertos with orchestral accompaniment, Bennett also made progress, during his first two years as a composer, in dealing with the orchestra alone. Davison, in after life, said that the first movement of a fourth Symphony, in A major, written in the winter of 1833–34, could take its place beside later works. Davison retained a warm interest in these early efforts. One evening, about the year 1870, when dining with Bennett in Bayswater, he found the score of this Symphony in a book-case and, on leaving the house, walked off with it. William Dorrell, who was with him, found great difficulty in getting him back to town, because he would stop at every lamp-post in the Bayswater Road to read a page or two of the manuscript. Davison once took the writer up to his bed-room, and showed him a collection of Bennett's unpublished scores, carefully kept amongst his linen in a small chest of drawers. He said that he often read them and could not bear to part with them in his lifetime. According to his direction, they were sent, after his death, to Bennett's family.

As in after years, so even as a student, Bennett was not an incessant composer. He wrote, at this time, on an average, three works in each year; taking in something like regular rotation, the Symphony, the P.F. Concerto, and the Overture. Dates on the scores show that a composition once begun was quickly finished; but a long time would often elapse before another was undertaken. The summer and winter holidays at Cambridge invariably furnished him with some fresh idea, and late in life he told an Academy student, who was one of his pupils for composition, that he thought, in his own case, the best of his work had been done in the holidays.

There were now many calls upon his time in London: his prescribed studies; the duty of hearing and taking part in much music; honorary work as a sub-professor; and outside engagements to furnish him with a little money; for though he still enjoyed free residence at the Academy, he was no longer a boy, and increased personal expense had to be met by his own exertions. Towards the end of 1833, he begged the Committee to grant him some relief from the strict rules of 'leave-out.' 'I have kept them,' he wrote, 'for upwards of seven years, but am now going out into the world, and wish to enlarge my connections.'

In the spring of 1834, he stood for the post of organist at St Ann's, then a chapel-of-ease to Wandsworth Parish church. There was a keen contest. When the electors met, the show of hands was not in his favour. His supporters demanded a poll, and issued a printed circular, which set forth his merits, and was backed by many signatures. On April 3rd, 'The public offices of Wandsworth' were open 'from 7 a.m. to 7 p.m.' for the voting, with the result that Bennett headed the poll with 174 votes, and a majority of 67. His opponents then challenged the legality of the proceedings; the Vestry took Counsel's opinion; the election was ruled in order; and the successful candidate, on his eighteenth birthday, secured an income of thirty guineas per annum. He held the appointment for one year; he diligently practised the organ in the hours between the Sunday services; and, towards the end of the time, the *verger* condescended to inform him that he had noticed great improvement in his playing. He would amuse himself, in after-life, by quoting the flattering opinion of this dignitary, and would at the same time speak of his slender means, at the time he first took the situation, which often obliged him to leave his gloves, in lieu of toll, as he crossed the bridge on his way to church. His next engagement was at a proprietary Chapel in the neighbourhood of St James's Park, and therefore more easily within his reach. He practised the organ much later in life, going to the Hanover Square Rooms when he could find a spare hour, and probably hoping to take part in organ performances given in connection with the Bach Society. In his last days, he startled the writer by the facility with which he played and pedalled difficult passages from Bach's organ-works on a pedal-piano which happened to be in his house a short time for a student's practice. As he got off the stool, he seemed to notice his listener's look of surprise, for he indulged in a merry laugh, and said, 'You didn't know I could do that.'

Besides Sunday work, he found pupils, though as yet only at low fees. He was employed at a ladies' school at Edmonton. He also taught at Hendon; for when the old 'Greyhound' Inn of that village was demolished some years ago, and a sketch of its traditions appeared in a newspaper, mention was made of Sterndale Bennett having, as a very young man, taken frugal meals there on his lesson days. To 'The Greyhound' at Hendon he would sometimes repair with his family, in the busy years of after-life, for a holiday, stolen from the toil of teaching, in the early days of summer.

His nineteenth year (April 1834—April 1835), during which he held his appointment at Wandsworth, was in all directions well-employed. Composition, though no great amount of time was spent upon it, showed an increase of power. In May he wrote a charming Overture to *The Merry Wives of Windsor*, for a concert given by Gesualdo di Lanza, a teacher of singing. But a much more important composition followed. The first movement of a P.F. Concerto, No. III, in C minor, was completed at Cambridge in August, and the other movements were added in October. This work afterwards served as his musical passport to Germany, and greatly conduced to his early reputation as a composer. A Song, 'Gentle Zephyr' (long after included in a set of six), and a Canzonet 'In radiant loveliness,' sung, with orchestral accompaniment, by Miss Birch, also belong to this year. They were the first, and for some years remained the only vocal compositions which he issued. At the same time he wrote his first solo pieces for the piano: a study in F minor, and a Capriccio in D minor dedicated to Potter. The Capriccio was much liked by his friends Davison and Macfarren. The latter knew it by heart, and played it a great deal at home, to the distraction of Mr

Macfarren senior, who did not share his son's admiration for the piece. The Overture to 'Parisina' which Bennett sketched[1] in twenty-four hours, under no pressure but what the flow of the music itself may have caused, was dated March 1835. This Overture eclipsed anything he had so far written for the orchestra alone, and was the only Academy work of that class that he selected for publication. It is a very early example of a successful use of the modern orchestra by a British composer[2].

About this time, Attwood wrote to Mendelssohn:— 'We have recently had a new establishment here which is entitled the Society of British Musicians, in the hope of bringing forward native talent. I hardly need say that Bennett stands pre-eminent.' At the concerts of this society, Bennett's Academy Symphonies, Overtures, and Concertos were freely introduced; but he was now to be brought forward in a sphere offering much greater distinction. One day in 1835, just before his nineteenth birthday, intelligence of a startling kind reached the Academy. Mr William Dorrell told the writer that it took everybody's breath away, and that amidst a scene of great though suppressed excitement, the question went round the house in a sort of whisper: 'Have you heard the news? Bennett is to play at the Philharmonic!' Sir George Macfarren wrote, fifty years later, of the performance:—' He played not his latest Concerto [C mi.] and that as yet of highest aim, but, by choice of the Directors, the one in E flat [No. 2], which, with all its grace, and its greater popularity of character than the other has never taken such hold of general esteem. This was a notable, I think unique instance of the composer and player of a work at one of those exclusive concerts being a youth still at school, still profiting by instruction, still obedient to discipline, and

---

[1] *Sketched.* He used the word when he had got to the stage of writing out the first violin-part alone, from beginning to end of a movement. Later, he gave up this practice, and filled in the pages of his score as he went along.

[2] Sir George Macfarren remembered that Potter, on first seeing this Overture, questioned the propriety of using the key of B for the recurrence of a melody which is first given in A, especially with reference to its relation with F♯ minor, the primary key of the piece; but on Bennett's explaining that he had wished to employ the same register of the violoncello for the cantabile phrase in both places, Potter accepted the reason as sufficient to justify the tonality.

fulfilling tasks among his fellows. I well remember his rapturous reception.'

The seal of approval set upon his playing by the Philharmonic audience, and the composition of the C minor Concerto in the previous year, placed him on a level where further instruction seemed superfluous; but he lingered on at the Academy, 'a quasi-student,' as he was afterwards described by one who was much with him at the time. When Bennett was examined before a Committee of the Society of Arts in 1865, he answered questions put to him on this subject by Sir Henry Cole :—

Q. Was not ten years an unusually long time to remain at the Academy?
A. Yes, very few remained so long, though some remained for eight or nine years.
Q. Were there any special circumstances which induced you to stay so long?
A. I did not wish to leave, and they very kindly kept me there.
Q. At your own expense, or that of the Academy?
A. At the expense of the Academy.
Q. In respect to both living and tuition?
A. In both respects.

Towards the end of his residence, he was allowed the unique privilege of a private sitting-room. His work had previously been done in the school-room, where the practice-pianos were kept, and used simultaneously. Order was maintained by an ex-Sergeant of the Guards, whose favourite sentry-post was at the back of Bennett's cottage-piano, where he would stand motionless hour after hour looking over at the boy's fingers. The study now specially assigned to Bennett long lingered in the memory of his friends. Sir George Macfarren, addressing the Academy students in 1879, directed their attention to a window next the buttress of the concert-room in which they were assembled :—' I can point you,' he said, 'to the window of the room where Sir Sterndale Bennett wrote some of the Concertos and Studies which you play, and in which you are heard to greatest effect. The room itself is not there, now that the dimensions of the building have been expanded * * *; but

I feel that his influence rests there, that his spirit hovers over us, and that we should try to do what he accomplished, and in that trial we shall at any rate do our best and gain what success we may.'

Davison, though not a student of the Academy, was a constant visitor. It was his delight to search old bookstalls for P.F. Sonatas which could not be found elsewhere. Such treasures he would take straight off to Tenterden Street; for, though he was himself a pianist, he liked to get his first impression of a piece through the medium of Bennett's remarkable sight-reading—remarkable, that is, for what seemed to his companions a prima-facie grasp of a composer's meaning. Davison has written in *The Musical World* of a day when he had unearthed a Sonata of Dussek, and had then found Bennett in 'his comfortable study at the Academy, cheerfully lighted, warmed with a blazing fire, and with a splendid new Broadwood "Grand" just presented to him on the part of that munificent firm.' In this room, in 1835, were written: a fifth Symphony, in G minor; a Sestet for pianoforte and stringed instruments; some P.F. Studies; and a Concerto for two pianofortes in which Macfarren and he combined, contributing alternate portions. The P.F. Studies were played, one by one as they were written, to Macfarren, and to him they were dedicated. Amongst them is one in E major which was a favourite piece of its composer. He liked it, as he afterwards wrote, because he had composed it in his room at the Academy 'without getting up from the table.' When Mendelssohn first heard this study at Düsseldorf, he said to Davison, in reference to its concluding passages: 'The man who can develope like that ought to be happy.' The Sestet was first played at a musical party in the rooms of Charles Coventry, the publisher of Bennett's early works. J. B. Cramer was present and after hearing the work and the composer's interpretation of it, remarked: 'We have had no one like him since poor young Pinto.'

Then, again, about this time, Davison was the first to hear Bennett play three new pieces, 'The Lake,' 'The Millstream' and 'The Fountain'; and, when asked by the composer if they might be called 'Musical Sonnets,' he advised the title 'Musical Sketches.' Davison told the writer that this private performance gave him the only opportunity he could remember of hearing Bennett strike a wrong note; nor did the pianist let the slip pass without comment, for as he got up from the instrument he said: 'You must not tell them that I can't play my own music.' The 'Three Musical Sketches' always ranked among the most effective of his minor works. 'You should have heard him play them himself,' became a very common saying in after years. Schumann wrote that his playing of 'The Fountain' created an effect 'almost magical.' When Bennett, later in life, was walking with a friend through the village of Grantchester near Cambridge, he showed the mill-stream which, as he then said, had suggested the second of these pieces.

In the New Year, 1836, he sketched[1] a 'Dramatic Overture' at Cambridge, and this was followed by a P.F. Concerto in F minor (an unpublished work), the last movement of which he was finishing on his twentieth birthday, April 13th. In the same month, he appeared at the Philharmonic for the second time, playing his Concerto in C minor.

And now, under happy auspices, it was arranged that he should pay his first visit to Germany. The Lower Rhine Musical Festival was to be held at Düsseldorf at Whitsuntide. Mendelssohn was to conduct it, and his Oratorio, 'St Paul,' was to be produced. Herr Carl Klingemann, of the Hanoverian Legation in London, Mendelssohn's intimate friend, was going over to hear the new work. These projects were the subject of conversation at an evening party in London. There Mr Henry Broadwood overheard Attwood expressing a wish that it were possible for Bennett to accompany Klingemann, and at once said, that if the difficulty was one of expense, he would most gladly furnish the means for the journey. Klingemann also took charge of Davison, whose parents fell in with his desire to be Bennett's fellow-traveller. They reached Düsseldorf in time to attend all the full rehearsals of the Festival music.

Mendelssohn received the two young strangers most kindly. He would call early at their hotel to rouse 'the

[1] The 'sketch' exists. A neatly-written Violin-part. He did not fill in the Score.

lazy Englishmen,' and to chat with them, as they dressed, before his duties for the day began. When the Festival was over, he made music, or played billiards with them. He taunted them for not going farther when they had come thus far; so, acting on his suggestion, they did not return with Klingemann, but, before leaving, took a short trip up the Rhine. On this excursion Bennett conceived the idea for his Overture 'The Naiads,' and when he got back to Düsseldorf he wrote the opening bars on a sheet of music-paper which Davison preserved as a souvenir of the happy time. Bennett had taken with him from England specimens of his work, in the hope that Mendelssohn might approve of them, and receive him as a pupil. When Mendelssohn had examined these compositions, he spoke to Davison in no doubtful tones, assuring him that he knew of no young composer in Germany, of Bennett's age, with equal gifts; and this, which Davison told the writer, is confirmed by two letters written by Mendelssohn to English friends, the first addressed to Attwood, and dated, Düsseldorf, May 28th:—

'I avail myself of Mr Bennett's departure for London to send you these lines, and to tell you how grateful I am to you for having procured me his acquaintance. I know it is owing to your advice, that he went to visit the festival, and therefore it is to you that I ought to address my thanks for all the pleasure he gave me by his compositions and his playing. I think him the most promising young musician I know, not only in your country but also here, and I am convinced if he does not become a very great musician, it is not God's will, but his own. His Concerto[1] and Symphony[2] are so well written, the thoughts so well developed and so natural, that I was highly gratified when I looked over them yesterday, but when he played this morning his six studies and the sketches, I was quite delighted, and so were all my musical friends who heard him. He told me that you wanted him to stay some time on the continent and with me. I really do think it impossible to give him (advanced as he is in his art) any advice which he was not able to give himself as well, and I am sure if he goes on

[1] No. 3 in C mi.
[2] No. 5 in G mi. (MS.).

the same way as he did till now, without losing his modesty and zeal, he will always be perfectly right and develope his talents as his friends and all the friends of music may desire; if however he should like to live on the continent for a while, and if he should stay at Leipzig, I need not say that I should feel most happy to spend some time with such a musician as he is, and that at all events I shall always consider it as my duty to do everything in my power to assist him in his musical projects, and in the course of his career, which promises to be a happy and blissful one. Have once more my thanks for the treat which I owe to your urging him to visit this country, and I only hope it may have given him also some pleasure to assist at the festival here.'

Mendelssohn wrote a little later to Klingemann[1]:—

'I have told him [Bennett] that about teachers there is, in his case, nothing more to be said by any one. Nevertheless, he still wishes to come, and you can imagine what a pleasure it will be to me to become acquainted with him more closely and for a longer time. *But*, I cannot take any money from him without being a Music-Judas. Moreover, I am certain to gain as much pleasure and profit from his society, as he from mine.'

On his return to London, Bennett made his last appearance as an Academy student at the pupils' concert in July, playing the Concerto in F minor which he had finished before going to Düsseldorf. At the rehearsal, he found that the slow movement failed to arouse interest. Brooding over this throughout the day, a fresh musical idea suddenly came to him. He accordingly burnt the midnight oil, and the last work done in his Academy study had happy result. Next morning, he brought down a new slow movement with band-parts copied out, and collected the house-orchestra to try it through with him. This movement, which he called 'Barcarolle,' became one of the most admired of his compositions. The Concerto in which it was first placed was never printed, but the 'Barcarolle' was subsequently published as the slow movement of another Concerto, also in F minor, a work which will be referred to later.

[1] Original letter is in German.

And now, in the hour of leave-taking, he did not omit some expression of gratitude to Mr Hamilton, who had been the first agent in bringing him to the Academy, and had since watched over him, for more than ten years, with parental care. He received the following reply:—

MY DEAR BOY,
I appreciate most sincerely your kind feelings conveyed to me in your letter just received.

Be assured I feel the most lively interest in your Welfare and Success whether Professionally or otherwise; and in whatever way it were possible for me to evince my Affection and Regard you know me well enough to be assured that you have only to point it out to ensure my warmest exertions. If in very early life I was of any service to you, be assured, my dear Boy, you have amply repaid me by the great (though to me not unexpected) success which has hitherto distinguished your youthful Career. Go on and prosper, and above all never forget the *Giver of all good Things*. If you have been blessed with superior Talents, if you have had the means of cultivating those Talents, and still have kind Friends raised up to enable you to bring them to Maturity; Remember the great Debt of Gratitude you owe to *Him* who has not only given you those Talents, but has raised up those kind Friends for you, and *who alone* has enabled you and will, I fervently pray, long continue to enable you to be an ornament to your Country, and an object of Pride and grateful Recollection
to your very sincere
and attached Friend,
FREDERICK HAMILTON.

Royal Academy of Music,
 7 *July* 1836.

To W. Sterndale Bennett,
 Student of the R.A. Music.

CHAPTER IV.

LEIPZIG.

October 1836—June 1837.

æt. 20, 21.

SOME weeks of the summer of 1836 were passed by Bennett at Grantchester near Cambridge. He invited Alfred C. Johnson, who had been his pupil at the Academy for the last three years, and whose parents had shown him much hospitality in London, to stay with him in his country lodgings. Mr Johnson wrote, in 1882, the following reminiscence:—'Grantchester was a favourite spot of his, and I spent two happy summer vacations with him there. I remember being struck, as a youth, by his peculiarity of repeatedly asking me to come out into the fields at the back of the cottage, when he would go off into a rhapsody as to the beauty and stillness of the scene, with the beautiful old village church close by, and in the distance King's College Chapel rising above the surrounding foliage. Afterwards he would lie down on the grass, fall into a reverie, and say what I would not a word could I get out of him. Suddenly when little expected, and I was interested in a book which, from experience of his peculiarity, I had taken care to provide myself with, he would jump up, saying, "Come, let us go in," and no sooner in doors he would set to work at his scores and at the piano, trying some of the ideas he had worked out in the fields.'

In this way, while Johnson read his book, Bennett completed his Overture 'The Naiads,' and he wrote from Cambridge to Davison on Sept. 15 :—'If you go to Coventry's *to-morrow* you will find my Overture which I have sent to him to-day—get it copied—and all that sort of thing, and I will come up next week.' Later in Bennett's life, someone doubting the correctness of a note in this Overture referred the matter, in the vestibule of the Academy, to the composer; but the latter, with a seeming want of concern, said, as he ran out of the house, 'Oh I don't know; you had better ask Davison, he corrected the parts.'

Notwithstanding the care taken during the progress of composition, he showed himself, in some ways, unconcerned with the fate of his music, after it had left his hands. This has been commented upon by Davison, both in print, and in letters written to Bennett himself. It has been said, for instance, that not only did he abstain from making any advances of his own towards getting his works heard, but also that he did not go out of his way to assist in their being well performed, and that, too, even if he were conducting them himself. Though he made three editions, writing new scores, of 'The Naiads' within a twelvemonth; three, if not four, of the Overture 'Parisina' in the course of three or four years; and took similar trouble over other of his compositions; yet, what he describes to Davison in the above letter as 'all that sort of thing' was often left in a more or less undecided state, which has occasionally given trouble to editors, performers and teachers of his music. About certain concomitants he was particular. He acquired a clear and even beautiful musical handwriting at a time when such neatness was not the rule in England. Though he had no studio in his own house, or study table with its fixed appurtenances, yet he liked his quire of music-paper to come from a special maker, and, when about to write, would go out and buy a bottle of his favourite ink. He paid attention to titles and title-pages, and would consult Signor Pistrucci, whom he constantly met at the schools they both attended, about Italian terms, hitherto unused in music, which he wished to introduce into his pieces. But, with all this, he allowed his works to issue, with needed indications of tempo, or marks of expression often wanting, and with typographical errors overlooked. He was a painstaking editor of other composers' music, but not a good one of his own. If his publisher sent him a proof of one of his short pieces, you would see him make one or two corrections on the first page; he would turn over, and when half-way down the second page, his face would assume a fixed expression, his head would begin to sway a little as if he were again at work upon the music itself; and when he came to the end, he would lay the piece down, having entirely forgotten the object for which he had taken it up. When Moscheles received a copy of Bennett's Caprice in E major, he returned it to the composer, and wrote: 'The pleasure I felt in reading this very spirited and interesting composition was only disturbed by finding on almost every page about half-a-dozen errors of the engraver. I have marked them down and send you the adjoining copy that you may derive the advantage from it of having them corrected, and I shall hope to be favoured with another copy in due time.'

On leaving Cambridge, Bennett said his last farewell to his grandfather. The old man died early in the next year—his grandson being then in Germany—struck down by an epidemic of influenza which was said at the time to be the most terrible visitation to this country since the Great Plague. The maternal grandfather, James Donn, who had died long before, had left money, and Bennett now looked forward, on coming of age in six months time, to a sum of four or five hundred pounds as his share of the property. It was this prospect that helped him to make arrangements for going to Germany, and the money furnished his chief means of support for the next two or three years.

Correspondence with Mendelssohn now began:—

LONDON, *October 3rd*, 1836.

MY DEAR SIR,

I presume you are by this time at Leipzig, and I have taken the liberty of writing to you to say, that I intend to leave London in about a fortnight to spend the winter in the same town with you. I should have wished to have been at Leipzig at the beginning of September, but I feared you might not have returned from the Hague, and indeed I am now not certain that this letter will find you, I can but *hope* that it will. I have been quite uneasy since I left Düsseldorf, as I have felt such an anxiety to profit by your good advice to me in my professional pursuits, and now nothing will stop me from being with you as soon as possible. I shall wait only to know from you that you are residing in Leipzig, and whether I may presume upon the kindness with which you expressed yourself towards me when I last saw you. I am very sorry that I am unable to go to Liverpool to hear your Oratorio; although it will suffer materially from the loss of Malibran, I have no doubt that every possible justice will be done to it. The Choruses[1] went off *magnificently* at Manchester and most likely the same Chorus-Singers are engaged for Liverpool. I will bring you a correct account of its performance, which I shall obtain from some friends who are going. You cannot form an idea of the great sensation the death of Malibran has excited in England. She was buried on Saturday at Manchester. The people in England are very much enraged with De Beriot[2] for leaving her directly she died and not being present at her funeral.

You will much oblige me by writing to me immediately, as I wish to lose no more time, and also to know positively that you are at Leipzig. If I can execute any commissions for you *here*, pray let me know and I shall be most happy to do so. London looks at this time most miserable, we have had nothing but rain during the last month. As for Music there is none to be heard for *Love or for Money*. Attwood has been out of town for three months, but I believe he returned yesterday. Since I left Düsseldorf I am sorry to say I have been idle[3], but I must make up my lost time when I get over to Leipzig. I have written my address[4] on the other side of the letter, and shall be most happy to hear from you as soon as possible.

  My dear Sir,
    Yours very truly,
      W. S. BENNETT.

---

[1] i.e. the choruses of other Oratorios. 'St Paul' was not performed at Manchester.

[2] Mdme Malibran's second husband.

[3] He need not have said this. Besides the new slow movement for his Concerto, he had written the Overture 'The Naiads,' and 3 Impromptus for the Pianoforte.

[4] He was staying with the publisher Coventry, at 71 Dean Street, Soho.

LEIPZIG, 10*th October*, 1836.

MY DEAR SIR,

I receive your letter of the 3rd this moment, and hasten to write to you in return, as you wish to have an immediate answer. I have come back to this place about three weeks since, and shall stay here during the whole winter till April of next year. How happy I shall be to see you here, I need not repeat, because you certainly know the esteem I have for you and the pleasure it will give me to become more acquainted with you and your talent, and I can only repeat in this respect the same things which I said to you at Düsseldorf. Mr Lipinsky told me some days ago he was sure you would come over, but I did not believe it, as I had not heard from you for so long. I was the more glad when I received your letter, and so are many of my friends and of the musical people here, who long to see and hear you. The musical season has begun pretty well here, the orchestra perform the Symphonies in very good style and with the greatest zeal, and I hope you will have some pleasure of your residence here. It is at least now one of the best and most animated musical places of this country, and I trust I shall have some of your orchestral music performed as it ought to be. Pray bring your Symphony and the Concertos, if possible with the instrumental parts, with you; if you do not, we shall be obliged to have them sent after you. Will you have the kindness before you leave London to enquire at Mr Novello's whether he has answered my last letter, and if not whether he will give you the answer to the many questions I put to him. You would also oblige me if you would ask Mr Klingemann if he has a letter or something else for me. Excuse the trouble and let me hope to see you soon here, and to see you in good spirits and healthy and happy, as I always shall wish you to be.

If you see Mr Attwood, pray remember me *very* kindly to him, and also my best compliments to Mr Davison (has he received my Psalm, which I gave to Mr Novello for him?).

Yours very truly,
FELIX MENDELSSOHN BARTHOLDY.

His Arrival

Four days after receiving this letter, Bennett started from London, sailed with favouring winds to Hamburg in sixty-five hours, and thence proceeded by coach, via Berlin, to Leipzig, at the average rate of five English miles an hour. No wonder that when a few weeks later a 'steam-carriage' arrived from England for the first German railway, he shared the curiosity of the Leipzigers, and paid his four groschen with the rest to stare at the interesting novelty.

On Saturday, October 29, about mid-day, he found himself at the Hotel Russie, Leipzig, feeling very lonely and friendless; but a note, sent in the afternoon to announce his arrival, was immediately answered in person by Mendelssohn, who took him off to his own lodgings, and did not leave him again till he had seen him thoroughly comfortable. The same evening, he was taken to the Hotel de Bavière, then a favourite resort of the musical circle. Before Sunday was past, he had made friends with Ferdinand David, the violinist and leader (Concert-Meister) of the Gewandhaus orchestra; with Stamaty, a young French pianist; with Eduard Franck of Breslau; and with a Scotchman named Monicke, a professor of languages, who, at Mendelssohn's request, took him under his wing, acting as his guide and interpreter, and his instructor in the German language. Of another acquaintance, he wrote home to Davison:—'I have found a new friend, a man who would be just after your own heart. How I wish you could know him. His name is Robert Schumann.'

After a few days, he took lodgings in the house of Dr Hasper, Katherinen Strasse 364[1], and became a subscriber at the Hotel de Bavière, where Mendelssohn, with Schumann by his side, dined regularly during this winter. The landlord of the house was the genial Julius Kistner, who some years later succeeded his brother Friedrich as manager of the music-publishing firm which still bears their name.

During his visits to Germany, Bennett kept journals. The entries are short and simple. A few extracts will give, in his own words, his impressions of his new surroundings. Where art is concerned he is temperate in the expression of opinion, and always independent. He does not meekly acquiesce in everything that a land of music puts before him.

[1] In 1881 the house was No. 15.

[Journal.] *Oct.* 31*st.* I have dined again with Mendelssohn to-day, and also met Mr Monicke, who afterwards took me to his chambers for coffee and cigars. He showed me my way to the theatre, which I entered at half-past five. The Opera began at six. The price of admission to the boxes or the stalls is sixteen groschen (two shillings). The Opera was one of Marschner's entitled 'Hans Heiling.' I cannot say that I think it was in any way well performed, but I like some of the music and I admire also some points of the orchestra which altogether is *rather* more musician-like than our orchestras in England, though it is far inferior in *force* and *spirit*.

Nov. 4*th.* Mendelssohn gave me a ticket for the concert last night. The Symphony [Mozart in E flat[1]] was performed really well. The band is rather small, but quite perfect and possesses great animation. Mendelssohn played Beethoven's Concerto [in G] very splendidly and his two cadences were magnificent. The people were enthusiastic. [The overture to] 'Oberon' was not so well played as I have heard it in London. I mean as regards the style of playing it. I have this afternoon been to the rehearsal of 'Israel in Egypt' in the Church. Upon consideration, I do not think that they understand the manner and style of playing this Oratorio, but I will say nothing until I hear it performed on Monday. I have made my bow to Miss Clara Wieck[2], a very *clever* girl and plays capitally. She played me a Concerto which she had composed. Altogether it wants *weeding*, but I wish all girls were like her. So much for Clara Wieck.

Nov. 5*th.* I have been again to the Church to hear 'Israel in Egypt' and still have the same opinion with regard to its performance.

Nov. 8*th.* I was too late to get a good place in the Pauliner-Kirche last night, although I went at half-past five, and as the Germans are very rude in pushing you about in all directions, I contented myself by standing under the orchestra. Altogether it might be termed a successful performance. The singers for the soli parts were anything but good, the orchestra wanted point, and the organist was

---

[1] The works to which he alludes are identified by programmes given in the diary.
[2] Afterwards Madame Schumann.

continually lagging. However, the people seemed pleased, and that is everything. 'The Horse and his Rider' was the best performed of the Choruses. £150 was taken and each person paid two shillings.

Nov. 9th. I was dressed by nine o'clock this morning —pretty well for me. After dining at the hotel, I went with David, Schumann, and Mendelssohn to play billiards at some gardens a little way out of the town—where afterwards heard some waltzes played by Mr Strauss's band. They tell me that the master of the gardens, Mr Queisser, is the finest trombone player in Europe.

Nov. 12th. Yesterday and to-day Mr and Mrs Paul Mendelssohn were of our party to dinner. Stamaty and Schumann came to-day and I played to them. The weather is not so cold as when I first came here, though the Germans wonder I don't wear a cloak, which in truth I would, but that they laugh at my little cloak so much.

Nov. 13th. The Quartetts of last night were played capitally with the exception of the Bass. That of Haydn [in G], I did not much like; it must have been written when he was either childish in youth or in age. The last movement has some beautiful points in it. I don't remember having heard it before. The beautiful Quartett of Mozart,

came like wine after water. The slow movement was very much out of time. But the Quartett of Beethoven [in E mi., Rasoumoffsky] laid hold of you by the ears. I should think that the Scherzo was one of the most beautiful things ever written. The Trio is certainly a *little too* much of a good thing.

Nov. 22nd. Now then for my first appearance at a German private dinner. Dinner at one. Very wet day; impossible to keep clean boots; however, by the utmost care, I managed to walk to Dr Haertel's without getting very dirty. Left my hat outside the room. David says, 'No, you must take it in the room with you.' This is something new. Our party consisted of my friend Monicke,

Professor Falkmann, Mr Brockhaus (the large bookseller), Mr David, Dr Haertel and his brother, and Mrs Haertel. At any rate a dinner here is a very different thing from a dinner in England; no asking people to take wine; the dinner wine is on the table and you must help yourself or you know the consequence. I was placed by Mrs Haertel who speaks English very well, and indeed there was more English than German spoken during the meal. I had the felicity of taking from each dish first, which was not a very enviable situation, as from their being quite strange to me, I did not know whether to take much or little, and I had no example set me. However, I made no very great mistake, as I could see from those that came after me. The only accident which occurred to me was that the footman handed me a pie with a kind of fish-slice which I began very dexterously to use on the dish, but Mrs Haertel stopped me and said, 'I beg your pardon, sir, use the spoon, the man is quite wrong,'—so after all, it was not my mistake. After eating for an hour we removed into a room and drank coffee, chatted for a few minutes, and left Dr and Mrs Haertel to enjoy domestic quietude. The house is the most splendid I have seen for a long time. It is called a Palace and is worthy of the name. I like Mrs Haertel very much *indeed*.

Nov. 23rd. Went with Schumann this morning to be introduced to one Mr Kistner, a music-publisher here, and afterwards to a Madame Voigt, who was dining at half-past twelve.

Nov. 28th. Called [yesterday] on Mendelssohn who introduced me to Madame von Goethe, daughter-in-law of the Poet, who was with her son (a student of the University here) at his house.

Kind attentions followed introductions. Herr Friedrich Kistner came round, in a few days, to Bennett's lodgings, bringing, as a surprise, proofs of 'Sketches' and 'Impromptus' engraved from English copies; and the first sight of his music in a foreign edition, coming unexpectedly, gave great pleasure to a young composer. Walther von Goethe, 'the grandson' as he was often styled, did his duty under difficulties, and paid a formal call. 'He speaks English,' writes

Bennett, 'a *little better* than I do German, and I don't speak at all.' But von Goethe met the emergency by bringing with him Dr Tauchnitz, who entered the room with a dictionary under his arm; and, with the ice thus broken, the two young men, the one as full of fun as the other, soon found common interests; nor was it long before they were playing their pranks together, to the delight of their older friend, the silent but smiling Schumann. Frau Henriette Voigt, who is now remembered as one of the earliest admirers of Schumann's music, with her husband, Herr Carl Voigt, a prosperous merchant, at once adopted Bennett as a member of their family party, giving him a permanent seat at their Sunday dinner table, and a hearty reception at all times; nor does Bennett forget to mention choice cigars, specially reserved for his use by Frau Voigt, which cigars he regarded as a set-off against the trial of taking his place at the piano; for this lady was a fine amateur pianist, and music was often brought forward.

'I am making friends,' he writes, 'at the rate of ten miles an hour'; but it must have been by personal rather than musical qualities that he at first found favour. Ten weeks passed before he was called to appear in public, and he escaped when he could from playing in private society. Of an early visit to the Voigts he writes, 'I paid my respects to Mr and Mrs Voigt and played a little to them'; but, on the other hand, 'I went to the von Goethes, talked and drank tea, but would not play; what a fool I am!' He finds a party at the house of Herr Brockhaus less agreeable than the one at Dr Haertel's, and though he gives no reason, it was doubtless because he was obliged to go to the piano; for Herr Brockhaus has written of the same evening in his diary, 'Bennett, the English artist played very well (sehr brav) and I much enjoyed his rendering of an Adagio by Beethoven.'

Between Schumann and Bennett, sympathetic and even intimate relationship dates from the first days of their meeting. If there is any truth in a statement that Schumann was by nature unsociable, he at any rate quickly attached himself to this young stranger, coming to his rooms, prevailing upon him to play the piano, taking him as the companion of his daily walks, and within a fortnight of the acquaintance, writing to his home in Zwickau: 'There is a young Englishman here, whom we meet every day—William Bennett—a thorough Englishman, a glorious artist, and a beautiful poetic soul.' Schumann, with a respect for England engendered by a study of its literature, was predisposed to welcome a musician coming from a land of poets. Full of fancy, he found pretty ways of showing his interest in Bennett's nationality. The word William had perhaps no over-familiar look or sound to German senses, and Schumann wrote about the coincidence which had given Bennett the same Christian name as Shakespeare. To this little piece of extravagance he clung, often writing 'William Bennett,' to the exclusion of the name Sterndale which others used[1]. When Bennett first stepped on to the platform of the Leipzig concert-room, Schumann had just overheard the remark, 'Ein englische Componist—kein Componist.' At the conclusion of the P.F. Concerto, he turned to his prejudiced but now converted neighbour with the query, 'Ein englischer Componist?' and received the reply, 'Und wahrhaftig ein englischer.' To this application of the old play on the words *Anglii* and *Angeli* he also clung, calling Bennett in correspondence 'an angel-musician.' But Schumann's fancies were prompted by realities. He readily held out his hand to an Englishman, but especially to one whose character as an artist was congenial to him. As editor of a musical journal, he was crusading against the superficiality which, not the least in what concerned the pianoforte, characterized the prevailing music of the period. Anxiously looking to the future, he was insisting that the works of the Great Masters must be taken as the source from which new beauties could alone spring. To combat 'the latest phase of the arch-foes of art,' which was 'the result of a mere cultivation of executive technique,' was one of the objects for which Schumann had taken up his pen. In the young Englishman he saw a firm adherent to his own principles. That performance should be subsidiary to music was no axiom at the time; but

---

[1] i.e. in correspondence and press notices. This was pointed out to the writer by Herr Gustav Jensen, who, however, in his edition of Schumann's letters and criticisms has sometimes supplied what he called Bennett's 'Rufname,' Sterndale, where it had been omitted by Schumann.

Bennett has written that he held that view, and Schumann, in a critique, has given him credit for acting on the conviction. As a student of the older masters, Bennett would be found by Schumann already far advanced, and, in this respect, the education he had received in his own country, might well take a German by surprise. Schumann, after knowing Bennett for two months, took him as a subject for his editorial article in the New-Year number of the *Neue Zeitschrift für Musik*, writing appreciatively of his early compositions, and of his general musical acquirements, and in a tone suggesting personal regard. He wrote in conclusion :—

Much else I might tell you— * * * —how he knows Handel by heart—how he plays all Mozart's Operas on the piano so that you can see them actually in front of you—but it is himself that I can no longer hold at bay. He keeps looking over my shoulder, and has already twice asked: 'Now what are you writing there?' I can only add, 'Dear friend, if you but knew.'

The diary duly records Christmas festivities, with the Christmas-tree, and other German customs, to which Bennett is introduced by the hospitable Voigts. The New-Year, 1837, arrives in severely seasonable garb; the excitement of sledging excursions is enjoyed; and then he finds himself face to face with the horrors of public performance in a strange land.

[Journal.] *Jan. 14th.* Received a visit from Mr Kistner in the name of the Concert Directors to ask me to play at the concert next Thursday. *Of course consented.*

Jan. 15th. Feel very uncomfortable at the thought of playing next Thursday.

Jan. 18th. Rehearsal in Gewandhaus, and I played my Concerto in C minor pretty well.

Jan. 19th. Good God! To-day I must play in the Gewandhaus. Horrible thought! However I must.

It was the custom of the Leipzig public to receive a new-comer in dead silence. It was not an uncommon occurrence for a performer to leave the concert-room without that silence having been broken. On exceptional occasions, positive marks of disapproval were forthcoming. Bennett had already been witness to the fact that judgment in the Gewandhaus was not tempered with mercy. He, however, successfully passed the ordeal. Mendelssohn—as was remembered by Herr Eduard Franck—pronounced the performance 'meisterlich,' and he wrote of the general feeling about it to his sister: 'Bennett played his C minor Concerto amidst the triumphant applause of the Leipzigers, whom he seems to have made his friends and admirers at one stroke; indeed, he is the sole topic of conversation here now.' Schumann described the Concerto and the effect produced, but without special reference to the playing, probably considering that in the case of a pianist-composer the idea of the music and its rendering was indivisible. He wrote :—

'After the first movement, a purely lyrical piece, full of fine human feeling, such as we meet with only in the best master-works, it became clear to all, that they had here to do with an artist of the most refined nature. Still, he was not rewarded with that general thunder of applause, such as only bold virtuosos excite. Expectation was visibly awakened, more was demanded, people wished to make the Englishman understand that he was in the land of music. Then began the romance in G minor—so simple that the notes can almost be counted in it. Even if I had not learned from the fountain-head, that the idea of a fair somnambulist had floated before our poet while composing, yet all that is touching in such a fancy affects the heart at this moment. The audience sat breathless, as though fearing to awaken the dreamer on the lofty palace roof; and if sympathy at moments became almost painful, the loveliness of the vision soon transformed that feeling into a pure artistic enjoyment. And here he struck that wonderful chord, where he imagines the wanderer, safe from danger, again resting on her couch, over which the moon-light streams. This happy trait set at rest all doubt respecting our artist, and in the last movement the public gave itself wholly up to the delight we are accustomed to receive from a master, whether he leads us on to battle or to peace[1].'

Bennett himself dismissed the occasion in few words :—
'Last night I played in the concert at the Gewandhaus, and according to all accounts made a satisfactory *debût*. I did not play so well as I can do when I am thoroughly com-

---

[1] Translated, from the German, by F. R. Ritter.

fortable. I had a bad *clavier*, not *strong* enough. However, I was perfectly satisfied with the whole affair. To-night I go to the masquerade in the Theatre.' With a weight off his mind, he could enjoy himself for a few hours in the guise of 'A Spanish Inquisitor.'

In the diary of this first visit to Leipzig, there is one name not so continually mentioned as might be expected. Bennett met Mendelssohn in general society; dined most days at the same table with him; and attended the concerts conducted by him; but of close personal association there is not much trace for some time. He noticed the quiet deference shown by Schumann and others to the leader of the musical circle, and was himself impressed with the distinction of Mendelssohn's personality. 'I cannot describe what I mean,' he would afterwards say, 'but Mendelssohn's entrance into a room caused a check, and everything seemed different.' So Bennett, at first, modestly kept at a little distance. He would naturally be unwilling to encroach upon the private time of a great man busily occupied. Then, again, in these months, the thoughts of Mendelssohn's spare moments were not so free as to be given exclusively to his Leipzig entourage. The rehearsing and performing at the Gewandhaus under Mendelssohn's direction, and the successful result, would help to dissipate Bennett's shyness; so between the parts of the next concert he went into the orchestra to have a chat with the conductor, and the few minutes thus spent prepared the way to more intimate friendship. Miss Jeanrenand, to whom Mendelssohn was soon to be married, had just arrived in the town on a visit to some friends, and was seated in the concert-room. She was now pointed out to Bennett, who, after expressing his own admiration for the young lady, began to teaze her betrothed about the impending sacrifice of liberty. Mendelssohn, who was (according to the diary) 'mad with happiness' broke out in singing the words, '*Hang* the liberty;' and this phrase thenceforward became a friendly watchword which passed between himself and Bennett when they met or corresponded.

Bennett being now a centre of interest, the compliment was paid him of placing his new Overture, as an attraction, on the programme of the extra concert given annually 'for the poor.'

[Journal.] *Feb.* 13*th*. Yesterday they rehearsed my Overture (Naiades) in the Gewandhaus. It did not please me—too much noise, so to-day at the second rehearsal I dispensed with the trombones and like it all the better. To-night I shall direct it myself as Mendelssohn wishes me to do so.

Feb. 14*th*. My Overture was received with good applause last night. I directed it myself, and did not know what to do with my left hand. I rather liked it myself, but I do not think the people understood it, with all the compliments which were paid me. In the second act of the concert was recited part of the Faust by Goethe, with music by a Prussian Prince named Radziwill. On this account, Schumann, and Goethe (the grandson), Armstrong, and Franck, with myself, adjourned to Dr Faust's cellar, otherwise Auerbachs Keller, where the Devil and Dr Faust are said to have had their meetings. There are some curious old pictures of the Doctor and the Devil, and the place seems very *sulphurish*.

A little Canon, now in the library of the 'Gesellschaft der Musik-Freunde' at Vienna, was written by Bennett on the day 'The Naiads' was first played, and probably in Auerbachs Keller, as he would scarcely have been in the fit humour for it, while the verdict on his Overture was in suspense.

Another relic of playful hours is the beginning of a German play, dedicated to Schumann and Walther von Goethe, which Bennett wrote amidst the exercises for Mr Monicke, and in which the University student (von Goethe), the Editor (Schumann), and the Englishman (himself), figure in the list of Dramatis Personæ.

The concert season closed on March 13th with a performance of the Choral Symphony, which in Bennett's opinion 'did not go well.' Then he spent a few happy 'breakfast-mornings' with Mendelssohn, 'playing a good deal to him,' and receiving, as a parting gift, the autograph score of the 'Hebrides' Overture. Mendelssohn, whose marriage was imminent, now left Leipzig. In the past twenty weeks, Bennett had spent little time in composition. The diary tells of a Symphony having been started on some 'rascally German music-paper,' but there is no further trace of the music. The statement, sometimes made, that he did regular work under the guidance of Mendelssohn, is false. As an exceptional circumstance, a pair of rather formal notes passed, to arrange an interview for the conductor's perusal of the 'Parisina' Overture, before its performance at the Gewandhaus; and either at the interview, or after the work had been played, Mendelssohn suggested that it should be lengthened. Bennett, on his return to England, acted on this advice, but with no successful result. His London friends, on hearing the new edition, were of one mind that he had spoilt the work, and he then restored it to its original shape. The fact is, that Bennett did not get, or did not take, at this time, the chance of spending with Mendelssohn musical hours such as he later enjoyed; and it was only towards the end of the twenty weeks which they had been spending in the same town, that the lost opportunity was realized. Either Mendelssohn was too busy to seek out Bennett, or Bennett too timid to approach Mendelssohn. The latter, conscious that Bennett held aloof, reproached him for it, saying at last, 'You are *always* with Schumann.' This remark, which Bennett repeated more than once in hearing of the present writer, would only refer to personal intimacy. There was no professional rivalry between Mendelssohn and Schumann; no dream that their names would come to be placed in opposition by partisans; and, indeed, little foresight, at this particular time, that Schumann would become a celebrated musician.

After Mendelssohn's departure, Bennett stayed on in Leipzig for another three months, and set to work on some pianoforte compositions. On Mendelssohn's wedding day, March 28th, he was finishing the last movement of a Sonata in F minor, to be dedicated to the bridegroom, whose health was no doubt drunk by Schumann and himself at a little dinner they took together that day in a country village. A fortnight later, Bennett was holding festival on his own account.

[Journal.] *April* 13*th*. Twenty-one to-day. Can hardly fancy myself a man, but I'll be hanged if I am not, at least according to law. Thank God for all things. I look back in my life and wish I had done much more, but nevertheless I have not been a regular scamp, and won't now if I can help it. Got up early this morning and found my room ornamented with green, and a wreath of flowers from Julius Kistner. I can't help wishing myself in England, perhaps an ungrateful wish.

A Birthday Breakfast.

At half-past eleven my visitors began to arrive. Monicke, F. Kistner, Franck, von Goethe, Dr Hasper, Schrey, Cayard, Schumann, and afterwards Benecke. Eating began at twelve and drinking afterwards. A cold breakfast out of the Hotel de Bavière, as I could not get a hot one. Schumann gave me a letter of Martin Luther, Mrs Voigt one of Weber, von Goethe gave me his Grandfather's works, Mrs Cayard sent me a silver cigar-case, and lastly Mr Kistner presented me something in a basket with a laurel wreath, which looked like a *Tea-Caddy*, but turned out to be a box containing a silver cup and plate from the Concert-Direction. No wonder with all these attentions I should have been *wondrously merry*. We finished with coffee at three. In the evening went to a party at Monicke's, where I saw cake on the table illuminated with twenty-one candles, which, I believe, is a German custom. A jolly day altogether—Never come again—That's certain.

Besides the Sonata dedicated to Mendelssohn, there belong to this time 'Three Romances' for the piano, which Schumann pronounced: 'a great step in advance as regards deep, even strange, harmonic combinations, and a bold, broad construction; resembling the earlier works in a rich flowing melody, and in the predominance of the melody in the upper part, but excelling them in their highly impassioned character.' Friedrich Kistner used, in afterdays, to greet Bennett by singing the melody of the first of these Romances. Then, again, a long 'Fantaisie' in four movements was written, and dedicated 'à son ami, Robert Schumann'; but, apart from the formal inscription, it was (according to Davison) intended as a *souvenir*, and expressly for Schumann's own playing, it being stipulated in fun that the composer must be sure to make it 'difficult enough.' Schumann found the 'Fantaisie' 'ringing with lovely melodies as over-richly as a nest of nightingales;' and though, through disablement of hand, he had long ceased to be a professed pianist, he was diligently practising the manuscript when Bennett left Leipzig. Bennett made himself acquainted with Schumann's early pianoforte works, knowing by heart some of those as yet in manuscript, and among them the 'Etudes Symphoniques,' which were about to be published and dedicated to him. It may be assumed that his renderings pleased the composer, who wrote later to his future wife that he hoped W. Bennett would join him in Vienna, because there were no pianists in that city with whom he was in sympathy so that many of his 'best thoughts' remained silent. The 'Etudes Symphoniques' had been written in 1834, but the last movement is said to have been a later thought. In it comes a fragment of the Romance from Marschner's Opera, 'The Templar and the Jewess,' in which Ivanhoe calls on proud England to rejoice over her noble Knights. 'It was an ingenious way,' writes one of Schumann's biographers, 'of paying homage to his beloved English composer[1].'

The diary brings this chapter to an end:—

May 28th. My poor Journal!! So many days and even weeks have elapsed, and you have never once been opened. And what have I been doing all this time? Visiting Princesses (Victoire and Julie of Schönberg) and Counts, re-scoring my Naiades, packing up my music for London. Been to breakfast two or three times with Count Reuss and smoked Turkey tobacco. Forgotten to mention that I have paid a visit to Madame Schumann[2] at Zwickau, fifty miles from here. I went with Robert Schumann and von Goethe. It rained the whole time. Have been in a regular *Sunday* humour to-day; quite happy and quiet.

June 10th. Well, I'm off on Monday. Beginning to pay my visits p. p. c. Count Reuss is gone away to Kreutz. Called yesterday on Madame von Goethe, dined with Benecke, and played at Cricket with some Englishmen, which made the Germans stare very much, as they never saw the game before—we had English bats and balls. *8 o'clock evening.* Schumann has been to spend an hour with me and drink a bottle of Porter, I am so sorry to part from him, for I think he is one of the finest hearted fellows I ever knew—My heart springs up when I think that I leave Leipzig on Monday, but yet I don't know whether it is with sorrow at leaving this place or joy at seeing my England again. I could never believe before that one was so fond of his own country—especially mine. As Sir Walter Scott says, 'Merry England which is the envy of all other countries and the pride of all who can call themselves her natives'—Amen, say I.

Leipzig

Adieu!

auf wiedersehen!

---

[1] Article 'Schumann' in Grove's *Dictionary of Music.*
[2] Robert Schumann's sister-in-law.

CHAPTER V.

LONDON AND, AGAIN, LEIPZIG.

July 1837—March 1839.
æt. 21, 22.

BENNETT spent a month over his return journey. He stopped a day or two in Frankfort to see the Mendelssohns, and was delayed for a fortnight at Mainz by the non-arrival of proofsheets which Kistner wished him to correct before leaving Germany. He occupied his time in making a four-handed arrangement of 'The Naiads,' but got a little cross as the days went by. The unforeseen expense taxed his travelling money, and he was forced to pass ten dreary days at Rotterdam before he could get a further remittance from England. It was not till the middle of July that he found himself under Coventry's hospitable roof in Dean Street, and was writing to his Aunt: 'I cannot tell you how glad I shall be to get quietly to Cambridge, where I rather hope to spend *some months* with you, that is until the musical season begins again in London.' From Cambridge he wrote[1] to Schumann on August 26th:—

MY DEAR FRIEND,

You really were most kind to send me such a charming letter. You show yourself, my dear fellow, in so happy a mood, and I trust that your joy springs from the heart. Yes! as you say, your style is no longer that of an *Editor*, but of a maiden of eighteen years. I have so often had you in my thoughts, wishing at the same time that you

[1] The original is in German.

were with me here. Ah! England! dear land of *Whig* and *Tory*. In London I only spent three weeks, and then came on to this place, which, as the weather continues to be fine, still looks quite heavenly. Do come and stop with me for six months. Say *yes*, and I will fetch you.

Coventry and Hollier will gladly print your *Etudes*. I have been playing them a great deal and with much enjoyment.

Here, assuredly, is a bar of very great beauty. I play it at least a hundred times a day.

To-morrow I am going to London for a day or two, and shall so meet Mendelssohn, for I know he is now there. I shall be travelling farther on September 14th— to Birmingham—and then I will write again to tell you about the Festival. * * * *

Thalberg is now the god of Englishmen. For a lesson of forty minutes he gets *two guineas*—no trifling sum. Rosenhain of Frankfort remains in London, having, doubtless, discovered the fine colour of English gold. You are sure to have heard of the concert for Beethoven's monument. Moscheles played the Concerto in C major very finely. The Choral Symphony was also given.

Greet the Voigts for me, also my dear friend Walther von Goethe to whom I *will* send a manuscript. Is Stamaty in Leipzig? I have had no news of him. How, too, is Anger? And now, dear Schumann, before you quit this world, do visit England. I very often think of Zwickau, of your brother and of his wife. I must soon come and see you all again, so when I *can* then I *will*. Forgive the errors in this letter. It is my pen, not my heart, that

---

[1] In this quotation Bennett has omitted one or two accidentals, and the bass notes of the first two chords.

makes them. Write again very soon and believe that I shall never forget you.

Adieu Schumann,
Always and ever your friend,
W. S. BENNETT.

PS. I am hoping for a copy of your *Etudes* and for one of the *Carnival*. Give my best remembrances to Monicke, to Julius and Fritz Kistner. Tell David that he must come to England next year.

The autumn was a poor time for a young musician to start professional life in London. For all that could be found to do, Bennett might almost as well have passed the months at Cambridge. But he was persuaded to make an attempt; and he found a little work, as well as a very pleasing reception, waiting for him at the Academy. On September 15, he wrote to his Aunt, in explanation of a broken appointment:—

'This morning I gave a lesson at the Academy at nine o'clock and was detained there on business all the morning. At 2 o'clock there was a great meeting of *all the Students* to present me with a *piece of Plate* which I knew nothing of till then. It was presented with a long speech from the Principal, Mr Potter. Of course I am very delighted. * * * I will come to-morrow.'

A few days later, he started for Birmingham; but, the coach losing four hours on the road, he reached the Town Hall just as the performance of 'St Paul' was concluding. Two special attractions of the Festival still remained. Mendelssohn was to introduce his new P.F. Concerto in D minor, and to give a solo-performance on the organ. To those who heard such organ-playing for the first time, as Bennett probably did on this occasion, the revelation was astonishing. Mendelssohn played on the last day of the Festival, and, when he had finished, hurried away to catch the coach for London. Bennett went to see him off, and unable to restrain his curiosity, asked, 'How ever did you come to play like that?' It was an old story; there had been no royal road; and Mendelssohn replied rather sharply, 'By working like a horse.'

LONDON, *October* 14, 1837.

MY DEAR MR MENDELSSOHN,

We cannot let Miss Novello go to Leipzig without sending you a few lines, just to ask how you arrived in Germany. I sincerely hope that you found your wife and all friends perfectly well. I could see when you were in the coach at Birmingham, how delighted you were at the thought of going back, and wished many times to go with you. I think you must have been perfectly satisfied with your reception in England, which is said to have been the greatest since Weber produced his Oberon—they talk of you very much and with the greatest enthusiasm, and I am *very, very* glad, because *my Country* is getting musical. I am sorry to tell you that our Organist Samuel Wesley died two days since very suddenly, I believe you were with him at Christ Church where you played the organ. I have no more news to tell you, but I hope you will be so kind to write sometimes and tell me what is going on in Leipzig. I think I should like to send you something for the Concerts, if you would do it, but I will write again about it. *Und nun, noch eine Bitte* (*Schiller*). Will you accept the little gold *pencil-case* from me, which is very simple, but I hope you will like it. Your name is engraved on the top—Good-bye—Give my best respects to Mrs Mendelssohn and the Schunck family and believe me,

Yours very truly,
W. STERNDALE BENNETT.

PS. I rather believe *Blagrove* (an English Violin-Player) will pass through Leipzig and give a Concert, when if you could show him any attention you would much oblige me. He would like to know *David*. Will you give my remembrances to Schleinitz and David—Good bye, Good Bye.

[Mendelssohn to Bennett[1].]

DEAR BENNETT,

A thousand thanks for your most kind present, and for the great pleasure you have given me by it. Especially, too, for your kind thought of me and your

---

[1] Original is in German—dated at end.

friendly letter—in fact, for everything. The pencil is so graceful and elegant, and the monogram on it so pretty—'quite English' as they say here when they want to describe the essence of elegance and usefulness. I am delighted that you think of me in this way, yes, even a little ashamed by your kindness in making me a present when I should be grateful to be simply remembered by you. Please do think of me often, and let me see a sign of it now and then by a letter, which is sure to procure me a few happy hours. I hope that the new compositions which you mention will be a reason for your first letter; for I must beg you to send them *as soon as possible*. You know what pleasure you give to all musicians here by your works, and that you may rely on our performing them with the most loving care. Send them soon, very soon. Of your earlier Overtures I have already put down 'The Naiads' for one of our concerts, and should like to know soon what new things I could place on the programmes. Everything is going on here in the old way which you know, and which has its good and bad sides. Your friends here are all well. I often meet Schleinitz, David, the Schuncks, who all return your greetings many times over, and often speak of you with friendly interest. Schumann I now see very seldom, for it was at the hotel that I always used to meet him, and I have quite given up going there now. But how nice my home now is, what charm my wife ('hang the liberty!!!'), has brought into my whole existence, what delight into my life, you should come and see that for yourself, and I only wish that you would do so soon. * * * This winter is again quite madly full of music and musicians, just like last year if not worse. Clara Novello is creating a tremendous furore. The public is quite beside itself when she sings with such perfect intonation, such ease and such reliable musicianship. Half Leipzig is in love with her. The people clap her wildly and the other night they even shouted 'Da Capo' until she had to come and sing again. This is quite an exception with us Leipzig folks! Next Thursday we are going to do the Messiah in St Paul's Church, to-day a singer, Mdlle Schlegel, is giving a concert, the day after to-morrow the violinist Vieuxtemps will give one, a few days ago Kummer the violoncellist gave one with the clarinettist Kotte from Dresden, next week the pianist Taubert from Berlin, then Herr Taeglichsbeck from Hechinghen, Herr Schuncke, Herr Eichler, &c. &c. &c. &c. &c.—my head quite buzzes from it all. I have not yet been able to begin composing, and yet am very anxious to do so. Let this be my excuse for an incoherent letter; I find it difficult to write even that much, but I have been wishing for a long time to thank you for your pretty present and your kind letter. Continue your kind friendship and write again soon to

Your friend,
FELIX MENDELSSOHN BARTHOLDY.

LEIPZIG, 11 *Nov.*, 1837.

By the end of the year, Bennett was occupying rooms on the first-floor front of 'Portland Chambers,' 75[1] Great Titchfield Street, his friend Davison being settled in the back rooms on the same floor. Davison's brother told the writer that Bennett kept his chambers in very nice order, and showed himself (as was always the case later) careful and proud of his possessions. When his companions admired the contents of his sitting-room, he would laugh with pleasure, and say, 'Yes, and it's all my own, you know.' In March 1838, he wrote to Mendelssohn :—'I wish you could see me at this moment in England and know how well I find myself in my little rooms near Great Portland St. where you used to live. Your picture hangs over my fireplace with the canon which you wrote on it at Düsseldorf. Davison is now in my rooms, we very often talk of you together and wish our happy *German days* on the Rhine to come again.'

He was taking a hopeful view of life, with little idea of the difficulty he would later find in making his way. Private pupils he might hope to get in greater numbers, as time went on; at present he was teaching two, then a third came, but no more. He was still in request at 'The Society of British Musicians,' his name appearing either as composer, pianist, or conductor, on the programmes of their four concerts in the early months of 1838. He played

---

[1] The house, still bearing the same title, is now (1907) numbered 93.

Mozart's Concerto in E flat, No. 14, on the opening night of 'The Vocal Concerts,' a new musical association which employed an orchestra. The revival of a Concerto of Mozart's involved trouble, but to him it was doubtless a labour of love to copy a full score from the band parts, as he did for the occasion. When the London season came, he took a bold step by announcing an 'Evening Concert,' for which he engaged ten of the leading English and German singers, as well as a full orchestra with Sir George Smart as conductor. A scheme of Symphonies, Overtures, Concertos, and Vocal pieces with orchestral accompaniment, was more costly, and at the same time less attractive to the general public, than the commoner form of programme with songs accompanied on the piano, and solo Fantasias for instruments. With concerts such as Bennett, and a few others provided, the only commercial question that arose was how much the loss would be. A well-established Professor could count upon his following of pupils and friends. For a young man, the risk was considerable, and Bennett, when excusing himself, a month before the concert, from performing a family duty at Cambridge, wrote:—'My concert is coming on, and absence from London at this time might mean ruin to me.' Whilst engaged in the preliminary business arrangements, he was also taking great pains over the composition of a new Caprice, in E major, for pianoforte and orchestra, which was to be played at the concert. Davison could point to a place, about 153 bars from the beginning of this piece, where progress had been checked, and would relate that Bennett woke him up one night, to show him how he had at length solved the difficulty. The event proved that Bennett had already many good friends; the favour of the Academy authorities was valuable; and May 25 saw the Hanover Square Rooms well-filled. If the music was of sterner quality than that usually offered at 'benefit' entertainments, in quantity at least it conformed to custom, and, in the course of several hours, the concert-giver could, without noticeable egotism, introduce two or three of his own works. Besides the new Caprice, he played on this occasion the Concerto in F minor, which had so far only been heard at the Academy. This work he again chose a month later for his appearance at the Philharmonic, which henceforth became an annual event. So also, except in one or two seasons, he continued to give his orchestral concert for the next ten years.

In an attempted sketch of his own life, abandoned when he reached the third page of a small note-book, he wrote of having tried at this time, but of having failed, to settle down in London. He wished once more to go to Germany, and especially, as he put it, to gain closer companionship with Mendelssohn. His Leipzig friends were pleased at the prospect of having him with them again, and the Directors of the Gewandhaus concerts, hearing that he was likely to come, despatched a very cordial invitation. On July 27, he wrote:—

MY DEAR MR MENDELSSOHN,

In reply to your very kind and handsome letter I beg to say to you that nothing short of Death or severe accident shall prevent me from shaking hands with you at Leipzig about the middle of October. I have read over your letter several times and assure [you] that I have a heart to appreciate all your kindness and generous feelings and if I have not the power to express all to you that I feel, you must give me credit for having it in me. * * * I go to Cambridge this day and shall remain until the end of September. * * * I am about finishing a new Concerto expressly for your Concerts and which is therefore *not* the same Concerto which I played at the Philharmonic but in the same key, and I will also bring my Caprice, and a new Overture (if possible)—and some little fishes—*and so, no more of myself.* * * *

In the cottage at Grantchester, again with A. C. Johnson as his companion, he completed his new Concerto in F minor; the slow movement, 'A Stroll through the Meadows,' being dated Sept. 26, 1838. On his way through London, he tried the Concerto with the Academy orchestra before a small audience; on October 5 he started for Leipzig with two young musicians, Gledhill and Pickering; and on October 15 he found himself at the Hotel de Bavière, whither his many friends hurried to see him.

This second visit to Leipzig, lasting twenty-one weeks, was a close facsimile of the former one. Similar concerts, the same amusements, and nearly the same associates appear again. There was, however, no Schumann this time, for he had gone to Vienna; Walther von Goethe had left the University and had returned home to Weimar; but Bennett now became very intimate with Count Reuss, whose acquaintance he had made towards the end of his first visit. The Count, who afterwards became 'His Highness, Henry II, Prince of Reuss-Koestritz,' had passed some years of his early life at a school in Yorkshire, and seemed to Bennett quite an Englishman. He often came to Bennett's rooms, his approach being heralded by a servant bearing his long pipe and other materials for smoking. He took Bennett to show him his future Principality, and to introduce him to his family, and as a New Year's present in 1839 gave him a handsome album, which eventually became full of interesting autographs and sketches, and proved one of its owner's choicest treasures. Bennett, after seeing Count Reuss upon a certain occasion of great solemnity and sorrow, wrote of him :—' What a noble fellow he looked, and I am sure he is a noble fellow.'

Three days after his arrival in Leipzig, Bennett wrote :— 'Yesterday with Gledhill and Pickering I dined at Felix Mendelssohn's—the first time since he had become a housekeeper. How very happy he seems in his new station and how much he deserves to be happy.' Mendelssohn, when urging Bennett to come over again, had written : 'We would have more music together than the first time,' and this promise was now fulfilled. The weekly music-parties, which Mendelssohn had instituted at his house in Lurgensteins Garten, gave regular opportunity; but pleasanter still to Bennett were the Friday mornings when, the Gewandhaus concert having taken place the night before, the conductor had breathing-time, and would invite him to breakfast and to spend a few hours playing or discussing music. Some days that music would be their own. Just at this time Mendelssohn had many fine works to show, and, among them, Bennett writes of hearing him play: 'the new and beautiful 42nd Psalm;' the 'really glorious' E flat Quartet; the 'very compact and charming' Military Overture; and 'the new Rondo in D major.' The meetings were not always at Lurgensteins Garten, for Mendelssohn was beginning to treat his young friend, seven years his junior, on an equality now, and liked to pass a little time in Bennett's lodgings at Lawyer Klein's in the Tuch-Halle. The Rondo in D major was there played, to the accompaniment of 'Cheshire cheese and bottled porter.'

On Bennett's side, the year 1838 was not an unproductive one. He had brought to Leipzig his new Caprice and Concerto. The Overture 'The Wood-nymphs' was written at Leipzig in November; a P.F. solo 'Allegro Grazioso' on December 16 and 17; and on Christmas morning he played with Mendelssohn his 'new little Duets' (Three Diversions, Op. 17) which he had composed 'in the last few days.' It was when reviewing these Duets that Schumann wrote:—'Foreign lands give us so little just at present; Italy only sweeps over to us her butterfly dust, and the knotted outgrowths of the wondrous Berlioz frighten us all. But this Englishman, among them all, comes nearest to German sympathies; he is a born artist, such a one as Germany herself possesses few to boast of.'

Whilst enjoying himself at Leipzig, Bennett had not forgotten his absent friends, Schumann and W. von Goethe. To the former he wrote:—

Nov. 11th, 1838.

DEAR SCHUMANN,

Unless I begin by writing to you, you may not write to me at all, and I want to hear as soon as possible how you are in health, how you like Vienna, and how your whole life goes on. I think you know that I came here a month ago and I have hoped day after day to hear news of you. I am lodging in the Tuch-Halle, and Pickering, an Englishman, is at Madame Devrient's[1]. Why are you not with us? I have here seen for the first time your Fantaisie-Stücke and they greatly delight me. Madame Voigt plays your music very industriously, but to my mind with too great *hardness*. I have a new Concerto and

---

[1] Schumann's former lodgings, which, on leaving for Vienna, he had reserved for Bennett.

Caprice with orchestra, and am now writing an Overture. I do not expect to play in public till after Christmas. * * *.

Now, dear Schumann, do write a few lines at once, so that I may know you are well and happy.

Your friend,

W. STERNDALE BENNETT.

Bennett wrote to Schumann, probably also to W. von Goethe, in German. The latter, as if to return the compliment, replied in English, which is here given without emendation.

WEIMAR, Dec. 10th, 1838.

MY DEAR FRIEND,

You cannot imagine how much pleasure your charming letter gave to my; indeed I am very happy that you do not forget your old German friends and the nice time we spent together. I have composed a great deal but till now nothing is printed. How do you like Schumann's 'Davidsbündler Tanze?' Some of them pleased me very much, but some——Oh, no!!!!! I should be very greadful if you would send me the titles of your new compositions. At Weimar I am banished in a musical Syberian. Mrs Shaw turned all the heads in Weimar. The Gran Duke danced from pleasure on his hands, and the Erb-Prinz on his head; you see the whole Weimar is upset. Will you not come to Weimar and spend the Christmas heare, my mother joins me in this wish and can offer you a room, pray come, we should be really rejoiced. God bless you, me dear friend. Write to me soon and tell me if you know anything of Florestan and Eusebius[1].

the foolish

WALTHER.

PS. To write this letter, I wanted three hours and a half. O friendship!!!!!

Bennett did not go to Weimar. He was full of engagements at Leipzig. Christmas Eve, with its Christmas tree,

---

[1] Meaning *Schumann*, who, as a writer, assumed these names.

was spent as before with the Voigts. Frau Henriette Voigt did not live to see another Christmas. In her short acquaintance with Bennett she became sincerely attached to him. During the summer of 1837, she paid a round of visits with her husband to friends in various German towns. Before starting, she commissioned Fraülein Böhm to paint a miniature portrait of Bennett, who was then in Leipzig. She wanted to show his likeness to her friends when she played his music to them. The miniature served its purpose, and Fraülein Böhm, according to a letter of her friend, Herr Hofrath Rochlitz, 'smiled quite prettily' when she heard that her 'Bennett' had given pleasure in Cassel. 'Ah yes,' she said, 'when a person has something in him then there is something to paint, and others observe it—that is quite natural.' In this way Frau Voigt brought Bennett to the notice of Spohr in Cassel and then wrote to Fraülein Jasper: 'This Arch-priest of true art * * * is especially noble in his recognition of others. Thus he takes a true delight in our little Bennett's compositions which I have had to repeat very often. The dear little fellow [Bennett] has written me a German letter, which I have just answered.' Rochlitz, then the doyen of German musical critics, wrote to Frau Voigt when she was at Weimar, and after telling her of Fraülein Böhm's pleasure at the success of her miniature, added: 'Should the Princess[1] invite you * * * I urge you very much to put forward "Bennettiana," and especially do it in this case, because the Princess from early childhood has cherished a fixed predilection for eminent English genius.' These extracts from letters (kindly supplied by Herr Gustav Jansen of Verden) point to a warmth of appreciation and encouragement which a young Englishman found in Germany, but of which he would know little in his own country. Bennett afterwards wrote of Frau Voigt: 'She was an excellent pianoforte-player, with whom I was very intimate, and who played my music much better than I could play it myself.' In later life, he would often talk to his children of the Christmas Eve of 1838, and of the good-hearted friends with whom he spent it, and he would point to some little book-shelves, hanging in the dining-room of

---

[1] Maria Paulowna, later Grand Duchess of Weimar, mother of Empress Augusta.

his London house, which had been their present to him on the occasion.

On Christmas Day, a dinner, after the English manner, was given at the Hotel de Bavière, the preparation of which was a source of amusement coupled with anxiety to those who arranged it. Doubt as to the arrival of a cod-fish, (a luxury at one time specially associated with Christmas Day in many English families), which had been ordered from Hamburg, caused great uneasiness. The Committee, in their efforts to explain red-currant jelly, at least impressed the cook with the importance of the subject, and a magnificent mould of transparent gelatine accompanied the hare. Few mistakes, however, were made; all passed off well; and Herr Brockhaus has described the entertainment in his diary:—

'Our late meal to-day was the result of an invitation from the English circle to a *Christmas-dinner*, signed by Monicke as President, and Sterndale Bennett as Vice-president. The latter brought with him one of his pupils, and by degrees has been building up quite an English circle. Besides the seven hosts there were Clauss, Voigt, Schunck, Mendelssohn, Preusser, David, and myself. The society was very lively, and to this, excellent eating and drinking, almost too splendid for an English dinner, no little contributed. First came the taking of wine with each other, quite according to English fashion, and after *moving-the-cloth* we got to the speeches, Monicke and Bennett responding for the hosts, Mendelssohn and Schunck for the guests. I was also obliged to return thanks for the toast of "The Town of Leipzig," but I got myself well out of the difficulty (tho' I was not the worst speaker of English in the company) by beginning, "Gentlemen," then playfully passing on to German and with a "Merry old England for ever" finishing amidst great applause.'

In the first days of the New Year, 1839, Bennett was preparing for an appearance (his second) at the Gewandhaus concerts. He showed his new Concerto to Mendelssohn. In the previous summer, whilst at Grantchester, he had revised the slow movement—headed 'A stroll through the meadows'—which had failed to please when rehearsed at the Academy in 1836 as part of the earlier Concerto in the same key of F minor. This piece, in its revised form, he was now intending to place in his new work, but while discussing it with Mendelssohn, he also played the 'Barcarolle,' the movement which had proved successful when substituted for the other in the earlier Concerto. When Mendelssohn heard the 'Barcarolle,' he said, 'Oh Bennett, *that* is what you must play,' and, in consequence, 'A stroll through the meadows' was again rejected, and the 'Barcarolle' then remained a fixture in the later Concerto. Bennett played the new work at the Gewandhaus on Jan. 17, upon a fine piano expressly sent over by Messrs Broadwood, which piano was then retained by the firm of Breitkopf and Haertel, as a model to be followed in the manufacture of their own instruments. He wrote to his friends of the result of his performance and the reception of his music:—

LEIPZIG, *January 23rd*, 1839.

DEAR GOOD SCHUMANN,

I have been wishing very often to write to you again, but have waited till I had made my appearance in public, so that I could tell you all about it. At last week's concert I played my new Concerto in F minor. It was very well received, and I myself was kindly and heartily greeted. I am, on the whole, quite content. The Concerto is to be printed at once, and I will see that a copy is forwarded to you in due course. A new Overture (which is called 'Waldnymphe') will be played at the Gewandhaus to-night; I think it is the best thing I have so far written. * * * I am now contemplating a Symphony for the Philharmonic Society of London.

The only thing I miss here, dear Schumann, is your presence. In about a month's time I shall set out, with *David*, for London. That makes it impossible for me to come to Vienna; but how delightful it would have been for me to be always able to pass an hour with you, talking over music and musicians, and then sometimes about our everyday concerns. But you really must come to England. We would make you very welcome.

Of your newer compositions, I always place the 'Davidsbündler' first. They certainly are very charming. Why do you not compose something for the orchestra?

Mrs Shaw is, I think, coming to Vienna in March, and, if you will let me, I will give her a letter of introduction to you.

Are you anxious about a composition for the Supplement?—for a later number?—because at present I have too much on hand, and I should like to do it properly for you.

Adieu, dear good Schumann,
Ever and anon
Your friend
W. S. BENNETT.

The above letter was written in German. In his own tongue he had written, at greater length, a few days before, to Davison.

LEIPZIG, *Jan.* 19*th*, 1839.

MY DEAR DAVISON,

I can write to you now without any degree of fidget, as I have got over all my troubles for the present. If you knew how much I hated going before the Public under any circumstances, you could imagine how very uncomfortable it is to walk before an audience, eight hundred miles from your own home. However, thank God, I played my new Concerto the day before yesterday with the most brilliant[1] success, and what pleased me most was that the composition was well understood, I am convinced, and the public seemed to think the playing a second consideration, and in which I am sure they are right. The Barcarolle created a great enthusiasm, and also the pizzicato in the first movement. I am sure I never wrote anything that was better received altogether. Another thing is that I was received, when I went on, with great applause, a thing quite out of order here. To sum up all, my dear Davison, you may congratulate me and do not think me vain in telling you all this. * * * I shall leave Leipzig, on

[1] This epithet was modified by being thoroughly scratched through, but is just traceable.

my return to England, on the first of March, and hope to find you and all my friends quite well and jolly. I have written three duets on purpose for you and L. to play together. David is coming with me to England, and I am sure he will do great things. * * * I hope my chambers are warming for me. I long to have my feet on my own fender. For God's sake show this letter to nobody. What I have told you about myself must go to no one else. I long to see you again. * * * Adieu, my dear fellow,

Believe me,
Yours very sincerely,
WILLIAM STERNDALE BENNETT.

Bennett's opinion, given in the above letter, on the relation between composition and performance, was echoed by Schumann in a critique written on the same Concerto after its publication. In referring to its principal Movements, Schumann wrote:—

'They offer nothing new in form, or, to speak more correctly, they seek novelty not in any startling effect but rather in the absence of all pretension. Thus at the conclusion of the Soli, where in other concertos the cadences[1] succeed one another in quick succession, Bennett interrupts the cadence and allows it to die away, as if he himself wanted to prevent all clapping of hands. In the entire concerto he never aims at bravura and applause. It is understood that the composition alone shall be the principal thing, and that virtuosity of execution is of secondary importance[2].'

If Bennett in this or other works did anything to limit the distinction of the Soloist, he did not spare him much in the direction of difficulty. His pianoforte music has generally been considered, even by pianists of the highest rank, to make its own special exactions. Schumann noted the difficulties of the F minor Concerto, but judged them to be of an intellectual rather than mechanical kind and to particularly require the faculty of welding the Solo instrument with the orchestra. Ferdinand Hiller, in a brief but beautiful obituary notice of Bennett, which he contributed

---

[1] Or 'trills.' Schumann's word is 'trillen.'
[2] Translated by J. V. Bridgeman, for *The Musical World*, June, 1856.

to the *Kölnische Zeitung*, recalled this particular performance at the Gewandhaus, and wrote, 'On his visit to Leipzig in the winter of 1838–39 his playing excited the greatest astonishment.' It is a satisfaction to insert this side by side with Schumann's remarks, and to know that such a result could be produced without any resort to extravagant 'tours-de-force.' Hiller summarized the playing as 'perfect in mechanism, and, while remarkable for an extraordinary delicacy of nuance, full of soul and fire.'

The 'pizzicato in the first movement' which Bennett told Davison had found favour, occurs in some passages where he used (as he did in some other concerted works) melodic phrases of single notes for the piano, 'having evidently conceived the idea,' as one critic remarks[1], 'of giving a cantabile effect to the percussion sounds of the piano by opposing them to the still shorter and sharper sounds of the pizzicato [on the stringed instruments].' He had introduced this at greater length in the rejected movement, 'A stroll through the meadows,' in which much of the solo part, representing the 'stroller,' employs only one note of the piano at a time. It is as if he felt that his favourite instrument could vie, in a succession of single sounds, with the tone and expression of any other, or even of the voice. Whether there was or was not any originality in using the piano in this way[2], there is no doubt that even in the few bars where he did so in the opening movement of this Concerto, his remarkable legato-playing and an unsurpassable richness of tone were shown to great advantage, and even with striking novelty of effect. An eminent Leipzig pianoforte teacher came to him at the time, and begged to be initiated into the secret. Bennett was pleased at this, but had no explanation to offer.

With Ferdinand David for his travelling companion, he started for home on March 2nd. His twenty-third birthday was at hand. The two years and nine months, which he had passed since leaving the Academy, had been a time of comparative freedom, from which he had derived lasting benefit. Health, which, according to Davison, had often

---

[1] Article 'Bennett' in Grove's *Dictionary of Music*.
[2] Sir George Macfarren writing of the Concerto, in 1871, considered this particular effect 'as individual as it is felicitous.'

caused anxiety to his friends, now seemed established. He had enjoyed the advantage, during the many months spent at Leipzig, of making several valuable friendships, and of mixing in a highly cultivated general society to which a young musician of his day had easier access in Germany than in England. But the means which had contributed to this were now exhausted, and he was face to face with the stern necessity of making his own living.

PART II

A YOUNG MUSICIAN IN LONDON

CHAPTER VI.

PORTLAND CHAMBERS.

1839—1841.

æt. 23—25.

In the romance of *Charles Auchester*, Sterndale Bennett is introduced under the name of Starwood Burney, and the authoress writes of the young musician, on his return from Germany, as bringing the whole force of music to his feet, pupils flocking to him in large numbers and deeming themselves lucky if they could obtain twenty minutes of his valuable time. The real tale, as told by the figures of account-books, is a different one. Fact was less ready than Fiction to bestow its favours, and many years were now to pass before Sterndale could stand in Starwood's shoes.

Among those watching Bennett at this time, no one showed deeper interest than Mr Thomas Holdsworth, a solicitor by profession, a great lover of music, an early patron of the Academy, and a warm-hearted friend to many of its students. For the past year or two, Mr Holdsworth had been managing Bennett's little business matters, had corresponded with him during his visits to Germany, and had lately written to Leipzig:—'I do believe most truly, that I rank high among your friendships, but I should be unworthy of that, if I were not to act the part of a true friend. I know your mental resources and riches are great and the mine is scarcely opened, but I look with anxiety to your return, because now you are leading a species of idle life, and on your return you will be imperatively called upon to work the work of drudgery, viz. Tuition—as the real resources of the day and week.' When Bennett read this, he had just been composing and performing at Leipzig, so that he could demur to the word *idle*. Mr Holdsworth offered the conventional explanation; he had not used the epithet 'in its ordinary sense;' but he continued his friendly exhortations. He was aware that Bennett had, so far, paid scant attention to money matters, and he doubted whether there would be found, in combination with an artistic temperament, a capacity for routine work. That such capacity could be aroused by necessity was soon shown; but Mr Holdsworth was not the only person who was mistrusting Bennett's power of settling down to business duties. The young musician probably had no innate disposition towards them, and it may be imagined that the harness which in after-life became so heavy and yet was worn so patiently chafed rather sorely when it was new. Bennett did not argue with Mr Holdsworth about the particular way in which a living ought to be made. There was no suggestion, on either side, that the British music-market could support him as a pianist or composer. It was assumed that, in his case, teaching could alone give security, and that other art-work should be pursued without reference to money. In the numerous musical establishments of Germany, well-accredited musicians could, quite early in life, find places as Capellmeisters, and thereby ensure not only subsistence, but also lives of continuous artistic activity. Without expatriation, an alternative which had been already suggested and rejected, there was no such opening for Bennett.

Ferdinand David wrote to Mendelssohn from London on Bennett's twenty-third birthday, Ap. 13th, 1839:—' Of Bennett I see a great deal. While travelling with him I came to realize the full charm of his personality. He is a man from whom I should like never to be parted. I cannot imagine the woman who would not wish to marry him. His compositions are, it appears, but little known here. They still see in him nothing beyond the *Academy student*. Heaven knows how he, with his unassuming manner, will make his way forward in this place. There are few Englishmen who would not deem a man insane, if he told them, that here was a musician of higher type than Mori, or Lindley or their other authorities. He keeps in very good health, looks well, and is in capital spirits.'

Works such as Bennett had been producing could not spread his name far in England. His pianoforte music which helped to make him known in German homes could in the same days do little for him here. Nevertheless, his own country had given him a share of the best things at her disposal, and he had already, in a limited but not insignificant degree, obtained a footing which many young English musicians of the time might envy. The present extent of his fame might be measured by the diagonal of Hanover Square, starting from the north-west corner in which stood the Royal Academy of Music, and reaching to the opposite one, in the south-east, where, in the Queen's Concert Rooms, five or six hundred connoisseurs attended Philharmonic concerts. In this neighbourhood he had for some time been a young man of mark, attracting notice as a specialist. British composers had been earning their reputation by vocal music. The Philharmonic Society since its foundation in 1813 had not, in the course of twenty-seven seasons, placed more than nineteen orchestral pieces of home-growth on their programmes. Cipriani Potter and Bennett were the only native composers who had been represented by a series of such works, and Bennett's four Concertos and three Overtures, which were played between 1835 and 1839, gave him an exceptional prominence, within a select circle of musicians and amateurs, on seven different occasions.

His countrymen applauded, but were less ready than the Germans to acknowledge him as a graduate in his art. At Leipzig, he had from the first been accepted as a young master of his craft and 'a present value' had been set upon him. Schumann took him as he found him, using the words 'whatever his future may be' and some time afterwards, when he saw the word 'promising' applied by another critic, he harked back to the days when he had first met Bennett, and retorted: 'With us and in other places he has already for six years taken place as a master.' In England critics gave their opinions tentatively. 'Let us reserve our judgment,' they seemed to say. 'We want a great representative English musician. When this promising young man can become that, it will be time enough for us to acknowledge him.'

William Ayrton, a musician by profession, but also a man whose general cultivation admitted him to the best literary circles in London, was at this time regarded as the foremost writer of musical criticism in England. With regard to Bennett, he went to two extremes, treating his Overtures with contempt and derision, but warmly praising his Concertos and the playing of them. After hearing the new Overture 'The Wood-nymphs'—perhaps, however, coarsely performed—at the Philharmonic, Ayrton described it as 'a discharge of musical artillery in the shape of drums, seconded by blasts of *trombones* and *trumpets* that seemed to realise all that we have heard of a tropical tornado.' Then, after ridiculing the title, he added: ' Seriously, we regret that the Directors should have been so blind to the interest of the composer as to bring the work before such an audience. So very clever and promising a young man ought to meet with every kind of reasonable encouragement, but judicious and true friends would have hinted to him that his present production is the dry result of labour, that it evinces not a particle of that genius which appears in one or two of his other works, and that in prudence he ought to have laid it by, not for so long a time as Horace recommends in a somewhat analogous case, but for a couple of years at least.'

In curious contrast to this English opinion, Schumann wrote of the same work:—

'The overture is charming; indeed, save Spohr and Mendelssohn, what other living composer is so completely master of his pencil, or bestows with it such tenderness and grace of colour, as Bennett? In the completeness of the whole, we forgive and forget all that he has overheard of those masters' tones, and I think he never before gave us so much of himself as in this work. Essay measure after measure; what a firm, yet delicate web it is from beginning to end! How closely, how nearly everything is united here, while in the productions of most men we are accustomed to find gaping holes as wide as one's hand! Yet this overture has been blamed for too great length of treatment; but this reproach strikes all Bennett's compositions more or less; it is his manner; he must finish everything, even to the smallest detail. He also repeats often, and note for note, after the conclusion of the middle period. But let any one try to alter his works without injuring them; it will not do; he is no pupil, to be improved by touching up; what he has thought out stands firmly and may not be displaced.

'It is contrary to Bennett's simple-minded, inwardly poetic character, and to his corresponding inclination, to set great levers and weights in motion; the splendour of decoration is foreign to him; he loves best to linger in fancy on the lonely shores of the lake, or in the green, mysterious wood: he does not grasp at drums and trombones, with which to sketch his quiet yet lonely happiness. He must, then, be taken as he is, and not mistaken for what he is not,—namely, the creator of a new epoch in art, a hero whom it is impossible to fetter,—but a genuine, deeply feeling poet, who passes on his peaceful way, all untroubled because a few hats, more or less, are raised and waved in his honour; but whose progress, though no triumphal chariots may await it, shall be at the very least embellished by the wreath of violets that Eusebius here offers him[1].'

In judging some of Bennett's earlier works, Schumann duly noticed similarities to the music of certain other composers. In no instance, however, did he do this, except by way of preface to insisting on an individuality which clearly asserted itself notwithstanding any such similarities. This individuality he observed not alone in most of the materials of the music, but also in the method of workmanship. He has expressed this concisely in a second notice of 'The Wood-nymphs,' where he compares the Overture to 'a bouquet, to which Spohr had given some flowers, Weber and Mendelssohn others, but to which Bennett had himself given the most, while the delicate hand which had designed and arranged them as a whole was his and his alone.' Mendelssohn, like Schumann, recognized this individuality. Mr J. S. Bowley, who was in Bennett's room at Leipzig when this same Overture was first played on the piano,

---

[1] Translated, from the German, by F. R. Ritter.

remembered how Mendelssohn called out continually as the music went on: 'Ah! that's Bennett, Bennett, *all* Bennett.' Some years later, Mendelssohn wrote from Leipzig: 'We play your "Waldnymphe" on Thursday next; I have just corrected the Programme, where they would spell your name with one t, and I would have waited till after the performance to tell you of it, but that I know beforehand what it will be. The piece is and always will be a favourite of the Public and the Orchestra, they will do their best to do it justice, and we shall all be happy with it and only wish for your being present. That is it what I would write on Friday and what I can do to-day as well.'

'The Naiads' and 'The Wood-nymphs,' from the dates of their first performance, long retained a place on the Leipzig programmes, being played alternately, season by season, for more than twenty years. They were much used in other parts of Germany. In England they had to wait. When they were ten years old, there came a sudden growth of orchestral concerts in London, and thenceforward they were constantly played, but they did not help their composer much in these earlier days when more publicity to his name might have been an encouragement.

As to Bennett's merits as a *pianist*, there had never been any doubt in Hanover Square. When comparisons were made, his name from first to last was placed in juxtaposition with pianist-composers of the highest rank alone. A fortnight after 'The Wood-nymphs' had been heard, he played his new Concerto in F minor at the Philharmonic. Ayrton found it 'an exceedingly clever composition, reflecting much credit on the Anglo-German school.' Then he added: 'The author performed it in a most skilful, feeling manner, his touch bringing to our recollection that of Cramer. Let him continue to imitate that great master of the pianoforte, and he will never want the suffrages of all admirers of eloquent music.'

So now, in 1839, he had gained, as a public performer, a place from which he might look for pupils willing to pay a good price for his lessons, and this was, for the time being, the pressing matter. Portland Chambers were not besieged, but when London was full and the musical world awake, with fifteen hours' teaching a week,—though that included poorly-paid work at the Academy,—he made a fair start, and Ferdinand David, at the end of the London season, wrote again to Mendelssohn :—' As for Bennett, I cannot say enough in his praise. Even as each day passes, he seems to grow more lovable, more industrious, more manly ; and he is a veritable jewel in the muddy soil of the art-world. He is also doing well materially, has a good number of pupils and, in a quiet way, is sure to succeed.'

This might be said in July, but ten or twelve weeks of comparative plenty were annually followed by forty of scarcity. Remunerative work throughout the year would only come when some of the coveted appointments in the best finishing schools for young ladies could be obtained, but such appointments were professional prizes beyond the reach of a young man. If Bennett's teaching remained in a small compass, it was due to no want of attention on his part. He confessed, when afterwards writing of the time, that he had occasionally been tempted 'on a very rainy morning' to shirk an outside lesson and enjoy himself at home with his 'beautiful pianoforte;' but his account-books show that there was little irregularity, while they suggest, at the same time, that there was a good deal of patience. For nearly two-and-a-half years he remained continuously at his post, while during that time there was only a single week, and that a Christmas one, in which no lesson was given. Mr Holdsworth must have looked on approvingly. Holidays were short and taken seldom. There were no more summers at Grantchester. Some young provincial teacher would make use of vacation time to come up for a little supplementary instruction, and Bennett must needs be in the way to pick up the crumbs. A narrow income, of which by far the greater part was made in three months of the year, could not last out a twelvemonth, without a thriftiness not yet acquired. There is no story to tell of starvation or garret-life ; but ends did not always meet, and he would say to his friend, who perhaps had help from home, 'I can't think, Davison, how you always manage to have money in your pocket.'

Davison's mother, a distinguished actress, but here only introduced as another kind mentor, with a motherly eye on Portland Chambers, wrote the following birth-day letter to Bennett :—

My dear young Sir,

Having been told that you once were heard to express a doubt of ever saving a guinea, I assume the privilege of better and longer experience to assure you there is nothing impossible to the firm resolve. You are now blessed with youth, health, and extraordinary talent, but consider,—health uncertain, the world full of change, and the Public a many-headed monster! Then reflect, how sweet is independence, when supplied by your own industry and careful management. I would not have you a miser, nor yet a spendthrift. There is ever a middle course to be pursued in every transaction through life's troubled round, which if followed will ensure you the approval of your heart, and the admiration of those whose good opinions are worth the cultivating—for the rest *care not*.

For your steady friendship to my dear James, of which he ever makes grateful mention, accept his mother's thanks. I understand this is your natal day. May you live in the cheerful enjoyment of many such. I have to request your acceptance of the accompanying pocket trifle, to be used as a kind of savings bank—as old ladies say—to provide for a rainy day. You will keep it for my sake; and when the hands that worked it for that purpose are under the grass green turf, and the heart, which once beat in the warmth of truth and friendship, is still and cold; you will perhaps think of me, and at the moment you do so, leave a little deposit as a tribute to my memory and a tacit acknowledgment that you neglect not my advice.

With every good wish for many returns of Good Friday to you and your best affections

I remain, dear Mr Bennett,
Yours very truly,
MARIA R. DAVISON.

Though Bennett had at this time no guineas to deposit in a satin savings-bank, he had at least the faculty of saving with the most affectionate care anything that was given to him as a keepsake. Mrs Davison, whose handiwork still lies where he placed it in his dressing-case, lived to be an old lady, and to see her young friend making his way.

But the subject of bread-winning may be left awhile; for Bennett could see in his call to teaching, a higher purpose than his own maintenance. Schumann, in special reference to the pianoforte music of the day, had already written:—'Were there many artists who worked with the same intention as Bennett, then no one would need to be anxious any longer about the future of our art.' Now certainly in England the condition of pianoforte music at this time gave cause for anxiety in some minds, and there was pressing need of men ready to join a minority in opposition to a predominant party. Celebrated pianists had lately done much towards popularizing the pianoforte among that class who could afford to attend expensive entertainments. Thalberg and other exponents of the modern Fantasia had cast a spell over hundreds in this country who would not under less seductive influences have stopped their chatter to listen to pianoforte-playing. To these remarkable players must be given the credit of establishing the pianoforte as an instrument that could be played by itself in English concert-rooms; nor can they be blamed for entirely absorbing, as they did, that increase of interest in pianoforte performance which they had themselves accumulated. For years and years the Fantasia held its supremacy, while the solo masterpieces of the great composers were struggling to obtain a hearing in the concert room. Meanwhile the duty of preserving and disseminating the classics of the pianoforte remained chiefly with teachers, but only with a faithful few who maintained that pianoforte music could and must be taught, to whatsoever pupil, with serious intent. There was little music-teaching which was not going with the stream of fashion. The essential of a teaching-piece, as of a concert-piece was the parade of the performer. Compilers of potpourris modelled on the favourite form abounded, and even composers of high merit consented to assist in stocking the young ladies' portfolios with glittering tinsel.

Bennett tried, in 1839, to write an article on the state of affairs in the pianoforte-world. He noted the important part which pianoforte-playing was taking in England as a branch of the musical art, and the powerful influence which the fashionable players and composers of pianoforte music were exercising. He looked back with regret to days of yore when the pianoforte had been subservient to music, and deplored the present subserviency of music to the pianoforte. He admitted that astonishing feats must be accomplished by the pianists who desired the applause of the multitude; but he contended that the Great Masters had not been afflicted with such blindness to the capabilities of the instrument as was now being imputed to them by the admirers of this modern school of playing. He was exasperated at hearing Mozart and Beethoven being freely spoken of as pedants.

He was able, however, before laying down his pen, to find consolation in an encouraging omen. Certain publishers were now showing themselves willing to try the experiment of placing within easy reach of teachers and students good music which had for many years been difficult to obtain. Thus one firm had been printing Beethoven's pianoforte music with Moscheles as editor, and was now advertising Czerny's edition of Bach's 48 Preludes and Fugues, with English fingering, at the price of a guinea-and-a-half, three pounds having hitherto been thought a fair sum to ask for an old copy of them. Lonsdale announced another English edition of the same Fugues, and roundly asserted his intention of printing all the instrumental works of Bach. In fact, the Leipzig Cantor was for the moment quite prominent on the advertisement sheets, beside the composers of Quadrilles and 'Morceaux de salon.' Coventry, possibly at the instigation of Bennett, with whom he was very intimate, appealed to Mendelssohn to be his editor of Bach, and engaged Potter to prepare the P.F. works of Mozart. The need of such a movement as this was clearly expressed by Davison when he welcomed the edition of Mozart with the words, 'It will no longer be necessary to wait for auction-sales to obtain such music.' Davison wrote further of the general ignorance of Mozart's pianoforte music amongst amateurs, and praised Coventry for filling up 'a lamentable chasm in the musical literature of this country.' The previous difficulty of finding music in England may be illustrated by instances of the pleasure which attended the discovery of buried treasures. Davison, at the end of a long life, would talk of the happy day on which he had found Dussek's Sonata, 'L'Invocation,' on a book-stall, and had then taken it off to the Academy to introduce it to Bennett, and to hear it played by him. Bennett too, in his later days, would recall the delightful sensation which had come over him when he 'discovered' one of Mozart's Sonatas, in F major, in the library of a country-house. 'I felt,' he said, 'as if I had found a diamond.' He soon himself joined the band of editors and took a share in the revival of the 'classics.' He selected forgotten Sonatas of Haydn, Clementi, Dussek and others, which Coventry brought out in a serial called 'Classical Practice.' This venture met with just sufficient success to repay the cost of publication. Coventry's business lay mostly in the provinces, where some of the early Academy students were now settled as teachers, and such works as Bennett selected came as godsends to professors of high aims. Kellow Pye, an excellent musician and charming pianist, wrote from Exeter to Portland Chambers, in a tone of distress, imploring Bennett (his old school fellow) to keep him informed of any new publications of value. Judging by the progress of the 'Classical Practice,' such music, for some time to come, could be but thinly scattered. Coventry continued to issue the Sonatas, but only at long intervals, and in the end the serial did not reach beyond twelve numbers. But the newer as well as the older pianoforte music, if described as classical, or if suspected of bearing that character, did not travel quickly. A little time back, it had taken four years to sell 114 copies of the first book of Mendelssohn's 'Lieder ohne Worte'; and the publisher Wessel was now obtaining no return but disappointment for printing the works of Chopin.

Miss Bettina Walker, who made Bennett's acquaintance when he had been teaching for twenty years, has written of his telling her that 'from the beginning of his career as a professor he had set his face against teaching any but classical music,' and this remark implies that he himself thought his attitude had been exceptional, and that he had not found it an easy one to assume, at any rate in relation to amateur pupils. As a young Professor at the Academy he at once attracted a class of advanced professional students, to whom he could lay down the law, and for whom the choice of music was not limited by considerations of its difficulty or abstruseness. Thus to this class he immediately taught the works of Bach, including the Concertos. But there was a greater demand on the courage of his opinions when he decided to force on young amateurs music which was at the time regarded as severe and not adapted for use in society. He was not taking the shortest road towards making a living. He certainly insisted on what he considered classical music being the foundation of work for all pupils. The new editions of such music came opportunely to his assistance, but when the Sonatas had been prescribed there was no profusion of subsidiary attractions. Compositions of Weber and Hummel seem to have been easily obtainable, and he used a few of the early pieces of Mendelssohn. He did not as yet entirely withhold modern Fantasias; he may have recognized their value for the development of technical skill; but, even if in using them he deviated from his principles, he gave way very seldom. He had known many of these Fantasias by heart, and had played them with as much brilliancy, in Davison's opinion, as the composers themselves; but this was a reminiscence of early student days; he never played them in public, and taught them so little, that he may easily have forgotten that he had taught them at all. To the sixteen young ladies who took lessons during twenty-one months from March 1839 to December 1840, he distributed sixty-five pieces. Fifty-three of these were by Haydn, Mozart, Clementi, Dussek, Beethoven, Weber, Hummel, Cramer, and Mendelssohn. Eight more were Studies and Rondos by Aloys Schmitt, Herz, Döhler, Czerny and Hünten; two were Fantasias by Herz and Kalkbrenner; and two were compositions of his own. He was only on the threshold of thirty-five years' work as a teacher. An opportunity may occur later in these pages of showing how he extended his course of instruction. For the present, as has already been said, his pupils were not numerous; his work with them cannot have occupied much of his time; a single lesson given at the distance of East Sheen might take up the best part of a day and unsettle his mind for the rest of it; but for many months of the year he had much freedom. What else was he doing? What, especially, was he doing as a composer?

PORTLAND CHAMBERS
Great Titchfield Street

CHAPTER VII.

COMPOSITION IN PORTLAND CHAMBERS.

1839—1841.
æt. 23—25.

ON his return from Germany in 1839, Bennett left for a while Concertos and Overtures, and turned his thoughts to other forms of composition. In his correspondence during the next year or two, an Opera, an Oratorio, a Symphony, Chamber music, and Songs are all mentioned as under consideration. He once told Mendelssohn that he thought his own sphere as a composer lay among the smaller forms of art. Mendelssohn disagreed with this limitation, and further said,—probably with England specially in his mind, —that small works would attract no notice, until something on a large scale had been accomplished. At this very time, there was much talk about English Opera, and Bennett would naturally be expected by his London friends to attempt success in the line which so many of his countrymen were following. In the summer of 1839, Coventry, the publisher, drew up an agreement with him to purchase the copyright of an Opera when composed, and the name of a librettist is mentioned in the document.

No libretto ever reached Bennett, but it is unlikely that he would be eager to see one. Attempts during the next three years to establish English Opera in London met with little success; the 'books' provided in those days by English librettists would not appeal to him; and, moreover, he was not strongly drawn towards dramatic composition.

His thoughts were not much in theatres. His friends considered him illiberal in his attitude towards operatic music. Davison dragged him off one night from Portland Chambers to hear a French Opera, and was much annoyed because no expression of opinion could be got out of him as they walked home. 'You might say something one way or another,' was Davison's last appeal, but there was no response. John Ella remarked that his own appreciation of 'the lighter wares of the French and Italian schools' was not shared by Bennett, and wrote: 'Our countryman is too rigid in his opinions on art to suit our views entirely.'

Though there was some want of sympathy with particular schools of music, Bennett was not really illiberal. When he chose 'The Opera' as the subject of a course of lectures delivered later in life, he showed himself ready to pay just tribute to Italian and French composers; speaking of Rossini as one of the greatest geniuses that the musical world had ever known; and of Boieldieu, Herold and Auber as 'those three splendid men under whose influence a School had arisen as new as it was beautiful, expressing French feeling and temperament to the very letter.' But any real interest in a theatre which he had allowed himself to take in his earlier years, seemed afterwards to explain itself as springing from his love for Mozart, and for Mozart's Operas he certainly did retain not only a musical but a theatrical regard, liking to recall his memories of them as seen on the stage. He would, for instance, picture to himself the opening scene in *Il Seraglio*, would hum the refrain of the Air which Osmino sings in the fruit-tree, and would then burst into laughter at Mozart's idea of making his own lovely phrase the object of Belmonte's mockery. When he talked of such things he would speak of his friends, the Seguins, by whom, at one time of his Academy life, he had been taken a good deal to the Opera. It was at their house that he became acquainted with Michael Costa, who, like the rest of the Seguin circle, admired the boy's rendering of the Operas on the piano. About the year 1870, Mapleson, the manager of Her Majesty's Theatre, gave Bennett a pressing invitation to write an Opera. He was flattered and pleased, quoted the remark made by Sebastian Bach under similar circumstances, but did not appear to treat the matter in a serious light. He would often play some attractive strains of melody and harmony, and then say, as if in sport, 'That's the opening of my Opera;' but he had long learnt to take a lofty view of what was necessary for the larger forms of art, and the last remark he made upon the subject was, 'If I had been Mozart, I would have written an Opera.'

One fact about him may have escaped the notice of his opera-loving friends. Apart altogether from music, and, perhaps, for no clearly defined reasons, he found the theatre itself uncongenial with his feelings. On his German tours, he heard for the first time, and recorded in his diaries the pleasure which he, of course, felt in listening to the music of such Operas as 'Alcestis,' 'Il Seraglio' and 'Oberon.' Yet it was from Germany, and in reference to attending the Opera-houses there, that he wrote home in 1842: 'I cannot bear theatres.' Sir Arthur Sullivan, when a boy, often took supper at Bennett's house after a music-lesson, and noticed with surprise that if he himself mentioned anything in connection with a theatre, his master's manner at once checked the subject. In after years, Bennett would occasionally go, as if in duty bound, to hear a new Opera; but during the performance he would sit taciturn and moody, and would be quite unlike himself. So also if he could be persuaded to go to the play-house to see a popular comedy, those who hoped for his being amused would be disappointed. Once inside the theatre, he would relapse into silence, could not enter into what was going on, or make himself companionable. He had, perhaps, in some degree, that puritanical objection to the stage which was still, in his own generation, wide-spread in this country; but he did not himself give any clue to the cause of his dislike.

A correspondence in 1839—40 about Handel, kept him in touch with Mendelssohn, who was then hoping to bring out an edition of that master's Oratorios, with an added organ-part, in order to facilitate their performance in Germany. Bennett was asked to help by examining the manuscripts in the Library of Buckingham Palace, and by undertaking the not easy task of procuring copies of English editions. Walsh's edition was out of print, and the plates were scattered all over London. The letters which passed on this subject touched also a little on matters personal to the writers. Bennett, however, was none too communicative about himself. In October 1839, Mendelssohn, when announcing the birth of a daughter, wrote:—' I cannot begin the letter immediately with Sampson[1] and Handel, but rather with my wife and *children*. * * * I know that you do not only partake of my musical pleasures and sorrows, but also of the domestic ones of which life and happiness depends. * * * I wish you could be with us and spend some quiet evenings or breakfast-mornings with me and have a chat about everything. Something at least you ought to write me about yourself, your life and works in your next letter; you are so very " einsylbig" about all this, in the last.' The Handelian researches, in which Bennett was proud to take part, may have prompted him towards sacred composition of his own, and early in the New Year, 1840, he wedged into a long letter about ' Samson,' a little sentence about himself:—' And now, my dear friend, I am writing an Oratorio, and already have done a great deal which I should like to show you, particularly a little Chorus which I have this morning written. I assure you I want some of your encouragement to make me prosper in such an undertaking.'

The contemplated Oratorio was begun with no overweening confidence. ' God give me strength and health,' he wrote to Kistner, ' and *ideas* to finish it.' He afterwards referred to his studies, at this time, of the choral works of the Great Masters, and in such occupation, as also in writing sacred music himself, hours were profitably spent to future advantage; but the Oratorio never saw the light. This episode in his life is a little disappointing. If he could have finished such a work in the fifteen months he first assigned for it, and if the merit of the whole had been equal to that of the part he did write, then, may-be, he would have gained, early in life, wide repute in an Oratorio-loving country. But to this particular project there was a drawback. He started on an insecure basis, without a fixed libretto. Having chosen a symbolical subject with the title of ' Zion,' he filled pages of a note-book with texts from the

---

[1] Mendelssohn, in his letters, has liked occasionally to retain the spelling of Handel's time.

prophecies of Isaiah and Jeremiah, which he selected as likely material; but notwithstanding the assistance of a scholarly friend, Dr Weil, no complete or definite design was ever arrived at. By degrees, he wrote an introduction and several numbers in connected sequence, whilst he apparently trusted to the chance of his subject developing as his work proceeded. With such indistinct purpose, progress proved slow. Two or three years later he made a revised edition of the completed part and was still adding to it. He fully meant, sooner or later, to finish his task. He was not the man to abandon lightly any intention once formed. Indeed, this Oratorio, a string Quartet, and the work he was engaged upon when death overtook him, are the only examples of important undertakings left unfulfilled. 'Zion' remained a hope until he found some of his subject embodied in the work of another composer. An Oratorio employing such texts as, 'The harvest is past, the summer is ended,' and 'Zion spreadeth forth her hands,' could not be continued after the appearance of 'Elijah.' He had the satisfaction of hearing two of the shorter Choruses from 'Zion' sung nearly thirty years after they were written. He placed them in his later work, 'The Woman of Samaria,' produced at Birmingham in 1867. One of them, in six parts, was redemanded, on that occasion, by the President of the Festival.

While sacred music was under consideration in Portland Chambers, Friedrich Kistner of Leipzig was expecting new works for publication. When fifteen months had passed since Bennett's departure from Leipzig, he grew impatient, and wrote in July, 1840[1]:—'Though I received in due time your favour of the 12th Feb., nevertheless I expected till here but in vain the promised manuscrits, in consequence of which I am really very much afflicted. All your friends here are asking at least every weack for new compositions from Bennett, and you know that my shop is such a kind of musical parlor, for there is the whole day a coming of musical men in order to learn any news, and I am obliged allready since a very long time to answer their askings, "there is a plenty of manuscrits from our friend Bennett just now upon road," (but they never arrive!). * * * As I am told by the newspapers that

[1] The words are given here without emendation.

the postage is now put at a lower rate in England, I shall send you innumerous letters till I receive the promised manuscrits—depend upon!'

Kistner's entreaties were persistent, but, for the time being, unavailing. With the exception of a 'Notturno' for the piano, afterwards called 'Genevieve,' the autograph of which was reproduced in *facsimile* in the *Allgemeine Musikalisches Zeitung*, Bennett parted with no music to a publisher between his twenty-third and twenty-sixth birthdays. This long silence set his German friends wondering, and he had to attempt explanations. He could write of works contemplated; but Kistner wanted to meet an immediate demand, and feared that the interest so far shown could not be maintained without fresh material. Then Bennett had to make excuses. To descriptions of festivals and concerts in Germany, he replied, 'Oh, that I were there,' and then went on to hint, as he could only do to a foreigner, that his surroundings were not inspiring. 'You know,' he wrote (Feb. 12, 1840), 'what a dreadful place England is for music; and in London I have nobody whom I can talk to about good things; all the people here are mad with Thalberg and Strauss, and I have not heard a single symphony or overture in a Concert since last June.'

Out of harmony with prevailing musical tastes; entirely absenting himself, for instance, from the Italian Opera; thinking it necessary, as he told Kistner, for his own progress in the right direction as a composer, to be very careful what music he listened to; and even avoiding conversation and arguments on musical subjects with his more eclectic companions, Bennett was drawn much within himself, and found a solitary but safe refuge in his piano and his musicbooks. In public life, even in by-ways, he was as yet little wanted. Between his annual performances at the Philharmonic in 1839 and 1840, eleven months passed during which he only took part in seven concerts. He conducted four, with a small orchestra at the Marylebone Literary and Scientific Institution, and played at three, two of which were at Clapham and Stepney. To the paucity of such engagements he does not refer in his correspondence. He would not himself notice it. There was nothing different to expect. Still, the fact remains that, except in his own study, or while engaged with his few pupils, he was living in a musical atmosphere which if not positively depressing to him, certainly cannot have been exhilarating.

Music had no natural place in London. When the coterie of wealthy persons who patronized it in the season had dispersed, and the continental artists had gone away with well-filled purses, music vanished too, or what was left of it was too scattered to be noticeable. Then, till spring returned, the few musical magazines that were printed, having nothing of passing interest to report, filled their columns with essays, biographies, and 'chit-chat from the continent.' Music was for one section of society and did not enter into the regular life of the Londoner. It might cross his path occasionally; at the dance, at the public dinner or other convivial meeting; not much in church, for the congregations of most London churches were vocally dumb, and allowed four ladies and gentlemen in the organ-gallery to act as their proxies. Jackson's 'Te Deum' in F, sung week after week by the hired quartet, represented to many a Londoner the English School of Church music. There were Cathedral Services; but Ecclesiastics, timid of the influence of music, withheld the means for its full support. When, later, the choir at Westminster was strengthened, Sydney Smith, as a Canon of St Paul's shrank from the example. 'Cathedrals,' he wrote, 'are not to consider themselves as rival opera-houses; we shall come by and bye to act Anthems. * * * It is a matter of perfect indifference to me whether Westminster bawls louder than St Paul's[1].'

When Bennett first went to Germany, he must have been prepared to find music more widely cultivated there than in England, but room was left for surprise at the extent of the difference. In letters home, he noted the contrast between the two nations in the amount of respect shown to the art by intellectual people, and he also observed that in Germany a love for it in its more advanced forms, was to be found in all classes. On the evening when he made his *debût* at Leipzig, he espied the man who blacked the boots at his lodgings, sitting in the gallery of the

[1] From letter,—in possession of J. S. Bumpus, Esq.,—dated Aug. 21, 1844, to W. Hawes, Master of the choristers then 8 only in number.

Gewandhaus, and in conversation next morning discovered that this humble individual looked forward to a Symphony-concert as an occasional treat. Such revelations were heart-warming, though they brought jealousy as well, to an English musician. In this country, anyone holding such views as Bennett did, moved amongst his fellow-creatures, both at this time and for many years to come, painfully conscious that the art he venerated was for the majority non-existent, and was by many, even by those of the highest culture, treated with brusqueness as the mere adjunct to ceremony, or despised as a frivolous pastime. In the best literature of the day, if music was noticed at all, such notice was seldom to its advantage.

That a dull artistic environment could tend to crush a musical spirit, is a theory which claims passing notice, for though it is too vague to be much pressed here, Bennett advanced it again later, and did so at a time when he was not excusing himself to a publisher. He was, however, no great grumbler. If, in after life, as for instance in lectures, he said anything about his own country, it was always rather to defend it as a musical nation, and to speak of progress witnessed in his own time; or if in conversation he became more critical, it would, at any rate, only be of the existing state of music that he would talk, and not of how that affected the musician or himself.

Of London, as a place of residence, he was a true lover. He could enjoy the bustle of its busy streets, and the beauty of its out-lying districts. When he could take Kistner to Richmond, or Marschner to 'The Spaniards' at Hampstead, then he was the proud Londoner. In his older age, he went so far as to say that he thought he could compose better in London than elsewhere. 'In the country,' he added, 'composition generally ends in taking a walk.'

The excuses sent to Kistner from Portland Chambers came to an end, and he said at last: 'I can hardly tell you the reason why you have not received anything from me to publish, although I still say that I have plenty on hand for you.' The question which he thus gave up trying to answer, thenceforward became a crux to others than himself; for notwithstanding the great facility for composition which the friends of his youth thought he had shown at the Academy, notwithstanding Schumann's impression that he could 'accomplish anything with sportive ease,' Bennett was not to be a voluminous composer. Davison could point to movements of Symphonies which had been written in Tenterden Street *currente calamo* and without premeditation, but Bennett himself, if such facility were referred to in after years, would then shake his head in disapproval, and he once said that he could only compare the production of a composition to the acutest form of bodily pain.

Much was expected from him, more indeed than he seems to have felt he had the power to accomplish. A little later than the time now under notice, he was again in Germany and was writing home letters to his future wife. He then dwelt upon the difficulty he foresaw in satisfying these expectations of others. Referring to the anxieties of an art-career, he wrote :—' I should be very ungrateful to complain, for I am sure no one ever went through life, as far as I have gone, meeting with more kindness and encouragement ; but the difficulty is to answer the hopes of one's friends, who are always too sanguine.' He recurs to this point more than once in the same correspondence :—' This year (1842) I must do a good deal, for my *too sanguine* friends are expecting much from me, and I must not totally disappoint them.' Then he wrote again :—' You will hear many people speak of me in different ways, some of my most *sanguine* friends will say much more than is proper for you or myself to believe, and others will (as a kind of balance) abuse me more than perhaps I may deserve. I trust you will believe that I am neither on the one hand too much excited or satisfied, nor on the other likely to be depressed or discouraged.'

He used to say that a composer should never allow himself to write below his proper level; that, if he did so, his reputation would be more likely to rest on his bad work than on his good; that one single careless publication might rise up in judgment against him hereafter, and utterly condemn him. These were his views. They may read like truisms, but they were not accepted as such by many of his time. There was to some the temptation, to others perhaps the necessity, of making a little money, which was quite as easy, or indeed easier to find by common-place work.

Bennett, as an artist, never succumbed to the temptation of money; nor did any wish for popularity or publicity prompt him to swerve from the narrow path which seemed to him to lead to the ideal.

He became very cautious. That can be noticed in him as soon as he returned from Germany, after his first visit, when he may have realized that the Germans set a higher value upon him, than he had hitherto placed upon himself. On his way home in 1837, he was detained at Mainz, and wrote thence to Kistner, that he was spending the time in reading German poetry, and would send him some songs soon after he got back to England. At the end of the year he wrote that he had composed twelve, and would send them over at the first opportunity. He always afterwards said, that what with finding words with which he thought he could deal, and then finding appropriate music which had at the same time some independent interest of its own, song-writing had been to him more difficult than any other form of composition. From the day that he first wrote to Kistner on the subject of songs, though he kept alluding to it in further letters as being still in his mind, it took him just five years before he could, after much consideration, selection, and rejection, hand his first set of six songs to his publisher. It was, perhaps, a wiser mode of proceeding than if he had issued sixty and left it to the public to make its own selection. Some may see in this a diffidence or a delay and therewith find fault, but others may see a constraint which they can commend. At all events, the songs themselves, when they did appear, were thought very satisfactory.

He wrote a Pianoforte Trio in 1839, which was fated to be a good deal played in the future, and to find many admirers. By its simplicity and comparative brevity it illustrates, as some of his later works also do, his desire to keep in what he deemed his proper place, and to avoid entering the lists with the greatest masters. Of this work he wrote to Kistner:—'It is rather small, and only fit for *Kammer-Musik*, * * * one movement I hope you will like better than anything I have done.' Then the diffidence, or the caution, appears again. He played the Trio in public the year after it was written, and promised to send it to Leipzig for publication, but he could not make up his mind.

'You are keeping what you do,' Kistner then wrote, 'a secret between yourself and your London friends.' Letters show that the manuscript was constantly on the point of starting, but it did not set out for six years.

Davison, when he became a musical critic, often found fault with what he called Bennett's 'want of productivity.' 'We have no patience with it,' he once wrote, 'whatever the cause may be;' but with the cause he did not deal, though he had been in as good a position as anyone to fathom it. He ended by saying that the matter had always been a puzzle to him for which he could find no solution. When Bennett, in course of years, became busily occupied in other directions, it was generally assumed that there was not enough time left for composing, and he would sometimes himself say so. Dr John Hullah, for one, thought that 'the curse of English music, pianoforte-teaching' must be held responsible. But Bennett's heavy work did not fall to his lot till his thirtieth year was passed, and this slow production was noticed long before that time. There is no period of his life at which it comes clearer to view than in these early days at Portland Chambers, when for two-thirds of each year he was not giving, on the average, more than six lessons a week; and yet his compositions came no more quickly then, than they did later, when he was in full work as a teacher, and was also discharging the duties of public appointments.

If one may now anticipate and take his life as a whole, there was a rate at which he issued his works, which, though slow as compared with that of other composers, was so nearly uniform as to suggest that it was regulated by some natural law within himself, and that it was not, in the long run, much influenced by outside circumstances. Throughout life, in his career as a composer, and as if in fulfilment of Schumann's prediction, 'a genuine and deeply-feeling poet' he pursued 'his peaceful way.' His progress was not always visible, but it was not a case of the slumbering hare; sure steps were being taken towards a goal; and in the end, for Bennett endured to the end, he left behind him a set of works representative of many departments of composition, the catalogue of which is as neatly moulded in form, as are the items themselves which it includes. Forty-two works, many of them in small dimensions, written in forty-two years, were not enough to keep him, during his life-time, in that continual evidence which others desired; but looking back through the vista, there are no prominent gaps in the sequence of production, and the total amount of work left may be taken as characteristic of a man always trying to assess his gifts at their true value, and to use them in some due proportion to their nature and extent. Surely, if not among musicians, then among poets, some parallel case to Bennett's can be found. It has been suggested to the writer that Bennett was 'the Gray of music.'

He had a kind of unwillingness to commit his ideas to paper. He explained this by saying that when once written down they became stereotyped in his mind, and that then revision proved to him a matter of great difficulty. Revision, in his case, had to be done before the pen was touched. Up to his thirtieth year, he did make new editions of some of his manuscripts, but where comparison with the older ones is possible, the alterations seen are in points of orchestration rather than in the music itself. Later works he did not alter, and, even in the course of first writing them, he made few erasures or changes of intention, such as may be seen in the manuscripts of other composers of his time. He once saw a student working at a harmony-exercise with a pencil and india-rubber, and he objected saying, 'No, you must use ink, and get the habit of making up your mind, before you write anything down.' He himself often spent a great deal of time in making up his mind before he wrote anything down, and the hours he gave to composition, or to attempts at composition, cannot be measured by the amount of music-paper he filled. In his later life, those who had the opportunity of being much near him, of sitting by his side in his carriage as he went long distances to his pupils, of taking silent walks with him, and of spending country holidays in his company, cannot but retain the opinion that few consecutive hours passed, without his brain being hard at work on its musical imaginings, and this no doubt had always been the case.

Mrs Meredith, the housekeeper at Portland Chambers, afterwards kept a lodging-house of her own, and Bennett would recommend it as a residence for musical students. When he became Principal of the Academy, she liked to talk of him to a younger generation, and to tell how frequently, on opening the front door, she had discovered him in a state of trance, and had watched him, as he passed her without notice and walked mechanically to his room; but to this she would add, that, when he came to himself and could not remember having seen her, he always came down and made her a pretty apology. Frequent fits of a complete abstraction, which would sometimes seize him quite suddenly, changing the one man so wide-awake and full of observation, into another whom nothing could disturb, told those who watched him that Bennett was at work, and gave them the impression of an industrious composer.

He did not, however, readily accept the thoughts passing through his brain. Nor did he often get, according to his own statement, an idea that would give him the impulse, or justification, for starting a composition. Here he may have been too critical, for it is well-known that some of his best music came to him when he was writing under pressure, and when, to bystanders, no difficulty in evoking it was noticeable. Still, when left to himself, he took full advantage of freedom of choice. How far he succeeded in finding fresh or striking openings for the principal movements of his compositions is not to be said here, but the point was certainly one that he kept in view. All his composition-pupils at the Academy have remembered the advice he gave them on this subject; how he would say that the works of the Great Masters could be identified by the first sound heard, whether a chord or a single note, and how he would give them many startling examples. An eminent German Capellmeister, who was staying at his house and heard him enunciate this theory, was sceptical, but it only took Bennett two or three minutes to convert him. It became, at one time, a favourite diversion of his, when he had musical friends around him, to go to the piano to play such an opening chord or note, and ask the name of the work; but he liked, in turn, to be tested himself, and his answers would come like lightning.

In the case of his own compositions, which it is perhaps needless to say were not introduced in his musical game, he took no credit for the principal ideas or subjects. A remark he made more than once was that they came 'at such strange times;' and then he would go on to say, that it had always been a little bit of a mystery where they came from and why they should come to *him*. The duty of choosing from them was felt to be his own, and he took it seriously. In his very last days, when he was sitting in his garden at St John's Wood, he said, not in conversation, but as if the result of a train of thought had, without his knowing it, escaped his lips:—'My life has been spent in rejecting musical ideas.' He said this very gravely, in no tone that could be taken to imply regret, but rather resignation, and as if he were preparing for the day when he would be called upon to answer for the use of his talents.

This brief summary of his own life, as given by himself, and to himself, in the hour of self-examination, seems to show him regarding composition, or the preparation for composition, as having been one of his most engrossing occupations. The narrative of his active life will not, of itself, give sufficient evidence of this. Much else he did, as the sequel will certainly show, for the sake of music other than his own. Even as a composer, he did much besides rejecting ideas. But the reader will now have, in advance, some explanation, and that partly from his own words, why in many pages of this story his work as a composer will be lost to view.

When Kistner could not get what he wanted from Portland Chambers, he ventured, in one letter, to ask his young friend, 'Is idleness the cause?' Here one may borrow from Mr Holdsworth and reply that there was no idleness at the Chambers 'in the ordinary sense of the word.' Bennett besides being a composer and a teacher was also a pianist, and that demanded a great deal. His friends have vouched for his industry; they even complained of it at the time, because it was the cause of their seeing so little of him. An outer baize-covered door protected his room, and no amount of knocking would unearth him. He was known to be within, because the piano was in incessant use. He was described by his friend John Jay, one of those who had reason to remember 'Bennett's knocker,' as having been 'a slave to the pianoforte.' Yet there was little outside encouragement to such devotion, three years passing while only four invitations to play at important concerts arrived.

Summer months of 1840 found him in constant attendance at the sick-bed of an old school-fellow, George Richards, a poor young violinist befriended by Coventry who was always ready to turn his house in Dean Street into a hospital. Three years before this, Bennett had dedicated 'Three Impromptus' as a tribute of affection to W. P. Beale, an esteemed pianist, then being nursed by Coventry in an illness, which, like that of Richards, proved fatal. When it is seen later that Bennett's business relations with Coventry as a publisher turned out unsatisfactory, it will be understood why he was ready to sacrifice a good deal out of gratitude for the kindness which he, like others, had met with from the warm-hearted 'little man of Dean Street.'

In the autumn of 1840, Bennett went to Birmingham to hear the 'Lobgesang,' and on September 30th had the pleasure of welcoming the composer to Portland Chambers, Mendelssohn inscribing the address and date on a set of his own Overtures. A few days later Bennett was writing to Carl Voigt:—'I have had a very happy time at Birmingham with Mendelssohn and his "Lobgesang." What a wonderful thing! * * * I hope to come to Leipzig next year, and be happy once more.'

In October 1849, Sir George Smart introduced the Overture, 'The Wood-nymphs,' at the Hull Festival, urging the band at the rehearsal to particular effort, as 'it was seldom that a native work found place on the programmes of similar musical gatherings.' As to the result, Sir George wrote to Bennett that 'the audience evinced their good taste by *silence* during the performance, and by loud and deserved applause after it.' The mention of *silence* by one with such experience of musical performance, towards the close of a long career as a Conductor, is interesting. The notion that instrumental music was placed on miscellaneous programmes for the sake of resting the singers, and of relaxing the prolonged attention of the audience, was very prevalent in England. Sir George Smart was probably noting the advent of a novel interest.

One day, Davison found on a book-stall a dilapidated piece of music, shorn of its title-page, and without trace of its author's name. He took it home, called a council, and was much interested to hear Bennett's reasons for dismissing, one after another, suggested composers. It was at last admitted that there must be some remarkable writer of pianoforte music who was unknown to Portland Chambers. On reference elsewhere, the piece was recognized as a Sonata by the lamented young Pinto. This was the musician to whom, thirty years after his death, J. B. Cramer found in Bennett the first young Englishman worthy to be a successor[1]. The tattered Sonata was soon reprinted in the 'Classical Practice' series, and it headed the programme of a unique concert which Bennett, assisted by other pianists, gave in 1841 in Coventry's rooms, 'hoisting the banner of classical sonatas,'—as an enthusiastic correspondent of *The Musical World* put it,—'and entering upon a crusade against all manufacturers of fantasias, etc.'

		Played by	
Sonata,	A ma., Op. 3	W. S. Bennett	Pinto.
,,	E flat, 'Les Adieux'	R. Barnett	Beethoven.
,,	B mi., Op. 40	W. S. Bennett	Clementi.
,,	A mi.	Cipriani Potter	Mozart.
,,	G ma., Op. 35	W. Dorrell	Dussek.
,,	C♯ mi., Op. 27	W. S. Bennett	Beethoven.

If solo Sonatas were ever meant for public performance, the occasions on which they had been so used in this country must have been very rare for many years previous to the date of this little manifesto. At any rate, it is not easy to find them on programmes given in musical journals.

When recalling these bachelor days, Bennett's friends one and all remembered his useless and aggravating *knocker*. They would then go on to give a reminiscence of a contrary kind. On his birthdays, four of which were passed in Portland Chambers, the baize-door was thrown wide open, Davison's rooms were annexed, and in imitation of the happy day on which he had come of age at Leipzig, he held high festival. William Dorrell, in his old age, still talked of this. 'Everybody,' he would say, 'remembered April 13th.' 'We all went,' wrote Grattan Cooke, 'whether we

---

[1] See p. 39. Cramer's remark was handed down by Davison.

were invited or not.' It was a merry gathering of old school-fellows round one who later proved himself, and was perhaps already, the focus of Academy 'esprit de corps.' Among these early friends were some who were ever ready to show their personal devotion to Bennett by loyally assisting him in serious projects of later life; but there is a time for work and a time for play, and April 13th was reserved for the latter.

Grattan Cooke, the well-known oboist, would be quite in his element. He was a good 'entertainer,' a rapid pen-and-ink caricaturist, and humorous even to a fault. The tales of his ludicrous behaviour in an orchestra are many. At rehearsals he was uncontrollable. One day he left his place, and was next seen struggling up the concert-room with a long ladder. He had resented the introduction of a very high note for his oboe in a new composition, and had gone for assistance to enable him to reach it. Bennett had a favourite tale of Cooke calling out to Platt, the horn-player, who had failed in one or two attempts at an awkward passage, 'Try it from the other end, Platt!' When telling stories of Academy life, Bennett would imitate the young oboist busily plying his fingers on his instrument, but also using any moment at which his right hand was disengaged, to manipulate the double-bass pegs, temptingly within his reach, to the mystification of the player on the lower tier of the stage.

Another birthday guest was Adolfo Ferrari, the son of eminent musical parents, who had begun life as a surgeon, but had soon exchanged, as he would say, 'healing for howling,' had entered the Academy, had thence gone to Italy where he appeared with success as an opera-singer, and afterwards for many years resided in the house of the great singing-master Crivelli, acting as his assistant-professor. He was full of fun and frolic, and many a bright hour did Bennett, in the course of thirty years to come, pass with his dear friend 'Ferry.' Ferrari was one who continued to keep Bennett's birthdays in observance, and in later years would spend weeks beforehand in preparing his annual gift; at one time turning, after repeated failures, a bâton light and slender enough to suit his friend's taste,— it was used to conduct the Philharmonic Concerts for many seasons;—and at another time training, to execute pretty cadenzas, a young parrot which, in due course, became attached to Bennett, learnt to echo his laugh in a sweet *sotto voce*, and, in the end, pined rapidly away, refusing all food after its master's death.

Another comrade, a very serious musician, but also an amateur 'entertainer,' was Robert Barnett, who by a combination of drollery, nervousness, and beautiful pianism had the characteristics of a John Parry. But John Parry himself may have been of the party, for he was an old Academy student, knew and appreciated Bennett, and assigned him a place of honour in a comic song, by the side of Thalberg and Liszt, as one of those composers with whose music the over-taxed young lady of the boarding-school would have to struggle before she could pass out as 'finished.'

'The birthday entertainment,' according to Sir George Macfarren, 'beginning with a breakfast party and lasting all day, was most convivial, he (Bennett) having that excellent quality in a host of setting each of his guests to say or do something which would show him to best advantage.' Bennett had his own little 'show' of conjuring tricks with accompanying narrative, and character-sketches, with which he could bring down the house at the Leipzig parties, and which he enjoyed exhibiting occasionally, in domestic circles, throughout his life. An effective spur to the merriment of others was his own laughter. 'Have you seen Bennett laugh?' was a question put by Signor Ferrari, in later years, to Miss Frances Cox, when she had recently become Bennett's pupil. The sound of his laugh 'gleeful and childlike,' as Miss Bettina Walker has described it, had great musical charm; but the eye was also attracted, not alone to his face which glistened with gaiety and sometimes bore a pretty sly look, but also to his figure, which the laugh permeated, his whole frame vibrating, though without contortion, whilst, as if to control himself, he would pass his arm rapidly to and fro across his back, then press one hand firmly to his forehead, and finally interlocking the two hands would rub them together lengthways with great vivacity, till the fun seemed to escape through his wide finger-tips. At all times of his life he could, when in the vein, keep a small company of intimate friends at a high pitch of mirth for hours together, and without effort. It was not always, at the end, that anything he had said could be remembered to account for this; but the fact was that, with all his seriousness, he never lost the naiveté of childhood, and therein lay the secret of the fascination which held those, and they were many, who delighted to be the companions of his play-hours.

The spring of 1841 brought Ferdinand David again to London. In the summer Count Reuss came over and spent some time with Bennett. Then the latter became drawn again to Leipzig, and determined to set out in October to spend the winter there, and to get, as he wrote, 'a new spirit and enthusiasm, *not to be found in England.*' Where he could look for the means to do this, unless perhaps, through the offer of some generous friend, cannot be conjectured. There was not much winter work to leave behind, and he arranged that a brother professor should take his private pupils during his absence.

Now, however, came another interest which could compete even with Leipzig. His journey was postponed, and he continued to take his class at the Academy till Christmas. He had found a new tie to his old home in Tenterden Street in the person of Miss Mary Wood, who was residing there to study under Mrs Anderson, and who was a very bright and charming girl in her seventeenth year. It was at one of the subscription Balls which Lord Burghersh used to arrange for the financial benefit of the Academy, that 'soft eyes looked love to eyes that spake again;' but Bennett could only be sure of his own feeling and courtship was at the time impossible. One or two Academy concerts gave opportunity for presence in the same room, and for exchanging a few words about musical studies; but that was all, and Bennett wrote afterwards of 'a miserable half-year of suspense' while waiting till the Christmas holidays would give him the chance of taking a bold step, with doubtful hope, and of learning his fate. He had not miscalculated. Lady Thompson (then Miss Kate Loder), who had invited Miss Wood to spend part of the same holidays in Bath, remembered the pride and pleasure with which her young friend and fellow-student confided to her that she was the object of Bennett's choice.

Thus accepted; having obtained the consent of Miss Wood's mother to a correspondence; armed with manuscripts for the encounter with Herr Kistner; as the year 1841 closed, Bennett, in the highest of spirits, was on his way to Germany, directing his first steps to Cassel, in order to introduce himself to Louis Spohr, at that time the acknowledged 'doyen' of German composers.

CHAPTER VIII.

HESSE-CASSEL, LEIPZIG, BERLIN.

Jan.—March, 1842.

aet. 25.

IN this chapter use is made of a series of very long letters written by Bennett to his future wife. In after-life she was on the point of destroying them; she had already torn one or two of them in shreds, when, sacrificing her own feelings,—for they belonged to her 'love-letters,'—she stayed her hand, tacitly sanctioning thereby the purpose to which they are now put. If Bennett, for a time, seems to be talking more about himself than usual, it must be remembered to whom he was writing. In fifty-six quarto pages of minute handwriting closely wire-woven with crossing, the passages here given are but an infinitesimal part of the whole and have in their original place no appearance of egotism. So, too, in a journal kept at the same time, the accounts of his own musical doings are none too prominent amid descriptions of the places he visited and of the people, other than musical, whom he came across.

English musicians of his generation did not often see one of their number starting on an artistic expedition to a foreign country. His associates did not allow the occasion to pass without some demonstration of interest. He thus described his departure from London to Miss Wood: 'As soon as I had finished my letter (on Thursday last) to you, I started for the Coach office in Regent St. where I found many Academy friends, including Dorrell, Patey, Smith, Goodban, Dunsford &c. I took leave of Dorrell there, and Dunsford and Patey rode on with me towards the Elephant and Castle where I, to my astonishment, found my faithful friend *Dorrell* again. He had taken a cab and got there before we did. You can't tell how that pleased me! The *three* then rode with me a long way further, and we had a long farewell while the coach was being properly packed. However, I was obliged to say Good-bye at last and took my place inside the coach. We were thirteen hours getting to Dover!'

The journey from London to Cassel, which, by way of Calais, was a little over 600 miles, had still to be taken, for the greater part of the way, under old-fashioned circumstances. A third of the distance could now be traversed by train,—this was new to Bennett,—from Ostend to Liége, and again from Aix to Cologne, at a speed of nearly fourteen miles an hour. But coach, boat, and diligences over the other 400 miles reduced the average rate, whilst actually on the move, to 7 miles an hour. Then again the journey could not be continuous, and though Bennett at each stage took the next available conveyance he spent five-and-a-half days in reaching Cassel. There were exciting moments on the way. A night-ride between Liége and Aix, 'in a horrid diligence at four miles an hour,' kept the travellers in a constant state of alarm. It was mid-winter; the roads were covered with frozen snow; many steep hills lay in the track; the vehicle was top-heavy with luggage. Accident seemed, at every turn, inevitable. The crisis came when, on a narrow bridge, the coach-wheels stuck fast in a rut. The passengers, expecting to be hurled into the depths below, clamoured to be let out. The conductor insisted on their keeping their seats while the diligence was being jerked into position. There was no catastrophe, but Bennett on arriving at Cologne wrote: 'I assure you we (the passengers) considered ourselves very lucky to get over this part of our journey.' A final ride of thirty-five hours covered the distance, viâ Frankfort, between Cologne and Cassel.

[Journal.] 'Römischer Kaiser, Hesse-Cassel, 3 o'clock Mittwoch, *Jan.* 5, 1842. * * * On my arrival here [at 9 a.m.], immediately sent my cards to *Spohr*, Hauptmann, Madame de Malzburg, and Frank Mori. * * * I received messages from all. * * * Since dinner have paid my visit to Spohr, who has always been represented to me as a *cold, haughty* person, but whom, I am proud to say, I found quite the reverse. He has a very pretty little house *all to himself*, in a little garden, and as soon as I entered I heard the violin going, but found that it was a pupil playing; he received me very kindly; talked with him about his new Symphony which we are to have at the Philharmonic this next Season, and other matters. * * * To-morrow evening I shall hear under his direction "The Templar and the Jewess" of Marschner, though, as he told me, he wished me to hear "Fidelio" which was to have been given, but in consequence of the illness of one of the Singers [was] postponed; he received the message to this effect whilst I was with him, and the coolness with which these Germans take these matters perfectly astonishes an Englishman, at least it does me. *Now* I only want to see *Cherubini*, and I shall know the only three great men left in our Art, viz. *Spohr, Mendelssohn* and *Cherubini*. * * * Wednesday night, 11 o'clock. Have been to the concert given by Frank Mori this evening, and met Spohr there, who introduced me to his wife with whom and himself I sat the whole evening. * * * Talked a great deal with Spohr about musical matters, about his Symphony in D minor (which I like better than anything of his) and which he told me he wrote twenty years ago in London. * * *'

'*Jan. 7th.* * * * Went last evening to the theatre, which is a very nice building but like all German Theatres very badly lighted. * * * I was in the stalls behind the Orchestra, and between the acts Spohr came and talked to me about the Music and situations of the performers in the Orchestra. The Stringed instruments are all on one side and the Wind instruments on the other; the Basses in the centre. I only wish our Wind instruments in England would play as well in tune as they do here. The singing was not good. I wonder our English singers do not learn German and travel, I am sure they would have great success.'

On January 8, he wrote to Miss Wood:—'There is here a Madame de Malzburg, one of the aristocracy of Hesse-Cassel, who is a great friend of mine, and plays my Sketches by memory and other things, * * * and last evening I made my first appearance in Cassel at a large party in her house. Spohr was there and got up one of his double Quartetts for me to hear, he also played one of his single Quartetts. I never heard such playing in my life. He is now nearly sixty years old, but has the greatest energy. I promised him in the morning that I would play and I found the parts of my Caprice in my portmanteau, so I took that and trusted to my memory for the Pianoforte part. You would have pitied me if you had seen the curious Pianoforte I had to play on, and I had not touched one since I left London. However I knew it was no time to make apologies, and off I started with everybody round the instrument. Something made me *very determined*, and I got through with capital success. They would not let me get up from the Pianoforte, and I must now play, " Der See, Der Mühlbach, und die Quelle," which is in English, " The Lake, The Millstream and the Fountain." The young ladies play these little sketches here, and so Spohr said to me, " They all play them differently, and now you must settle the point ;" and then after I had played them, there was a *great uproar*. After supper, once more the ladies begged Spohr to ask me to play again, I played them my "Allegro Grazioso" and one of Mrs Anderson's pieces[1]. * * * Altogether it was perhaps the most gratifying time I ever spent in my life, and I only looked round the room for my *Mary Wood* to make my happiness complete.'

'*Jan.* 9*th* [letter continued]. * * * I have been received here by the musical people like a Prince ; when I go to the theatre Spohr leans over the Orchestra and talks to me as if I were his son. He paid me yesterday his visit at my Hotel but I was unfortunately not at home ; he sent me, however, a note, inviting me to tea at his house and afterwards he took me to a Society, or kind of Club, of which he is a member, where I found many people smoking pipes and playing cards (in the German fashion). I was obliged also (only imagine) to play *three games of billiards* with him, and had the pleasure of being very well beaten by him, although I managed to win one game. I afterwards

---

[1] Mrs Anderson had accepted the dedication of his 'Suite de Pieces,' a work recently written.

supped with him at the same place as his guest, and he brought me home again, and in all respects he has behaved to me as if I were really his son. He talks to me about music as if I knew as much about it as he did. * * * To-night I think I shall go and spend the evening at Madame de Malzburg's. * * * Yesterday I found on her pianoforte my *three diversions* which she played with me uncommonly well. There was also a volume on the pianoforte with Bennett on the back. All these things make me very vain, and I must get back to England to bring me to myself again.'

[Journal.] '*Jan.* 10*th.* Paid my Abschieds-Visit to Spohr this morning and stayed nearly an hour with him. He has behaved all the time I have been here with the *greatest* kindness, *and I won't forget it hastily.* * * * Afterwards went to my favourite Madame de Malzburg, whom I like very much indeed and I never met a more amiable lady in my life. They want me to come back this way and I will if I can. Mr K. supped with me this evening and talked about Theory and Counterpoint enough to serve *half-a-dozen* Academies. I must not forget to mention that the Austrian Ambassador sent me a most polite message to spend the evening at his house, but I declined as I had to send my luggage to the Post-office and had no *coat* to go in. * * * I am now going to bed, and start to-morrow morning at half-past five. I cannot however close this book without a most grateful feeling for the great kindness I have experienced during the few days I have been in Cassel, and I shall always retain the most pleasant recollections of my visit.'

'God save Spohr, Mdme de Malzburg, &c. &c. &c.'

Bennett remained, throughout life, constant in his loyalty to Spohr, always maintaining that the Cassel composer, when at the zenith of his powers, had written music which gave him a right of succession in the dynasty of Great Masters. In forming such an opinion, Bennett was not conscious of deriving any assistance from the comparison of one composer with another; for he regarded the rare mastery which attests greatness as an absolute quality, and used to say that it was far too pronounced in the individual who possessed it to allow of any uncertainty in recognising it. He strongly resented any discussion upon the relative eminence of the great men who had in their turn helped to raise the edifice of Music; so that all there is to say with certainty about his estimate of Spohr is that he placed him in a first class, that class being one within which, in his opinion, no order of merit was feasible. He wrote, however, in reference to the great musicians:—'I do not confound genius with mastery;' and he may possibly have valued Spohr for what he called 'mastery' rather than for what he called 'genius.' He certainly thought him a great master of orchestration, especially admiring him as one who could, when he chose to use his means frugally, lay them out to the best advantage. In a lecture at Cambridge, in 1871, after quoting Mozart's G minor Symphony as an example of marvellous power and pathos displayed with sparing use of instruments, he next put forward the score of Spohr's 'Scena Cantante' as a study of modesty with grandeur. His mention of these two composers in such close sequence, though it only refers to a single trait which he recognised in both, is of itself sufficient to give some notion of his respect for Spohr's mastery. But he was no blind hero-worshipper. He did not consider a Great Master outside the pale of reverent criticism, nor did he think that a Master had his genius perpetually within call. One day he had been studying a newly-arrived instalment of the Leipzig edition of Bach's works, and as he gently placed the volume in his book-case he sighed and said, 'Very disappointing.' Such a man was not likely to be afflicted with musical manias, and the violent mania raging at one time in this country for Spohr's choral music, and more especially for that which he wrote in his declining years, only affected Bennett in so far that he thought it had done Spohr harm. When the reaction came, he would say angrily that the English people had got tired of Spohr, because they had only admired his defects. It was not, however, the populace alone who were fickle to Spohr. Bennett lived to notice with pain some apostasy among musicians who in earlier days had been the composer's adherents, and he did not understand turncoats. In one of his letters to Mendelssohn, he asserted of himself that he was never liable to hasty impressions, but that he could not forget anything that had once gone to his heart. He was not then referring to music, but his constancy as a musician was very marked, and a particular instance of it may be seen in his attachment to Spohr's D minor Symphony, the work to which he gave a preference in his Cassel diary. He seized opportunities of reviving it at his own orchestral concerts in London. As soon as he became one of the Philharmonic Directors, the Symphony after long neglect immediately reappeared on the Society's programmes. The same thing happened, many years later, when he was appointed the Society's conductor. Mr Paul David, who, during the last ten years of Bennett's life, was intimately acquainted with him, has written of the same Symphony:—'It was a favourite work of Sterndale Bennett, who was never tired of humming its spirited and melodious themes[1].' Sir George Grove, when recalling the last occasion on which he had met Bennett, said, 'He talked to me of Spohr's Symphony in D minor.'

In his work as a pianist and pianoforte-teacher, Bennett could not offer the same liege service to Spohr as to other great musicians. It was probably this disability which led him to take every chance of expressing his respect by word of mouth. Chary as he was of conversation on musical subjects, whenever Spohr's name was mentioned in his presence he would always open his lips, and give some token of his fidelity. He certainly kept the promise which he made to himself in Cassel, not to forget *hastily* Spohr's personal kindness to him.

He left Cassel at 5.30 a.m. on Jan. 11. After 'a cold langweiliche Reise' he reached Leipzig at 2 p.m. next day, and took up his quarters at the Hotel de Baviere. Within an hour of his arrival, Kistner, David, Verhulst, Monicke, and Schumann had been to see him. Two Cambridge undergraduates, H. H. Pearson and Novelli, whom he already knew, arrived from Dresden the same afternoon. Mdlle Meerti, the singer engaged for the winter season at the Gewandhaus, was staying in the Hotel, and sent down a note to solicit his help at a concert which the Directors were to give for her benefit on the following Monday. 'Poor girl,' he wrote, 'she had been refused

---

[1] See Article 'Spohr' in Grove's 'Dictionary of Music and Musicians.'

by everybody and was waiting for me to come, therefore I am very glad to be of any service, although I had wished to have turned myself round first.' On Jan. 13 he wrote to Miss Wood : 'To-night (Thursday) I am going to one of the grand concerts to hear Spohr's new Symphony[1] which will be given for the first time, and which afterwards I put in my portmanteau and bring to London for the Philharmonic.' [Journal.] *Jan.* 15*th.* 'Dined yesterday (Friday) with Voigt, where I met Schumann and his wife. We afterwards sledged it to Connewitz, a little village two miles from Leipzig. How interesting it is for me to renew the acquaintance of Schumann whom I have not seen for nearly five years.' Invitations to dinner at noon and to 'Thee und Butterbrod' came 'pouring in fast.' On Saturday he dined with the Davids; on Sunday with the Schumanns; on Monday he played his Caprice in E major with orchestra at the Gewandhaus and accompanied Mdlle Meerti in her songs; on Tuesday he went to the Buchhändler Börse to hear a few bars of an Overture of his own which he thought was being very well played, and then hurried off to a large music-party at Mdme Haertel's which brought a gay week to a close. Dr Haertel pleased him very much by offering to send to his rooms one of the new grand pianofortes recently made by the firm of Breitkopf and Haertel. These instruments had special interest for an Englishman, because they were after an English model, and he wrote :—'On my former visit to this town I ordered for them a Broadwood Pianoforte from London, and they have made Pianofortes exactly like them, which are very successful.'

He now set out to find Mendelssohn who was residing in Berlin.

[Journal.] '*Jan.* 21*st*, Berlin. * * * Left Leipzig at six o'clock yesterday morning and arrived here at two. * * * Called on Mendelssohn at 5 o'clock—not at home. Went then to the theatre [Gluck's *Alcestis*], and before two acts were over, he came and found me out. He took me afterwards to the Singing Academy, where I heard part of a Mass of Cherubini's, which I did not like very much. Saw Spontini there. Capital Society, about 200 in the

---

[1] (Op. 121) for 2 Orchestras.

chorus, chiefly amateurs. Breakfasted and spent the morning with Mendelssohn, had a little music and a great deal of talk. Kinder than ever to me. * * * This town is very dull. * * * Sent a card to Liszt, and one to the British Embassy[1]—all very grand. * * * Oh England! never mind, March will soon be here.'

All the journals which Bennett kept when abroad, show him as constantly attacked by sudden fits of home-sickness.

He had recently been elected one of the seven managing Directors of the Philharmonic Society. Mendelssohn had been asked if he could contribute a new work for performance during the coming season, and had replied to Bennett early in December 1841:—'I do not know whether I can have anything ready. * * * Should I have anything, it would be finished by the time of your arrival, and I would then ask you to take it back to the Society.' Mendelssohn, at the exact time predicted, had a work ready. He finished it on the very day of Bennett's arrival in Berlin. It was the Scotch Symphony.

Bennett then wrote to Miss Wood:—'I am reckoning greatly upon our Philharmonic season, and trust that as I am now partly responsible, we shall have good success. All the musicians that I meet here are congratulating me on being a Director, and I am sure I did not think anything of it before. When Mendelssohn saw me in the theatre, almost the first words he spoke were, "Why, Bennett, I really don't see you are any prouder," and I could not think what he meant.'

[Journal.] '*Sunday, Jan. 24th, eleven o'clock.* Breakfasted with Mendelssohn this morning and he played me his new Symphony which I hope we shall play at the Philharmonic next Season. I like it very much already and I am sure with the orchestra it will be very successful indeed; he tells me he has never played a note of it to anybody. * * * Dine to-day with Madame Mendelssohn sen. * * * *Sunday evening.* Met nearly the whole Mendelssohn family. * * * After dinner went over to Mendelssohn's lodging to hear once more his new Symphony and I am sure I shall always like it.'

[1] The Earl of Westmorland, founder of the Royal Academy of Music, was Ambassador at the time.

When Mendelssohn was leaving his mother's house in the afternoon after dinner, he said, 'Now, Bennett, you must come and let me play the Symphony once more, you do see through music so quickly.' Bennett would himself relate this with modest pride, and he could, confidentially, show places in the Scotch Symphony where the composer, who liked him to criticize, had adopted his suggestions. The same evening, there was a long talk about the Philharmonic. This opened the question of Mendelssohn going to England to take part in the Society's concerts of 1842. For the past year or two the Directors had been trying, but without success, to secure his services. Accordingly, Bennett had now been asked to use his personal influence, and a few weeks later he was able to say that he had 'persuaded' Mendelssohn, and that he thought the Philharmonic ought to be 'very much obliged' to him.

Another invitation which Bennett gave at this time, and which he did not hesitate to give on his own responsibility, has great interest. He wrote to Miss Wood from Leipzig on Jan. 18:—'Clara *Schumann*, who is married here to a friend of mine, is one of the finest players I have ever heard, and is altogether an extraordinary person; you may perhaps have heard of her as Clara Wieck. I want her to come to England and I have answered that she shall play at the Philharmonic, but I fear I shall not be able to persuade her.' Nor did he, and the reason of his failure is easy to find. A classical pianist, like Madame Schumann, would not, at that particular time, secure enough engagements in London to meet the expenses of her tour. Later in his life Bennett negotiated for six years before he succeeded in bringing Madame Schumann to this country for the first time.

After a few days in Berlin, he returned to Leipzig. [Journal.] 'Leipzig, *Jan.* 25*th*. Arrived from Berlin last night about seven o'clock; dined and dressed and managed to hear the third part of Verhulst's concert. * * * Schumann supped here this evening. Capital fellow! Mrs Shaw arrived from Berlin and paid me a visit in my rooms. Count Reuss also here to-night.' Then three weeks passed in which he had social engagements every day. He worked in the early hours of the morning, but towards mid-day his

rooms were 'full of people,' so that he was prevented from completing a new P. F. Concerto which he had begun in London in view of playing it at Leipzig. He was a great deal with Count Reuss, with Mrs Shaw and her husband, and with the Schumanns. There was, of course, music. He heard performances of his 'Naiads' and 'Wood-nymphs' and was invited to play at two of the Chamber Concerts which the Gewandhaus Directors had lately added to their scheme. In reference to one of these concerts, he wrote :—
'Mendelssohn's Quartett I *really do like*; *only perhaps not so much* the last movement. * * * I had a very bad headache and came home to the Hotel between the Acts and so missed my everlasting favourite, Mozart's Quintett [in G mi.]. I returned however soon enough to hear

The programme of the concert shows that the Quartet of Mendelssohn was the one in D major. The original manuscript of the work, given to him at this time by the composer, always remained one of Bennett's most valued possessions. In after-life, as an exceptional mark of favour to one or other of his pupils, he would take it down from his book-case and show it, together with the autograph score of 'The Hebrides,' the Album in which he kept his letters from Mendelssohn, and the other Album, given him by Count Reuss, which contained a water-colour drawing by Mendelssohn of the Thomas-Schule at Leipzig.

On his former visits to Leipzig, a warm attachment had sprung up between Bennett and the members of the Schunck family, with whom Mendelssohn also was on terms of close intimacy. Their family circle had lately gained a charming addition through the marriage of Herr Julius Schunck to Mdlle Jeanrenaud, Mendelssohn's sister-in-law. Bennett described his first meetings with this lady in a letter to Miss Wood. Here he shows himself in the opposite moods of seriousness, or perhaps shyness, and of gaiety. A young lady, who moved in this same set, has given her remembrance of him, under these two aspects, in a letter which will be quoted presently. To Miss Wood he wrote :—

'I went out the other day to a dinner-party and met for the first time a Mrs Schunck (the sister of Mrs Mendelssohn), who had married a friend of mine, Mr Julius Schunck, since I was here. I suppose she expected me to be jumping over all the tables and chairs in the room, for I heard afterwards that she was disappointed in finding "such a serious person," but a few days afterwards I spent the evening at her house and made noise enough for ten people, and she seemed quite delighted and begged me to visit them very often as she found me "very merry," so I have set my character to rights there.' A few days later he wrote of her in his journal, 'How I do like Mrs Schunck.'

Trains were now running from Leipzig to Dresden in four hours, so Bennett went over with Carl Voigt to spend three days amid pictures and porcelain. He also anticipated a rare musical treat. Mendelssohn had given him a letter of introduction to Schneider, telling him that he would hear the Organ Fugues of Bach played 'better than by anybody in the world.' The great organist, however, was too unwell to trust himself in a cold church, so Bennett came away disappointed. He found himself not altogether a stranger in Dresden, and wrote: 'I had a curious scene in a music-shop here. I went to order something and kept walking about the room and at last came and leant over the counter and looked at the music-seller, and he started back as if I were a ghost and exclaimed, "Is it, is it, is it, Mr Ben- Ben- Bennett?" I made my bow and said that was my name, and had a hearty shake of the hand, and I asked where we had had the pleasure of meeting one another. I then found out that he had only seen my *Leipzig portrait*, which proved to me that it must at any rate be something like.'

He went for a second time to Berlin. [Journal.] '*Feb.* 16*th*. Have been spending the evening with Mrs Mendelssohn where I met the whole Mendelssohn family. Mrs Hensel played some of her new compositions and played them charmingly.' Of another evening (Feb. 21) he wrote to Miss Wood :—' I went to a small music-party at Mendelssohn's where I met all his family and some other musical people. He played three pieces and then insisted on my playing. I *never was so alarmed before*; not at him, for we have played too often together, but at his sister, Mrs Hensel. However, he was getting rather angry, and I played very well as it happened, and they were very generous in their applause. I never was frightened to play to any one before, and to think that this terrible person should be a lady. However, she would frighten many people with her cleverness.'

[Journal.] '*Feb. 22nd.* * * * To-day I have been dining with Mendelssohn, and played him my Songs. Mr Liszt made his appearance to take farewell of Mendelssohn, and he played me the few bars of *most extraordinary* harmony, which he had written for me on a sheet of paper I sent him this morning, but which I have not yet got. * * * To-night spend the evening with Taubert.'

Bennett wrote of the pleasure he found in making Taubert's acquaintance, and how the mutual knowledge of one another's music served as an introduction to their chatting together as if they had known each other all their lives. Liszt showed him some kind attentions; but unfortunately Liszt seems to have been very bitter against England at the time. He abused the country 'very unmercifully' to Bennett, saying that there was nothing to be found there but 'manufacture and brutality;' so that the Englishman's patriotic feelings were wounded. As, however, Liszt cannot possibly have meant to offend Bennett, and was, at the time he made the remarks, drinking his health at dinner, one can only imagine that he was intending to sympathize with a refined artist who had to make his way in the art-world of London.

On February 23 Bennett returned to Leipzig, and wrote to Miss Wood of a 'delightful journey' of eight-and-a-half hours which he had taken with Mendelssohn from Berlin. 'The weather was very fine, and we talked and laughed the whole way. He (Mendelssohn) brought with him a whole stock of provisions, and a bottle of Madeira, *twice past the line*, and when I said, "Whose health?" he replied, "Miss Wood." On Thursday next * * * he gives his new Symphony and directs the concert, and I expect it will be the fullest of the season.'

The Scotch Symphony was produced at Leipzig on March 3. Bennett played his F minor Concerto the same evening. After the concert he attended a large supper-party at Madame Frege's, Mendelssohn also being a guest. He wrote in his journal at midnight: 'Miserable all day—always am the day I am going to play. Concert very brilliant to-night. Mendelssohn's Symphony was the great attraction, and I liked it excessively. Never played with more comfort to myself; Barcarolle immensely applauded, very happy this evening.' He also wrote to Miss Wood, 'Mendelssohn told me that I played better than he had ever heard me. Are you pleased?'

The same evening is incidentally mentioned in a letter written forty years later to Bennett's friend and pupil, Mr Arthur O'Leary, by a lady with whose family Mendelssohn was closely connected, and who was present both at the concert and at the supper-party after it. The letter, however, goes further, picturing Bennett amongst his Leipzig friends, and especially by Mendelssohn's side.

'Sterndale Bennett,' this lady wrote, 'was a frequent and welcome guest at our house, and I often met him and Mendelssohn together. Their relations to each other were those of surpassing friendliness. Each loved and respected the other, and Mendelssohn felt the highest pleasure not only in the eminent gifts, but also in the characteristic and amiable nature of the young artist. One can say that Mendelssohn, like an elder brother, shared in his strivings and successes, and always supported him readily with his counsel in the most loving way. Their intercourse was most cordial and intimate. They were both given to pleasantry and Bennett in particular was as a rule in the mood for all manner of fun. The German language, still unfamiliar to him though he studied it industriously, German life and customs all gave rise to laughable mistakes and witty remarks. Within the circle of his more intimate friends, Bennett's childlike merriment was irrepressible. He was fond of performing divers conjuring tricks, and his anecdotes and comical stories were received with roars of laughter. In large assemblies he was reserved and retiring, but very popular, all considering themselves fortunate in counting him among their guests. His first[1] appearance

[1] Not his *first* appearance, but perhaps the first occasion on which this lady heard him.

at the Gewandhaus was a decided success. The refined grace with which he gave the second movement of his Concerto—entitled "Barcarolle," if I mistake not—inspired the audience with enthusiasm. Mendelssohn rallied him on this occasion about a nervousness which had made him accelerate the time, though he was greatly pleased at his triumph.'

The relationship of an elder to a younger brother, which this lady's memory has given to Mendelssohn and Bennett at the ages of 33 and 26 respectively—bringing to one's mind a like happy association half-a-century before between Mozart and Storace with the same difference in their ages—seems also traceable in Schumann's mind when he wrote of them as contemporary musicians sharing a common inheritance, and not as master and disciple. 'No one,' he wrote, 'desires to call Bennett a great genius, but he has a great deal of one kind of genius;' and certainly, in Schumann's opinion, Bennett was worth speaking of in the same breath with Mendelssohn. This is to be seen in the first as well as in one of the last of his criticisms on Bennett. Thus, in 1837 he wrote:—

'The first thing that strikes every one in the character of his compositions is their remarkable family[1] resemblance to those of Mendelssohn. The same beauty of form, poetic depth yet clearness, and ideal purity, the same outwardly satisfying impression,—but with a difference. This difference is still more observable in their playing than in their compositions. The Englishman's playing is perhaps more tender, more careful in detail; that of Mendelssohn is broader, more energetic. The former bestows fine shading on the lightest thing, the latter pours a novel force into the most powerful passages; one overpowers us with the transfigured expression of a single form, the other showers forth hundreds of angelic heads, as in a heaven of Raphael. Something of the same kind occurs in their compositions[2].'

Now, five years later (1842), Schumann reviewed at great length the 'Suite de Pieces,' a set of elaborate Pianoforte Solos which Bennett had completed in London before starting for Germany:—

[1] The word in the original is 'Bruderähnlichkeit.'
[2] Translated from the German by F. R. Ritter.

'The resemblance of his compositions to those of Mendelssohn has often been remarked; but those who think they have sufficiently designated Bennett's character by such a remark, do him great injustice, and betray their own want of judgment. Resemblances are common between different masters of the same epoch. In Bach and Handel, in Haydn, Mozart, and Beethoven in his earlier period, we find a similar aim, like a bond of union between them, and which often outwardly expresses itself, as though one were calling unto the other. But this inclination of one noble mind to another should never be misnamed imitation, and Bennett's likeness to Mendelssohn is involuntary. Yet Bennett's works have continued to increase in originality; and in the one that lies before us, we are merely reminded of the artistic striving that inspires him in common with Mendelssohn. We think more frequently of older masters, into whose nature the English composer seems to have penetrated. The study of Bach and of Domenico Scarlatti, whom Bennett prefers among pianoforte composers[1], has not been without influence on his development. And he is right to study them; for he who desires to be a master can only learn this from masters. * * *'

Schumann here observes 'increase in originality' and fresh influence of 'older masters,' so one may think that Bennett had done himself no harm by abstaining for two or three years from writing pianoforte-music, and then, as it were, starting on a new track. Davison, in his review of these pieces, thus noticed the change:—'In this work Mr Bennett has altogether abandoned the accompanied song style which characterises the majority of his previous compositions for piano solo. We are not sorry for this, since, in addition to its rescuing him from the accusation of monotony, we find in the *Suite de pieces* a strength and energy which are not compatible with the style we have alluded to. * * * The fifth [piece] reminds us, we know not why, of some of the quaint lessons of Domenico Scarlatti. * * *' Bennett had certainly tried in Portland Chambers to extend his knowledge of Scarlatti's music.

---

[1] A more literal translation of Schumann's sentence would be 'The study of Bach, and of the clavier-works of D. Scarlatti for which Bennett has a particular fondness has not been without influence on his development.'

THE GEWANDHAUS CONCERT-ROOM
LEIPZIG

He had searched for it. Knowing that Lord Fitzwilliam's library, bequeathed to the University of Cambridge in 1816, contained works of the composer, he made enquiries in 1840, but received the disappointing reply that the music-library was stored away pending the completion of the Fitzwilliam Museum.

Bennett now saw the last of Germany for many a long year. This visit, especially, furnished many treasured recollections. His reception by Spohr; his introduction to the Mendelssohn family, to Madame Hensel and her husband the painter, and to Mendelssohn's other brother-in-law the mathematician Dirichlet; his meeting with Spontini, Meyerbeer, Taubert, Schneider, and other musicians in Berlin and Dresden; his joyous day's journey with Mendelssohn from Berlin to Leipzig; all such things were often to be thought of and recounted. The evening on which the Scotch Symphony was first heard, and on which he played his own Concerto, was never forgotten by him, and he was justified in recalling it with some pride. On the one hand, Mendelssohn had come from Berlin to preside over a single concert, on the spot which he had made peculiarly his own. He conducted his new work at a desk wreathed with laurels, and was received with all the honour due to a great master giving to the world a glorious masterpiece. On the other hand, Bennett played his Concerto amidst universal applause, and the lady who wrote of the evening forty years afterwards had not forgotten Mendelssohn's pleasure at his young friend's 'triumph.' Opportunities of distinction came rarely to an English pianist of the time, and Bennett would, in later days, speak of his connection with this concert as one of the chief events of his life.

He remained in Leipzig a few days longer, took part in all the social festivities held for welcoming Mendelssohn, heard the new 'Antigone' music at the theatre, and then travelled straight through to England, to be present, in his place as one of the Directors, at the first Philharmonic concert on March 14.

CHAPTER IX.

THE PHILHARMONIC SOCIETY.
THE MUSICAL SEASON OF 1842.

March to July, 1842.
æt. 25, 26.

THE Philharmonic Society of London, an institution with which Bennett was closely connected during the greater part of his life, was founded in 1813, i.e. three years before his birth, and thirteen years before he began his studies at the Academy. The movement which originated the Society, gave a new direction to the musical taste of this country, and prepared the way, by the introduction of fresh models, for that extension of musical education of which he was one of the first to reap the benefit. The Philharmonic accepted him, while still a youth, as one reared under the same influences as itself, and thenceforward to the end of his life regarded him as the English musician who came nearest to its own ideal. He, in turn, for the best part of forty years, followed with the deepest interest the Society's work; grateful, no doubt, as time went on, for success gained under its auspices, and tied to it by the memory of happy associations; but beyond any such self-concern, always very jealous for its reputation as the chief home in this country of a school of music which he piously venerated.

The Society had been the outcome of a strong desire on the part of certain eminent musicians to see concerted instrumental music, and especially orchestral music of the then modern type taking up a fixed abode in England. The last decade of the eighteenth century was marked by the visits of Haydn and the production of his Symphonies at Salomon's concerts; but Salomon found it impossible to keep alive the interest in such music which Haydn's presence had aroused, and in 1799 abandoned the attempt. The nineteenth century opened with no promise of progress. This country was at a crisis when it could give little attention to home affairs of any kind, and art could look for no encouragement. It was not alone to instrumental music that the check came. Haydn's Oratorio 'The Creation,' produced here in 1800, took no hold until it was revived thirteen years later, a few days after the first Philharmonic concert. In the month of March, 1813, music in this country awoke to a new life. The aristocracy at their 'Concert of Antient Music' had been steadily preserving Handelian traditions, and in the course of long programmes of vocal music had listened to the Overtures and Concertos of Handel, or Corelli, or Geminiani; but modern music could not, by their rules, appear on their scheme. The Philharmonic Society was a union of professional musicians; but they would never have attained their purpose had it not been for the fact that they came forward, in this instance, simply as music-lovers. They had no material interests of their own in view. They did not aim at the production of their compositions; for few of them wrote concerted instrumental music. They looked for no prominence as performers; for they at first excluded from their programmes works in which soloists were conspicuous. They had no thought of pecuniary gain to themselves; on the contrary, the Members and Associates resolved to support the undertaking by their own subscriptions, and to accept no remuneration for any services which they rendered at the concerts. Bennett, in his later life, liked to tell, in praise of these pioneers, how he had heard that some leading musicians of the day, who were not professed orchestral players, renewed the practice of instruments learnt in their youth, and enlisted in the ranks of the Philharmonic band to help the Society on its start in life. So admirable a spirit courted success, and success both artistic and financial came. There was a rich store of music ready for performance, little of which, save the almost forgotten Symphonies of Haydn, had been heard in England before; but the Society was ambitious to concern itself with the present as well as the past, and with the security of accruing funds entered into negotiations with celebrated living composers, engaging them to write new works and inviting their presence at concerts. Thus between 1817 and 1829, all the world being then at peace, Cherubini, Spohr, Weber, and the youthful Mendelssohn, were in turn welcomed to the Philharmonic platform. The advent of Spohr in 1820 led to a repeal of the law forbidding Concertos with a soloist, and thenceforward many European artists of renown performed at the concerts, the first introduction of a modern pianoforte Concerto by Moscheles, in 1821, creating a remarkable sensation. Of paramount interest, however, was the co-operation of Beethoven as a composer, culminating in his dedication to the Philharmonic of his Choral Symphony. Fortunate, too, was the Society who could find means to contribute to 'the comforts and necessities' of Beethoven in his last illness, and who could place on its records the grateful message he sent back, eight days before his death, to 'the noble English.' Thus, when the Philharmonic came of age in 1833 (an event which it celebrated by commissioning the composition of seven new works) it had made history and acquired prestige. Foreigners eyed with favour an institution which took delight in honouring them, whilst English musicians regarded election as Member or Associate in the light of a professional diploma granted with authority, and scarcely obtainable at the time in any other way.

Bennett's adoption by the Society came early, and his promotions followed quickly. Performances of his works, after his debût in 1835, were given annually. He was elected an Associate in 1838, at the age of twenty-two, and being in Leipzig when he heard the news, he immediately ran off to Mendelssohn to tell him of his 'good luck.' He was raised to the rank of Member in 1840, and at the end of 1841 was appointed one of the seven Directors, as also one of the seven Conductors of concerts, for the next year's season. The conductorship, though it only entailed presiding at a single concert, was an honourable post for him, seeing that in the first year he held it, when he was twenty-six years old, he was the colleague of Sir George Smart, Sir Henry Bishop, Potter, Lucas, Moscheles, and Mendelssohn. In his other office as Director, to which he was annually re-elected until such time as he declined to serve further, he was able to make himself useful. His views were not always in accord with those of the majority of his colleagues, as his correspondence will show; though why he disagreed with them he does not definitely state. One cause of variance, however, can be made plain. When he first joined the Board, the Society, which was entering on its thirtieth year, was passing through a time of depression. It no longer had the monopoly of instrumental performance in London; the material prosperity of earlier years could not be maintained; and for some time past accumulated savings had been drawn upon to cover deficits. Business had to be thought of as well as art. It had come to pass that the Directors were not necessarily selected because they were the most learned of the Members in that branch of music which was the speciality of the Society. Certainly, in framing their programmes, whether it was that they thought to please and attract a larger public, or whether they only listened to the dictates of their own tastes, they often admitted musical works and performances which were out of keeping with Philharmonic traditions. There were items on their programmes of which a man as strict as Bennett could not possibly approve. It was, however, an awkward duty, for one who himself figured as a pianist and composer at the concerts, to give opinions on the merits of others. He therefore set to work quietly, though he was by no means inactive. His connection with Germany was the first source of his practical usefulness to the Society, and from that same connection he derived the most pleasure in his new position; for, with no further prospect of travelling himself, he could still keep in touch with his German friends. Philharmonic business led to much correspondence between Mendelssohn and himself. That correspondence supplies some of the best material available for following his professional and also his private life during the next few years. It will be used as the groundwork of this narrative, which will now be resumed in March, 1842.

Bennett, after his return from Germany, moved from Portland Chambers to 42 Upper Charlotte St, Fitzroy

Square[1], where his friend, Mrs Johnson, was residing with her two sons, one of whom, Alfred Croshaw Johnson, has been already mentioned as his pupil and his visitor at Grantchester. Mrs Johnson had lately been left a widow; her house was beyond her requirements; and some friends of hers, who also knew Bennett, suggested that she should admit him as a member of her family. The proposed arrangement promised well for him; it would increase his expenditure; but he would be in a better position to receive pupils, and in the handsome rooms assigned to him he would be able to give little concerts or music-parties. All this he explained in letters to his aunt at Cambridge, writing: 'I hope to see a few *carriages* before my door in the course of the season;' and, again, 'It seems more of a home than I have been latterly used to; no more Chamber life for me!' At the same time another home was ready to welcome him at Southampton where his future mother-in-law dwelt. Thither he now went to spend an Easter holiday. Miss Wood had only just completed her seventeenth year, so there was no talk of an immediate marriage; nor would his present means have allowed of it. Her father, a Commander in the Royal Navy, was abroad, and was not expected home for two years. Meanwhile, Bennett must work and have something satisfactory to say to Captain Wood on his return. From Southampton he wrote to Mendelssohn, using note-paper with a view of Netley Abbey upon it. Mendelssohn had been delighted to hear that Bennett was engaged, and had never ceased to sing 'Hang the liberty' when they were together in Berlin.

SOUTHAMPTON, *April* 2, 1842.

MY DEAR FRIEND,

I hope you will be so good to notice well the *picture* on this sheet of paper and if you remark the name of the town I have written underneath you will be able to tell where I am now and what the object of my visit to this part of the world is. I am just going back to London but I thought I should very much like to write to you from this place, and after this little introduction I must begin to

---

[1] Now (1907) 92 Charlotte St. On the east side, the 4th house south of Howland St.

talk about other things. I am beginning to be very anxious about my box which contains the parts of your Symphony and I shall be very much obliged to you if you will immediately after you receive this send a few lines to Kistner and enquire if he has sent it off, for I am very anxious that the rehearsal of your Symphony should take place as soon as possible. * * * I hope if you have made the alterations which once you spoke to me of, you will write me full directions. * * * If you can, do tell me the very day you are likely to be in England as I will come and meet you if possible. I always regret that I did not see you the day I left Leipzig and hope you received my letter from Mainz. I delivered all your dispatches most punctually and delivered them all in the Philharmonic concert room where many asked for more letters than I had to give them. * * * I find the Philharmonic going on in the same way as ever, I have already spoken on some little matters and hope to effect some improvement, but I must do it very quietly. I arrived in London on the morning of the first concert from Dover. I had a very bad journey all the way from Mainz to England. I was abused in one of the newspapers that I was absent from England when the first programme was made and indeed it was a very bad concert. I am very unsettled at this moment as I am changing my lodgings and hope in about *eight weeks* to welcome you in Upper Charlotte Street, Fitzroy Square (No. 42). *A young Lady* wishes to thank you for the Song you wrote for her and so I have promised to leave some room in this letter. I hope your visit to Leipzig did not very much fatigue you and that I shall see you well and happy in England. Pray write soon.

With best remembrances to Mrs Mendelssohn and your family,

Believe me ever
Yours sincerely,
WILLIAM STERNDALE BENNETT.

Bennett, having failed to find Mendelssohn when he called to say Good-bye to him in Leipzig, had written from Mainz: 'I very much regretted it, wishing to have a *chat* with you for a quarter of an hour and to thank you for all your kindness to me when I was at Berlin and many other things which I must say to you when I see you in London. Amongst *these other things* I most especially wished to ask the favour of your playing over Six pieces (which Kistner is now engraving) and to see that they do not publish *all* the wrong notes which I am afraid in the hurry of writing them out I made. And will you also be so good as to mark any *Pia.* or *For.* which you may think necessary, for I know I have not marked them sufficiently and I fear I shall not be able to correct the proofs and send them back in time to be printed. Do pray excuse this most *inhuman* request. * * *'

Mendelssohn wrote from Berlin, on April 15 :—

MY DEAR BENNETT,

Mr Kistner writes me yesterday (dated 12th April) that he sent your box *last week* via Hamburgh to you, I hope accordingly that it will reach or has reached you safely. I have made all those alterations in my Symphony which I intended (two principal ones in the 1st movement and some other trifles in all four) but I need not make any remarks about them, or give new directions, it goes all by itself. I hope you will keep your kind promise and superintend the rehearsal as paternally as possible. * * * Thanks also for your very welcome letter from Mayence; you know what pleasure it will always give me to know your new things earlier than other people[1], and although I am usually but very indifferent a corrector I will on this occasion screw up my capacities to an extraordinary pitch and hope to drive Kistner mad with wanting flats and sharps which I shall find out. But till now I have not got them; he writes in his letter from yesterday that he will send the proofs 'nächstens.' I am very anxious to get them and play them over again and again.—You see in this letter that I am in a dreadful bustle and have thousand unmusical things in my head (*for you use*[2] *to know it whenever you look at my face,* and therefore

[1] It seems strange that Bennett should not have played or shown his 'Suite de Pieces' to Mendelssohn whilst he was in Germany.
[2] 'you *use*,' i.e. 'you are wont.' Mendelssohn has employed this obsolete present tense in other correspondence.

I believe it will be the same with my letters) businesses, and Concerts, and Quartetts and everything. * * * And now enough. We are all quite well; Cecile sends her best compliments, anticipates much pleasure from her intended visit to your country, and has English lessons and reads English books, Marriage in high life, &c., with a vengeance. *Remember me kindly*[1]; write the days of the Philharmonic, farewell, and excuse the stupidity of this letter and of its author

       Yours always,
     FELIX MENDELSSOHN BARTHOLDY.

Bennett to Mendelssohn.
      April 25, 1842.
    42 UPPER CHARLOTTE STREET,
      FITZROY SQUARE.

MY DEAR FRIEND,

  Your kind letter of the 15th inst. I received on Saturday last and as to-morrow is foreign post-day I herewith send you the dates of the remaining Philharmonic Concerts. * * * You will see by this that you will have plenty of time to do as you like at Düsseldorf and still be with us at the *sixth Concert*, or if this does not agree with your plans, then you can in any case be with us for the two last and help us through with your aid to finish the season well. I cannot tell you how glad I am that your coming to my country amounts now to a *certainty*, and you know how happy the musicians here will be to welcome you and none more than myself. The box has not arrived but I hope to hear of it every day and immediately I get your Symphony, we will have a good and serious rehearsal. We played your Midsummer-night at the last concert (which Mr Potter directed) and I never heard it better played in England. They played it dreadfully slow at the rehearsal, but I hinted to Mr Potter as to the Leipzig time and he adopted my suggestions. Molique played at the last concert and has also brought a new Symphony which is to be played at the 5th concert. They have also asked me to play but I wish very much not to play until you come and the night you give your Symphony I should like *to*

---
[1] i.e. to Miss Wood.

be of the party, as at Leipzig. But will you let me know whether you will play first or whether you will have the Symphony and then play at the succeeding concert? Everything shall be as you wish, at least I am sure the Directors will arrange all to your satisfaction. I regret much that our Directors are at variance with Moscheles and I will tell you the whole affair when I see you. We are not able at present to give Spohr's new Symphony in consequence. *Entre nous* I am not at all satisfied with my colleagues and fear you will not find us very much improved in spirit and enterprize. I have kept very quiet because I could find no good opportunity of giving my opinion of their general arrangements which are far from being good, but all this when I see you. I am much obliged to you for your kindness in consenting to correct my proofs and hope you will not have too much trouble although my *fear* outbalances my *hope*. Then in three or four weeks I shall see you and you know how happy I shall be. Many thanks for all things. I think you will find me making love to a *vast extent*. I know you will wish me to prosper in all such happy affairs and although I shall retain my liberty some time longer, I begin to feel that I could give it up without *much* hesitation. With best compliments to Mrs Mendelssohn and your family,

Believe me, ever *and a day*,
Yours very truly,
WILLIAM STERNDALE BENNETT.

In one of the letters which he had recently written to Miss Wood from Germany, Bennett mentioned that he had just been buying a good deal of music for his library. He had perhaps received from Kistner a little money for his compositions which he could invest in that way. One day in Berlin he walked into a music-shop and ordered straight off, 'all the works of Bach;' but when he related this incident in after-life, it was not with reference to a well-filled purse, but to the scarcity at the time of published works by that composer. When he was leaving for England he placed his new purchases in a box, which he asked Kistner to send after him as soon as the orchestral parts of the Scotch Symphony for the Philharmonic were ready to be packed in the same. Kistner despatched the box in the early days of April to travel viâ Hamburg. As the weeks passed and Bennett saw no box he became very uneasy, the more so because in the course of the time a terrible fire had broken out and raged for some days in Hamburg. By the middle of May the matter was serious. The performance of the Symphony was fixed for the sixth Philharmonic concert on the 30th; Mendelssohn, after conducting a Festival at Düsseldorf, would only reach London in time for a final rehearsal on the 28th, and Bennett had pledged his word that he would himself prepare the Symphony in advance. Happily, however, the music had escaped the flames; and, though the disordered state of Hamburg had caused long delay, the precious box arrived just in time for a score of the Symphony to be copied from the parts, and for a special rehearsal to be called, which rehearsal Bennett conducted on the 26th. He thus kept his promise to his friend, and had for himself the satisfaction of co-operating in the production of the new work. It would, of course, mean a great deal to him, to appear as Mendelssohn's representative before the Philharmonic orchestra at this rehearsal, and it would help to confirm his position as one of the Society's conductors, in which capacity he had appeared, for the first time, ten days before. It was, however, now known that the Symphony would not be wanted for performance till the seventh concert. Mendelssohn, exhausted by the fatigue of the Düsseldorf Festival, had asked for a respite and postponed his journey. This postponement was a disappointment to Bennett, for he played his F minor Concerto at the sixth concert and had hoped that Mendelssohn would be conducting. When the Scotch Symphony was given on June 13, he was 'not one of the party, as at Leipzig,' which he had wished to be.

Of his personal intercourse with Mendelssohn during this visit to England there is little to be said, save that he shared with a host of others the wide-spread pleasure of the time. Mendelssohn had arrived by June 2, on which day he attended an orchestral concert, given by Miss Dorrell and her brother, which Bennett was conducting. William Dorrell remembered that as the conductor was leaving the artists' room to enter the concert-room Mendelssohn ran after him, saying, 'Here, Bennett, I have forgotten something,' and that he then took a little case from his pocket and presented, in the name of the Gewandhaus Directors, a valuable diamond pin. Mendelssohn wrote to Kistner on June 5 :—'I gave Bennett his pin during a concert, he stuck it in, thereupon immediately conducted an overture of mine, was vastly delighted, and all the performers were mightily impressed by your beautiful gift. They said, they too would like to come to Leipzig.'

Mendelssohn had brought his wife to see England and to visit relations and friends; his social engagements were innumerable; but he was ubiquitous, and A. C. Johnson remembered him as often running into Charlotte Street to find Bennett. Thalberg would also sometimes be there, and, when playing to Mendelssohn and Bennett, would not mind their rallying him about certain features of his music or performance; but would himself jest back, and enjoy what they said in the most good-humoured way. The Philharmonic season, with Mendelssohn's assistance at the last two concerts, ended brilliantly on June 27. A finishing touch, however, was still wanting. It appears that there had been a hope that the musical circles of London would combine to celebrate Mendelssohn's presence in their midst by some public festivity; but there was a lack of unity, and the failure to carry out such a scheme, when once it had been proposed, had a sorry look. The Philharmonic Society, anxious to perform their own duty of hospitality, at the last moment hurriedly arranged a whitebait dinner at Greenwich. Mendelssohn, on receiving their invitation, came to Charlotte Street on Wednesday, July 6, and wrote on a sheet of Bennett's music-paper :—

At the end of the London stay in 1842.
July 6th.

DEAR BENNETT—I am so very sorry not to find you at home! We leave England on Saturday or Sunday and I must beg you to excuse my not coming to Greenwich on Friday with the Directors, as it is so near to our departure and the principal reason is that they asked me to play the

Organ in Exeter Hall for the distressed manufacturers on Friday also and I declined it because I was going, and therefore I think it would not do to accept of any other engagement. So pray make my apology and give my best thanks to the Directors, and may health and happiness be always with you and with all whom you love and *vice-versa*. (There is also some selfishness in this wish you see.) And so good-bye, auf gutes Wiedersehen.

Always yours,

FELIX MENDELSSOHN BARTHOLDY.

I like the red room!!

Bennett, on reading the above, must have rushed off to consult his colleagues and to get the impossible Friday altered to Saturday on the chance of Mendelssohn's postponing his departure. A fresh invitation must have been immediately sent, and Mendelssohn wrote next day:—

DEAR BENNETT,

Our journey *is* postponed and so I will certainly come and dine with you at Greenwich. But tell me where and when we meet on Saturday.

Always yours in dreadful haste,

FELIX MENDELSSOHN BARTHOLDY.

Thus the Philharmonic saved its character for hospitality, and at the dinner on the 9th, Mendelssohn—according to *The Musical World*—assured his hosts that he would do all in his power to promote the interests of their Society. This was not a mere post-prandial 'sentiment,' but a real promise afterwards fulfilled. Then on their way home from Greenwich Mendelssohn and Bennett made another appointment. Miss Wood was still cloistered in Tenterden Street for her last term, and there had been no opportunity for introducing Mendelssohn to her. A concert or rehearsal at the Academy on the coming Monday would give such a chance, and this explains the following affectionate letter[1].

---

[1] The original is in German.

LONDON, *July* 11*th*, 1842.

MY VERY DEAR BENNETT,

I had hoped till the last moment to be able to come to the Academy, and now it is late at night and I have not been! I am terribly sorry, please do not be angry with me.

I enclose cards, my wife's and my own, for Miss Wood. If she thinks as I do, she will not care for them in the least, but I trust she will care somewhat for our warm good wishes for her happiness and prosperity, and these will be her faithful companions now and always—of that I hope that she feels no doubt.

These wishes are also at the same time wishes for you, dear Bennett. Your two persons are united, and wishes for you may be united too. Good-bye, my English visit is at an end once more—it was a happy one. Good-bye, may we continue as close friends as ever, and meet again soon.

Ever yours,
FELIX MENDELSSOHN BARTHOLDY.

CHAPTER X.

CORRESPONDENCE WITH MENDELSSOHN.

August, 1842—December, 1843.

æt. 26, 27.

In August, 1842, while Bennett was staying 'in the house of Mr J. W. Davison[1],'—which probably means that he was, at the time, enjoying rural pleasures at Davison's parental home in Brixton—he wrote one of his best known pieces for the pianoforte, first called 'Rondo Grazioso,' but afterwards called 'Rondo Piacevole.' This was 'the little P.F. Rondo in E major' which he referred to in his next letter to Mendelssohn.

SOUTHAMPTON, October 9th, 1842.

My dear Mendelssohn,

I shall avail myself of a quiet hour at this place to write you a few lines to ask you how you are, to find out *where* you are, and when I am likely to hear anything about you. I am here since Thursday evening and am going back to-morrow (Tuesday); you may imagine that these few days are passing happily enough, and I find it such a relief from the bustle of London to put myself in the railway carriage and come and walk on the *Pier*, not alone I assure you. I have heard nothing of you since you left our shores which were so very sorry to part with you. My *Mama-in-law* has your picture, which is now before me looking as happy and as gay as ever, as I trust you are.

---

[1] So stated by Davison himself in the programme of a Monday Popular Concert; but Davison had no house of his own at the time.

I have still my *liberty* and shall keep it still some time, but I do begin to agree with you and could now heartily sing with you 'Hang the liberty.' I wonder when I shall see you again and whether I shall be myself or not. I often wish to transport myself to the *Thomas-Mühle* and run up your staircase, but I hope all this will come again some day. I am writing to-day to Kistner to tell him that I cannot agree with Miss Birch, as she wishes to remain in London during the months of January, February and March. I have only just received her answer and I am not very well pleased at the indifference she displayed after the trouble I had given myself to ask your Directors to make her an offer. What think you of Miss Dolby, if she would come? and I think she would. * * * I remain in London this winter and am determined to work and send you over some new things, amongst others an Overture which must be for the Gewandhaus and which I hope to send you before the year is out. I am doing much to my Oratorio and have written just now a long Chorus, which I am rather satisfied with. My little P.F. Trio in A major I must also publish, and I have a little P.F. Rondo in E major the proofs of which are ready and I am wanting to send it to Kistner, which I hope you will like, not a very grand fellow nor a very merry one, but has something about it, which I think would please you. I will send you the English copy of my 'Suite de Pieces' whenever I have an opportunity and thank you once more for correcting the German edition. Spohr's new Oratorio 'The Fall of Babylon' according to the newspapers has made a sensation in England. I have neither heard nor seen a note of it, nor heard any opinion which I could have faith in or value. Edward Taylor is now at the head of Music in England and so you know what our hopes must be. I cannot give you any Philharmonic news, but I think we shall make some important changes next season, at any rate we shall have our eight concerts as usual. I suppose this letter will find you at Leipzig although I have heard nothing as to your plans. * * *
Do write to me when you have time; you know my dear friend what pleasure it always gives me to hear from you and what you are doing, and what is the musical state of Leipzig, if *healthy as ever*. Shall we have you next year

for the Birmingham Festival? I hope you will tell me what new things you have done and *for my sake* send us something for the Philharmonic next year. Pray give mine and Miss Wood's best compliments to Mrs Mendelssohn and kiss your children for me. Let me hear that you are really well and happy, remember me to the Schuncks, Davids, Schleinitz, &c., &c., and hoping to hear from you very soon, believe me, my dear Friend,

Yours most sincerely,
WILLIAM STERNDALE BENNETT.

Vergessen Sie nicht die noten von Bach für mich.

In November, Bennett announced a scheme of 'Classical Chamber Concerts,' a title which he later changed to 'Performances of Classical Pianoforte Music,' as being a closer description of their speciality. He was about to extend his work, and to do his duty, as a pianist, in a direction little tried so far by others in England. Chamber-music in which the pianoforte takes part had not yet found much place in concert-rooms. The Philharmonic Society had from the first included it in their programmes, but generally in the form of a Septet or Sestet. Similar works for a smaller combination of instruments such as P.F. Trios, and Sonatas for pianoforte and violin had been seldom played in public. The violinist Dando, and others following his example, had for a few years past given concerts of string Quartets. A P.F. Trio was a usual item on their schemes, so that just a few of such works had lately been brought to a hearing; but a vast number of masterpieces were quite unknown except to professors and a few highly-cultivated amateurs. A great pianist could gain at the time little distinction and certainly no money, by taking part in concerted chamber-music at a concert; and yet if such music was ever to gain the appreciation it deserved, pianists of high order were wanted to illustrate its beauty; men who would be patient in looking for even an educational result, without thought of material advantage, and who were willing to lend their powers to the furtherance of Music in her serious aspect, foregoing the applause given to *ad captandum* feats of virtuosity. Bennett was such a pianist, and there were none too many like him in his earlier days.

Of solo-performance on the pianoforte, only two forms were at this time recognized by the concert-audiences of England. Pianists were heard in Concertos with orchestra, or if they played without accompaniment, were expected to exhibit themselves in astonishing *tours-de-force*. The 'Recitals' by Moscheles in 1837 and 1838 may be quoted as striking exceptions sufficiently rare to prove the general rule. In Bennett's case, from the day in 1831 when he had first attracted notice at a students' concert, he was for about eleven years heard in Concertos with orchestra; and up to his twenty-sixth year the only solo-pieces played by him before a London audience were the above-mentioned Sonatas given in Coventry's rooms, and a selection from the 'Lieder ohne Worte,' at a concert of T. P. Cooke's. The modern 'Fantasia' was the only sure passport to the platform, or to the aristocratic salon. From Leipzig in 1842 he had written home about the Chamber-concerts lately added by the Gewandhaus Directors to their syllabus. Even there he found 'a small audience,' but he noticed with satisfaction the great attention paid to such music, and was delighted because one of the movements from the Violin Sonata, in B♭, of Mozart, which he played with David, set 'all the old ladies nodding their heads.' Then, too, for the first time, though nearly twenty-six years old, he was invited to play Solos of his own composition. He wrote of this fresh experience to Miss Wood: 'It is something quite new for me to play in this manner, for I do not very much like to play without the orchestra.' Yet he was pleased with the result. 'I stepped up [at the end of the concert] and played first one of my *new pieces* in E minor and afterwards my Sketches which the people applauded very much.' Thus encouraged abroad, after his return to his own country, he gave his first series of three concerts at the beginning of the New Year, 1843, in his drawing-rooms at Charlotte Street, before an audience of about 100 persons; introducing Trios, Violin and Violoncello Sonatas, playing Preludes and Fugues, Sonatas, and new compositions of his own. On March 3 he wrote to Mendelssohn: 'In the month of January I gave three little chamber-concerts in my own rooms and played a great deal from a great many authors. I played amongst other things your Violoncello Sonata, your Prelude and Fugue in E minor and your Seventeen Variations, some of Handel, Bach and Scarlatti, Sonatas of Beethoven and Spohr's new Trio.' As a concert-giver, he always took great interest in the selection of the vocal music, suggesting to his singers songs in keeping with the general character of his programme. In accounts of his concerts this point was often noticed in his favour. At the third concert of this first series he asked Miss Masson to sing Beethoven's 'Lieder-Kreis,' which had not, as far as he knew, been heard before in this country. After telling Mendelssohn about the concerts, he continued his letter with a change of subject:—'Now then let me talk a little on domestic affairs and thank you for your kind mention of Miss Wood (my dear Mary, as I call her). I saw her a fortnight since, and in another fortnight I hope I shall be with her at Southampton again. I generally pay a visit once every month and remain two or three days. She is indeed a dear girl and promises everything for my happiness, and I now can scarcely believe that you and I ever argued about losing *liberty*, for I am now as anxious to lose mine as you were in 1837. I think I shall be married next Christmas and shall be so delighted to introduce my little wife to all my good friends at Leipzig and I hope they will be hers. She studies your language with great perseverance. You must forgive me for talking in this *love-strain*, but I know you can appreciate my feelings and I assure you I am *more in love than ever*, hang the liberty.'

Mendelssohn replied on March 10:—'Thank you for your very kind and welcome letter which I received yesterday and which gave me such a pleasure! Particularly the passage which relates to the liberty and its hanging. God may give you so much happiness as I enjoyed those six years since I am married. I cannot wish you more for I believe there can be no more in the world. And give (not write) my kindest regards to Miss Wood (your dear Mary, as you call her), and write my wife's with them, and tell her, she must soon come and visit your German friends, who are hers.'

The Philharmonic season of 1843 was now approaching. The Directors had hoped that Mendelssohn would again assist, and had sent him a formal invitation; but in writing to Bennett on the subject, he referred to the recent loss of his mother, as the cause of abandoning all idea of coming to England this year. The Society's prospects were now very gloomy, and the best that Bennett could write about the disappearing capital was, 'We still have a little to lose.' He has been credited with suggesting to his colleagues, at this juncture, that they should apply to Spohr, and the application was successful, Spohr consenting to come over towards the end of the season. Bennett himself took part in two concerts. He conducted the fifth, at which the 'Lobgesang' was given, and at the sixth he played a new Concerto in A minor (unpublished), on which he had been engaged for eighteen months. It was the sixth and last Concerto he wrote. His first idea was to limit the work to two movements, and he named it not Concerto, but Concert-Stück. After playing it at the Saturday rehearsal he changed his mind, and composed a slow movement for the Monday concert, with an orchestral accompaniment sufficiently simple to be played without rehearsal. *The Musical World* described the Allegro as 'full of passion and grandeur,' and the Finale as a 'rondo presto of untameable spirit and untiring energy.' Spohr arrived in London just in time to grace with his presence a 'Soirée d'artistes,' which Bennett gave in Charlotte Street, and which, according to Davison, attracted 'a brilliant galaxy of celebrities.' It was certainly an interesting evening. Spohr was a grand 'lion' who had not been seen in London for twenty years. Dreyschock, whom Bennett had met at Leipzig, and whom he thought 'a very wonderful player as far as difficulty was concerned,' was in the company; but there was also a pianist of very different character, the boy, Charles Filtsch, who was spending in London two months of his short life, and, though only thirteen years of age, was influencing musical taste; for he was the first to make the music of his master, Chopin, properly understood by some of the musicians in this country. Charles Hallé, who was to give his first concert in London a few days later, was another guest; and

Moscheles brought with him Ernst, the violinist, who had arrived the day before on his first visit to England, and at this gathering in Charlotte Street made his entrée into English musical society. A third great violinist was asked and he accepted, but named a fee of fifty guineas, so that poor Bennett, whose annual income at the time scarcely exceeded four times that amount, was placed in the awkward position of having to withdraw his invitation.

On July 3, Spohr played and conducted some of his works at the Philharmonic, and on the 13th the Society gave an extra concert by royal command, the Queen attending and Spohr directing the whole performance. The Directors could congratulate themselves on another successful close of a year's work, but there was still cause for anxiety. A stroke of good fortune, which would have some lasting effect, was sorely needed.

In August, Bennett was in country lodgings near Southampton 'composing very hard;' finishing an Overture, which he christened 'Marie du Bois,' in allusion, it may be assumed, to the name of his future wife. He was also making some revision of his new Concerto, which he allowed Coventry to advertise as *in the press*. He wrote to Kistner in the autumn: 'I have ready for the engraver my new Concerto, which I performed last season at the Philharmonic Society and which I have since altered.' The Overture 'Marie du Bois' (afterwards used for 'The May-Queen') and the Concerto (or Concert-Stück) in A minor were two works which he continued to like himself, and he made second editions of both; but, though Kistner still pressed for music, Bennett held back, kept the Overture in manuscript for fifteen years, and never published the Concerto, though he was thinking of doing so up to the time of his death.

In October he found himself at Portsmouth, climbing the side of H.M.S. *Tortoise*, replying to the challenge of a sentry, and being conducted to the cabin of Captain Wood, who had just returned from New Zealand. 'It was rather a *nervous appearance* for me to make,' he wrote to Mendelssohn, 'but it is all happily over, and there is another step to our marriage.' In the same letter—dated November 6th—he unfolded to Mendelssohn a scheme

which he had proposed to his Philharmonic colleagues:—
'*Now then for business*, and I hope to explain myself distinctly for I have an important subject to write upon. I write in strict confidence. The Directors of the Philharmonic have privately charged me to write to you on the subject of their concerts next year. They feel the great and lasting advantage the Society derived from your presence at their season in 1842 and they further wish to express this by again securing your appearance amongst us *next* season. We much wish if possible to have *one Conductor* and it would be *all and everything* to us for you to be that Conductor. I do not know how your arrangements and plans are ordered at Berlin, but could you be with us as Conductor of our *entire* season? I will at once answer that every arrangement shall be framed to meet your views. Our first concert will be on the 25th March and the last on the 8th July. We will endeavour to make your sojourn in England as comfortable and happy as possible. Let me know your opinion upon the subject as soon as possible, but I do not wish you by any means to say "Yes" or "No" immediately, but let us know what hopes there are.'

Mendelssohn, unable to foretell how his duties at the Prussian Court might shape themselves, could not at once write the words 'Yes, I come,' as he wished to do; for he chose to regard the invitation as a great honour. The Philharmonic Directors were quite content to wait four months for a definite reply, hoping to secure his services for at least part of their season. 'Let us have as much of Mendelssohn as we can get of him,' was the message they sent him through Bennett.

In a further letter of December 9, Bennett submitted to Mendelssohn, in delicately chosen phrases, the business details of the Philharmonic appointment. He then broached another subject:—'Now, my dear friend, I must take advantage of this opportunity to tell you that I have proclaimed myself a candidate for the Musical Professorship at Edinburgh which Sir Henry Bishop has just resigned, and I should be so glad and obliged if you could give me a testimonial which I might send to the Authorities at the University.'

Similar requests were cordially responded to by the Earl of Westmorland, Sir George Smart, Dr Crotch, J. B. Cramer, Cipriani Potter, Moscheles and others; Spohr and Reissiger testified to a high reputation in Germany; and Mendelssohn, who was one of the earliest to reply, wrote in his brotherly way: 'I send you here the letter about the Edinburgh professorship. Really, I felt ashamed while writing a testimonial for you; *I* for *you*. I think you do not want such a thing from anybody—however you wished me to send it, and there it is. I wish you may have the success you deserve—you will then get that situation and more.'

This was the testimonial:—

BERLIN, 17 *December*, 1843.

MY DEAR FRIEND,

I hear that you proclaimed yourself a Candidate for the musical Professorship at Edinburgh and that a testimonial which I might send could possibly be of use to you with the Authorities at the University. Now while I think of writing such a testimonial for you I feel proud and ashamed at the same time—proud, because I think of all the honour you have done to your art, your country and yourself and because it is on such a brother-artist that I am to give an opinion—and ashamed, because I have always followed your career, your compositions, your successes with so true an interest that I feel as if it was my own cause, and as if I was myself the Candidate for such a place. But there is one point of view from which I might be excused in venturing to give still an opinion, while all good and true musicians are unanimous about the subject: perhaps the Council of the University might like to know what *we German people* think of you, how we consider you. And then I may tell them, that if the prejudice which formerly prevailed in this Country against musical talent of your Country has now subsided, it is chiefly owing to you, to your Compositions, to your personal residence in Germany. Your Overtures, your Concertos, your vocal as well as instrumental Compositions are reckoned by our best and severest authorities amongst the first standard works of the present musical period. The public feel never tired in listening to, while the musicians feel never tired in performing your Compositions, and since they took root in the minds of the true amateurs my Countrymen became aware that music is the same in England as in Germany as everywhere, and so by your successes here you destroyed that prejudice which nobody could ever have destroyed but a true Genius. This is a service you have done to English as well as German musicians, and I am sure that your Countrymen will not acknowledge it less readily than mine have already done.

Shall I still add that the Science in your works is as great, as their thoughts are elegant and fanciful? that we consider your performance on the Piano as masterly as your Conducting of an Orchestra[1]? That all this is the general judgement of the best musicians here, as well as my own personal sincere opinion? Let me only add that I wish you success from my whole heart and that I shall be truly happy to hear that you have met with it.

Always yours sincerely and truly
FELIX MENDELSSOHN BARTHOLDY.

One may be sure that so delightful a document, reaching Bennett on Dec. 23, would make the last days of 1843 happy ones for him.

---

[1] Mendelssohn had occasionally asked Bennett to conduct the orchestra in the Gewandhaus on evenings when he himself was to play the pianoforte. The critic Davison, in after years, often quoted this fact as an instance of Mendelssohn's confidence in Bennett.

CHAPTER XI.

MARRIAGE.

CORRESPONDENCE WITH MENDELSSOHN.

1844—1846.
æt. 27—30.

THE year 1844 opened with exciting prospects for Bennett. His marriage was now imminent; he had a chance of election to the Edinburgh professorship; and he could look forward to a musical season which would probably be brightened by the presence of Mendelssohn. On Jan. 8 he resumed his concerts in Charlotte Street, and on the 10th he was at Crosby Hall in the City, where he had been engaged to direct, during the winter, monthly performances of chamber-music. On the 13th he set out for Edinburgh, anxious to obtain, in view of marriage, an honourable post with a fixed stipend, and likely to bring in its train more employment than he could as yet find in London. In addition to his testimonials he had obtained good personal introductions. Mendelssohn—though this, Bennett himself may never have known—had written on his behalf to influential Scotch friends. He was welcomed by a section of the electors as the best-equipped musician in the field. Of the other candidates one alone was a formidable opponent. This was John Donaldson, who, though he had abandoned the profession of music for that of the law, was well known in Edinburgh, where he resided, as a man of considerable ability, and as one who had studied the physical side of musical science. A few of the electors, regarding Donaldson as too little, and Bennett as too much, of the practical musician, were reluctant to support either, and the question was how this third party, if prevailed upon to vote, would turn the scale. Bennett remained in Scotland a fortnight; he paid a flying visit to his young friend A. C. Johnson, who had just settled in Glasgow as a teacher of music; and he returned to London with the impression that the votes for the Professorship, as far as they were promised, were equally divided between Donaldson and himself. The election was not to take place till the end of March.

On March 3, Mendelssohn found himself able to accept, in part, the Philharmonic conductorship. He wrote next day to Bennett:—'Since yesterday I have the certainty of being able to come over to you; and this morning I receive Mr Watts' official letter. There is superstition for you and for me. I have written to him with how great a pleasure and how thankfully I accept the honor the Philharmonic Society will do me, and that I shall come—if possible in time for the 29th April—if not, certainly for the last 5 Concerts, and that I anticipate such a treat, such a happy time from my stay in England! The same I must write to you, and thank you! And do that from my heart!

'Now let me ask a favour; it is to correspond very regularly with me during the 6 or 7 weeks of my stay here, as there are many, many things which I should set right before my departure and which depend on your answer and letters. So pray write me *always* at least 2 or 3 days after you receive my letter; I will do the same, and I hope that you will be kind enough to grant me that favour, and perhaps we may thus do some good to your Society.'

Long letters accordingly passed about programmes and the chance of introducing unknown works. Mendelssohn, having first asked what English music would be available, undertook to find German novelties. Timely news reached him that fourteen MSS. pieces by Beethoven—music to 'The Ruins of Athens' and 'King Stephen'—had just been found at Vienna. He at once procured for the Philharmonic an offer of the copyright of this music with the right of first performance in England for the modest sum of £15. He suggested the two earliest Overtures to 'Leonora' and a MS. Finale from the same; a Suite by Bach; Schubert's Symphony in C; a Symphony by Gade;

and 'other good new things' from which a 'choice' could be made. Last, but not least from the English point of view, he hoped to be ready with music of his own. All this, coupled with the expected advent of many eminent artists, foretold a memorable season. One of its most interesting episodes was heralded by the following letter from Mendelssohn to Bennett:—

BERLIN, 10*th March*, 1844.

MY DEAR FRIEND,

The bearer of these lines, although a boy of 13, is one of the best and dearest friends and of the most interesting acquaintances I have made since long. His name is Joseph *Joachim*, and he goes to London to visit his uncle, Mr Figdor, a merchant; he is born at Pesth in Hongaria. Of all the young talents that now go through the world I know none that is to be compared to this Violin-player. It is not only the excellence of his first-rate performance, but the positive *certainty* of his becoming a first-rate artist, if God grants him health and leaves him as he is, which makes me feel so much interest in him. In fact while I write to you I think the impression his performances made on me very much like the one I still have of your Concerto at the Hanover Square Rooms, when you wore the green jacket. He is not so far advanced in Composition yet, but his performance of Vieuxtemps', Beriot's, Spohr's Concertos, his playing at sight (even the 2nd Violins of difficult Violin-quartetts I heard play'd by him in the most masterly manner), his accompanying Sonatas &c. &c. is, to my opinion, as perfect and as wonderful as it may be. Besides he is an intelligent, well-educated, good-natured fellow. I think he will become a yeoman in time, as both of us are. So pray, be kind to him, tell him where he can hear good music, play to him and give him good advice, and for everything you may do for him be sure that I shall be indebted to you as much as I can be.

Auf Wiedersehen,

Very truly yours,

FELIX MENDELSSOHN BARTHOLDY.

Pray introduce him to Blagrove, if you think he will be kind to him!

On March 30, the Edinburgh electors found themselves unable to decide on the choice of a Professor. Bennett, having already postponed his wedding, to await their decision, did so no longer. Easter placed a few days at his disposal. He was teaching in London the day before Good Friday, and was married at All Saints Church, Southampton, on Easter Tuesday April 9, being within a few days of his twenty-eighth birthday, while his bride was just nineteen. They were driven with postilions, on the first stage of their journey, according to the usage of those days, and they then took train from Winchester, *en route* for the City of London, where Bennett had a concert engagement in Crosby Hall next day. He was in no position to put off any work, and at once returned to Mrs Johnson's house, where his first year of married life was spent. On May 2, Mendelssohn wrote:—'I shall leave Frankfort for London on Monday next and hope to arrive on board the Antwerp steamer on Thursday morning. Thank you for all the pleasure I anticipate from this visit; Bennett married, and plenty of music, and spring-time—Hurrah! Auf Wiedersehen!'

At the Philharmonic Concert on May 13, which was the first of five that Mendelssohn conducted, Bennett played his own C minor Concerto, and *The Musical Examiner* wrote:—'The superb Concerto of Sterndale Bennett, perhaps the masterpiece of its composer, was enthusiastically received. Bennett never played better, his tone sounded at the further end of the room as full and clear as if we had been seated at his side; in this particular—in what an eminent pianist who was present happily termed a dignified composure in executing passages of any extent of difficulty —and last not least in a noble, fervid, and unaffected style of expression this great English pianist has no superior and but few rivals: we were delighted to hear him achieve so great a success in the presence of his warm friend and admirer, Mendelssohn, who conducted the Concerto with evident interest and unflagging attention.'

Bennett had married on a small income, and he would afterwards refer to the economy which it was necessary to practise in Charlotte Street. His young wife refused to attend the interesting concerts now going on; for though

MRS W. STERNDALE BENNETT
From a water-colour drawing

admission to them was free to her, conveyance to and from the concert-room was not. However, they gave their first dinner-party, though perhaps only to one guest. Mendelssohn had apparently been asked to name his own day, and the following letters were written on Friday, May 17.

> My dear Bennett
>
> Shall I dine to-morrow with you and drink 10 pints of porter? Or rather not?
>
> Yours ergebenstly
>
> Felix Mendelssohn Bartholdy
>
> Friday
> 4 Hobart Place Eaton Sqre
>
> No answer from Edinburgh till now!

To which Bennett replied:—

42 Upper Charlotte St
Fitzroy Square
May 17. 1844

Mr Chairman & Gentlemen.

I propose that my friend Felix Mendelssohn Bartholdy come and dine with me tomorrow (Saturday the 18th) at half past five of the Clock All you of this opinion, hold up your hands —

{ — Mary Anne Bennett
  William Sterndall Bennett

Nota Bene
   Mr Watts will *not* trouble himself to send a Circular —

XI]   *The Decision at Edinburgh*   161

Mendelssohn and Bennett must have had some joke between them about the formalities of English committee-meetings. A letter of Mendelssohn's drawn up in form of a Resolution will be given later. The negotiations which Bennett, in the name of the Philharmonic Directors, conducted with Mendelssohn, were confirmed by the official circulars of Mr Watts, Secretary of the Society. Hence the allusion in Bennett's postscript.

The election at Edinburgh had come to a dead-lock, but a fresh candidate now came forward. This was H. H. Pearson (a friend of Bennett's)[1], a young graduate of Cambridge, son of the Dean of Salisbury, a student of medicine as well as of music, and destined under the name of Pierson to become a composer of mark both in England and Germany. He was acceptable to those who would vote for neither Donaldson nor Bennett, and in the eyes of Bennett's supporters, was, as a musician, preferable to Donaldson. Some one must obviously now give way, and Bennett was asked to do so. Mrs Bennett wrote to her husband's aunt on June 3:—'I am sure you will be anxious to hear who is the successful candidate for the Professorship at Edinburgh. My dear husband resigned his claims on Thursday last, through the advice of his excellent friend and warm supporter, Professor Jameson, who feared that his interest had been much divided by the new candidate, Mr Pearson, who has from Sterndale's resignation gained the vacant chair. My dear husband I am happy to say [? bears] the disappointment much better than I expected, and begged me to tell you he is perfectly contented to remain in London, where he is sure better things are waiting for him.'

On the same day that this was written, just eight weeks after her marriage, Mrs Bennett met with a terrible accident. 'Her husband'—so writes A. C. Johnson—'was out at a concert, and she had gone to a press in her bedroom with a candle, and in some way set fire to her clothes. She came screaming down the stairs, when fortunately my mother and brother who were in the dining-room rushed to her assistance, putting out the flames that were surrounding her. She was very much burnt and confined to

---

[1] He translated Uhland's 'Maien-Thau' (May-Dew) for Bennett when the latter set music to it.

bed for a month. It was of course a great shock to her husband on his return from the concert.' Her recovery, if recovery it could be called, was slow. Bennett was assured at the time that he need not 'fear any ultimate injury to her constitution;' but he, later in life, believed she had suffered such injury, for she never again enjoyed the same health as before. In relating the accident to his Aunt, he wrote: 'You may be assured that with all this, Edinburgh has cost me very little thought.' His pleasure in the musical season was checked. He cancelled what engagements he could, to sit, as he told his aunt, with his 'dear invalid,' but he was necessarily in attendance at certain concerts. At the Philharmonic, on June 10, his Overture, 'The Naiads,' was played, and he was presented for the first time to Prince Albert. He gave his annual morning concert on June 25. Mendelssohn contributed a novelty to the programme in the shape of an extended version of his Variations in B♭ (Op. 83) re-arranged as a Duet[1], which he played with Bennett from the manuscript. Mendelssohn had undertaken to conduct the whole concert. A contretemps which occurred was, for him, nothing but a chance seized to show further kindness. When the audience arrived there was no band. Costa had detained the players over-time at an Opera-rehearsal. Mendelssohn saved the situation by starting Bennett's concert with the vocal music, and himself accompanied on the pianoforte, from the full score, several pieces which should have been sung with the orchestra.

The Philharmonic was now enjoying its stroke of good fortune, and taking a new lease of life. *The Musical World* wrote:—'It was a lucky thing that Sterndale Bennett was chosen a director. He saw that only great efforts could rescue the Society from annihilation. He infused new spirit into its endeavours. He brought over Mendelssohn in 1842. He brought over Spohr in 1843. He has persuaded Mendelssohn to come again in 1844, and these wise proceedings have saved the Philharmonic.

---

[1] The Duet was published posthumously as Op. 83a. The following note appeared on the English edition. 'Originally composed for one performer, but subsequently re-composed for two, and performed by the Author and Mr W. S. Bennett at the concert of the latter in 1844.'

Motive of Mendelssohn's Visits

Bennett has been zealously seconded in his endeavours by Mr Anderson, a director whose indefatigable perseverance, excellent judgment and admirable business habits have been of inestimable service. To these gentlemen we are inclined to think the Society is mainly indebted for its happy restoration to health and vigour. Bennett has suggested—Anderson[1] has carried out his suggestions. The judicial and executive forces of the Society are concentrated in their two persons.'

The writer of the above would have been more exact, if he had used the word 'persuaded' in connection with the year 1842. The persuasion which Bennett, for some reason or another, was obliged to use in the first instance did not seem wanted in the second. Still, these two memorable visits of Mendelssohn to London can be set down chiefly, if not entirely, to Bennett's agency. Mendelssohn did not come the less readily from having a trusted friend on the Directorate who would do his best to have everything arranged in consonance with his wishes. When he received the second and more important invitation, offering him what was virtually a new office, viz. the conductorship of the Philharmonic for an entire season, he wished, as it has been said, to accept at once. But he did not do so without making some preliminary enquiries of Bennett. The letter in which he made them is lost; but Bennett's reply shows how particularly Mendelssohn desired an assurance that he would not, by accepting a professional appointment in London, be interfering with the interests of others, or be doing anything contrary to the wish of the English musical profession. Without such assurance he could not count on fulfilling the main purpose for which he came to London on these two occasions—the unselfish and generous purpose of lending a helping hand to English musicians. But on this subject a word or two more will be said later.

Bennett advertised his new Overture, 'Marie du Bois,' for his morning concert in 1844, but he withdrew it, and in the summer made a new edition. He doubted its suit-

[1] G. F. Anderson served the Philharmonic, as Honorary Treasurer, from 1840 to 1876. He was Master of the Queen's Private Band, and both he and his wife, an eminent pianist, had considerable influence in the musical profession. He came to rule the Philharmonic with an almost despotic sway, but with unremitting zeal and with no small measure of success.

ability for a concert-piece; told Mendelssohn that he could not bring himself to like it (i.e. as a Concert-Overture for the Gewandhaus); wrote of it to Kistner as being a theatre-work; and therefore, no doubt, thought he had found the right place for it, when he used it, as he afterwards did, for his Cantata 'The May Queen.' Towards the end of the Overture he has written on the score:—'August 6th, 1844— The Tower Guns firing for the birth of a Prince or Princess —Tuesday morning one o'clock (just at these bars).' Later in life he became known to the musical Prince, H.R.H. the Duke of Edinburgh, whose birth at Windsor is thus recorded on the pages of 'The May Queen.' To convey such intelligence to London, the electric telegraph was used that night for the first time.

There is nothing else to notice in the first year of Bennett's married life except that, as it passed on, the amount of his teaching began, by very small degrees, to increase. Then, with some assistance from his wife's parents, he furnished a house in Russell Place[1], Fitzroy Square, and moved to it in March, 1845. He was close upon twenty-nine years of age. Account-books continue to tell the tale of very narrow circumstances.

The Philharmonic Society, keeping to their new arrangement of having a single Conductor, appointed Sir Henry Bishop for the season of 1845. Something, it may be assumed, went wrong, and he retired after the third concert. Bennett's pupil, W. S. Rockstro, was starting for Leipzig, as a student, and in a letter introducing him to Mendelssohn, Bennett wrote on May 9:—' * * * I want sadly to hear from you, it is a long time since I saw your handwriting. *Moscheles* has been elected to conduct the five remaining concerts of the Philharmonic this season, Sir Henry Bishop having resigned. I am very glad that it has been so settled for the concerts have been very bad hitherto. * * * I send by Rockstro to Leipzig a Sestett for P.F. and stringed instruments. I wish you would find some opportunity to try it when it is printed and tell me how

---

[1] Russell Place, now called Fitzroy Street, is a continuation northwards of Charlotte Street. Bennett's house, then No. 15 but now No. 19, in which he lived for 14 years, is on the west side, and is the third house south of London Street. Daniel Maclise, the painter, lived next door in the second house from London Street.

FROM THE OVERTURE TO 'THE MAY QUEEN'

you like it. I wrote it long since in 1835, but have been renovating a bit. I have really some new things just finished. My concert takes place on the 24th June. I shall indeed wish you with me as on the last occasion. My wife is only pretty well. I fear she has never recovered her sad accident. * * * I have got a new house close to my late residence and should so like to see you in it. Let me hear from you soon, do pray! I think of you much and hope you do not forget me. I will write to you soon again, if I do not hear from you, and tell you plans I have for visiting Germany next year. Now for the present Good-bye.'

Mendelssohn wrote[1] from Frankfort on May 26:—
'* * * Many thanks for the letter which Mr Rockstro brought me. He is a nice young man, but is very homesick, and was very nearly becoming quite melancholy here. * * * I could not resist my curiosity and asked him to show me your Sestett, even before its publication in Germany. It has been a very great treat to me, and I thank you for the pleasure I have had from merely reading it through. As soon as it is published I hope to play it and then get to know it more thoroughly. At present, merely from reading it, the Andante is my favourite part. "Sehr Bennettisch." And how much I am looking forward to the new things you promised! And most of all to your plan of visiting Germany with your wife! Do carry that out and tell me more about it soon. It is most unfortunate that your dear wife is still suffering from the consequences of that terrible accident. So bring her to Germany, try the effect of change of air, of a different doctor, of the many friends you have here. I trust that this will do her more good than any Baths or other cure-systems. With us all is well again, thank God. * * *

'What I hear of the management of the Philharmonic concerts does not particularly please me. I am afraid that neither Moscheles nor any one else can permanently improve matters there. But enough for to-day. * * *'

A visit to Germany was nothing to Bennett now but a pleasant dream. To make a living and develope a teaching-connection demanded his continuous attention

---

[1] The letter is in German.

throughout the year. If he spared a few days for a holiday at Cambridge or Southampton, he would come up to town in the course of it to give a single lesson rather than disappoint or offend any one pupil. He was now coming into greater request as a pianist, and was playing at many important concerts. He ceased for two years to give Chamber concerts in his own name, probably could not afford to give them; but he was engaged to direct long series of the same at Greenwich, in a Lecture Hall which was under the management of Mr (afterwards Sir) John Bennett. He continued to murmur to Mendelssohn about the Philharmonic, writing on July 24:—'We had the annual meeting the other day and chose new Directors for next year. * * * I am not at all glad to have anything to do with them but at any rate I was not able to decline. I am sure next year there will be a great uproar about who is to conduct.' Then again he wrote in November:— 'The Philharmonic Directors have engaged *Costa* to conduct their concerts with which I am *not very well pleased*, but I could not persuade them to the contrary, and am tired of quarrelling with them. They are a worse set this year than we have ever had.'

Bennett had promised to send his Overture 'Marie du Bois' for performance at Leipzig, and in April, 1846, he wrote to Mendelssohn from Southampton:—

'* * * I should have written to you and sent you my overture according to promise, but I really could not make up my mind to like the overture and think it good enough for the Leipzig Public who have always been so kind to me and are certainly entitled to the best I can do whatever that is; and I do not despair of renewing my friendship with them if I have health and strength and more time to devote to composition than I have just now, but you know what England is, and how we must work to keep up our houses, and living even on the most economical scale. * * * And now about the Philharmonic, I dare say you have seen all the flaming accounts in the newspaper about Costa and our grand doings, but if you were here and able to judge for yourself, you would not say that he was the greatest Conductor in the world. I am quite alone in my opinion upon these matters in the Direction and am sick to death with the Public who pretend to be so clever. But I want you to come to England and let me get some good spirits by talking to you and then I want to try to come to Leipzig next year. * * * And now may I not talk to you about my *little boy*[1] now nearly four months old and a dear fellow. * * * I was going to write to you soon after he was born but I found out that you knew all about it and I was disappointed that I could not tell you first myself. * * * Now then good, dear friend—Good-bye. The sea is roaring at my windows. Write soon to me. * * *'

Mendelssohn to Bennett[2].

I played the above last night, saying to myself at the same time, I must write to him at once and tell him:— The principal thing in your welcome letter, and for which I thank you most, is and remains that you mean to come to Germany next winter and to come here. That is the very best thing that could happen to us, and I think that for yourself and your dear wife also, it will be good and pleasant—or must she stop at home with the baby? * * * And just *next* winter, not a bit later, your coming, and your playing, and your conducting would be exactly what is wanted. Therefore, come, come—that is the main object of this letter.

If anything can be done to make your stay, either here or in Germany generally, easier or pleasanter, and if it is in my power to contribute anything towards that end, I hope that I need not tell you how glad I should be to do it.

---

[1] His first child, Charles Sterndale Bennett. A second son born in 1847, and a daughter in 1848, completed his family.

[2] The original letter is in German. The music is the opening of the Barcarolle from Bennett's 4th Concerto, the MS. of which is headed 'Rowing Time.'

Think over this, for you know this country almost as well as your own, and we often say with pride that you are half at home with us. If all is well, I hope to see and talk to you in England in August, but it will only be for a short time, for my wife cannot come with me, she wants to stay with the children, and I do not like to leave her and them for long. * * * I hope also to have my new Oratorio ready to bring with me—how glad I should be if it pleased you.

But do come to Leipzig again next winter. That is the principal thing, as Cato of old would say.

You need not write to me any more about the Philharmonic. The few words in your letter were more than sufficient for me, and I had always thought that it must be so. Bad enough, and it makes me feel sorry for your countrymen.

'Hang the liberty' how is the little boy? Has he got a tooth? Is he like you, or like his mother, or like both? Does he cry enough? (I consider that a very important point according to my experiences.) Is he already obliged to do conjuring-tricks[1]? (I hope not!) What are his Christian names? Is he fair or dark? Blue or black-eyed? I ought to be able to tell my wife all these particulars.

But come here next winter, says Cato[2].

Your friends here are well: David, Schleinitz, the Preussers, Julius Kistner &c. When they hear W. St. Bennett mentioned their hearts seem to enlarge; they are one and all your loyal and attached friends. Fancy what it would be if I could say to them: He is coming here next winter!

Therefore do come! And give a thousand kind messages to your dear wife and the little boy, and keep your friendly feeling for

Your

FELIX MENDELSSOHN BARTHOLDY.

---

[1] Mendelssohn would have in his mind Bennett's own conjuring-tricks.
[2] Cato, by the persistent use of his famous dictum 'Delenda est Carthago' kept a prime duty before the Romans. Mendelssohn imitates this by reiterating the main idea of his letter, viz. that Bennett must come to Leipzig.

CHAPTER XII.

THE UNFORESEEN STROKE.

1846—1847.

æt. 30, 31.

BENNETT's position at the Philharmonic, as long as it had given opportunities of association with Mendelssohn, had brought him both pleasure and pride. It was now bringing him into a very different relationship. Much advantage was likely to accrue and in the end did accrue to the Society by the appointment of Costa as conductor. The Directors would have been glad to get him sooner if the Manager of the Italian Opera would have allowed him to come. At the Opera, where he was as yet best known, he had acquired a great name and had won the confidence of the largest and most influential section of the musical Public. With the complete equipments of a musician, he had also the attributes of a ruler of men; and, while firmly establishing his own place, gained absolute control over a set of players who soon learnt the lesson that their livelihood depended upon their loyalty and obedience to their chief. Difficulties which had previously arisen between conductors and the Philharmonic orchestra would surely vanish when he came on the scene. Nevertheless, Chorley and other critics raised an objection to his being chosen for this particular post. They thought that an Italian, a conductor and composer of Italian Operas, a composer who had gained his chief, as yet, success in the higher forms of Ballet music, might be—they probably knew that Costa avowedly was—out of sympathy with much, and with some of the finest of the music he would have to conduct at the Philharmonic. This was the ground on which Bennett opposed his election. Earlier personal intercourse between Costa and himself had been of a friendly kind; though there could be little artistic sympathy between the one who did not admire Beethoven, and the other who seldom entered the Italian Opera House. Costa would be sure to hear of the single vote given against him at the Philharmonic. As the concerts under his direction went on, Bennett did not join in the chorus of unqualified approval. He said so in the last-quoted letter to Mendelssohn. Any words of criticism which may have passed his lips would not lose force when they were passed on from the tongues of the mischief-makers, of whom there were plenty about, to the ears of the conductor. Then, again, Bennett himself was thought by some to be the man who ought to have been chosen. Musical papers had pressed his claims. Moscheles, when he heard of Sir Henry Bishop's appointment in 1845, wrote in his diary:—'How is it possible to prefer him to Bennett, who is so immeasurably his superior?' It may be imagined that Costa might regard Bennett, though his junior by eight years, as a possible rival. He might suspect, since re-election of a conductor took place annually, that some opposing party would attempt a change. One here conjectures the seeds of that hatred which Costa ultimately felt towards Bennett, the virulence of which is scarcely to be accounted for by the spark that, as will presently be seen, caused the explosion. Bennett, however, had never expected the office for himself. He mentioned no such hope in his letters to Mendelssohn, but named Lucas, who was, like Costa, eight years older than himself, as one likely to be appointed. From the English point of view, Bennett, however well-qualified in other respects, was too young to expect a public position of importance in the musical world. He must, with patience, wait his turn. As a well-timed encouragement, however, he now received a valuable testimony to his qualifications. In the first year of Costa's conductorship at the Philharmonic, when the Italian seemed to be carrying all before him, Moscheles was on the point of leaving England after a residence of twenty-three years. He invited Bennett to conduct his 'Farewell' concert.

The direction of important Benefit concerts, when an orchestra was employed, had always been regarded as one of the rights of the leading conductor of the period, so that Moscheles, by departing from custom on this occasion, was thought to be paying Bennett a significant compliment. Davison described the concert as a 'leave-taking' which brought with it 'many cheers and many tears;' and he wrote of Bennett's association with Moscheles on this day as 'something to be remembered with pride by every Englishman.'

On August 23, Bennett wrote to his aunt: 'Mendelssohn was with us yesterday, and I am going on Tuesday, if all be well, to Birmingham to hear his new oratorio.' It was no common occurrence for Bennett to attend a provincial Festival. He was only present at five or six of them in his life, and then (except in the case of a Festival that he conducted himself) only for the sake of attending one or two of the performances. When young he could not easily afford such excursions. Later he disliked, probably had never liked the excitement incident to large gatherings. He did not, however, miss the crowning event of the century in the annals of our musical Festivals. He was not off duty this August, but after teaching five hours on the Tuesday he went to Birmingham with his pupil, William Rea, and heard the 'Elijah' on Wednesday. He met the composer. Sir Charles Stanford has heard the tale of a happy supper-party at the 'Woolpack' hotel, where his father, Mr John Stanford, and Joseph Robinson, of Dublin, merrily entertained Mendelssohn and Bennett; Rea did not forget an early walk taken with his master and Mendelssohn on Thursday; and Bennett's then prompt return to work is recorded in his teaching-books.

Bennett's German friends were still hoping that he might fulfil his project of spending with his wife the coming winter at Leipzig. So when Mendelssohn returned to Germany he wrote once more. With charming delicacy he here resorts to a joke in order to veil the generosity of his intention. Desirous of removing any difficulty which ways and means might present to the Bennetts, he offers them the hospitality of his own house during the whole time of their visit.

LEIPZIG, 28 *Sept.* 1846.

MY DEAR BENNETT,

I have come home very happily and found my wife and children in perfect health, and everything looking as well as I might have wished, and now as I am comfortably settled again since the last few days I called a meeting, consisting of Cecile and myself, and we passed the following Resolution:

Resolved

That Mr and Mrs Bennett are most earnestly, sincerely, and heartily requested by Mr and Mrs F. Mendelssohn Bartholdy to accept of a very small room at the Königs Strasse No. 5[1] for their residence from December to April next (if possible) in order to afford the aforesaid Mendelssohn Bartholdys the opportunity of seeing as much as possible of the aforesaid Bennetts during the aforesaid residence; and that, as this small room has an entrance of its own, and no communication with the remainder of the lodging, the said Bennetts will be quite at liberty to go out when they like, and to come in again when they like, and to see whom they like, without giving trouble to, or experiencing trouble from, the other inhabitants; and that it would be considered by Mr and Mrs M. a very great pleasure to come if Mr and Mrs B. would say yes, and come and stay with them as long as they can stay in Germany.

The favour of an Answer is requested.

I see I have not been able to make out the true Style of an English Resolution, and the end is very much like the 'invitation à la danse.' But never mind; you understand what I mean by the stupid jest, and that I should be so *very happy* (in good and best earnest) if you and Mrs Bennett would accept of our invitation and spend some time with us, and that Cecile joins most sincerely in this invitation! Now try what you can do! I might have sent a round Robin if I had allowed Monicke, and the Schuncks, and the whole Concert-Direction, and the Voigts, and I do not know whom not to subscribe them-

[1] Mendelssohn's house is generally given as No. 3. Perhaps the offered room was in an adjacent house.

selves to a petition to you; but I wanted to have it all by myself, and I hope you will consider of it! As this letter is not only directed to you but also to *Mrs Bennett*, I wish you would talk the whole matter over with her, and settle it, and write, 'We come on such and such a day' the very same hour when this note arrives at your house. * * * And now my dear friend let me have a favorable answer, and with many good wishes to Mrs Bennett, and to young Bennett (meaning not *you* but the stout boy)

I am and shall be always yours,

FELIX MENDELSSOHN BARTHOLDY.

Madame Mendelssohn added her own words of invitation at the end of her husband's letter, so that Mrs Bennett may very likely have written to her some temporizing answer pending the decision. Otherwise, the date of the following reply from Bennett is later than might be expected.

Bennett to Mendelssohn.

Nov. 16, 1846,
LONDON, 15 RUSSELL PLACE,
FITZROY SQ^{RE}.

MY DEAR GOOD FRIEND,

How often have I postponed writing *this letter*, do not think me ungrateful for your kindness, this is not the case and never will be. I wish I could write to you in real happiness to say that I proudly accept your warm invitation for Christmas, but circumstances will otherwise and I must submit, although more reluctantly than I have ever done to any circumstances in my life before. I have been hoping for weeks past so to arrange matters of business and see my way clear for a happy holiday with you at Leipzig, and my wife has joined me in my happy anticipations, but we are obliged to forego all at present. I cannot tell you how much we feel this disappointment, and nothing but an assurance from you that you do not think us ungrateful to you and Madame Mendelssohn will in any way relieve us. If I were near you now I would not hesitate to let you know the many reasons which oblige us to remain at home for the present and so enjoy a holiday with more comfort at a future time, and will you believe me that no trifling reasons keep me from that happy roof in the Königs Strasse. My business at this time is much increasing and requires my constant attention, and as I am becoming a family man, I dare not longer rely upon chance and I fear that were I absent at the beginning of the new year, I might lose much; but all this appears to me, as I am now writing it, *so dreadfully worldly*, and so ungenial to all I ever feel upon these matters, that I will not write another word about it, save from my heart to thank you again and again for the proof of your valued friendship which you have given me—which if I live to be an old man I will even then think of as vividly as I do now—and so God bless you. And now, are you coming to us in April? and will David come? Alas, poor Alsager has suddenly left this world and will take no more interest in the Beethoven Quartett Society for which amongst other things I understand David was coming. * * * But why do I write such a miserable letter, for indeed I ought to be happy and thankful for all I enjoy. Remember me to all my kind friends in Leipzig

and ever believe me

Yours sincerely

WILLIAM STERNDALE BENNETT.

Bennett's 'business,' as he called it, which had been slightly but perceptibly increasing each half-year since his marriage, had in the autumn of this year taken a sudden leap. The departure of Moscheles from London might well account for this. The problem of bread-winning had demanded Bennett's patient attention for seven years. Its solution was at hand. His obvious duty, at this juncture, was to remain at his post and to secure the new connection of pupils placed within his reach. He could not close his regretful letter to Mendelssohn without some expression of thankfulness for material benefits. His prospects were bright and he could at least hope to see Germany again in the near future, and thereby gain stimulus to his artistic pursuits. But it was not to be. Mendelssohn's words, 'Just *next* winter, not a moment later' proved only too true.

In April, 1847, Mendelssohn again came to England

for performances of 'Elijah.' Returning from one of these at Birmingham, Davison was his travelling-companion to London. Their conversation in the railway-carriage was much about Bennett and his position as a composer in England. 'Ah,' said Mendelssohn, 'he ought to come out with some large work, and say, "Here I am, I am *Bennett*";' then after singing the second subject of the last movement of the 'Suite de Pieces,' he added, 'For he is *so* gifted.' This was the more impressed on Davison's memory, because Mendelssohn, being at the time careworn and depressed, was talking in so serious a tone. Schumann in his criticism of the same 'Suite de Pieces' had urged Bennett to similar effort, but the latter did not put the same value on his own powers, and having at length placed his unfinished Oratorio on the shelf, for the future took the view that works of colossal proportions should be left to the greatest masters of the art. Moreover, two events were approaching to cast shadows, for a time, both on his private and his artistic life. The one event brought grief, the other injury. He was to lose a friend, and find a foe.

'A quiet hour' on Sunday afternoon, May 2, which Mendelssohn appointed to spend at Bennett's house, was the last that they are known to have passed together. Six months later, the intelligence of Mendelssohn's death came, with the full severity of suddenness, to his English friends. Bennett's pathetic letters written at the time to Ferdinand David and Kistner contain passages which cannot be re-handled here. The beautiful reply in which David described Mendelssohn's last hours has already been published.

Among those who had lived in artistic and personal sympathy with Mendelssohn, there were some—Ferdinand David was certainly one, and Bennett another—who could not, in after life, bring themselves to talk freely about him. Time never dimmed their mental picture of a great personality. The same change, noted with curiosity by Bennett, which used to pass over his companions and himself when the living Mendelssohn came into their midst, was still to be observed when, after his death, he entered their minds. Nothing could more powerfully reflect Mendelssohn's *greatness*, as it had appeared to men who were themselves not without distinction, than their restraint of manner and speech at the mention of a name which was in use by others as a household word. Mendelssohn's nature repudiated that open obeisance which has not proved displeasing to some remarkable musicians. He was very strict about the observance of such forms of courtesy as are due from one man to another, but in his intercourse with his brother-artists he liked to be treated on terms of musical equality, and he allowed no reference to be made to intellectual superiority. Nevertheless, the deference which is compelled by, and is a proof of superlative greatness of mind and character was paid to Mendelssohn quite as surely as if it had been expressed by outward acts of homage. Bennett would say that Schumann was one who, in his quiet way, uniformly showed reverence to Mendelssohn. In this innermost circle there was no parade of adulation. The ranters and sentimentalists who after Mendelssohn's death swelled the crowd of his worshippers in England were not of the true Mendelssohnian pattern. They would have felt quelled in the presence of Mendelssohn's real friends.

Bennett outlived Mendelssohn twenty-seven years. So long a time did not pass without his writing something about him as a musician, or without his occasionally introducing an anecdote about him in conversation with favourite pupils or at his own fireside. He referred to him in lectures, though more briefly than to some other musicians. He had to curb feelings, some of them injured ones, when speaking in a public place. Mendelssohn's death had opened the door to virulent attacks upon his reputation by certain leaders of musical thought in Germany, and this had given great pain to those who were mourning the loss of 'a just man made perfect.' Bennett had by some means acquired the notion that the Germans had not treated Mendelssohn in any too generous a manner during his life-time. He was, however, not to be drawn into controversy; so that, though bold in asserting Mendelssohn's absolute merit, he did not go the length of illustrating that merit by naming contemporary musicians and making comparisons. Writing some ten years after Mendelssohn's death, he dismissed Germany with the single remark, 'I do not scruple to assert that Mendelssohn was more thoroughly appreciated by the English than by his own countrymen.' At the same time, he was not quite content with the view taken of Mendelssohn in England. He thought it was not sufficiently comprehensive. He admitted, in 1858, that in Oratorio, Mendelssohn had 'taken a place in the hearts of the English, second only to Handel;' but he wanted more acknowledgment of the manifold nature of Mendelssohn's work, urging that he had proved himself 'grand in all departments of the art,' and that he had contributed 'such glorious and finished masterpieces to the art in all directions.' In this variety of successful achievement he could see one feature of resemblance between Mendelssohn and those great musicians whom he placed highest, and could perhaps contrast him or hope that others might contrast him with contemporaries who were either specialists, or who had not shown themselves so successful as Mendelssohn in so many branches of composition. His conviction that Mendelssohn deserved to rank as one of the chief representatives of the classical school was unalterable. The last words which the present writer heard him speak on a musical subject were in reply to the question whether he remained firm in his belief that Mendelssohn was one of the great masters. He then solemnly attested his faith, saying slowly and with much seriousness, 'Certainly, one of the *greatest.*'

More than once, when lecturing, he referred in grateful terms to the services which Mendelssohn had specially rendered to the English. He wrote, in 1858, of the unique influence which Mendelssohn's music—he was alluding more especially to chamber and pianoforte music—was exerting in English homes:—' Even young ladies who steadily adhere to the superficial music of the present day find place in their repertoire for many of the works of this illustrious man. This fact amidst all my grumbling consoles me and leads me to hope that the mind and heart that can feel and love Mendelssohn will cease to enjoy the ephemeral and unintellectual music which is so abundant and for which I cannot disguise my utter contempt.' He did not hope in vain. High authorities have since traced in the successful appeal which Mendelssohn's chamber compositions both vocal and instrumental, made to the English, the origin of that wide appreciation which gradually came for the similar works of his great predecessors and contemporaries.

Bennett also spoke of 'the gain to English art by the never-too-often repeated visits of this great man,' and of the *love* which, to his own knowledge, Mendelssohn had entertained for England; a love that so distinguished him (as Bennett well knew, though this he did not publicly say) from many other foreign visitors who showed their aversion to everything pertaining to this country except its money. Prince Albert, who was well-placed to observe, and well-qualified to comment on existing musical conditions, called Mendelssohn, in 1847, 'a second Elijah * * * encompassed by idolaters of Baal.' No wonder that the few musicians in England on the classical side valued the actual presence in their midst of this great prophet of their own creed. There are full records of his Birmingham and Philharmonic triumphs; he has himself described his gracious reception by Queen Victoria and her Consort; but it must also be remembered that this much-fêted man, in what he called a 'time-eating country,' spent hours in humbler places giving a helping hand to musicians who were striving to do good, though little noticed, work. Dando, the violinist, treasured to a ripe old age the memory of this noble yet lowly minister of Music having played for him at his little Quartet-concerts in the city; and a study of Mendelssohn's doings during the nine weeks he spent here in 1844 reveals other like acts of encouraging support, many more of which, done privately, have passed into oblivion. Bennett could not speak at length on such matters, while thinking of his own connection with them. He drew his pen through the words, 'ever ready to cheer and encourage the young artist,' and wrote instead, 'Had I not known him so intimately, I might have trusted myself to talk more of his vast claims upon our affections.'

In course of time he saw with disapproval that the English idea of Mendelssohn was being corrupted by sentimentality and romance, and he wrote in 1858, 'One would greatly welcome a faithful biography of Mendelssohn.' Shortly after his own death in 1875, a lady gave the following reminiscence. 'He (Bennett) was not an enthusiastic man. In speaking not long ago to the writer of these pages[1] of his friend Mendelssohn and all that had been written of him, he said, "I knew and loved the man himself too well to like to see him so absurdly idealized.'" Some of Bennett's little stories about Mendelssohn seemed to be told with the express object of reducing him to a reality. Two of them, though he told them as against himself, he often repeated, because he admired the sharp decisive manner in which Mendelssohn answered questions which he deemed needless. On first going to Leipzig, being under the impression (which was probably, in general, a correct one) that Handel was less familiar to the Germans than to the English, he asked Mendelssohn whether he knew a great deal of his music, and Mendelssohn snapped at him with the reply, 'Every note.' So, too, when relating how his surprise at Mendelssohn's organ-playing had led him to enquire by what means it had been attained, Bennett would always give the answer, 'By working like a horse,' in the tone of a tart rebuke. Then he would talk of Mendelssohn's manly vigour, as *e.g.* of his strength as a swimmer, without mentioning the more feminine graces which rhapsodists had attributed to their ideal musician. He said, again, that he had often been struck with Mendelssohn's practical business qualities, which he could not understand his possessing. He would sometimes qualify his statements, in the one direction or the other, in order to give the real Mendelssohn. Of this Mr W. Crowther Alwyn, who, in Bennett's later days, studied composition under him at the Academy, records the following instances:—'On discussing one morning, during the Composition class, an impromptu characterization of Mendelssohn's pianoforte-playing, with which he was in profound disagreement, he said, speaking very earnestly and with deep feeling: "It was not playing that *could* be criticized. At times it seemed to send a thrill through every fibre of my body—but he did not always play alike, for, after all, he was human." Again, he said that Mendelssohn's personal appearance was often insignificant, not such as would attract passers-by in the street—but that, at other times, he had the appearance of an *angel*.'

[1] *Fraser's Magazine*, July 1875.

Although Bennett's musical tastes, and principles as an artist were determined quite early in life, and were causes rather than effects of his congenial association with Mendelssohn, yet it is certain that he was much strengthened, at the outset of a career which his conscience made a hard one, by the fellow-feeling and approbation of this elder brother. When he wanted counsel, Mendelssohn, who was not only older but who had been surrounded from his youth up with a greater variety of educational and social advantages, was able and ready to give it. Bennett acknowledged his debt, when he wrote in 1844: 'How much all my professional life has been influenced by your friendship;' but the friendship, as their letters have shown, was no mere professional alliance. They shared, as Mendelssohn wrote, 'not only musical pleasures and sorrows, but also the domestic ones on which life and happiness depend.' Bennett would sometimes quote adages and maxims which Mendelssohn had received from his father for the guidance of life, and which the son had recommended to the use of another; and when doing this he would reproduce the pious reverence of tone in which the son had uttered his father's sayings. This gave the impression to his hearers that his conversations with Mendelssohn must often have taken a very serious turn, and that music was not, perhaps, the greatest thing that bound them together. When Bennett, after hearing of Mendelssohn's death, wrote to David and Kistner, he expressed himself mindful of the many valued friendships, including their own, which still remained to him; but, without fear of being misunderstood or of hurting feelings which were sure to agree with his own, he could write of Mendelssohn, 'I have lost the dearest and kindest friend I ever had in my life.'

PART III

A HARSH REBUFF. QUIET SPHERES OF ARTISTIC USEFULNESS

CHAPTER XIII.

RUPTURE WITH COSTA AND THE PHILHARMONIC. OCCUPATIONS AS A TEACHER.

1848.
æt. 32.

MENDELSSOHN, after writing 'Elijah' for England, was accepted here, without further hesitation, as a great master of Oratorio. He had given music in this case not to a musical sect or confraternity of connoisseurs, but straight off to the heart of a whole nation whose musical sentiment, in its widest and most genuine form of expression, he thoroughly understood. Wherever Handel was known, he was now admitted, and if not before his death, then at least very soon after it, his name attained a celebrity in England more far-reaching than that of any other modern composer. So great and secure a fame, won by a culminating masterpiece, gradually drew more attention to his other achievements, and the ultimate appreciation of his work, on its many sides, balanced if it did not outweigh the vulgar prejudice permeating English society against music described, and oftener than not *jeeringly* described as 'classical.' But the war between real and inane music lasted for many long years. It was not during Mendelssohn's life-time that his instrumental chamber-music made any great way here. His pianoforte Solos were not much taught and they were very little played in public. Statistics of Bennett's career as a pianist help to prove that. From the time of his settling down in Portland Chambers in 1839 to the time of Mendelssohn's death in 1847, he played at eighty-three concerts in London and the suburbs. Twenty-five of these were orchestral, fifty-eight of them chamber concerts. Of the latter, sixteen were not of sufficient importance for musical papers to record them, or for the programmes to be preserved; they are only noted in his engagement-books. But the remaining forty-two gave him as much opportunity of introducing good music as was afforded to any other classical pianist, and he would be as much disposed as any one, when he himself chose the music for his own performance, to pay a fair share of attention to Mendelssohn. What was the result? In the nine years, but chiefly within the last four of them, he took part in Mendelssohn's concerted chamber-music ten times, and he played Solos, or groups of Solos of his composition on eleven occasions. This was all that the circumstances of the time permitted him to do for Mendelssohn in that particular direction, and it is not to be discovered that others did nearly so much. Shortly before Mendelssohn's death, Davison, when referring to a performance of his music by Bennett, wrote:—'In the absence of Mendelssohn himself, our young countryman is his fitting representative, and indeed the influence he has had in diffusing a knowledge of and creating a love for the works of the greatest of modern composers is only calculable by those who, like ourselves, have watched his career from earliest boyhood up to the present epoch.' Davison would here refer not only to influence as a public performer, but also to Bennett's private exertions in student-days, and later among pupils, to win adherents to classical music. Old companions, who got some of their earliest impressions of the works of great masters through the agency of his playing, might well retain a special remembrance of his introducing Mendelssohn's music to them as it arrived. Certainly they retained the wish to get from him such first impressions. Mr J. S. Bowley has written of interesting evenings spent in Berners Street with G. A. Macfarren who, in bachelor days, would get Bennett to his lodgings when any new works of Mendelssohn's reached England, so that the old 'set' might know them through his playing —his '*singularly* beautiful playing,' as Sir George Macfarren himself summed up his memory of Bennett's pianism when he wrote or spoke about it in after life.

In the last weeks of 1847, and in the early part of the New Year, concert-givers naturally devoted themselves to paying tribute to Mendelssohn's memory. From this time may probably best be dated the beginning of the more quickly spreading influence of his music. Bennett, as a public performer, did not identify himself with Mendelssohn's music—except perhaps, with a single volume of it—more than with that of other great masters. But with the wish to make his playing a part of his teaching, he made use of some of Mendelssohn's simpler strains to attract a song-loving public to a deeper love for the pianoforte and for legitimate pianoforte music, than that which had been awakened by the Fantasia with its substratum of Italian Opera Airs. He early saw in the 'Lieder ohne Worte' the most potent philtre to use. The first time he played a Solo at a London concert, in 1838, he introduced a selection of these pieces. It was a novel and a bold idea to venture on to a public platform with music apparently so simple; and Davison, who had perhaps been sceptical, wrote: 'The performance of these "Songs without words," as they are called, told better than we expected.' Bennett had no further chance of playing an unaccompanied Solo in London, till he started his own Chamber concerts. In 1844 he played the 3rd book of the 'Lieder' in Charlotte Street; in 1847 the 4th book in the Hanover Square Rooms; and in the same year he still further tested the effect of such music, by introducing the 5th book as a relief to the heaviness of a long orchestral concert. After Mendelssohn's death, he played a selection of the 'Lieder' at a 'memorial' concert given by himself, and was then immediately invited to do the same at five such 'memorial' concerts given by others. John Hullah asked him to do it in Exeter Hall. Some of Bennett's friends wondered at his being ready to attempt delicate solo-work in so large a building, and tried to dissuade him; but he was determined to take part in the concert, and the fears of others were really groundless, for indeed, by the distinctness of his playing, he could produce as telling an effect as any pianist of his time. Violinists who accompanied him in Concertos spoke afterwards of the pleasure it used to give them to combine with one whose meaning was always so clearly

defined, while critics wrote of the exceptional ease with which they listened to him from the back of a concert-room. Then, too, his tone and attack were quite *per se*, surprising those who heard him for the first time. Advanced students of composition who worked under him in later days found their attention 'arrested and compelled,' when he went to the pianoforte to give short illustrations in the course of his teaching. About this, one of them now writes:—
'An indelible impression was left upon my mind by the playing of a few bars of a Sonata of Mozart on a single occasion.' A clergyman who, as an undergraduate, had heard him play in Cambridge spoke in later life of never having heard 'a piano *sound* like it,' and the surprise of this anonymous critic was also felt by Mr R. S. Burton, the well-known organist and chorus-director of Leeds, who independently used the very same words, 'I had never heard a piano *sound* like it,' when he was recalling the moment at which he was seized by the sound of the opening of the 'Duetto' from Mendelssohn's 'Lieder.' Kellow Pye remembered 'the tone of his touch as marvellous.' H. C. Banister, a man of acute sense and fine musical intelligence, when describing to the present writer his first meeting with Bennett, said: 'I was standing near him in a window, and, while thinking of something he had said, did not notice that he had left my side. Suddenly I was startled and could not, I assure you, realize what had happened. He had gone to the pianoforte and touched the keys. I had not the least idea, on the first impression, what the instrument was. It might, for all I knew, have been an organ or anything else. The sound produced was quite new to my experience.'

To return now to Hullah's 'memorial' concert in Exeter Hall. On a bench, some distance behind that which Mrs Bennett and her friends were occupying on the occasion, sat a burly countryman whose enthusiasm for the vocal music was unrestrained, and whose comments were made in a stentorian voice *pro bono publico*. When Bennett's turn came, this loquacious gentleman let every one know that he had not come there to see 'a fellow twiddling his fingers on a piano.' Mrs Bennett's party were, of course, anxious as to what might happen next; but they were soon relieved. When

Bennett touched the instrument there was immediate silence. Then by degrees came little grunts of satisfaction from the bench behind, which continued to increase in intensity, till the end of the performance came, and the lusty lungs of a new convert to the pianoforte led the cheers which acclaimed Mendelssohn's music as interpreted by Bennett.

On May 15, 1848, Bennett played at the Philharmonic concerts for the thirteenth and, unluckily, for the last time. No harbinger of ill-fortune appeared that night to warn him that his career as a Concerto-player was virtually at an end. He was at the height of his powers and achieved a success as marked as on any previous occasion. He chose Mozart's D minor Concerto, contributing his own Cadences and adding the necessary embellishments with rare taste and discretion. 'His performance,' wrote Ayrton, 'was in true keeping with so noble and dignified a composition. His feeling taste, so opposed to the prevailing style of most of the pianists of the present day, reminds us of a great retired performer. That the mantle of J. B. Cramer has fallen upon our countryman is the general opinion. May he long continue to wear and deserve it.'

Ayrton had been predicting for some years that this mantle would fall on Bennett. By clothing him with it this evening, he probably paid the very highest compliment he could imagine, and paid it to a man with whom he had little personal acquaintance, and of whose musical efforts, unless they concerned the pianoforte, he had written with a pen always cold and sometimes cruel. From Cramer, Bennett may have inherited, with other things, his legato-playing. In a notice of one of his Chamber-concerts, written some years later than this, Davison said: 'Surely no such legato-playing has been heard since the days of Dussek and Cramer.' But there was another quality on which Davison always laid great stress in reviewing Bennett's performances. Among the numerous critiques upon them which he has left, there is scarcely one to be found, which does not contain one of the words 'energy,' 'fire,' 'animation,' or a combination of two or all of them. Ferdinand Hiller's recollection, that his playing was 'full of soul and fire,' has already been given, but may be repeated here to support Davison.

A month or two before Ayrton gave Bennett the mantle of Cramer, Davison had written, in reference to his playing Fugues by Bach and Mendelssohn :—'The *legato* which is so eminent a feature in his style was employed to advantage in the Bach, and the *fire* which makes him as unlike John Cramer (the model to whom critics will insist upon comparing him) as one pianist can be unlike another, was marvellously well bestowed upon the Mendelssohn.' Davison, however, when thus disagreeing with Ayrton, does not seem to do more than insist upon adding something to his view, and one cannot afford to put out of count an equality with so great a pianist as Cramer, when the suggestion of that equality comes from a critic who must have heard that master in his prime, which Davison can scarcely have done.

On May 14, the day before the Philharmonic performance, Mr Otto Goldschmidt called at Russell Place with a letter of introduction from Bennett's old schoolfellow, C. A. Seymour of Manchester. Bennett gave Mr Goldschmidt a ticket for the concert. A few years after Bennett's death, his friend and former pupil, Mr Arthur O'Leary, read a Review of his master's life before The Musical Association. Mr Goldschmidt contributed a reminiscence, which Mr O'Leary related as follows:—'An eminent musician, now resident in London, who happened to arrive here a day or two before he [Bennett] played Mozart's D minor Concerto at the Philharmonic, in 1848, was recently speaking to me of this performance. Passing through Paris he had just heard, with delight and enthusiasm, Chopin, at the last famous concert given by that composer on the eve of the February revolution. This notwithstanding, the finish of the English pianist, his exquisite tone and touch, combined with masterful conceptions of the composer's intentions, was for him a new revealment, the memory of which is still fresh in his mind.' Here Bennett's name occurs by the side of another great master of the pianoforte, not exactly by way of comparison, but at any rate as worthy to be used in the same sentence. Mr Otto Goldschmidt often confirmed this remembrance, in conversation with the present writer, and a few weeks before his death cordially sanctioned its being recorded here in Mr O'Leary's words. He also desired to add that he retained a particular recollection of the *warmth* of Bennett's playing, as well as of the grace and propriety of the embellishments which he introduced where necessary in the Concerto.

But Bennett was to play no more Concertos of Mozart. The twenty volumes of their scores, which a copyist in Germany had transcribed to his order, were to remain idle in his library. Now comes a story which must be told at full length, in fairness to others concerned as well as to himself. The occurrences which it relates had a serious and lasting effect throughout the rest of his life.

A fortnight after he had played the Mozart Concerto, with Costa of course conducting, his Overture to 'Parisina' was down for performance at the Philharmonic concert of Monday, May 29. He did not himself attend the rehearsal on the previous Saturday. Davison, who was present at that rehearsal, has thus recorded what happened :—'The overture was tried through twice by Mr Costa, who took great pains with it, * * * but busy-bodies * * * went to Mr Bennett the same evening [Saturday], and buzzed in his ear that his overture had been ill-rehearsed, which was untrue, and taken too slow, which was true.'

Now considering how easily Bennett was satisfied, at any rate in later life, when the performance of his own works was in question, it does not seem quite characteristic of him, that the report of the 'busy-bodies' should have troubled him as it did. One day at the Academy, years afterwards, a friend told him that a Professor was giving his pupils a reading of the 'Rondo Piacevole' quite at variance with precedent. Bennett only laughed and said, as he ran out of the house, 'Oh, let them play it as they like.' It was perhaps a pity that he did not apply the same philosophy to the pace of 'Parisina.' But for the fate of this Overture he may have felt a special anxiety. From the number of editions and autograph scores that he made of it in the few years succeeding its appearance, it may be inferred that he set some value on it himself, and had spared no pains to perfect it to the best of his ability. 'It has not,' wrote one critic, 'the sparkling beauties of its more graceful sister, "The Naiads," or the inimitable variety of its other sister, "The Wood-nymphs," but it is a composition of graver style and deeper thought.'

Nine years had passed since the Overture had been played at the Philharmonic, and it was therefore on a fresh trial as a comparatively unknown work. If, by its graver character, it was less likely than his other compositions to gain quick appreciation, a careful and sympathetic rendering was a necessity to its success, so Bennett's uneasiness was natural; but the rehearsal was over, and it was late to devise any means of influencing the performance of the music.

So Sunday passed. On the Monday afternoon he was busy with a long spell of lessons at the Academy. He may have been intending to go to the concert, but, if so, certainly not in time for its commencement. As evening drew on, his anxiety increasing, it occurred to him that he might ask Charles Lucas, who lived close by, and who, as a member of the Philharmonic orchestra, was sure to be at the Hanover Square Rooms in good time, to make a suggestion to Costa about the 'tempo' of the Overture. Lucas was a Director of the Society, and it was certainly not without precedent that the interpretation of the music should form an occasional subject of friendly conversation between the Directors and their Conductor. Lucas, especially, on account of his wide knowledge of orchestral music, and because he was one of Costa's most valued colleagues at the Opera, was an authority from whom Costa took advice as to the interpretation of any instrumental works with which he was unfamiliar. Bennett accordingly wrote to Lucas a note, somewhat hastily worded, but clearly written in pencil on a double sheet of note-paper, and neatly folded in three-cornered shape. He did not despatch it in hot haste. When his work at the Academy was over, he took the note home. Mrs Bennett then took it to Lucas's house and placed it in his hands as he was putting up his violoncello in its case, and was on the point of starting for the concert.

This note, which caused endless mischief, was afterwards kept, though presumably mislaid, by Anderson. After his death in 1876 it was found. Meanwhile spurious versions, injurious to Bennett, had appeared in public journals. It therefore seems expedient to reproduce the original.

Monday afternoon

My dear Lucas

You would very much oblige me if you would ask Costa to take my Overture a little faster. I have not been able to explain my idea of the time to him, but you have often done it, and I am sure he would not take it amiss —

The middle parts especially, with the Syncopations, want keeping up to time —

Be so good to do

this for me – it is of some
consequence to me –
Excuse Pencil
Yours truly
W. S. Bennett

R. A. Music
Monday.

all fast

C Lucas
54 Bemers St
Oxford St

Lucas, acting for Bennett in the simplest way that suggested itself, showed this note[1] to Costa. *The Musical World*, when reviewing, a few years later, the occurrences of the evening, attacked Lucas severely for taking this course. 'The letter,' the writer of the article insisted, 'was not meant to be shown to Mr Costa, and never should have been shown.' The contents, however, read by themselves, without knowledge of collateral circumstances, seem so innocuous, while time for consideration must have been so short, that there is something to be said for Lucas. His action, however, proved unfortunate. A verbal hint, based on his own previous knowledge of the music, might have been accepted; or even a suggestion made in the form of a *message* from Bennett—whose absence from, or delayed arrival at, the concert would have accounted for the intervention of a third party—might have been listened to; but when a letter was handed to Costa, at a busy time, on rather a delicate subject concerning his own professional work, and he found it addressed, for no motive that he could be expected to grasp at a moment's notice, to a person other than himself, some feeling of annoyance seems not altogether unnatural.

Now, when Bennett wrote, and Lucas showed the letter, they were unaware that Costa was already in a state of irritation about the Overture. The conductor when accepting office had stipulated with the Directors (of whom Bennett was one) that all music should be sent to him for study at some stated time before it was to be performed. The story goes that the score of Bennett's Overture did not reach Costa's house till the evening before the rehearsal. If sent by Bennett, a note would no doubt accompany it explaining or apologising for the delay. These orchestral works were as yet in manuscript; when lent for performance they were not always returned; and when wanted again it was not always easy to find them. The Philharmonic librarian may have been the person at fault. Still the fact remains that Costa's condition was not fulfilled in this case. It was said that he saw the score for the first time, when it was handed to him with his other music

---

[1] The original note is now in the possession of Charles Lucas's representatives who kindly lent it for reproduction here.

through the window of his carriage as he was starting from his house to the rehearsal.

Thus predisposed to imagine disrespect, Costa was in no mood to place any but the worst construction on the incident of the letter. Tales have been told of the effect produced upon him at the sight of it, how he burst out into a frenzy of rage, how he raved and stamped, and ground the poor little missive to dust beneath his feet. This, however, was not *all* true. The note, at all events, is still intact. But there is no doubt that he was terribly angry. He was greatly incensed with the words 'all fast,' written above the music, which he mistook for some insulting expression. He used strong language with regard to Bennett; seized upon the ambiguous phrase, 'but you have often done it' (by which Bennett meant that Lucas had often made suggestions to Costa), and settled the matter by saying to Lucas, 'If you have often done it, you shall do it now.' He refused to conduct the Overture, and Lucas was obliged to take his place.

On May 30, the day after the concert, Bennett wrote to Lucas :—'I scarcely know how to act. If I move at all it will certainly be to *complain*, and *that* I am unwilling to do if it can be prevented. My conscience tells me that I have nothing to answer for, but I cannot quietly submit to any such inconsiderate conduct as I at present think Mr Costa has evinced not only to me but the Society at large. If it can be shown me that I am in any way at fault, it will be my only satisfaction to offer the most ample apology, and on the other hand it appears to me that some explanation should be offered on the part of Mr Costa. I will not be too precipitate in the course I take, and I should be glad, if possible, that Mr Costa and myself should meet through the intercession of yourself or some other mutual friend. Otherwise it would perhaps be better for my colleagues to meet upon the subject, without either the presence of Mr Costa or myself, and fully consider the matter. The simple circumstances which gave rise to the unpleasant affair are as well known to you as to myself, and you will much oblige me by considering all the details and giving me your advice.'

On receipt of this letter, Lucas wrote to Anderson,

who agreed that the best course would be for Costa and Bennett to meet, when misconceptions could be cleared away vivâ-voce.

Bennett again wrote:—

15 RUSSELL PLACE, *June 2nd*, 1848.

MY DEAR LUCAS,

Many thanks for your trouble in this affair. I am still willing to receive and give an explanation, but cannot at present move further than I have done, and it is now for Mr Costa to express himself as anxious as I am for a meeting. Any *slight* which he may think I have put upon him is at the most imaginary; *that* which he has put upon me has been *real*. There has been time since Monday for him to have moved as well as myself, and still the matter may be, as I wish it to be, amicably arranged, in which case I would meet Mr Costa *by his wish* at the Hanover Rooms at one o'clock on Sunday with you and Mr Anderson. Otherwise, and with the fullest thought upon the matter, I must officially appeal to the Directors, and take my stand. * * *

Yours very truly obliged,
WILLIAM STERNDALE BENNETT.

C. *Lucas, Esq.*

There is no account of the further efforts made by Lucas and Anderson to mediate, but at any rate they had no success. From a few letters which Bennett had occasion to write subsequently to the Society, it is gathered that he had expected the Directors, after his proposal for a meeting with Costa met with no response, to give him some formal explanation of, or opinion upon, his treatment by the Conductor, but that such explanation, when he asked for it, was not forthcoming. There was now only one course left for him to take. He withdrew from the Society, ceasing to be a Director, and thenceforth, for eight years, refusing the annual invitation, which the Society continued to send him, to play at the concerts.

Since his twentieth year, the Philharmonic had been the centre of his public musical life in London. A rupture in his relations with it meant not only a withdrawal as a pianist and composer from the arena where high distinction could, in his case, most readily be gained, but also a severance of ties of the strongest kind, and the loss of such musical associations as he most highly prized. There is no doubt that he was deeply hurt, very little doubt that he did not emerge from the trial, if it was sent him as a trial, without showing something of a rebellious spirit. In reviewing his career as a composer, the blow seems to have fallen at a critical time. With his worldly position fairly secure, he had again been turning his thoughts to composition, which he could not, or did not, pay much attention to for the two or three years during which his teaching-connection had been so largely increasing. Early in 1848 he made a fresh start, wrote Sacred Duets, re-constructed and re-scored his 6th Pianoforte Concerto for his annual concert, and about the same time asked H. F. Chorley to write him the libretto, not of an Opera or Oratorio, but of a secular Cantata of moderate proportions for the concert-room.

But now, a smart stroke having laid him low, the critics hit him when he was down. In a fit of despondency, he tore the score of 'Parisina' into fragments, thus destroying his final edition of the work. Now, too, it may have been that he registered a vow that he would compose no more; for later in life he hinted that he had come to such determination, adding the words:—'I gave them nothing for ten years.' Nearly ten years did pass after Chorley wrote the libretto of 'The May Queen,' before Bennett produced the music. It is not, however, literally true that he wrote nothing for so many years; though, as a composer, he did retire into a quasi-private life. With the exception of a Violoncello Sonata for Piatti, he wrote nothing specially for public performance; but he quietly issued a series of pianoforte and vocal pieces, which, though they did not appear so often as to attract attention at the time to what he was doing, in the aggregate ultimately formed a material addition to the catalogue of his works. When speaking, many years afterwards, of some of the pieces which he had written at this time, he said he thought they were about the best things he had done, and that he was satisfied with them, because they did not seem to want any of their notes altered.

At the end of the London season of 1848, he went with his wife, not as usual to stay with her parents at Southampton, but, for the sake of greater retirement, to the sea-side village of Littlehampton. There he completely broke down. The death of Mendelssohn, to him the cause of deep and silent sorrow, was still an open wound. At the time of the Philharmonic trouble, he had just lost the best friend in whom he could have confided, whose advice, sympathy and encouragement would have been so affectionately tendered, and would have been so helpful. Mrs Bennett was seriously alarmed at the apparently utter collapse of his strength and spirits. He was just of the age at which his father had almost suddenly succumbed to illness, and though he soon returned to his work, he was so slow in becoming his usual self, that his wife's anxiety was of long duration. But if not robust, he at least possessed a sound constitution. Doubt might be felt whether the amount of his strength would prove commensurate with the amount of his work, yet from this time forth for about twenty-five years, illness only prevented his fulfilling his engagements for a few single days occurring at long intervals. When speaking of an arrangement he had made of his Songs as pianoforte Solos he said, 'I did them one day when I stopped at home for my annual cold;' but by the time he made this remark, even the annual cold was only a treat of by-gone days.

Since the completion of his thirtieth year his employments had assumed, both in nature and extent, the form from which in future they little varied. One year serves as the pattern of many that followed. In the first six months of 1848 he taught the piano for 950 hours; gave four concerts of his own; played or conducted at eleven others. He took part in the organization of the new Queen's College in Harley Street. There he delivered an Introductory Lecture on 'Harmony' in the spring, before taking classes twice a week in that subject. Continuing to teach in July, in August also, except for the fortnight's illness at Littlehampton, he had, by the end of December, brought up the total hours of teaching to 1632, without counting his classes at Queen's College. These figures, however, do not at all represent the time entailed. Towns such as Maidstone, Ipswich, Brighton, in all of which he taught in turn, were not in those days easily accessible; while the villages in the neighbourhood of London could not yet be called suburban; but Bennett still had to take his work wherever he could find it.

On the Brighton day, a policeman, on his beat, rang the door-bell at 4 a.m., and continued his peal till Bennett from his bed-room window answered the signal. Then there was a long drive to London Bridge to catch the 6 o'clock train. Eight or nine hours' lessons were given at one school in Brighton, and home was reached about 11 p.m. This was done for very many years, and he never forgot to bring back from a Brighton confectioner the cakes and sweetmeats for the weekly supply of his family. On ordinary days he left home at 8.30 and returned at 9 or 10 in the evening. In the London season days had to be lengthened. Charles Steggall, who was his pupil for the pianoforte, harmony, counterpoint, and composition for four years (1847—1851), took many lessons from him in Tenterden Street during summer months at 7 a.m. Steggall, on seeing whither his master next repaired, used to wonder how any inhabitant of Portland Place could be ready to take a lesson as early as 8. Bennett would often afterwards tell, in praise of the young lady who did so, that before receiving him, she had already attended to the breakfast of her brother, a future Lord Chancellor, who went very early to his Chambers.

Though hours were long and his life laborious, hard work, as long as it was free from worry, by habit became congenial. 'I have not,' he wrote to Charles Salaman towards the end of the year 1848, 'ten minutes in the week for my own amusement.' Nevertheless, he was patient and content. He seldom left home without saying or doing something of a playful kind, which started the day cheerfully for those around him, and he would run out of the house in the highest of spirits, whenever it was only teaching that he had to think of. Again, Mr William Dorrell often told the writer how much he had been struck by finding Bennett, after returning from a long day's work, always in such a good temper, and so merrily talking to his wife or to any old friend who took the last hour at night as the only chance of seeing him.

That such a life was possible, was largely due to the fact that Mrs Bennett, who had been trained in her girlhood, with a somewhat Spartan severity, to habits of industry, had worked conjointly with him since their marriage, by degrees relieving him almost entirely of correspondence and business matters. He took great pride in showing to his brother-professors the time-table in her handwriting of his day's work; then he would say, 'I have nothing to do with it, I only have to give the lessons.' Then, again, though for some time it seems to have been necessary to work almost continuously throughout the year, it was not always at high pressure. Lastly, the Sunday of those times was a day of absolute rest; a day of such stillness that you could, through many hours of it, have heard a pin drop in the bye-streets of London. The pianoforte in Bennett's house was not touched on Sundays; the only music he heard that day were the Chants and Hymns and Jackson's inevitable 'Te Deum' in the Charlotte Street Church.

He had written to his mother-in-law in May, 1847:—
'I am very busy. I wake early in the morning, and have to begin the day immediately, and only wish for the evening to come as soon as possible—and then we are all fatigued and want to go to rest again. Polly is my faithful Secretary, she has much to do for me and directs me what to do in the day, for I trust to her written plan, which I carry in my pocket. * * * My little Charlie is a good dear little boy, and begins to love *me* very much, and I want him to love me more than he loves his mother, but you know there are many things in the way of this, his mother gives him oranges and cakes, and I never have these things in my pocket.

'My concert is coming on! Heaven help me! Everybody seems afraid of any speculation this Season—nevertheless, I do not fear. Thank you for the spears, arrived quite safely, and you will be pleased to see the way in which we have *slung* them up in the hall. I am delighted with my collection. * * * And now I come to the fourth page, and my report to Professor Moseley is still unwritten, and to-morrow will be Monday, and till next Sunday I shall be the property of the world at large, so "Good-Night."'

One morning he unexpectedly found a hired brougham at his door, which his wife had taken the responsibility of ordering, and on the future use of which she insisted. He demurred, saying that it could not possibly be afforded; but he had to give way, and in the little carriage which he, soon after, bought for himself he spent a great part of his life. In the long drives to his work, it served for his reading-room, full of newspapers and sometimes books. In it he studied counterpoint; tried to learn Latin; prepared lectures; and mentally practised the pianoforte—that being the only method, as he afterwards said, which circumstances allowed him for perfecting some of the most difficult music to be played at his Chamber-concerts. In this carriage he composed or sifted his musical ideas probably as much, if not more, than in any other place. It served him, too, for a dressing-room and even for a dining-room. Foot-warmers, hot plates, and a bull's-eye lantern were constant accompaniments. The lantern was often wanted on his return journey from Miss Lowe's school at Southgate, which journey, in the foggy season, he took on foot by the side of his horse. At least half his week was spent in rural places, and this added to the brightness and healthfulness of his life. In the spring and summer he came home with his carriage full of flowers, and the country-schools vied with each other to be the first to present him with his favourite lilac-blooms.

And the pianoforte-teaching itself, to which in those days so many applied no other word than 'drudgery,' was by him considered a high calling. How mean the occupation was in the eyes of the world must at times have forced itself to his notice; but Bennett's work lay much at the Academy, at colleges and schools, and among professional pupils. He was never a fashionable music-master. His other private pupils were, as a rule, real music-lovers, who engaged him because they wished to work seriously at the best music; who knew something of his value as a musician, so that they looked up to him and treated him with courtesy and respect. He spent his days not only in the society of the countless number of pupils whom he influenced, but also in continuous association, through the medium of the music he taught, with the great masters of his art. He taught school-girls who were almost beginners; but, as far as could be seen, he took the same interest in them as he did in advanced students whom he was preparing for the concert-room. When he was selecting teaching-music from its special bookcase before starting on his rounds, he would often speak of the beauty of some small and simple work of one of the great masters as he put it in his portfolio for one of these younger pupils. In a school where he taught for many years, and for many consecutive hours at a sitting, it was found 'impossible to gather from his manner which was the most or the least clever pupil, so thoroughly did he interest himself in each individual[1].' One who worked with him for some time has written:—'From the zest with which he went into every special beauty of the composition which was being studied, it would have been difficult to realize that he was not just entering a new and enchanting region instead of (as was the case) walking over well-trodden old familiar ground[1].'

His patience, a quality which even the youngest scholar can appraise, was proverbial amongst his pupils. One, and she not the least distinguished of them, looking back on her own career of twenty-five years as a teacher, said: 'In hours of irritation, I used to think of Bennett, and so possessed my soul in patience.' He was found strict, at times even severe. Personally he was thought by many to be rather difficult to approach. There is little recorded of any definite systems of instruction. Music, rather than the playing of it, seems to dwell in the memory of his pupils. 'He taught me to like Beethoven' has been said or written by many. Not a few have gone much further and sinking music altogether have preferred to speak of the strong influence for good that their music-master had upon their lives.

In 1848, the Rev. F. D. Maurice drew up the syllabus of studies for the new Queen's College, Harley Street, introducing subjects which had so far found no place in a woman's education. Bennett had no need to urge the claims

---

[1] Vide *My Musical Experiences*, by Bettina Walker.

of music in general. Professor Maurice had a strong conviction that, however desirable the new departure might be, it ought not to be taken at the expense of Art and Music. Bennett, however, was anxious, as he always had been, that instrumental music should have some recognition in this country analogous to what was given to vocal music. In view of writing to Professor Maurice and pressing this point, he set down in a pocket-book some memoranda, which admit of being arranged as follows. It may be explained that such jotting in a pocket-book or on the backs of letters was one of the occupations of his carriage-life.

'The Pianoforte master has his share in educating the mind of his pupil. The disposition of a pupil cannot be concealed even in a Pianoforte lesson. If you describe pianoforte-playing as an *extra* study in your prospectus, you will give the impression that it does not take its place in the general course because it is a *light* study, which it is not. It is not right that it should suffer in esteem with other subjects of education, simply because it is necessary to teach it individually and not in classes. The Pianoforte does not yield to the voice in its power of expression, and it is fully as capable of exciting great and noble feelings when legitimately used. The instrument has been chosen by the greatest masters as the sole exponent of many of their greatest works. If I had the time to undertake the duties, I should consider the post of Professor of the Pianoforte in your College, of equal honour to that I hold for Harmony and Composition.'

At the outset of Bennett's career, it was assumed by his advisers and by himself that there was no other way open to him for making his bread than as a teacher. In the end he was said to have sacrificed himself too much. Some blamed him for this, but not all. The Rev. H. R. Haweis wrote 'In Memoriam' of him, in 1875:—'In these days our young men complain of drudgery. They are poets and have to keep accounts; they are men of genius and sensibility and pass their time in turning over other people's money. Remember then that Sterndale Bennett passed the greater part of forty years in incessant drudgery. He the master—the worthy friend and brother-in-art of

Mendelssohn and Schumann, with a reputation as wide as the civilized world, and a commanding genius the lustre of whose work does not grow pale beside those of the greatest gods of music—this man spent habitually about eight or more hours every day of his life in teaching children and all kinds of pupils the rudiments of music. Some regret this, and from an artistic point of view it is to be regretted, but from a moral point of view it is not. His example rebukes the idle, the discontented, the conceited grumblers to be found in all grades of society. He taught once more the lesson left us by the Divine Man, who was called the Carpenter's Son—the importance of lowly duties—the power of unpalatable toil—the Grace of Common Work.'

CHAPTER XIV.

THE BACH SOCIETY. CHAMBER CONCERTS.

1849—1855.

æt. 33—39.

Though Bennett's works were heard no longer at the Philharmonic, they now gained a footing elsewhere. New orchestral societies were being established and his Overtures came into great request. 'The Naiads' was played at the Gloucester Festival in 1847; was repeated at Worcester and Hereford in the next two years; and in 1848 was placed on a programme at Windsor Castle, a compliment rarely paid to British music. In 1849 he was summoned to Court, where he had not been seen since boyhood, and he played, by Prince Albert's wish, two movements from his F minor Concerto, and his 'Three Musical Sketches.' In the course of the next few years other pianists began to play his pianoforte music. Special mention may be made of Alexandre Billet, who gave a prominent place to Bennett on his programmes and brought to light some of the earlier works which the composer himself had never played in public. So now Bennett, whether by express intention or not, left his interests as a composer in the keeping of others, while he lent his services almost exclusively to the music of the Great Masters. He abandoned the old-fashioned plan of giving an annual orchestral concert. He gave the last in 1849. Securing greater patronage than usual, he handed the profit of £80 to 'The Governesses' Benevolent Institution,' that being an institution in whose work both he and his wife were deeply interested. The tales of distress heard within its walls prompted the desire to equip young women more completely for a calling which often came to them as a necessity and found them ill-prepared. This movement for the higher education of women was started by the foundation, in which Bennett took part, of the Queen's College, Harley Street.

On Thursday evening, October 18, 1849, as Bennett was leaving the Academy he asked his pupil, Charles Steggall, to join him in his walk home. As they walked, he unfolded a project which he said had been in his mind for some time. He pointed out that while the Organ and Clavier works of Sebastian Bach were well known to many English musicians, few knew, few seemed even aware that there existed the great works for chorus and orchestra left by that master. He went on to speak of the 'Grosse Passions-Musik' and other works possessing the character and proportions of Oratorios, and expressed his conviction that such works would surely find acceptance in England if once they could be made known. It was his ambition, he said, to initiate some movement which would arouse interest in this unknown music. As a first step, he asked his pupil to undertake the duties of an honorary secretary. A few days later, he saw Steggall again and asked him to invite certain musicians, whom he named, to a meeting at which his project might be discussed. On October 29, E. J. Hopkins, Robert Barnett, Oliver May and F. R. Cox met Bennett and Steggall in Russell Place, when the following resolutions were passed:—

'That a Society be formed to be called "The Bach Society" having for its primary objects:

'(1) The collection of the works of John Sebastian Bach, including as far as practicable all the various extant editions, also copies of all authentic MSS., and all biographical works relating to him and his family, with a view of forming a library of reference for the use of members.

'(2) The furtherance and promotion of an acquaintance with his works amongst musical students and the general public by such legitimate means as may from time to time present themselves.'

The subject of musical performance was thus kept in reserve, but some more definite promise was afterwards deemed necessary to attract members. When the prospectus appeared in print, mention was made of 'performances, the frequency and extent of which must be governed by the means at the Society's disposal.' The promise of these performances proved very difficult to keep. In forming his Committee, Bennett looked to his Academy colleagues; also to organists, who were so far the chief exponents of Bach in England. Besides those present at the preliminary meeting, W. H. Holmes, W. Dorrell, John Goss, George Cooper, H. J. Lincoln, Henry Smart, C. E. Horsley, John Hullah, and the violinist Dando joined in the movement. Sir George Smart and Cipriani Potter, as representatives of seniority, were asked to set their stamp of approval by accepting office as Honorary Auditors. By the close of the year, regulations had been drawn up, and a room attached to the Hanover Square Rooms had been taken in which to hold meetings and store a library. Then the prospectus was issued and applications for membership were invited. There was no rush of applicants. The name of Bach, at the time under notice, was not one to conjure with. Indeed it was very little known, as was soon shown by the varieties of pronunciation which English tongues gave it. Bake, Back, Batch, Bash, Baitch, and Bortch were only a few of the first attempts. Mr Punch did not get it quite right, when he honoured the Society, soon after its institution, with a specimen of his amiable raillery.

'A BACK-HANDER.

'In this country there is a strong tendency in things to start up the more you put them down, and in fact if a thing is really good there is no quizzing it out of its vitality. We have occasionally indulged in a good-humoured joke at the expense of our rusty fusty friend BACH, the great composer of innumerable *Ops*, and whose sundry Schezzi in A, B, or C, are anything but ABC work to those who conscientiously try to "render them." Such however is the tenacity with which the *virtuosi* keep in what may be called the BACH ground of the musical world, that a "BACH Society" has sprung, or rather toddled, into existence. This Society we believe invites an audience, and has such a thorough-going way of BACH-ing its friends, that there is nothing to be heard but BACH during the whole evening. We shall expect to find the BACH enthusiasm ultimately reaching such a height that the BACHITES will be satisfied with nothing less than a BACH attic in which to hold their meetings.'

The first candidate for election to the Society was a young lady, then in her eighteenth year, who had been an amateur pupil of Bennett's for the pianoforte and the theory of music for the past two years. Her name was destined to become prominently associated with the Bach movement in England. She wrote to Mr Steggall:—

8 ST JOHN'S WOOD ROAD,
Dec 22, 1849.

DEAR SIR,

Mrs Bennett has just informed me that ladies are admitted as life-members of the Bach Society. I beg to enclose my subscription, and shall be glad to feel myself among the *early* subscribers if you will do me the favour to insert my name.

I remain,

Yours very truly,

HELEN FRANCES HARRINGTON JOHNSTON.

Miss Johnston headed a list of six members elected on January 24, 1850. The next lady to follow her example was Miss Dolby, who proved a pillar of strength to the Society in its earlier efforts. She lent a great mind as well as a rich voice. When the Society reached the stage of public performance, Miss Dolby was the English singer who could from the very first render Bach's difficult Solos so that they touched the hearts of the uninitiated. The Society hoped to announce itself in some special way on March 21, the anniversary of Bach's birth. A suggested banquet was opposed as an extravagance, and as having no touch with the memory of a man who had not himself known much of the pleasures of the table. A festival performance of music was then decided upon, and a sub-committee undertook to arrange it. But the pioneers did not as yet realize the difficulties in front of them. To obtain performers, or to find music to perform, for any concert on a large scale proved hopeless. So, as Mr Punch said, the Bachites had to be content to 'toddle into existence.' But they kept the birthday. Chappell lent them a room in Bond Street, where, on the evening of March 21, they had their first 'trial' of music. Henry Smart conducted 'The Motet.' Dr Steggall told the writer that this Motet had been edited by Angel of Exeter under the title, 'Honour, Glory and Blessing,' and that it was the only vocal work of Bach with English words which could be found in print at the time. Doubt has since been expressed whether Sebastian Bach ever wrote the Motet which represented him at this opening ceremony. The Society, with no fixed abode, save the 'Bach-attic' for its library, wandered round from Chappell's to Coventry's, thence to The Hanover Square Rooms, and on to St Martin's Hall, thus continuing its work throughout the musical season. There were thirty-five members when the practices began; of ladies, there were only four; but the assistance of Academy students was obtained, and, before long, the Rev. Thomas Helmore gave willing and active aid, bringing with him the children of the Chapel Royal, who lived under his charge. Two more Motets were arranged with English words. Their rehearsal gave great trouble. Henry Smart conducted, while Bennett supported the Chorus by re-producing the scores on the pianoforte with a completeness and facility which surprised the musicians around him. The conductor, however, was at times in despair at the frequent break-downs of his forces. On one occasion, having laid the blame, in turn, on each section of the eight-part chorus, he at length threw down his bâton, and crying out, 'Bennett, I do believe its your —— piano,' provoked a roar of laughter, and restored good humour.

The centenary of Bach's death fell on July 28 of this year. The day of the week was Sunday, so the Society solemnized the occasion on the next evening. They gave a private concert at St Martin's Hall with the following programme, which does not enter very closely into particulars.

Part I.

Choral, 'God my King.'
Duet, Violin and Pianoforte.
Motet (E mi), No. 5.

Part II.

Choral, 'Farewell, thou orb of splendour.'
Concerto, Two Pianofortes.
Duet, 'Et in unum,' Mass in B minor.
Chaconne, Violin and Pianoforte.
Motet (B flat), No. 1.

At this concert the performers, whether enrolled as members of the Bach Society or not, gave their assistance as amateurs. Their names do not appear on the programme. Molique was the solo violinist, Bennett and Dorrell were the pianists, Henry Smart conducted, and stringed instrument players came forward to accompany the Concerto. There was no sale of tickets. On the evening before (Sunday), the Germans in Leipzig had marked the centenary by founding another Bach Society, which had for its object the gigantic task of publishing all the Master's works. The London Society now took one step in the same direction. They negotiated with Messrs Ewer for a publication of the Six Motets. The issue of these under the editorship of Dr Steggall, with English text by Bartholomew, gave great impetus to the practices. Eminent musicians, who had not sung since boyhood, joined the ranks. The volume of Motets was issued in June, 1851; monthly 'trials' were then appointed, and were regularly continued, during winter and spring, for many years. The untiring exertions of the youthful Miss Johnston ensured no further lack of material for study. She framed the course of her life in view of this special work; diligently learnt German at the new Queen's College; persevered with her study of musical theory under Bennett and Steggall; learnt the organ; and perfected herself in the art of lithography. She gradually produced, consulting Bennett at every stage of her progress, an English version of the St Matthew 'Passions-Musik.' She set up a lithographic press in her house at St John's Wood, and prepared with her own hands all the parts necessary for the practice and at last for the performance of the great work. The size and weight of the Bach portfolio which she had herself constructed, with many a cunning device for the better storing of her treasures, and with which the enthusiastic girl was constantly trudging between St John's Wood and Russell Place, stood for measures of her laboriousness and endurance. At the practices, whether as leader of any voice part within her compass, or as stage librarian, she was indefatigable and ubiquitous. Rather eccentric in appearance, with eyes beaming through large spectacles, and with her own ideas of dress, her youth was somewhat disguised. A violinist, unversed in musical chronology, attending the rehearsals for the first time, and astonished at the enthusiasm she displayed, seriously enquired of his neighbour, 'Is it *Mrs* Bach?' At one time later in life, she was summoned to India to fetch home her father, a Commander in the Royal Navy, who had been attacked with serious illness. She took her portfolio with her and got up a branch Bach Society among the sailors. That Bach should go into competition with Dibdin tickled Bennett's sense of humour[1]. Probably, however, a few Chorales were all that Miss Johnston would use in her appeal to the Navy; and it was part of Bennett's own creed that Bach's music was not for the cultivated musician alone. When he had been holding rehearsals of the B minor Mass in St Martin's Hall, he told his friend, the Rev. W. T. Kingsley, that it had been a great satisfaction to him to hear the street boys in Long Acre whistling the melody of the 'Sanctus.' But the Bach Society must now be left for a while, giving their occasional concerts on a still small scale, celebrating their master's birthdays, collecting, through the generosity of others and by their own expenditure, a valuable library, and struggling with the difficulties of the St Matthew 'Passions-Musik.' Bennett afterwards wrote of this music :—'Its introduction was effected *bit by bit*, one portion rehearsed over and over again, until performers and listeners began to find their way in it, and then some other portion ventured on.'

---

[1] No disrespect to Dibdin was implied. Bennett often instanced the bestowal of a Pension upon Dibdin as a remarkable recognition of the services rendered by a song-writer to his country.

WILLIAM STERNDALE BENNETT
AET. CIRCA XXXV
From a Daguerreotype

Bennett's Chamber Concerts had now for some time been recognized as a feature of London music. Such concerts were not at first fashionable enough to find a place during the London season. He gave three in the early part of the year, and after abandoning, in 1849, his annual orchestral concerts, he ventured on a fourth Chamber Concert in the month of June. It is evidence of progress, that as the years passed the dates changed and he ended by giving the series of three in the height of the season. The Hanover Square Rooms did not require a very large audience to fill them. For smaller concerts, a screen was dropped over the orchestra for acoustical reasons, and a platform was placed at the centre of the north wall, on to which the performers stepped from George the Third's tea-room. With these arrangements one found oneself in the drawing-room or music-room of some princely mansion, such a place as Haydn or Mozart must often have appeared in to play their Trios or Sonatas. It was a custom of the time for a concert-giver to send out invitations to brother-artists. If they accepted and came in large numbers, it was taken as a sign that the concert was important, and *éclat* was rightly thought to be added to the proceedings. By conforming to this custom and by securing about 150 subscribers, Bennett always had a sufficient audience. He engaged the best artists both vocal and instrumental, and did not expect to gain anything for himself. At first he incurred a slight loss, but, as time went on, interest grew and additional tickets were sold. Of a concert in 1852, *The Musical World* wrote:—

'The Hanover Square Rooms were densely packed with such an audience of connoisseurs and professors as, perhaps, Sterndale Bennett alone is able to collect together. Success was never more thoroughly merited. Sterndale Bennett was the originator (in 1842)[1] of these performances of classical Chamber-music, by the great composers for the pianoforte, to which the art and its professors are so much indebted, and which, of late years, have been so greatly in vogue. The best pianist, and the best composer for the pianoforte that this country has probably known, no one

[1] The scheme was advertised in 1842 but the first Concert was given in Jan. 1843.

could be more fitted to set the example; and if works once confined to the student's library, although acknowledged superior to anything else belonging to this special and important branch of the art, are now widely diffused and popular, it is certainly due to Sterndale Bennett, who was not only the first to venture on producing them in public, but, now that ten years have passed, remains without a superior among the foreign and English pianists who have followed in his steps.'

With a slight reservation the above tribute may be accepted. Moscheles and Charles Neate had both given one or two series of somewhat similar concerts in advance of Bennett. They did not continue to give them. Bennett took the work up again, and persevered with it. There is no hesitation in claiming for him that within a certain period (1843—1856) he was able to accomplish more than any predecessor or immediate contemporary, in awakening, by the beauty of his playing and his interpretative power, an appreciation in this country for the masterpieces of concerted Chamber-music in which the pianoforte takes part. He was no self-assertive pianist. A point admired by Schumann in his Concerto-writing, and often noticed by Davison in his Concerto-playing, was his rare power of uniting the pianoforte to the orchestra with due regard to the claims of each. In his playing of Chamber-music the same attitude was constantly referred to as something exceptional. The faculty of combination was one in which the pianist-composer had the advantage over the mere virtuoso, and over those who, in days when performances of Concertos and Chamber-music were far rarer events than they became later, had little chance of gaining such faculty by experience.

The violinists who helped him most frequently at these concerts were Blagrove, Molique, Sainton and Ernst. Vieuxtemps and Joachim also appeared. Dando took the viola when that instrument was wanted. Piatti, who joined him in 1849, remained from that time his constant colleague, and during a period of seven years there was no musician with whom Bennett seemed to have closer artistic sympathy. With such help, he produced the Violin Sonatas of Bach, playing them much with the fine musician Molique. Of

Mozart: three of the Violin Sonatas, one Trio, the Quintet with wind-instruments, and the Trio with clarinet were constantly played. Of Beethoven: all the published Trios, all the Violin and Violoncello Sonatas, the Quintet with wind-instruments and the Horn Sonata were included. The works of Mendelssohn for pianoforte and stringed instruments had been used, on their first arrival, to supply the special item in which the pianoforte took part at String-Quartet concerts, so that there is no particular interest attaching to Bennett's producing them, as he often did, at his own. Similar works by Dussek, Weber, Spohr and Hummel found occasional place. To sum up: He gave forty concerts; he drew from a repertoire of forty-five concerted works; and very few of these works, save those of Mendelssohn, had been played in public in England at the time he introduced them. Amateurs may have played them in private with great enjoyment to themselves; but it is a well-established fact that amateur instrumentalists who could give pleasure to others by the performance of such music were few and far between in those days. Classical Chamber-music to win its way to full appreciation required an introduction by first-rate artists.

Bennett himself was represented on his programmes by a 'Chamber Trio,' which modesty did not prevent him from often repeating; also, by a Sonata Duo for pianoforte and violoncello. He wrote this Sonata for Piatti in 1852. On the eve of the concert for which it was promised, he told his wife that he could not possibly finish it. She begged him to make an effort to keep faith with the Public, and sat with him through the night while he worked. Next morning he went out to his pupils and, after six hours' teaching, returned in the afternoon to complete his task. A letter from Signor Piatti (dated Jan. 12, 1882) to the present writer, refers to the composition and performance of the Sonata:—

'* * * Certainly my recollections of the friendly relations between your esteemed father and myself are very pleasant, and his genial character was so sympathetic to me, that I always felt very happy in his company, and I believe he felt so at ease with me, that a child could not have been truer and more natural in his conversation. * * * I had many and many a pleasant walk with him, and I must say that I have always found him the same good, kind and congenial companion and friend. * * * He did me the honour of writing a Sonata expressly for me, and I can't forget the hearty laugh he gave when, on the evening of the concert that it was to be performed, on my going to rehearse it, he informed me that it was not quite finished. That was about two hours before the concert. His piano was already gone to the concert, at least I think so, because he invited me to go downstairs in the Housekeeper's room, where there was a little cottage-pianoforte, and there he set at work to finish it and I to learn it. We could not rehearse it, being now the time to go to the concert. However, it went off very well and it pleased the Public very much. On this particular occasion he reminded me more than ever of the fine, crisp, diamond-like touch of Mendelssohn, and he never played better, nor the Sonata go so well as that night.'

The 'hearty laugh' with which Bennett greeted Piatti can only have been a cloak to underlying anxiety. One of the audience said, fifty years later, that he happened to pass the composer a few moments before he stepped up to play the Sonata and thought his appearance was that of a painfully nervous man. He passed him again half-an-hour later, and saw his face sparkling with gaiety. The marked contrast had fixed the evening in the observer's memory. Bennett often alluded to this occasion, in remembrance of Piatti's masterful readiness in musical performance, and of his matter-of-fact way of accepting a situation in which he could help a brother-artist out of a difficulty. Piatti played his part in the Sonata from the manuscript, while the composer trusted to his memory.

At these concerts, as also elsewhere, Bennett liked to introduce music for four hands on the pianoforte, or duets for two pianofortes. His friend Dorrell used to imitate the plaintive tone in which he had once said: 'Ah, Dorrell, how I wish I could do something for Mozart.' When the public performance of instrumental music began to spread in this country, and when the music of two or three generations was presented simultaneously for a first hearing, the works of Beethoven, of Spohr, or of Mendelssohn seemed to appeal more readily to the popular ear than those of

Mozart. In the case of Chamber-music and Solos for the pianoforte this was particularly noticeable. In the duet-playing, however, Bennett found a special and most fascinating aspect in which to present his own model musician. He understood that Mozart had himself invented the duet-playing on one pianoforte. The Duet in F minor, one of the two said to have been written for a musical clock, Bennett described, in a lecture at Cambridge, as 'the essence of music.' He placed it on many programmes of concerts and lectures in the course of his life. The Sonata in D major for two pianofortes gave a splendid opportunity of illustrating Mozart's genius not only in Hanover Square, but to less instructed audiences in Finsbury or Greenwich. Mendelssohn's Andante con Variazioni (Op. 83a) was another favourite item, recalling to his mind his own concert in 1844 when the composer had contributed the piece as a novelty, and had played it with him. Schumann's Andante with Variations (Op. 46) was produced, and perhaps heard for the first time in London at one of his latest concerts. In this duet-playing he was associated with other eminent artists. It enabled him to invite Moscheles, Cipriani Potter, Stephen Heller and Madame Schumann to assist him; also Robert Barnett, a pianist whose style was considered almost a facsimile of Bennett's, but whose nervousness prevented him from gaining eminence. Bennett, in after life, would often speak of the painful nervousness that had, in his own case, attacked him *before* public performance, but he said that it left him altogether when he seated himself at the pianoforte, and with such a suddenness that he seemed to *feel* it go, as if it were lifted by an unseen hand.

The music for his own solo-playing at the Chamber Concerts was not selected with a view of exhibiting his technical skill to its full extent; though the choice was no doubt sufficiently comprehensive to show what Sir John Goss termed 'his extraordinary power of illustrating the various styles of the Great Masters on the pianoforte.' In analysing a list of the Solos he played, it is found that Bach and Handel were the composers whose works he played the oftenest. Mozart and Beethoven were so well represented on his programmes by concerted music that he did not select largely from their Solos. Of Beethoven's Sonatas he limited himself to five. Of Mozart he played Sonatas in F ma. and A mi., a Romance in A flat, and a 'Tema e Variazioni' in F. Of Mendelssohn, the Preludes and Fugues were his great pieces. Mendelssohn played them to him in Leipzig a day or two before he sent them to a publisher, and in the same week wrote about them to Ferdinand Hiller and expressed a doubt whether they would be much played. One may imagine that he would make the same remark to Bennett, and that the latter would determine that it should be no fault of his if they were not well known. The Prelude and Fugue in E minor became a favourite *cheval de bataille*. The boldness of the acceleration with which he worked up the Fugue was enough to alarm some of his listeners. William Rea and Dr Steggall in the course of one such performance turned to each other and said simultaneously, 'He'll never do it.' Late in life, and when he had for many years entirely abandoned pianoforte-practice, he took it into his head one day to sit down in his Academy class-room and try his old favourite, for the sake of a student who was going to play it the same evening. Mr William Shakespeare, who heard him do this 'so magnificently,' gained thereby the impression that, 'as a pianist he must have been of the greatest,' and noticed that he still possessed 'a remarkable firmness of touch, splendid accent, wonderfully clear technique, and a style of phrasing as pure and fastidious as his own music.'

His playing of the 'Lieder ohne Worte' seems to have been regarded as an almost necessary sequence to his appearance at a concert. His object, when he first adopted them for public performance, has already been explained. He either played one of the books complete, or else three or four numbers which he would allow his friends in the artists' room to select before he went on the platform. He was generally obliged to play three or four more, and was seldom allowed to escape till the 'Duetto' had been heard.

Of other composers, Scarlatti, Paradies, Haydn, Clementi, Cramer, Potter, Moscheles, Fanny Hensel and Schumann were drawn upon, but to no large extent. For himself he did not do much. By an audience numbering many pupils and friends he was of course expected to contribute something of his own. By their choice, probably—the words *by desire* being often appended—he constantly played, from his earlier pieces, the 'Three Musical Sketches,' and, from his later ones, 'The Rondo Piacevole.' These he repeated to the exclusion of other of his works which he might, with advantage, have made known through his own renderings. It would, however, have been at variance with the main purpose of his Chamber Concerts to put forward the pianoforte too prominently as a solo instrument, or to draw disproportionate attention upon himself among the artists with whom he worked.

He continued the concerts till the year 1856. Then new duties, as will later be explained, obliged him to abandon them, and he ceased altogether to play in public. Other occurrences up to that date will be noticed in another chapter, but leave may here be taken of him as a pianist. His retirement, when it came, was marked by no 'Farewell' demonstrations. His work in this direction had for some years been singularly unpretentious and his greater days as a performer had long since passed away. The premature check to his career, caused by the wretched contretemps at the Philharmonic, was a source of much after-regret to his admirers. Schumann had written of him that he was 'Clavier-Spieler vorzugsweise[1].' To others who had taken the same view, regret would naturally come that Bennett, in his thirty-third year and in the fulness of his powers, should have discarded, to so great an extent, the branch of his musicianship on which, may be, his individuality was most clearly pronounced. Nevertheless, the thirteen years that included his more notable performances sufficed to gain for him an honoured name both in England and Germany, though not, perhaps, one of those long-lasting reputations which the verdicts of successive generations help to accumulate. A wide-spread fame he never sought. With no innate desire for prominence on any platform, he was not the man to seek for wider recognition by extending his travels in strange lands. His visits to Leipzig were not undertaken with public performance as their prime object. It is true that his mind was at one time set upon a tour

[1] F. R. Ritter translates Schumann's words: 'Bennett is a pianist above all things.'

through some of the other musical centres in Germany, but though Mendelssohn and the publisher Kistner encouraged the scheme he did not carry it out; while to a definite offer that he should go to Paris as an artist he at once turned a deaf ear. However, even if he had wished to travel, few were the places that would have welcomed or defrayed the expenses of an instrumental performer who was not ready to concede something, in his choice of music, to prevailing fashion, and to consider the interests, at least in some degree, of the sight-seeing section of a concert-audience. That fact can be seen in black and white, on the programmes of the period to which he, as a player, belonged. Nor is it certain that his playing, by the nature of its sentiment, would have appealed successfully to the temperaments of various nationalities. His very personality was not, perhaps, of that order which commands the vast and parti-coloured assemblage. The simplicity and unaffectedness of bearing which added charm, in English eyes, to the performances of his boyish days remained with him to the end, or only gave place, as years went on, to a grave dignity which befitted manhood. But such characteristics would not have helped him far in his way through Europe or the New World. It is better to think of him as stationed just where and just when men of his stamp were scarce and sorely needed, but also just where and when the ways of greatest usefulness could not all lead to high distinction. Still, whatever can or can not be said about his worldly fame, ample testimony remains, of which perhaps enough has been recorded in these pages, that he was a remarkable master of the pianoforte. His playing had for many that same magnetic attraction which had drawn the old Sergeant of the Guards to watch over his practice at the Academy. He possessed a marvellous faculty for revealing the grandeur or the grace of music to the uncultured and for converting the thoughtless to a belief in what he himself revered. No child could fail to realize the majesty of some ancient Chorale, as the broad impressive tones rose from his instrument and set the whole atmosphere of his house in vibration. But far away, on the other hand, he was no less able to captivate the sympathetic interest of some of the most illustrious musicians of his time. Schumann, writing to Simonin de

Sire in 1839, extolled Mendelssohn as the foremost of then living musicians. He made a special reference to his playing and then added :—' Next to him comes Bennett. And in what a way do they both play the pianoforte, like angels and with no more assumption than children.'

CHAPTER XV.

CORRESPONDENCE WITH THE SCHUMANNS.
GREAT EXHIBITION OF 1851.
REVIVAL OF THE PHILHARMONIC TROUBLE.
CONDUCTORSHIP OF GEWANDHAUS CONCERTS.
PRODUCTION OF BACH'S 'PASSIONS-MUSIK.'

1850—1855[1].

æt. 33—39.

FOR the three years succeeding Mendelssohn's death, no letters, of which this writer is aware, passed between Bennett and his German friends, except one, carefully preserved, written to him by Madame Mendelssohn. There was, however, no lack of opportunity for exchanging news between London and Leipzig. Julius Kistner and Monicke visited him in Russell Place; Mrs Bennett corresponded with Miss Annette Preusser; and there was now a constant passage of musical students between this country and the Leipzig Conservatorium. Bennett, when he at last took up his pen, did so with a very interesting object. He wrote to Düsseldorf.

LONDON, 15 RUSSELL PLACE,
FITZROY SQUARE,
Dec. 15, 1850.

LIEBER SCHUMANN,

Kennen Sie meine Handschrift? Are you really so near to old England? and will this letter find you in Düsseldorf? I want to know how all goes with you, and to make some plan to bring you and your good wife into our Land. Will you not come to our grand

[1] This chapter and the foregoing one supplement each other, both traversing nearly the same period of time.

Exhibition? and will you not come to exhibit yourselves to some very sincere and good friends!

I wish Madame Schumann to come and play to our English people who will listen to her, and applaud her with all their hearts—and if she will come, I will make some Concerts and *arrange* beforehand (voraus), all that is necessary. It is my present intention to have some new Concerts next Season, beginning in May and 14 days between each; perhaps you would come and your good wife would play at *two* Concerts, and I would give some of your compositions, and this could all be done in little time, and then if you liked still to remain in England longer, you would find many friends to interest you, and Madame S. would find many good engagements.

I must now be a man of business. Will you tell me (senza delicatezza) what Madame Schumann would receive for performance at two Concerts in London in May next, e.g., 14 *May* and 28 *May*, with condition that between those periods (zwischen der Zeit) she should not perform elsewhere in London, and that she should first appear at my Concerts? Let me know this immediately. If it were more convenient to you I could arrange for *June*, but I would rather have you in May.

If you will come, I will endeavour to give these Concerts and introduce your compositions, and renew our acquaintance, which (to me) will be the best thing of all.

Pray answer this letter *immediately*. If you do not come, I shall not give these Concerts, and pray mention distinctly the *terms*.

I want to see you and Madame Schumann and have some good music. This is the *second* letter which I ever sent to Düsseldorf, the first, I wrote to Mendelssohn in 1836.

Greetings from my Wife and self to your Wife and self.

Ever thine heartily,

WILLIAM STERNDALE BENNETT.

Schumann to Bennett[1].

DÜSSELDORF, *January the 2nd*, 1851.

DEAR BENNETT,
Your letter of Dec. 15th only reached me the day before yesterday, as a good ending to the year. What pleasure it gave me, to recognize your hand-writing; for often and always have I thought of you, and of the many delightful hours I have passed with you. We have the greatest desire to visit England, and we shall probably come. But first one thing: A musical Festival will be celebrated here on June 8th and, as it is the turn for Düsseldorf this time, the direction will be in my hands. Now this fits quite well with the dates given by you, the 14th and 28th of May. We would arrive in London in the beginning of May, and could be back again by the 1st of June, so that I should still be in time to direct at least the full rehearsals. The question now is, could we in so short a time earn enough to cover the cost of journey and living, which we estimate at £100 at least? If you think so, we should wish for nothing further.

Another thing I should like to mention. You will think it natural and you also touch upon it in your letter, that I should not like to remain idle at my wife's side, but should also like to show myself as a musician, namely as a Conductor, which is my greatest desire. Now could you negotiate this, as for instance with the Philharmonic Society, so that there might be some chance of bringing it about? I have many works, which I believe might find favour in England: 'Paradise and the Peri,' an Overture and incidental music to Byron's Manfred, a new Symphony lately completed, and much besides, which to you above all I should have such great pleasure in showing.

Would it perhaps be possible for you to fix the days of your concerts eight days *earlier*, upon the 7th and 21st of May, so that in the time between the 22nd of May and the 1st of June we could still undertake something, my wife perhaps play at a Philharmonic concert, or obtain other engagements.

Now will you turn this over in your mind, dear Bennett? We have, as I say, the greatest desire to come, and will

[1] Original letter is in German.

do so, if only there is a reasonable prospect *of our not being losers by it.*

And still a few questions: Are the concerts, which you give, *with Orchestra*? How many times would my wife have to play at each of them? On which days are the Philharmonic concerts fixed? Do you think I could bring about a performance of the *Peri*, if not in May, perhaps later on, if Mdlle. Lind would sing in it?

A thousand such things I should like to ask, and others too of a more ideal kind, and also how you fare yourself, and whether you are as happy in your life as I should wish you to be, and of myself I should have much to tell you, of my home happiness, and of my *five* children, and of my joyous impulses towards composition which are ever and ever prompting me. That must be spared for another letter! The greetings which you send us from your wife we heartily reciprocate as I myself do yours.

Your old friend,
R. SCHUMANN.

The continuation of this correspondence cannot be found. Bennett only gave his usual Chamber Concerts in 1851. He may have been advised that the year of the Great Exhibition would be unfavourable to musical enterprize, as did prove to be the case. It is known that the arrangement with the Schumanns was postponed till the following year, but again failed of accomplishment. Finally, ill-health prevented Schumann from fulfilling his desire to visit England. As will be seen, Bennett was able later to take part in carrying out some of the wishes expressed in Schumann's letter.

The Great Exhibition of 1851 was opened with a ceremony in which music found some place. Sir George Smart, in virtue of his office as Organist and Composer to the Chapel Royal, directed the musical proceedings, conducting the National Anthem himself, but gracefully resigning the bâton to Sir Henry Bishop for the 'Hallelujah' Chorus. The performances on the exhibited organs, which afforded continuous music as the Queen's procession passed round the building, were announced to be 'under the superintendence of Mr W. Sterndale Bennett.' Any recognition on a great public occasion was of value to a man whose name was, as yet, little known outside musical circles. Musicians found further work assigned to them by the scheme of the Exhibition. They hailed with pleasure an opportunity, which seldom came their way, of appearing as useful citizens side by side with the representatives of other arts and sciences. As judges of musical exhibits they entered upon their work with zeal. Bennett, who had been appointed a Juror, was constantly across Hyde Park and at the doors of the Exhibition by 6 a.m., the earliest hour at which he could gain admittance. Committee-meetings and the drafting of reports heavily taxed the time of his colleagues and himself. The satisfaction of joining in public service promised a sufficient recompense, but in the end they thought their labours had been ill requited. Their recommendations for the award of medals were not accepted in some important cases by a superior Committee of non-musical men, who were perhaps unprepared to consider improvements in the manufacture of pianofortes as of much importance to the progress of nations. Then came a long correspondence between Sir George Smart, Sir Henry Bishop, Cipriani Potter, the Chevalier Neukomm and Bennett, and a protest was sent to the Commissioners signed by six out of the ten musical Jurors. The question at issue appears to have been how far anything connected with a musical instrument could claim a high award as an invention. The protesting musical Jurors, whether they had just cause or not, were offended at being considered incompetent to decide that point. Added to this came another grievance.

For the ceremony at the closing of the Exhibition, the services of the Sacred Harmonic Society were accepted, but the Commissioners neglected to engage a Conductor. At the last moment Costa was applied to. He was out of town and wrote, that, even had it been possible for him to come, he would not have interfered with the prerogative of Sir George Smart. Little care seems to have been taken at the time in the treatment of musicians. The Commissioners accepted the services of a volunteer who put himself forward, and the feelings of those who had taken part in the 'Opening' proceedings were not worth a thought. On the day after the 'Closing,' Sir Henry Bishop wrote to Bennett:—'Sir George Smart, yourself, and I have been grossly insulted by the musical arrangements of yesterday. It is a question whether they were under the control of the executive committee or not. No matter by whom organized the insult is the same.'

Thus, on the whole, the Exhibition proved rather a disappointment to Bennett, notwithstanding much interesting work, and a deluge of invitations to hospitable functions in the City, Birmingham, Paris and other places.

His position as a teacher now seemed quite secure. Mrs Bennett had for some time been constantly refusing applications for lessons. In 1851, he being then 35 years old, she insisted on raising his terms for new clients. Timid of the consequences, as he afterwards said, it was with great reluctance that he gave way to her wishes; but she proved right. As old engagements gave place to new his income gradually increased; though so lasting were many of his connections that it took at least twelve years for his wife's idea to take full effect. Meanwhile the 1650 to 1700 lessons which he gave in the year furnished comfortable means for a small family, with a margin for generosity and a little margin for saving. He was also able to keep clear of money considerations in any other musical occupations in which he wished to engage. The scheme of life originally suggested by his old friend, Mr Holdsworth, was being followed to the letter. His work was still continuous throughout the year. He could not get ten days in succession for a holiday, even in the summer. Private pupils often kept him in town till the first few days of August had gone, and the middle of that month brought the young ladies back to their schools after the Midsummer holidays. In the summer of 1852, he took lodgings for his family at Windsor, going himself to and fro for a few weeks, and getting odd days free. From Windsor he dated several numbers of the 'Preludes and Lessons' (Op. 33), a work which he finished at Southampton at Christmas time. One of the 'Lessons,' in G minor, he had written for the album of Miss Wood in 1842, when he had just become engaged to her, but the others were probably quite new. The collection was said to be made for the pupils of Queen's College, Harley Street, and to them it was dedicated. Several of the 'Lessons' are very short, and Davison was quite angry about this, saying to Mrs Bennett that the book was a 'murder' of valuable ideas. Nevertheless, the little pieces are quite perfect as they stand; they were very welcome to many amateurs of the day; and Bennett himself used to play selections from them with telling effect.

The season of 1853 revived the Philharmonic trouble. Since 1848, the year of its occurrence, one work of Bennett's had been played, under exceptional circumstances, at a concert of the Society. Miss Kate Loder (Lady Thompson) selected for her performance in 1850 his Caprice in E major. Costa, at the entreaty of Mr and Mrs Anderson, whose niece Miss Loder was, agreed to conduct it, and did so. Towards the end of 1852, the Society elected Bennett as one of the Directors for the 1853 season. Anderson expressed himself confident that, after a lapse of nearly five years, the misunderstanding with Costa could be removed; so with this assurance, and with the knowledge that he had been elected a Director by an unusually large number of votes, Bennett consented to serve. But he soon found himself in the wrong place. Costa, far from fulfilling Anderson's expectations, refused to renew his engagement, unless a clause was inserted giving him liberty to decline conducting any work to which he might take exception. This condition was granted. Early in the season (1853), Miss Arabella Goddard was invited to make her debût, and she selected Bennett's Concerto in C minor. Costa refused to have anything to do with it. The Directors then asked Miss Goddard to choose a work by one of the great masters. Her first invitation had laid no restriction on her choice of music; as the change might seem to imply a slight on Bennett's reputation, she refused to make it, with the result that her engagement was cancelled. This incident, which caused much remark, and the old quarrel to which it was the sequel, were thus referred to in *Punch*[1]:

> 'Sterndale Bennett was Indignant with Costa
> For not playing Bennett's composition faster;
> Costa flew into Excitement with Lucas,
> For showing him Bennett's Order or Ukase,

---

[1] Mr Punch's comments on musical events, some of which are quoted in this book, were generally attributed to Shirley Brooks.

Haughtily Resigned the Seat which he sat on,
And Contemptuously told Lucas himself to Take the bâton,
Moreover Stipulated this year with the Directors
That Nobody was to read him any more Lectures:
Also, he made it a Condition Strict,
He was Only to conduct what Pieces of Music he lik'd,
Whereby this year Costa doth Prevent
Any performance of Music by Sterndale Benn't:
Likewise excluding the young and gifted Miss Goddard
Whom with Admiration all the Critical Squad heard :—
All to be Deplored, and without more Amalgamation
The Philharmonic will Tarnish its Hitherto Deservedly High Reputation.'

Miss Goddard straightway went off and played the C minor Concerto, under the bâton of Lindpaintner, at 'The New Philharmonic,' a recently formed institution which was bidding fair to become a formidable rival to the older Society. In June, Bennett was asked to play a work of his own at another rival establishment, 'The Orchestral Union.' He had not been heard of as a Concerto-player for some years, and this exceptional appearance proved his last in that capacity. *The Musical World* records a 'magnificent performance' of his Concerto in F minor, and a 'reception, by an audience filling the Hanover Square Rooms to overflow, which was a significant expression of public opinion about a recent event which has made much noise in the musical world.'

But Bennett now followed his quiet way, without being much exposed to the jars of public life. He was happy with his Bach Society, his Chamber Concerts, and in the composition of his pianoforte pieces. He enjoyed the work with his pupils, and his personal association with the host of old and young friends who clustered round him. His domestic life was delightful. Though he was much away from home, his wife managed to keep him in touch with the many who desired access to him. Weeks of comparative leisure came sometimes, when, if he could not leave London, he could pay a little attention to the duties and pleasures of society. A formal dinner-party would be given at least once a year; but there were also occasional evening parties in Russell Place when young people were gathered and at which his Academy pupils were made very welcome. On such occasions he took his full share in the entertaining. Impromptu dances would be proposed, very much for the

Immense Attraction!
The Pure Drama Restored!!
RUSSELL THEATRE
Fitzroy Gardens.
WEDNESDAY EVENING, JULY 13th, 1853.
MR. BENNETT

Has the honor to announce that, after great inconvenience and much distress of mind, he has at length prevailed upon

THE CELEBRATED
TENTERDEN COMPANY
TO PERFORM
FOR ONE NIGHT ONLY!!

At the above Theatre; and, regardless of expense, has also been fortunate enough, by no end of great persuasion and promises of payment, and at the risk of incurring an Action from a rival Establishment, to induce

THE CELEBRATED SCOTTISH ACTRESS,
MISS AUGUSTA THOMSON,

To assist the above Celebrites in personifying the well-known screaching Farce of THE

SPITALFIELDS WEAVER.

Harry Brown	-	Mr. JAMES THOMSON.
Darville	-	Mr. WILSON.
Dawson	(a Butler) -	Mr. CUSINS.
Simmons	-	Mr. SHARPE.
Adele	-	Miss AUGUSTA THOMSON.
Principal Footmen	-	Messrs. BENNETT and BARNETT.

The Female Aristocracy represented by
Mesdames FERRARI and BENNETT.

THE ORCHESTRA

Will be on an unusually small *scale*, much inclining to the *minor*, and it is to be hoped with few *accidentals*.

Principal Flute (with a peculiar BORE), Scene-shifter, Prompt-or-and-them, and willing to make himself generally useful in any capacity not menial,

Signor FERRARI.

FREE LIST WIDE OPEN!!!
CRITICS SUSPENDED!!
Manifestations of delight not forbidden!!

ADMISSION—UP THE GRAND STAIRCASE.
Seats preserved, but not warranted to keep throughout the Evening.

Vivant Regina et Princeps.

J. MALLETT, Printer, 59, Wardour Street.

sake of hearing him extemporize graceful dance-music. This side of his musicianship, according to Sir George Macfarren, had given pleasure to his friends in quite early days. He would invent musical games, and, with the aid of Arthur O'Leary, or some other favourite pupil for an accomplice, would, by his playing, accomplish thought-reading sufficiently miraculous to the lay mind. Charades were much in vogue at the time and his friend Ferrari was always ready to direct them. They together arranged a more ambitious performance and collaborated in the production of a full-sized play-bill here printed on a smaller scale.

Bennett had been cast for the *Butler*, but could not, perhaps for want of time, master his part, so resigned it in favour of his pupil, W. G. Cusins. His silent *rôle*, however, proved no sinecure. Hair-powdering and the donning of a gorgeous livery brought the nervous Robert Barnett to the verge of stage-fright. Bennett, by his merry encouragements, at last succeeded in pacifying him, and the entrance of the 'Principal Footmen' laden with trays and decanters of wine evoked a loud burst of the unforbidden 'manifestations of delight.'

A few days after this diversion, some friends in Leipzig wrote to tell Mrs Bennett that they might require her husband's holiday address. They hinted, at the same time, that a surprise, which they hoped might bring pleasure, was probably in store for him. The address for his brief vacation in August was to be Southampton; but, before going there, Bennett spent a few days, with his wife, in Derbyshire, on a pilgrimage to scenes and spots about which he had, in his youth, heard much talk at his grandparents' fireside. He now passed through, for the first time, the village of Ashford-in-the-water, the home of his forefathers. He played on the little organ in the church where they had worshipped, and was more than satisfied with his visit when he came across an old villager, sitting by the wayside, who well remembered his dear grandfather. This excursion delayed his receipt of an important letter which he found lying at Southampton when he arrived there.

LEIPZIG, *29th July*, 1853[1].

*The Concert-Direction of Leipzig
to Mr William Sterndale Bennett, Southampton.*

The undersigned Concert-direction still remembers with pleasure the time of your long residences in Leipzig and the active service you rendered as well as the kind feeling you showed to the Gewandhaus Concerts.

For these concerts, the direction of which has up to this time been taken by Capellmeister Rietz and Concertmeister David and Capellmeister N. W. Gade of Copenhagen, we are now anxious to obtain, for the next winter's season, an able conductor. The considerable fame which you, Dear Sir, enjoy in the musical world, and the abiding favour always accorded to you by the public here, make us wish and herewith to express the hope, that it may be agreeable to you to undertake in the coming winter the direction of our twenty subscription concerts, and of two extra ones the first of which, as you will probably still remember, is given by us for the benefit of the poor, and the second for the Pension fund founded for distressed musicians. As honorarium we offer you the sum of 1,000 thalers.

Although we cannot but see, that the granting of our request would entail many sacrifices on your part, among which the change of domicile for so many months would not be the least, nevertheless we hope, that the friendly remembrance of the time you passed here, and the fact, that in our concerts we still have, as before, the furtherance of true art as our object, may possibly lead you to lend an ear to our proposal.

Should our hope be realised, we should then count upon seeing you at the head of our orchestra from the middle of September of this year until the end of March, or beginning of April, 1854.

We shall hope as soon as possible for the news of your consent and please may we ask another favour, whether you can recommend an English singer whom we might be able to secure for our next season or for part of it? We should especially like to hear from you whether Miss Louisa Pyne, whom we have before invited, would be able to come and

---

[1] Original is in German.

allow us to hear her, and do you think she would obtain favour here?

Accept the assurance of our very great esteem and attachment, with which we remain
In the name and by the order of the Concert-Direction,
                                      DR WENDLER.

Bennett to Dr Wendler.

13 HANOVER BUILDINGS,
SOUTHAMPTON,
August 8th, 1853.

DEAR SIR,

Being from home on a journey, I did not receive your kind and flattering letter of the 29th of July until yesterday. It is difficult for me, even in my own language, to thank the Concert-Direction of Leipzig for the very high compliment they have paid me in inviting me to conduct their Concerts of next Season. Would my arrangements allow me to accept this invitation, I feel that such a circumstance would give me a new existence, and independently of the opportunity afforded me of mixing myself more with the poetry of my art, it would again enable me to enjoy the satisfaction of renewing those friendships which I had the good fortune to enjoy in former times. I have always looked back upon Leipzig as a second home, and indeed how could it be otherwise, when I found such kind friends, and amongst all enjoyed the protection of the illustrious man whose removal from the world we all alike deplore.

Your invitation must, however, remain unanswered for two or three days. I will write again on Wednesday next, and if I am obliged to decline the greatest wish of my heart, be assured that I shall regret it all my life in many respects.

I will not forget to give you my best advice about a Singer. I shall go up to London on Wednesday and make enquiries.

Believe me,
Dear Sir,
Yours very truly,
WILLIAM STERNDALE BENNETT.

Dr Wendler,
 Concert-Direction,
  Leipzig.

13 HANOVER BUILDINGS,
SOUTHAMPTON,
August 11, 1853.

DEAR SIR,

According to my promise I write again to you upon the subject which has so entirely engrossed my thoughts since the receipt of your letter. Unfortunately, however, I must now write contrary to my sincerest desire, and *with the utmost regret* decline the very kind and generous invitation of the Concert-Direction of Leipzig to conduct their Concerts next Season.

Since my last communication, I have been in London to look into my affairs, and find it impossible to release myself from engagements already made; indeed many parties with whom I had so engaged myself are now absent from the country and therefore cannot be made aware of the position in which your kindness has placed me.

I wish I could fully express how much I appreciate this new act of kindness on the part of my Leipzig friends, and how sorrowful it makes me to be compelled to decide so thoroughly against my inclinations. I do not despair however of being able to pay Leipzig a short friendly visit during the Season, and supported by this hope I must conclude with a thousand thanks to the gentlemen of the Direction, and hearty wishes for the continued prosperity of the Gewandhaus Concerts.

Allow me, Sir, at the same time to thank you personally for the handsome terms in which your communication was couched.

Believe me,

Dear Sir,

Yours faithfully and obliged,

WILLIAM STERNDALE BENNETT.

Dr Wendler,
　　Concert-Direction,
　　　　Leipzig.

P.S. I shall see Miss Louisa Pyne on Tuesday next, and will then write to you on *that* subject.

Mrs Bennett wrote (Sept. 2nd, 1853) to Miss Annette Preusser, of Leipzig :—

'* * * and my husband was so completely overwhelmed with the feelings of joy and pride at the receipt of such a testimony of friendship and good feeling, that he could have accepted *at once*, but at the same time came many business letters for the half-year, and then came the consideration of whether he was not pledged in honour to the large schools to attend himself up to Christmas at least, then, many of the Principals of these establishments were away and he could not hold communication with them, also having most responsible situations in the R.A.M. and Queen's College, all of which were recommencing in about a fortnight after the date of the invitation. You can well imagine how these things perplexed us, my husband immediately came to London, and then his difficulty increased by finding our friend, Cipriani Potter, away in Germany, and that heavy family affliction would meet him on his return home (from the death of his son by drowning on his first voyage to sea and of which Mr and Mrs Potter would be ignorant until their return as their whereabouts are not known by any one here). Mr Potter would have been the only one able to have assisted my husband in teaching for him during his absence, and this obstacle occurring seemed to be insurmountable. * * * I must assure you that it was a great, great grief to my dear Husband when he considered that it was his first duty to remain in England, for it was his fond wish to have come to Leipzig. * * *'

To the above obstacles, Mrs Bennett added others of a domestic kind, and wrote at great length in her anxiety to prove that her husband was not ungrateful. His Leipzig friends, however, were much disappointed. They had counted upon his coming. The Preussers had gone so far as to secure the first refusal of a residence for himself and his wife. There can be no doubt that he, too, was genuinely sorry to decline. So pronounced, so unique an honour, paid to an English musician by Germany, would have an additional value to a man who had, as yet, been offered no such position in his own country. Pecuniary loss, the temporary disturbance of his London career, might have been balanced by the prestige which such a connection would have given him on his return. But probably all was ordered for the best. Musical thought in Germany was already taking new directions, and it is difficult to conceive that Bennett could have adapted himself to or felt happy under the changed circumstances. A short visit paid to Leipzig twelve years later sufficed to convince him that the same unanimity of feeling on musical questions which had existed in the Leipzig of his young days had disappeared. On that visit he was most cordially received by the public; his old friends seemed scarcely to know how to make enough of him. Conrad Schleinitz said to him, in the Directors' box at the Gewandhaus, with serious earnestness, 'Ah, Bennett, you were the one we wanted, you ought to have come to us.' When he was leaving, delighted with the main circumstances of his visit, a crowd of well-wishers assembled at the station, and then it seemed so curious that, as the train moved out of their sight, his first words should be, 'Thank God, I never went there.'

If it may be said that Bennett was wanted in Germany, it can also be said, though this may not have been apparent at the time—that he was wanted at home. The winter which he might have spent in Germany 'mixing,' as he had written, 'with the poetry of his art,' but also perhaps, as he afterwards thought, entangling himself in its party strifes, was marked by artistic work in London of much interest and of abiding value.

The members of the Bach Society, after keeping the composer's birthday in 1852 by a public concert of Motets and Concertos, devoted themselves entirely to the preparation of the St Matthew 'Passion.' In the winter of 1852—53, progress in the choral music was made; in April, 1853, a set of solo-singers accepted an invitation to take part in the practices; and in the autumn Bennett settled down in a determined way to get the work ready for performance in the spring of 1854. Meetings which had so far been called 'trials' were now styled 'rehearsals,' and were held constantly for six months. A volunteer orchestra was enrolled and studied assiduously with the chorus and soloists. Instrumentalists found no less difficulty than vocalists, and accidentals flew about in all directions. Bennett's friend,

Mr Charles Sparrow, who represented the amateur element in the violin-department, looks back to the time with the words, 'How we *did* work!' The chorus of over 100 voices (considered a large one for the Hanover Square Rooms), as well as the orchestra, consisted almost entirely of busily occupied professional musicians and students. The amateurs had never taken kindly to the Motets and few had remained faithful. Bennett wrote of eminent Professors who viewed the reception of such music in England as hopeless. Davison looked on with great sympathy, but with no confidence. He wrote, as follows, in *The Musical World*:—

'A body of men, artists and amateurs commingled, banded together in pursuit of some beloved study, which, in its very nature, postpones, well-nigh indefinitely, all prospect of reward or public fame,—yielding unflinchingly time, labour, and talent, solely to a conviction of right-doing in the cause of art, is ever a gratifying subject of contemplation. We may criticise its efforts as inadequate to their purpose, we may consider its measures ill-chosen, we may even think its object chimerical; but we must always admit the sincerity of its devotion, and respect in it that unquestionable element of the artist character—unfortunately, yet but slow of development in this country—the abstract love of whatever is deemed great, apart from all question of its popularity and profit. In this favourable light does the Bach Society present itself to notice. The task that it has chosen is almost Herculean, its fulfilment lies far off in the future, and its reward, we fear, is anything but secure.'

Miss Stainer brought a little brother with her to sing at these rehearsals and at the performance. Thirty years later, Sir John Stainer—as the boy, in after-life, was known—referred, at a meeting of The Musical Association, to the important work which Bennett had done in laying the foundation of the study of Bach's music. He said:—'As a small boy I had the honour of being admitted as a member of the first [Bach] Society, and I can assure you that I have a most vivid recollection of the very great pains that Bennett used to take at rehearsals. I fancy, as far as my memory serves me, we used to meet at Tenterden Street for the rehearsal of Bach's 'Passion,' and sometimes in the music-room in Store Street. I remember the immense trouble and pains he took about it, and knowing how very often the day had been passed in very fatiguing work, this shows his great self-sacrifice to the cause of music, thus to have devoted his evenings to such laborious practice. In those days he had all the labour and anxiety of a pioneer.'

The undertaking was beset with financial as well as musical difficulties. The Bach Society had by this time, *on paper*, a list of 150 enrolled members. The majority of these had paid an entrance fee of two guineas, in return for which they had been promised life-membership. This fee was fixed, at the time when the prime objects of the Society were the formation of a library, and meetings of members for private study of music. The capital thus collected had been gradually spent on these objects. Annual subscriptions from other members had dwindled. A library could be no attraction to those who had retired in despair from the Motets. At the beginning of 1854, the Treasurer reported, that the Society's little capital was exhausted, and that he had heard nothing of any subscriptions. Thus the performance of the 'Passions-Musik,' on April 6, had to be self-supporting. Doubt must have been felt as to how many people would pay five shillings to hear it; the strictest economy was necessary in making the arrangements; no additional help could be called in at the last moment to supply defects in the orchestra and chorus. The performance reached no high standard of excellence; but the feat of getting through the work continuously was at least accomplished; and had the effort not been made, the Society could have held together no longer. As it was, interest was aroused. Even at the first hearing much of the music was greeted with 'loud bursts of applause and encores,' out of place, perhaps, but at any rate encouraging. Bennett had obtained a copy of the book of words as used by Mendelssohn for the centenary performance at Berlin in 1829. This he followed, except that he replaced a few of the omitted Chorales, and the two Contralto Airs, 'Ah, Golgotha,' and 'See the Saviour's outstretched arm.' The difficulty of finding Contralto singers in Germany may account for Mendelssohn having omitted these Airs. As sung by Miss Dolby, at this and subsequent performances, they were always redemanded.

Satisfied on the whole with the reception of the work, and wishing to have it heard again, before the awakened interest waned, Bennett decided on a second venture. A few professional friends joined him in guaranteeing the expenses; fresh rehearsals were started in the autumn; and a second performance of the 'Passions-Musik' was given in November. After these accomplishments, satisfactory as a first step, but too crude to convert certain eminent English musicians to a belief that Bach's choral works would ever find acceptance in this country, the Bach Society retired for a while to their private studies, continuing their winter practices and gradually getting into debt.

In July, 1854, Bennett attended, as an invited guest, a musical festival at Rotterdam. He crossed over with a party of friends, one of them being Miss Dolby who was engaged to sing at the festival. His name was known in Holland. At Leipzig he had enjoyed the friendship of Verhulst, who became the leading musician of the Netherlands, and who, according to Davison, retained to the end of his life a very special liking for Bennett's pianoforte music. As early as 1839, Bennett had been elected a member of the *Society for the Encouragement of Music* in the Netherlands, a Society which aimed at assisting young composers of that nationality, and he had subsequently, as a member, taken his share in criticising compositions submitted to the Society for publication. When asked by the same Society to contribute a pianoforte Solo of his own to an Album which they published, he responded in his most finished style by writing for them early in 1854 his 'Toccata' in C minor, Op. 38, which has generally been reckoned one of the most successful of his minor works, and which was, at all events, a grateful offering to Holland and his Dutch friends. As a recognition from another foreign country, he received, in 1851, a request signed by Berlioz and other French musicians to become an Honorary member of a new Philharmonic Society which they had recently founded in Paris. Attentions of this kind were consoling to an English musician of Bennett's time. He preserved and valued such diplomas, though he confined their exhibition to the walls of his dressing-room.

A year now passed (Nov. 1854—Nov. 1855) leaving no events to record, out of the usual course, in Bennett's life. There is, however, one letter of his, preserved by Madame Schumann, which belongs to the time and cannot be overlooked. When he wrote to the Schumanns in 1850, he invited them to concerts of his own. It might, therefore, be hinted that he had some business interest in the matter. The following letter is inserted because it can bear no such construction, and because there seems something to admire in the fact of one pianist[1] pressing another to come and enter his own preserves, while he merely asks for himself the privilege of preparing her way.

LONDON, 15 RUSSELL PLACE,
FITZROY SQUARE,
November 1st, 1854.

MY DEAR MADAME SCHUMANN,

I am flattered to think that a letter from me might be acceptable to you, and that you would not refuse to listen to my persuasions that you would soon pay England a visit and give the English people the benefit of your acquaintance and your eminent talent. I can tell you with the very greatest confidence that you would be received with enthusiasm and I think you would in every way be satisfied that you had at last paid a visit to London. For my own part it would be a great pleasure to me to be of the least assistance to you in your previous arrangements, and to make your stay in England as comfortable as possible—and if you will excuse me also saying one word upon *business*, I think you would make a very profitable journey. I should be glad if you would tell me when you would come and how long you would stay, and if you would give me leave to accept engagements for you, and how much for each Concert et cetera—then I would take care to have a good business prepared for you. Pray write to me this very soon—and if you will come first to our house, until we can get you a nice Lodging, it will give us very great pleasure to see you.

And now, I hope you will be able to tell me that my dear friend, Rob. Schumann, is recovering from his distressing illness. I have never ceased to think of this sad trouble and to make every enquiry, and latterly I was

---

[1] Bennett was still playing in public at the time.

delighted to receive better news of him. It will give me so much satisfaction, if you will not fail to tell me all you can upon this subject—and now, my dear Madam, with the kind regards of my Wife and myself, believe me

Ever yours sincerely,

WILLIAM STERNDALE BENNETT.

Madame Schumann gave favourable consideration to the proposal; but, as to the result, *The Musical World* of March 10, 1855, wrote thus:—

'CLARA WIECK-SCHUMANN.—A letter has been received by Mr Sterndale Bennett, with whom this eminent pianist was to have stayed as a guest during her proposed residence in England, stating that, in consequence of the precarious state of her husband's health, she has decided, in obedience to the advice of his medical counsellors, upon not visiting London this season.'

Madame Schumann's first appearance in England was destined to be more conspicuously associated with Bennett, than it would have been if it had occurred in 1855. The circumstances of his life now underwent a change, and at last, in his fortieth year, he was called forward to hold public positions of importance.

PART IV
CALLED TO THE FRONT

CHAPTER XVI.

PUBLIC APPOINTMENTS.

1855—1856.

æt. 39, 40.

COSTA, after having held the conductorship of the Philharmonic for nine years, resigned it at the end of 1854. His reasons were not published, but thenceforth he was completely estranged from those who governed the Society. His position in the musical world had become so high, and his following amongst amateurs so large and influential, that a diminished subscription list seemed a certain sequel, unless some very distinguished musician could be found to succeed him. The Directors searched the Continent and, after several disappointments, Anderson travelled to Zurich and secured the services of Richard Wagner. Sainton has been credited with suggesting this. Wagner came over, entered upon his work with great zeal, acknowledged the *esprit de corps* among the English players, and admired the wonderful tone of the stringed instruments. It was found, however, that neither his name, nor his conducting, nor as yet his works, were attractive to the English public. He had no chance, in the short hours allotted to rehearsals, of changing, to the extent he wished to do, the style of the orchestral playing. The band did not respond to him, while the Directors argued with him about his readings of the Symphonies. George Hogarth, who, as Secretary of the Society, was behind the scenes, wrote some years later that the Philharmonic season of 1855 'was on the whole neither pleasant nor satisfactory,' and that at its close 'Mr Wagner hastened to take his departure from England.'

The Society was now in serious difficulties. The members met, altered laws, reduced the number of annual concerts from eight to six, and relieved the Directors of the power or of the responsibility of nominating a Conductor. At a general meeting of members held on November 19, 1855, Bennett was elected to the vacant office. He accepted it, though not without hesitation. Past grievances might be forgotten, but he was being asked to take the helm of what many people thought a sinking ship. Davison wrote:—
'If Mr Sterndale Bennett makes a failure as conductor of the Philharmonic concerts, he does neither more nor less than peril his status as the most eminent Professor of music in this country. * * * The question is, *can he* succeed and in such an arena? We are inclined to think he *cannot*, and therefore regret that he should have consented to accept the post. * * * It is indisputable that the members of the orchestra *will not* (we don't say *can*not) pay the requisite attention to any other conductor than Mr Costa. * * * This was painfully felt by Herr Wagner last season, since who in his senses can deny * * * the shameful inattention of the band under his direction?'

The Athenæum and other journals added their comments on the disorganized state into which the band had drifted, as also on the secession of some of the leading violinists, owing to a dispute with the Directors over the positions assigned to them in the orchestra; and considered that Bennett was taking office at a most inauspicious time. Wagner had been rejected, and the shout of 'Costa aut nullus' grew the louder.

Notwithstanding these dismal prognostications, the 1856 season eventually proved very interesting from an artistic point of view, and successful from a financial one. Bennett, immediately after his election, was admitted to the confidence of the Directors and he eagerly entered into the plans of a new campaign. His interest in the Society was by no means limited to the special duty for which he was engaged.

The re-appearance in England of Madame Jenny Lind-Goldschmidt towards the end of 1855, after an absence of more than five years, and the announcement of a series of Oratorio and miscellaneous concerts which were to be given by her during the winter months, aroused much expectation, while concert-managers viewed with some alarm the effect that so powerful an attraction might have upon their undertakings. At the Philharmonic, it was wisely seen that possible advantage rather than the reverse might be derived from her presence in this country, and the Directors made bold to ask her to appear at one of their concerts. This, after due consideration, Madame Goldschmidt generously agreed to do; 'but, why did she agree?' wrote Davison, 'I can tell you. It was because her husband, Herr Otto Goldschmidt, himself an admirable musician, entertained a high respect for the genius and talents of Professor Sterndale Bennett who is more of a prophet in Germany than in his own country. For this reason and for no other (I have it from the best authority, that of Herr Goldschmidt himself) Madame Jenny Lind consented to sing for the Philharmonic Society.' When the announcement, couched in somewhat ambiguous terms, was made, that the great singer would help the Society, and rumour spread the idea that she would appear on more than one evening, the subscription list began to lengthen. Her absence on a provincial tour, during the earlier weeks of the London season, heightened the interest attaching to the few farewell performances to be given in June, before her final retirement, and the knowledge that one of these last appearances would be at the Philharmonic, with the constant promise of it on the programmes of the earlier concerts, kept the subscribers in a state of pleasurable excitement throughout the season. Madame Lind-Goldschmidt, having once consented, did not spare herself in fulfilling her promise. She did not limit herself to the one or two vocal pieces usually given at the concerts. Her singing, a few months before, in a performance of Schumann's 'Paradise and the Peri' at the Lower Rhine Festival, had made a deep impression upon her hearers, and it was now suggested, in the first instance by Mr Otto Goldschmidt himself, that this work should, with her assistance, be produced at the Philharmonic. The idea was at once seized upon. In close connection with it, another interesting musical event took place, by which a desire that Bennett had felt for years was at length gratified.

LONDON, 15 RUSSELL PLACE,
FITZROY SQUARE.
January 21, 1856.

MY DEAR MADAME SCHUMANN,

You will receive by this post a letter from the Directors of the Philharmonic Society to ask if you have the intention to visit England this summer. I am now the Music-Director of these Concerts, and I am so very anxious that you should perform at them.

Also I am very anxious to give the 'Paradise and the Peri' if Madame Jenny Lind will sing in it, and the Directors will invite her. Altogether it will be a very happy thing to see you in London, and I think you will be very satisfied with your visit. Would you also write a letter to Madame Lind to use your influence with her to sing in 'The Peri.' Pray let me know your plans as soon as possible, and believe me,

Yours very sincerely,

WILLIAM STERNDALE BENNETT.

I do not forget to think of my friend Robert. Do let me know if there is any improvement. What a beautiful work is 'The Peri.'

Again, a week later, he wrote to Madame Schumann: 'You must write and tell me when you can come, it would be very good that you should make your *debût* in England at the first concert on April 14. * * * We have a *Conferenz* at the Philharmonic Society next Saturday, and I wish to say that *you will come*. Write me all your ideas and questions and I will be sure to answer them, but be sure to come to England in April, and make your first appearance at the Philharmonic.'

Bennett conducted his first rehearsal on Saturday, April 12, and the first concert on April 14, his fortieth birthday occurring on the intervening Sunday.

An Opening-Night

UNDER THE IMMEDIATE PATRONAGE OF
Her Majesty.
HIS ROYAL HIGHNESS PRINCE ALBERT.
HER ROYAL HIGHNESS THE DUCHESS OF KENT.

PHILHARMONIC SOCIETY.

FIRST CONCERT, MONDAY, APRIL 14, 1856.

PART I.

Sinfonia in C minor (dedicated to the Philharmonic Society) -	- *Mendelssohn.*
Recit. {"E Susanna non viene"} Madame CLARA NOVELLO (Le Nozze di	
Aria {"Dove sono"} Figaro) - - - -	- *Mozart.*
Concerto in E flat, Pianoforte, Madame CLARA SCHUMANN (her first appearance in England) - - -	- *Beethoven.*
Overture (Don Carlos) - - - - -	- *Macfarren.*

PART II.

Sinfonia in A, No. 7 - - - - -	- *Beethoven.*
Recit. {"Sì, morir"} } Madame CLARA NOVELLO (Corno Inglese,	
Aria {"Ma negli estremi istanti"} Mr NICHOLSON) Il Giuramento	- *Mercadante.*
Solo, Pianoforte (17 Variations Sérieuses) Madame SCHUMANN -	- *Mendelssohn.*
Overture, "Preciosa" - - - - -	- *Weber.*

Conductor—Professor STERNDALE BENNETT.

⁂ *To commence at Eight o'clock. Doors will be open at Half-past Seven o'clock precisely.*

THE SECOND CONCERT WILL TAKE PLACE ON THE 28TH INST.

'The new conductor'—wrote *The Morning Herald*—'was received both by orchestra and visitors with warm and cordial recognition, from which it may be inferred that the appointment has been agreeable to the patrons of the Society. The office upon which Mr Bennett enters is one of responsibility and onerousness, but he is already well versed in its functions, although he has not of late been called upon to discharge them. It is time, however, that English interests should prevail, and that the foreign reproaches that we have no conductor worthy of the name, should be gainsaid by proof. * * * Mr Bennett, who was probably somewhat nervous, nevertheless acquitted himself well, and the reading of the music was everything that could be desired. The players seemed anxious to second the indications of the conductor by every possible attention.'

Madame Schumann had arrived a few days before the concert, and had taken up a temporary residence at the Bennetts' house in Russell Place, where she found a sympathetic welcome awaiting her. The illness of her husband, and her anxiety on his account, were distressing accompaniments to a sojourn in a strange country. Within an hour or two of entering the house, she betook herself to Bennett's pianoforte and played many pieces to Mrs Bennett and her family. The front dining-room, with a grand pianoforte from Broadwood's, was reserved for her own use. Old servants, living in the house at the time, remember how they were asked by the Bennetts to pay special attention to a distinguished lady who was coming to stay with them, and who was in great trouble. One of them remembers being sent all over London by her mistress to procure some lilies-of-the-valley, which proved to be the last birthday souvenir sent to Robert Schumann by his wife. Mrs Bennett was able to give great assistance to Madame Schumann in getting up her first pianoforte recitals and in securing a good audience, such being work that she had always done in connection with Bennett's own concerts. Thirty-three years later, when Madame Schumann addressed a letter, on the subject of Bennett's musicianship[1], to the present writer, she added a remembrance of Mrs Bennett in the words: 'Besides this, I never shall forget how kind your parents both were to me when I first came to England.'

Bennett's prediction of the favour with which Madame Schumann would be received in England was well fulfilled. The author of the article on Madame Schumann, in the first edition of Grove's *Dictionary of Music and Musicians*, had been misinformed when he wrote:—'Her reception in this conservative country was hardly such as to encourage her to repeat her visit, and many years passed before she returned.' As a matter of fact, she came the very next year, as also in 1859. Moreover, from the first

[1] The letter contains the words: 'My husband spoke so often of him [Bennett] as one of the Pianists he most admired.'

she was greeted with respect and admiration by the leading critics and with enthusiasm by the audiences. Schumann's music may have wanted time to make its way, but it was not left to a later generation of music-lovers to appreciate Madame Schumann as a pianist. *The Morning Herald*, after her first performance, wrote:—'It would be difficult to describe the effect Madame Schumann produced. It amounted to a positive sensation, even among those who are moved with difficulty, and are excited only when the illustrative genius is of the highest order.'

As the concerts of this year progressed, *The Athenæum* enquired why no music of Bennett's was introduced, seeing that the reason for excluding it no longer remained. Bennett, throughout the time in which he held the conductorship, frequently asked the Directors not to introduce compositions of his own. He would, indeed, have made some condition on the subject, as Mendelssohn is said to have done at Leipzig, only they would not listen to him. For one thing, the works of other British composers were seldom placed upon the programmes, and he would not like, whilst he was Conductor, to have a prominence given to his music if his fellow-countrymen did not share the honours. Constant complaints can be found in the writings of those times about the musicians of this country not combining, and seizing opportunities to further each others' interests. It is not so easy to find where such opportunities arose. Sir George Macfarren has written of Bennett in this connection:—'Somewhere about the year 1840 he had a concert in Hanover Square which, for some reasons I forget, was more notable than those previously given, and because it was so he asked to have a work of mine included, to mark our dear and old connection. In the same spirit in 1856, when appointed Philharmonic conductor, he specially urged the insertion of an overture of mine at the first concert.' It will be told how and why Bennett soon ceased to influence the choice of music at the Philharmonic; but it is worth notice that while he did so, he could put in a word for a compatriot. Another English overture, the 'Antony and Cleopatra' of Cipriani Potter, was heard at the third concert. Then a work of Bennett's did appear, but with an exceptional reason for its performance. Miss Arabella

Goddard, by playing his Concerto in C minor, carried the point on which she had insisted three years before, when Costa's condition, to conduct no work that he objected to, had led to the cancelling of her engagement.

The series of concerts closed with the performance of the 'Paradise and the Peri' on June 23. The work had been already performed on February 10 and March 8, 1854, under the direction of William Glover, in Dublin. It was now given for the first time in London. The German version of the poem, to which Schumann had set his music, had been retranslated for this occasion by W. Bartholomew, Moore's words being used by him as far as possible. Madame Schumann, who sang in the chorus at the concert, had actively assisted Bennett during the long and laborious rehearsals, upon which both he and all concerned had bestowed great pains. The better to rivet the attention of the audience, he had arranged a thematic programme. This may, at the time, have been thought an eccentricity, for it was not then printed[1].

The singing of Madame Lind-Goldschmidt was by itself sufficient to attract 'one of the largest and most brilliant assemblages' that George Hogarth had ever seen in the Hanover Square Rooms. 'The Queen and Prince Albert, with the Prince of Wales, the Princess Royal, and the Princess Alice were present, together with the Prince of Prussia, Prince Oscar of Sweden, and a numerous and splendid *cortége* of English and foreign nobility and gentry. Most of the musical celebrities now in London were among the audience.' The performance was praised by the critics; but three hours of music in a style as yet unfamiliar to English ears failed to hold the audience, and the work was very coldly received. 'With many beauties,' wrote Hogarth—that kindest and most cautious of judges—'it was on the whole laboured and heavy[2].'

Bennett has been credited, on the authority of many of his musical acquaintances, with a limited appreciation of

---

[1] The writer has the MS. with the names of Madame Lind-Goldschmidt and other singers who took part in the 1856 performance appended to the pieces they sang. It was printed and circulated with the programmes at a later performance which Bennett conducted in 1866.

[2] See Note, in Appendix A, on the conditions under which this performance took place.

Schumann as a composer. To this point some reference may be made later. Meanwhile it is a pleasure to record the care and interest he took in an early effort to introduce to this country the noble-hearted musician whom he always so lovingly spoke of as 'my own dear personal friend.'

The members of the Philharmonic Society, at their next general meeting, passed a unanimous vote of thanks to their Conductor for his 'zealous and able services.' The Directors addressed him the following encouraging letter:—

HANOVER SQUARE ROOMS,
June 28, 1856.

DEAR SIR,

We the undersigned Directors of the Philharmonic Society, at the close of a highly gratifying season, beg to congratulate you on the very great success which has attended your labours, and to thank you most cordially for your great and able exertions which have been of such essential benefit to the Society.

We are, with much esteem,
Your sincere friends,
G. F. ANDERSON,
&c., &c.

A few weeks after Bennett's appointment to the Philharmonic conductorship, and before he had entered upon its duties, the chance occurred of trying for another important post. By the death of Thomas Attwood Walmisley in January, 1856, the Professorship of Music in Cambridge University fell vacant. In past times this office had usually been bestowed, by an unopposed 'Grace' of the Senate, upon some eminent musician already connected with the University. Walmisley's death created a void which could not be filled up so readily. During the latter part of his life he had discharged all the chief musical duties in the University, playing on the Sunday at as many as eight services in the chapels of the three principal Colleges and at the University Church[1]. Cambridge had therefore now

[1] As a ninth duty of the day, he regularly conducted a performance of sacred vocal music in the Hall of Trinity College.

lost its sole musical representative, and there was no one at hand who could be regarded as his natural successor in the Professorship. It was therefore announced that the choice would on this occasion be made by open poll of the Senate, and an opportunity was thus given for free competition. Such a chance had previously occurred but once during at least a hundred years. No less than forty candidates made preliminary enquiries. Dr Whewell, the Vice-Chancellor, wrote on January 25, 'I am perfectly overwhelmed with applications for the Professorship of Music, and for the organist's place.'

Bennett took counsel with his valued mentor, Sir George Smart, but got no encouragement from him. Charles Edward Horsley was already in the field, and Sir George held that the influence which would support the member of so distinguished a family must prove irresistible. Bennett, nevertheless, decided to take his chance. He corresponded with Horsley, and a friendly rivalry was agreed on. 'Whatever may be the result of this election,' wrote Horsley, 'I am quite sure that it will make no difference in our friendly feeling towards each other, but rather cause us to rejoice that either should have succeeded in obtaining any position he desired.'

Bennett was, of course, not unknown in Cambridge. A man with so tender a regard for old associations was not likely to lose touch with the home of his early youth. It had remained one of the few places out of London where he had from time to time appeared as a pianist. This was mainly due to his friendship with Thomas Wood, a well-known music-seller in the town, and organizer of local concerts. About the year 1850, Wood had introduced performances of classical Chamber-music in 'The Aldermen's Parlour' at the Guildhall, and Bennett from that time had gone up once or twice a year to support his friend in the scheme, taking with him the artists with whom he usually played in London. 'The audience'—writes the Rev. W. T. Kingsley—'was small but appreciative, and the concerts were, without exception, the most enjoyable I ever attended.' Bennett's playing, and especially the interpretation of Beethoven's Trios with Molique and Piatti, are remembered both by Mr Kingsley and Mr A. D.

Coleridge to have been the subject of much remark among the small coterie which in those days clustered round Walmisley, and learnt from that many-sided man to admire the higher forms of secular instrumental music. Walmisley, though best known as an organist, was also a skilful and charming pianist, with much interpretative power. One day, when he was called upon to play at a concert of Wood's, he said very modestly to Mr A. D. Coleridge: 'It is hard upon me to have to play this music so soon after Sterndale Bennett.' Walmisley and Bennett probably met, or at least heard of each other very early in life, for they were both favourites of Attwood. They certainly knew each other in 1836 and 1838, when the young Cambridge Professor—a Professor of the University while still an undergraduate reading for mathematical honours—was a constant visitor at the cottage in Grantchester, where Bennett was writing his works for Leipzig. Walmisley always retained a warm appreciation of Bennett's musicianship, and took pleasure in introducing his compositions to the notice of Cambridge amateurs.

It was these disciples of Walmisley that now saw in Bennett the most desirable successor to their lamented friend. Among them were the Rev. W. T. Kingsley, Fellow and Tutor of Sidney, and three others who held high positions in Trinity, the Rev. F. Martin, the Rev. A. Thacker, and the Rev. W. C. Mathison. Another valuable supporter was Mrs Frere, widow of a former Master of Downing, noted for the fine style of her singing and for other musical accomplishments, of which her ready reading from score or figured bass was not the least remarkable. In her husband's life-time she had presided over an artistic *salon* at Downing Lodge, and, though now advanced in years, she had lost none of her vigour or of her position in the University as an authority on musical matters. Bennett's beautiful singing, in his earlier student-days, of Handel and Mozart, remained a tradition in Cambridge families. The writer has met men whose grandmothers had often talked to them about it. Mr Frank H. Henslow, in a letter from Madras in 1870, recalled his Cambridge friends of forty years before, and reminded Bennett of dramatic[1] and musical performances at Downing Lodge. 'I remember you,' he wrote, 'as a happy merry boy in a round blue jacket. * * * How well I remember your singing "Una voce poco fa."' There can be no doubt Mrs Frere's appreciation of Bennett dated from those early days.

His friends found it no easy task to explain their candidate to the Cambridge dons. As the sequel showed, some interest was excited, but no great number of resident electors went to the poll. A large majority, unversed in musical matters, would, if it were merely a case of choosing the best musician, leave the decision to those who had special knowledge; but there were other claims than mere musicianship which, if advanced, might lead to a more general expression of opinion.

Sir John Herschel wrote: 'I hear great things of Mr S. Bennett as a composer who will not be led out of harmony and melody by fiddle-de-dee, and moreover that he is in very high esteem as a master of composition, a very different thing from a "music-master." On these grounds he is sure of a certain support at Cambridge, but on these *alone* I should hardly feel quite clear that I ought to meddle with his election as Professor of Music at Cambridge.

'But if he is really disposed to raise that very low nonentity the Musical Professorship into a worthy and efficient position—by giving lectures in which the principles of the physical science of sound shall be made (as at a *scientific* University they ought to be) an integral feature (though of course a subordinate one), to illustrate these lectures by experiments, both physical and artistic (so far as a reasonable consideration of expense will enable him), to do, in short, for Cambridge what Donaldson is doing for Edinburgh; then in that case all I *can* do to forward his election, I will.'

Sir John Herschel's ideal candidate, able to do what Professor Donaldson had done, and at the same time to show himself a masterly composer, could scarcely have been found in England. But if a scientific man with some knowledge of music had come forward there might have

---

[1] Mrs Frere counted Mrs Siddons amongst her friends.

been, as at Edinburgh twelve years before, a warm controversy in Cambridge. Another question did arise which gave trouble to Bennett's supporters. A certain candidate came forward as the champion of religious music. He issued a florid address, advocating, in English church music, a reformation which the authority of a University Professor could do much to promote; disparaging secular music as a worldly amusement and sensual enjoyment; and descending to an electioneering artifice by mentioning 'a kind of patchwork church service selected from Mozart's Masses which he had heard, and which he understood was called "Bennett[1] and Mozart in E♭."' Here was a 'party-cry' which might appeal to clerical tutors, the great majority of whom, when outside a college chapel, had no notion of music other than that of a siren luring undergraduates to their destruction. Walmisley's old friends, who happened to know something of the extent of the candidate's musical acquirements, viewed with some alarm the progress he was making. He had a plausible policy. On the other hand, Bennett, the secular composer, the pianist, the 'music-master,' could not be said to have the usual qualifications which precedent associated with the Professorship. He was not known as a church composer. He had not even concocted the medley church service, the 'Bennett and Mozart in E♭,' for which his religious rival wished the electors to credit him. In due course, however, it proved possible to convince many that the candidate was not sufficiently versed in his profession to 'champion' or 'reform' any branch of Music, and when Walmisley's friends succeeded in proving this, he retired.

The electors included non-resident members of the Senate. Many of these were reached through Bennett's past and present pupils. Here Mrs Bennett left no stone unturned to help her husband, spending a month over continuous correspondence. To press his claims, Bennett himself did not do much. He issued a short address, and circulated the testimonials, without additions, which he had used twelve years before at Edinburgh. As the election drew near, he was persuaded to go up to Cambridge to do a little personal canvassing, and was supplied with a large

[1] Not Sterndale Bennett, but very likely to be mistaken for him.

number of electioneering cards with which to introduce himself. He endured two or three interviews. At the last of them the lady of the house expressed her desire for 'a more classical musician.' He then lost heart and went home.

In the end, the choice was known to lie between Horsley, Bennett, and Dr Elvey, Organist of St George's Chapel, Windsor. It was impossible, owing to the uncertainty of the non-resident vote, to gauge the chances, and the result was looked forward to with some curiosity. Bennett and his wife understood that the Horsley party were very sanguine of success. Dr Whewell wrote from Trinity Lodge on February 24: 'We are here growing more and more eager about the election of a Professor of Music. I have fixed Tuesday, the 4th, for the election. Mrs Frere is very zealous for Mr Sterndale Bennett; and, by way of falling in with her humour, I have asked her to come and stay with me here[1], and canvass the College and the University to her heart's content. I think too Lord Monteagle will come and vote, though I hardly know for whom. It is wonderful what a stir this election makes in London.'

Bennett went up to Cambridge to be present at the election, leaving his wife in a state of great anxiety. March 4, in Russell Place, was spent in dead silence until Mrs Bennett's tension was relieved by the receipt of a telegram from her husband's friend, Wood: 'Professorship of Music, March 4th, 3 p.m.—Close of the poll. Bennett one hundred and seventy-four[2]; Elvey twenty-four; Horsley twenty-one.'

Bennett's friends had come from all parts of the country. Members of the Goold family had crossed from Ireland. Mrs Frere made one of her last appearances in University precincts. Surrounded by a group of friends, she stood leaning on her crook-stick and watching with keen interest the progress of the voting in the Arts' School. When she subsequently spoke a few kind words, by way of consolation,

---

[1] Mrs Frere lived a few miles out of Cambridge.

[2] The identical number of votes which he had secured when he once before went to the *poll* (see p. 35). Newspapers, however, reported his votes at Cambridge as 173.

to Dr Elvey, she added: 'I am eighty-five years of age, but I can still sing up to A.'

The majority which Bennett had obtained by the middle of the day caused surprise on all sides, because a close contest had been expected. Suspense, however, continued till the arrival from London of another train which surely would, it was thought, bring up more voters for the other candidates. A rush was made to the Bull Hotel to meet the omnibuses from the railway-station. Only one drew up, and the Bennett party were greatly relieved to see, as its sole occupant, the somewhat diminutive Charles Steggall, who had come up in the hope of being among the first to congratulate his master. The bells of St Mary's were pealed in those days in honour of a new University Officer, so Bennett, when he had cheerfully done his duty by the Bell-ringers, retained, as a little souvenir of a red-letter day, the card which they had left upon him, and without further delay, returned to his work in London.

CHAPTER XVII.

THE CAMBRIDGE PROFESSORSHIP.

AFTER Bennett's election at Cambridge was announced in the newspapers, few hours elapsed before he was reading letters in which the writers mingled their congratulations on his success with their hopes of being the first to satisfy his requirements for a degree in music, and in the course of the next month or two he found himself besieged with enquiries as to the conditions on which such degrees were granted. In a book kept for copies of Cambridge correspondence, no drafts of replies to these earliest applications are entered. He was not as yet prepared to do more than acknowledge their receipt. Authorized information on the 'Proceedings in Music' as given in *The Cambridge Calendar* and a few other books was scant and vague. It would be necessary for him to submit doubtful points to the consideration of University authorities, and to draw precedents, if possible, from the rulings of his predecessors.

Meanwhile it was thought advisable that he should take a degree himself, and on June 16 Dr Whewell wrote: —'On your composing an Anthem for Commencement Sunday to be performed in St Mary's Church, I have reason to believe that the University will grant you the degree of Doctor of Music. I shall be most happy to forward the proceeding as far as it depends upon me.' The next day Bennett was in Cambridge making the needful arrangements for the performance of the as yet unwritten music. During the same week occurred long rehearsals of Schumann's 'Paradise and the Peri' in London. In the next week, on Monday, June 23, he gave seven hours' lessons, also took his classes at Queen's College, and conducted the

'Paradise and the Peri' at the Philharmonic in the evening. Tuesday he spent with his pupils at Brighton. Then the Anthem for the following Sunday had to be considered. Limiting his teaching on Wednesday and Thursday to thirteen hours between the two days, he gave the rest of his time to composition, Miss Johnston being at hand to superintend the copying. On Friday he only gave one lesson, and on Saturday afternoon the Anthem in several movements[1], with parts copied for a large double choir, was rehearsed in Trinity College Chapel under his own direction.

The Cambridge Chronicle thus referred to the music after it had been sung on 'Commencement' Sunday in the University Church:—'An anthem composed by Professor W. S. Bennett, as an exercise for the degree of Doctor of Music was performed. Mr Hopkins, organist of the University Church and of Trinity College, presided at the Organ. The subject of the Anthem was taken from the 15th Psalm "Lord, who shall dwell in thy tabernacle?" The conception of the composition is original and effective, the question "Lord, who shall dwell, &c." preceding each of the verses in recitative answered by a double choir. In one of the movements is introduced the English chorale "St Mary's," the University Church bearing that name. The placid character of the chorale is strongly contrasted by a declaration of the choir to another subject in strong unison. This is followed by an elegant movement of a pastoral character, which breaks into a massive original chorale at the conclusion to the words of the "Gloria Patri."'

The Anthem, though not musically elaborate, was designed on a scale showing due respect to the importance of the occasion, and it may be said, on the authority of the Rev. J. R. Lunn, that it made a favourable impression on those who were judging Bennett, as a writer of sacred music, for the first time. On the next day the Senate passed a 'Grace' authorizing the Senior Proctor to present Professor W. S. Bennett for the degree of Doctor of Music.

As an explanation of the fact that, in those days, the

---

[1] The Anthem is published, but in an abbreviated form.

conferment of a degree was reported twice over on successive dates in *University Intelligence*, Bennett made the memorandum :—'I took my degree of Mus. D. on Monday June 30th in the afternoon, and was "created" the next morning at half-past ten o'clock. The latter is a form seldom gone through by musical graduates.' Dr Whewell wrote on July 1:—'To-day * * * and * * * have been to the Senate House together, to see the great show of the Commencement, when the prize poems are recited, and all the ladies collect. The Senate House was full without being too full, and the gentlemen had the grace to let the ladies have the seats, so the house looked prettier than I ever saw it look before. Among the new Doctors we had Mr Sterndale Bennett, but he did not appear in the beautiful "singing-robes," as Milton calls the poet's official dress, which poor Professor Walmisley used to wear.'

The fine specimen of a Doctor of Music's gown which had belonged to Professor Walmisley, and before him to Professor Clarke Whitfeld, was later purchased by Bennett, and occasionally worn by him in the Senate House, or when conducting exercises for musical degrees. On this occasion, however, he wore the 'congregation-robe' of a Doctor of Laws. In so doing, as well as by suggesting, which he himself did, that he should be presented by the Senior Proctor, he was observing old traditions[1]. This was of a piece with the care he took in other ways, while trying to regulate the 'Proceedings in Music,' to avoid taking liberties with the few enactments he could discover.

The latest and fullest information about musical degrees, and about the Professor's connection with them, was contained in the following paragraph which is taken from a Report (published 1852) of the University Commissioners. It was probably contributed by Walmisley, for his name appears in the Report in connection with other information therein given.

'The University confers the degrees of Bachelor and

---

[1] Graduates in Music were not members of the Senate and had no 'Congregation-robes' assigned to them. When required in the Senate House, a Grace had to be passed, first, to admit them, and secondly to allow them to wear the robe of another Faculty. An old enactment, originating probably from the scarcity of Graduates in Music, provided that when no Doctor of Music was at hand the Senior Proctor should make the presentation.

Doctor of Music. The conditions for both degrees are the same, namely that the candidate be a member of some College, and that he satisfy the Professor of Music as to his proficiency in the art, *more especially*[1] by composing a solemn piece of music to be performed, at the appointment of the Vice-Chancellor, before the University.'

Bennett's correspondence shows how well he weighed each phrase of the brief text, and how he tried to make the most of it. The four points he took into consideration were as follows:—

(1) The nature of the 'solemn piece of music,' or 'Canticum' as it was elsewhere described.

(2) The relationship, if any, between the degrees of Bachelor and Doctor.

(3) Other tests of proficiency which the Professor might apply in addition to the Exercise; the use of the words *more especially* indicating that something else had been required.

(4) The construction to be placed on the condition that 'the candidate be a member of some College.'

In settling the nature of the composition required, he had the advantage of an old friendship with his predecessor's father, who had written to congratulate him on his election, and had, at the same time, offered any assistance in his power. The writer well remembers being present at a pathetic interview in the house of T. F. Walmisley at Westminster, when the veteran musician—a noted vocal composer—gave personal mementoes of his 'dear son' to Bennett, together with correspondence which had passed between Professor Walmisley, shortly before his death, and certain candidates for degrees. So in September (1856) Bennett was able to write to an applicant:—

'It is required of a candidate for a degree in music at Cambridge that he compose a "Canticum" which shall exhibit his mastery in the Art to the entire satisfaction of the Professor. The exercise hitherto exacted from the candidates for the degree of Bachelor is an *important* composition for five voices with full orchestral accompaniment.'

Then, again, in reply to a candidate's suggestion that, in

---

[1] These words are underlined by the present writer.

respect to the Doctor's degree, he was acting arbitrarily, and exceeding the conditions hitherto imposed, he wrote :—
'It is *not* doubtful that the Professor can adopt any test that he may think desirable, to assure himself of the requisite attainments of candidates for degrees in music at Cambridge. I do not dispute for one moment that your impressions consequent upon your interview and conversation with my predecessor, Dr Walmisley, are as you state them, still I must tell you that his *rule* (which I cannot wish to relax but would rather tighten) was to require from those wishing to become Doctor in Music, that they should write an important exercise for eight voices, with an accompaniment for a full orchestra. I have these directions in his own handwriting added to the testimony of the last Doctor made, a pupil of my own. In my opinion a degree in music in a University should be gained with great effort, and be the result of a series of successful works, the candidate exhibiting great research in the theory, and great facility in the practice.'

In the same letter Bennett announced his intention of advising candidates to apply for the degree of Bachelor before that of Doctor. No regulation connected the two degrees. *The Cambridge Calendar* reprinted from year to year an old statement: 'A Mus. D. is *generally* Mus. B.;' but even this had ceased to be true. The possibility of proceeding at once to the higher degree had in course of time lowered any value attaching to the other, and when Bennett became Professor the Bachelor's degree had not been taken for fourteen years. He determined to increase its importance, persevered, and succeeded in doing so. Apart from the traditional form of the 'Exercise,' it rested entirely with himself to determine the standard of musical merit, and this, from the first, he made sufficiently high for young men to feel content if they could satisfy him for the Bachelor's degree. He never disguised the fact, but clearly set it down in his syllabus of information that the senior degree could be taken alone. Nevertheless, when it became common knowledge that he was a difficult man to approach, the way in which he wished to be approached seemed also generally understood, and, as it turned out, no one, during the nineteen years of Bennett's Professorship, took the Doctor's degree who had not previously taken the other.

On two other doubtful points he first consulted the Rev. Joseph Romilly, the University Registrary, who had very courteously offered to place at Bennett's disposal the knowledge he possessed of University procedure.

LONDON, *October* 5, 1856.

DEAR SIR,

You gave me permission to trouble you upon any points connected with my Professorship. * * * Without referring to what has been customary, I wish to ask your opinion upon the following matters:

(1) Ought I not to examine the candidates themselves as well as their exercises, or at any rate examine their exercises in their presence?

(2) Could I not fix a day for my examination at *Cambridge*, and should not the candidate have previously entered a College?

To this the Registrary cautiously replied:—' I think you may demand of the candidates that they submit to a personal "viva-voce" examination over and above the exercise, as a test that they are really the composers of it. It seems to me that the examination should be subject to your approval of the exercise. I think you should arrange with each individual approved candidate to call on you, in London or Cambridge, according to the circumstances of his case.

'I do not approve of your idea that a candidate should be a member of some College. Such a regulation can only be made *by the University*, and I doubt extremely the University being willing to make such an enactment.'

But Bennett again wrote:—

'The University of Oxford has lately passed a Statute respecting degrees in Music, a copy of which I will procure and transmit to you. I am anxious that our degrees in Music at Cambridge should be equal in reputation to those of the sister University.

'I really cannot think it just, that candidates should be

entitled to examination without having paid any fees to the University (this is not the case in any other faculty as far as I am aware). Were they first obliged to enter a College, I believe they would reflect much more upon the chances of failure, and make themselves much safer. As it is, I am receiving so-called exercises from mere beginners, who try their strength with the chance of a very small penalty, viz., a confidential letter from me advising them to get instruction in the rudiments of the art, and there ends the matter; not, however, without much loss of time to me, and which time I cannot even have the satisfaction of feeling is spent in the service of the University. From Gunning's "Ceremonies" (I do not know how far this book is an authority) it would appear that the first step is to enter a College.'

The Registrary—whose letters cannot be quoted at enough length to show the great courtesy and consideration with which he treated the Professor of Music—still maintained that membership of a College was only necessary on the eve of taking a degree, i.e. after the candidate had been approved by the Professor. Bennett, therefore, waited for some fresh opportunity of pressing his point. He was, in the meantime, glad to get approval of his *examination*; but he was determined that this should be held in Cambridge, and that London should be no alternative place as suggested by the Registrary.

In the musical profession, University degrees had for some time been regarded as of no great value, by some even as things to be avoided. Scurrilous suggestions had often been admitted into musical papers, and those who mixed in musical circles often heard doubts expressed in conversation as to the methods by which such distinctions had been obtained. The whole subject had become somewhat 'uncanny.' Goss, the organist of St Paul's, when asked at this time by a lady-pupil why he was not a Doctor of Music, replied: 'Because I would rather not be one.'

It was therefore obviously desirable that the Professor's negotiations with candidates should be conducted with a certain amount of public formality. The University was evidently not prepared to lay down any scheme for musical procedure so definite as that which had just appeared at

Oxford. Bennett was limited to making the best of present conditions and within such limits the authorities were not unwilling to support his efforts.

He had to guard himself from fruitless work and unwarrantable intrusion. He could, in his preliminary correspondence, sympathize with, and write kindly to, the poor clerk, 'sick of the thraldom of the desk,' who begged to be excused 'the scores for separate instruments,' and to be allowed to present his 'accompaniments' in the form adopted in 'Novello's Oratorios' because it happened to be 'such a very busy time at the office.' He could be gentle and write of 'the great love of music' discernible in a 'first attempt at composition' sent him by one who had been 'a sailor for the last nine years,' but had received twenty-four lessons on the organ when a boy. On the other hand, he could not open his heart to the 'self-taught musician' just beginning to write music 'with a rapidity which astonished both his friends and himself.' He shrank from the gentleman who proposed to spend a day in Russell Place, bringing with him from the country not only the 'solemn Canticum' but also comic Operas on which he would like an opinion; nor did he eagerly respond to the candidate who was looking forward to 'a good long chat on church-music in general.'

So, on October 21, he wrote to Dr Whewell :—' Out of several musical exercises which I have received from those wishing to be graduates in music, one or two are likely to prove successful, but before I pass them I am anxious to examine the candidates themselves, and to issue a notice after the manner of other Professors. I therefore ask your permission to name the Public Schools under the Library (close to which there is a small room used as the music-library) as the place of meeting.'

Dr Whewell saw 'no objection' to the proposal; and the first examination was accordingly held in the Arts' School on November 15. A few days later Bennett wrote to Dr Philpott, who had just succeeded Dr Whewell as Vice-Chancellor, informing him that Mr E. Bunnett had passed the examination for the degree of Bachelor of Music. To this he added :—

'I shall await your pleasure as to the time and place of

Mr Bunnett's exercise. I suppose that prior to such performance he should enter his name at a College.

'This leads me to offer as a point for your consideration whether I should not in future be justified in declining to examine any candidate before receiving a certificate of his having entered a College. I cannot think that the authorities would require me to examine any but those who had in some way connected themselves with the University, and I shall be very grateful to you for your opinion on this subject, or if you should think fit, would you be kind enough to bring the matter before the Council?'

The Vice-Chancellor at once replied:—'I have no difficulty in answering the question you propose. The Professor of Music cannot be called upon to examine any person who is not a member of the University, and though in some cases, from kind feeling, the late Professor may have examined the exercises of persons who were not members of the University, the proceeding is irregular and ought not to be drawn into a precedent.'

Thus, before the end of the year, Bennett had a plan of action sufficient for his purpose. He then compiled a circular containing all needful information about entrance into a College, musical exercises and their performance, and the expenses of the degrees. Sir Henry Bishop, as Professor at Oxford, had suffered from the quantity of letters he was obliged to write to 'enquirers' from whom he heard nothing further. Bennett's circular proved a safeguard, not only to his time, but to his feeling of proper pride in his office. When, however, a man, as a member of the University, became a *bonâ-fide* candidate, Bennett spared no trouble, acting in all respects as if he were a College tutor, advising, if needs be, on the direction further studies should take to ensure success, and even at times giving something like actual instruction. Any such work for Cambridge he did most cheerfully. At a later period, when the publication of distinguished musicians' letters was coming into vogue in this country, he would laugh and say that the letters he had received from one candidate alone, during a series of years, would supply two good-sized volumes.

There was no stipend attached to the Professorship during the first twelve or thirteen years he held it, but before his time fees were paid by the graduate to the Professor in consideration of the latter having to conduct the performance of the 'Exercise.' At one time the Bachelor had paid five shillings and the Doctor twenty-five shillings, but these fees had afterwards been raised and in Walmisley's days they stood at five and ten guineas, sums more in accordance with those received for similar services by Professors of other faculties. Bennett may have accepted these payments from the first two graduates of his time, but it is certain that he returned them to the third, and then to all that followed, or destroyed their cheques; for the custom was so far established that, though it was not mentioned in his circular, the fees were generally sent to him. His reason for this course cannot be given with certainty. If the writer's memory is correct, Bennett was unable to find any enactment by which the fees were authorized; but apart from that, at a time when persons could still write of musical degrees as obtainable by purchase, he may have thought it well that at least the candidates themselves should know that he took no pecuniary interest in the matter. To them it had the advantage of reducing a rather heavy expenditure.

The Professor of Music might be called upon to furnish the music for an Ode when a new Chancellor was installed, an event which did not happen on the average oftener than once in twenty years. Otherwise, his only prescribed duty was in connection with degrees, and the discharge of it gave no great prominence to music, or to himself, within the precincts of the University. Much of it lay with unsuccessful candidates and was therefore invisible. But even those who became graduates, unless they were College organists, were practically aliens. Their degrees gave them no place in the Senate. At the Colleges where they entered their names, but never resided, they were unknown. There was a little flutter of interest when their Exercises were performed; but after receiving their titles as a mark of proficiency they departed, and were seldom seen again. A non-resident Professor, who attended to their wants alone, might remain almost as great a stranger as themselves.

Bennett wished, if possible, to be identified with music in Cambridge itself, hoping—as he had written in his address to the electors—to be found 'active and useful, not regarding his office as merely nominal, but remembering that the interests of a great art had been entrusted to his care.' The time was favourable to his purpose, for music during the past two or three years had been making distinct progress in the University, and his place was well prepared for him. In December, 1850, Walmisley had reported to the University Commissioners:—'Music is not cultivated to any great extent by members of the University, but I believe a taste for the art is rapidly increasing amongst us.' At the time this was written there is little doubt some change had begun to take place throughout the country in the attitude of educated men towards music. Among many general and individual influences to which this change might be attributed, one may be selected which would be very likely, in time, to reach a University. Years of hard work spent by such men as John Hullah, his supporters and followers, in pressing upon the clergy and schoolmasters the importance of music as a branch of education, may have already taken effect upon the rising generation of students. In 1853 the members of the University Musical Society were turning their attention to more important music than that which had so far generally appeared upon their programmes, and under the conductorship of Mr W. Amps, an undergraduate of Peterhouse, and a former pupil of Walmisley's, were practising great choral and instrumental works. When Bennett became Professor, three years later, there were in Cambridge, especially among the junior fellows of Colleges and the undergraduates, a goodly number of men with serious intention in their musical pursuits, who were capable of taking their measure of a musician, who were ready to appreciate Bennett, and to welcome his presence among them.

It being the custom for resident members of the University, including the students reading for honours, to stay up for two months of the Long Vacation, Bennett, in the first year of his Professorship, took advantage of this, engaged a furnished house in Addenbrooke Place, and spent his summer holidays in Cambridge. These holidays, for the past two years, had become much longer than before, owing to a change of arrangements at the schools where he taught. The short term of residence in Cambridge, though it involved some sacrifice of the needed rest and retirement which he could only enjoy at that season of the year, served a useful purpose. In the course of a few weeks he made many new acquaintances, and laid the foundation of many close and life-long friendships. The proverbial hospitality of an English University helped him on the way. For the time being he conquered his usual reluctance to play in private society, and readily assisted at musical parties designed for the purpose of 'lionizing' him. Music-meetings of another kind he forthwith arranged himself. Of these the Rev. H. T. Armfield afterwards wrote: 'The first start of Bach in the University was in a walk which I took with him in the Long (1856). Talking of "The Passion," he said: "If you'll go round and get the men, I'll go to London and get the parts and we'll rehearse it."—This we respectively did, and two or three times a week we rehearsed it under him in a Trinity lecture-room all through the Long. This led to a Bach Society of which I was Director. We gave a concert, and with a mad enthusiasm played actually four Concertos of his for two or three pianofortes in one evening.'

It must, however, be said that Walmisley had already diligently brought Bach to the notice of his amateur friends, and had prophesied a future for his choral works in this country. Another zealot was the Rev. J. R. Lunn, a young Fellow of St John's College, who in this same 'Long' was finishing a small manuscript copy of the 48 Preludes and Fugues as a pocket-companion for evening parties! and who also, with the aid of the diagram of a pedal-board painted on the floor beneath his pianoforte, was vigorously practising the Organ Fugues, to the mystification and distraction of the pupils of an eminent mathematical 'coach' in the rooms below.

During this Cambridge holiday Bennett made a further essay at sacred composition. In the Anthem which Dr Whewell had asked him to write, as a preliminary to taking a degree, he made no display of the academic learning which might be looked for in a diploma work. The University had not wished to examine their Professor or to ask him to prepare an 'Exercise.' Now, however, as if to show his skill in more elaborate form, he began an eight-part Motet to the words, 'In Thee, O Lord, do I put my trust,' borrowing for it the opening bars of the first Symphony which he had written for Dr Crotch in his boyhood at The Royal Academy of Music. It was probably while he was weaving in his mind this intricate texture, that he woke up one day from a reverie, to find himself seated in a room the surroundings of which were unfamiliar to him. The three houses in Addenbrooke Place were of the same pattern, and in a fit of abstraction he had entered and settled himself down in the wrong one.

The minute-book of the University Musical Society records a conditional promise on his part that he would annually conduct one of the concerts. The organists who had recently arrived to supply Walmisley's places were young men who had as yet no vested interests which Bennett could injure, while Mr W. Amps, the appointed conductor of the Society, a musical enthusiast whom Bennett at one time often spoke of as his probable successor in the Professorship, was so modest and retiring that he, perhaps more than any one else in Cambridge, was from the first only too glad to have the Professor's support. Bennett for some time continued to conduct the more important concerts and to take some part in others. Later, unless he received some very special invitation, he preferred to leave such work in the hands of the resident musicians.

To engage in performances when the amateur element so strongly preponderated was a new experience for him. The band and chorus of the University Musical Society presented, at the time, rather a motley crew. College choirs were at hand to assist; good solo-singers were generally attainable; among the members were men of intellectual ability, to whom the study and practice of music seemed to present little difficulty; the north of England, from which Cambridge draws so many of her students, contributed its due share of musical fervour. General culture and enthusiasm were, however, far in advance of actual performance, which was, and remained for many years, rough and imperfect. Music was a disturbance to the established routine of College life. Tutors and reading-men could ill afford time taken from the evening hours of teaching and of study. Rehearsals were irregularly attended. The constantly changing 'personnel' of a University prevented any steady improvement from year to year. Periods of prosperity and depression came in turn, according to the zeal and musical ability of the men of each period.

It often seemed strange that a man so sensitive, so noted for perfection of detail in his own performances, could find it tolerable to assist in such haphazard music-makings. 'Poor Sterndale Bennett,' the Rev. H. R. Haweis called him, when he wrote his reminiscences of these early concerts; and, as time went on, there were others who felt incongruity in so refined a musician taking part with them in their badly-balanced and imperfectly-prepared exhibitions. He was not in complete sympathy with the amateurs of the day in their public performances. He did not approve of the reckless way in which they attacked music far beyond their executive powers. When he congratulated his young friend, Armfield, on being elected President of the University Musical Society, he wrote: 'Hurrah! now we will have Haydn;' for the Cambridge orchestra preferred to lay bare its shortcomings in the Symphonies of Beethoven, to experiment on Schumann, and to give even Wagner his chance. But in such matters Bennett did not really interfere. He smiled, but only with great good humour when he spoke of them; and, indeed, he watched with keen delight the awakening of a love of music in a rising generation of Englishmen. His nature disliked any exuberance of expression, but he could make allowance for it in others when the feeling which prompted it was genuine. Late in life he paid a little tribute to enthusiasts in the words: 'When I hear the young men talk, I begin to wonder whether I myself was ever fond of music at all.' But whatever he felt or thought, when he was taking part in these concerts he certainly threw his whole energy into what he was doing, and he proved himself a most capable leader of irregular forces. After the first concert which he conducted, 'an old guest of the Musical Society' wrote to the newspaper: 'It was truly delightful to see the talented Professor of Music presiding over the band; his forces seemed animated with something of his own vigour, for rarely, if ever, have they more distinguished themselves than on the present occasion.'

There was a seriousness of manner, bordering upon severity, inseparable from Bennett when practising his art in public. Upon amateurs who found themselves for the first time under the influence of his musical personality the impression was very forcible. The presence of a master was felt. Easy-going enjoyment, ultra-expression of individual sentiment so dear to the heart of the half-trained amateur performer, vanished at the first stroke of his bâton, and the sight of his rigidly set face. Davison once wrote of him, after he had been playing a Concerto with a very unsteady orchestral accompaniment: 'The devil himself could not disturb the equanimity of our young countryman when he has once set out upon his path.' It was this equanimity, coupled with a determined insistence, which gave confidence to uncertain performers. A particular example of the wonderful control he had over himself was given by these concerts. When other musicians were occasionally invited to Cambridge to conduct their own works, their looks of anguish when they heard the orchestra strike up were involuntary and natural, but very alarming to the poor performers. Bennett's face, stern as it was, never betrayed the least sign of displeasure, or of his having taken any particular notice of failures and imperfections past remedy. No individual performer was ever disconcerted by any special recognition of what he was doing.

When the music was over he appeared in another aspect. He had the faculty, strengthened no doubt by long experience with pupils, of finding a few expressive words of temperate approval or encouragement. These never approached to flattery, seldom to unqualified praise. They were often humorous, or seasoned with a sprinkling of raillery. They were never twice alike, but adroitly adapted to the individual case, while they had a ring of truth about them that drove them home, fixing them as little treasures in the memory of those to whom they were addressed. He had no conventional epithets ready for use. He would probably have found himself quite unable to offer satisfactory congratulations to a great prima donna; a celebrated pianist, who often played his music, once reproached him for his coldness of manner; but where less was needed his little sayings were happily conceived. A young schoolgirl sending home her first impression of her new music-master wrote of him: 'When he speaks, he always seems to say something.'

To the musical amateurs of Cambridge, one of the places most closely associated with their remembrance of him would be the Sidney Combination-room, which the members of the Fitzwilliam Musical Society used as a green-room when they gave their concerts in the College Hall. There one could watch him, surrounded by many admirers competing for the chance of a word with him, or could notice how in corners of the room the attention of those who did not know him personally was rivetted to his face. The Rev. Arthur Beard, the conductor of the Society, who loved him with a brotherly affection, would gently place his hands on Bennett's shoulders and chat to him, content in return with the gentle laugh or expressive smile which would, as often as not, supply the place of words in his conversation. One evening a very young singer made his debût on the concert-stage in a performance of 'The May-Queen' in Sidney Hall, and Mr Edward Lloyd, for he it was, had not forgotten at the end of his brilliant career the kindly words which Bennett, with a rare prescience, had spoken to him at the start of it.

When Bennett was elected Professor, *The Athenæum*, in reporting his appointment, admitted that there was little to say against it, but suggested that he was adding fresh duties to those which already, if report could be trusted, gave him full occupation. This far-fetched objection would apply to most men chosen for important posts, and Bennett, like others, could rearrange his plans to suit new needs. He was quite prepared to make sacrifice of more lucrative employment in return for the honour and pleasure which his connection with the University brought him. Details of the first eleven years—after which steps were taken towards requiting his services—will be sufficient. Between March 4, 1856, and March 4, 1867, entries occur in his teaching-books—where they are placed to account for the omission of lessons—of 133 days spent in Cambridge, and there were times of the year when he could pay additional visits of which no entry in those books was necessary. He at least gave up, on the average, four of his regular working days in each term to Cambridge. In the earlier years the amount of time spent on the journey would not in these days be credited. If he went for a single day, an early start and a return by the night-mail were generally necessary. The hours he spent in Cambridge enabled him to do everything required, beyond what he could do by correspondence, in connection with musical degrees; to assist or be present at concerts; to appear at University functions or at such social gatherings as he was invited to in the Colleges. He certainly became as familiar a figure in Cambridge as any other non-resident officer.

As years went on he became well-known far beyond the limits of any musical circle. Striking changes, or rapid developments in the musical life of the University did not perhaps occur under his *régime*; but the degrees came to be regarded as desirable honours difficult to obtain; and, again, at a time when respect for music itself among the members of a learned society was only advancing by slow degrees, no man could be better qualified than he, even without any apparent effort of his own, to disarm prejudice and win converts. He moved in Cambridge with modesty, dignity and grace, an attractive impersonation of the art he professed.

CHAPTER XVIII.

DIFFERENCE WITH THE PHILHARMONIC DIRECTORS;
BACH SOCIETY; THE EARL OF WESTMORLAND
AND R. A. OF MUSIC.

1856—58.
æt. 40—42.

THE year 1856, bringing to Bennett the appointments at the Philharmonic and at Cambridge, dates a distinct epoch in his career. Seventeen years had gone by since he had settled down to regular work in London, and during that time, which proved in the end to represent nearly half his professional life, he had not found it easy to keep himself before the musical world. What he had done for the advancement of music, beyond the wide and wholesome influence as a teacher, had been chiefly the outcome of private enterprise and had been limited by the slender pecuniary resources at his command. Of the causes and extent of the discouragement which he felt as he approached and passed through middle life little can be said; for though he himself afterwards alluded to such feelings, he gave no sufficient explanation of their origin. There had certainly not been much at hand to brighten and stimulate the life of an Englishman holding the views he did. He had walked in a narrow path with few companions.

Now, however, at the age of forty, he found himself as well placed in his profession as he could desire to be, and he may be deemed fortunate, seeing how few were the appointments, except for organists, which this country had to offer to its musicians, to have obtained promotion, with the attendant encouragement, at the time he did. In one way, however, his new appointments made little difference to him. The fees received for the conductorship did not quite balance the expenses incident upon performing his honorary duties at Cambridge. For his livelihood, therefore, he had still to depend entirely upon teaching.

In the year 1856 he gave his usual series of Chamber Concerts. At the second, on May 6, Madame Schumann played with him her husband's Duet for two pianofortes and four numbers of the Opus 85. At the third, on June 3, he made his last appearance as a pianist in London. Early in 1857, Mrs Bennett wrote to one of his pupils, that it would be very difficult for him to manage concerts of his own concurrently with those of the Philharmonic. As he was by this time quite willing to give up playing in public altogether, he took that step, and later in life never seemed to regret having done so.

In anticipation of his second season at the Philharmonic, he was as anxious as he had been during the first for additions to be made to the Society's repertoire. When, in earlier years, he served on the Directorate himself, he had always urged this upon his colleagues. Thus *The Musical World* wrote in 1844: 'As a Director of the Philharmonic, Mr Bennett's influence has for the last three years acted most beneficially on the politics of that prominent musical body. We have observed immense improvements in the general character of the programmes.' Bennett, however, was now Conductor, not a Director, and his efforts to infuse some new spirit into the Society's doings met with a check, by means of some indiscreet tale-bearer.

Some time before the 1857 season began, he had written suggesting Beethoven's music to 'Egmont' and some other works as suitable for the Directors' consideration. A report then reached him that his letter had been received with strong marks of ill-favour. When he made inquiries as to what had really happened, Mr McMurdie, one of the Directors, wrote:—

'When your letter was read, it was agreed *una voce* that we must not establish a precedent for taking our Programme from the Conductor, whilst at the same time, we should be most ready to act on his suggestions, and meet his wishes. We then wrote to *Joachim*[1], and gave the order for the parts of "Egmont." On the following Saturday it was ruled that "Egmont" would be rather heavy for a first concert. (I gave no opinion myself, not knowing the work.) * * * Rest assured that you have the respect and esteem of one and all of our body. * * *'

Bennett replied on April 3:

'I am much obliged to you for your kind note, but it confirms my suspicions that the Directors are annoyed at my suggestions (for they were only suggestions, if you will have the note read again), and really this makes me feel most uncomfortable. * * * The Philharmonic has a very ready method of turning a warm-hearted active friend into a lukewarm machine. I am still undecided what to do. * * * PS. I trust in any case I may not have to conduct *Masaniello*. Is it not too un-Philharmonic and noisy? Pray help me and the concert in this respect.'

The same day, Bennett prepared the draft of a letter tendering his resignation, but did not send any such letter. The Directors, hearing what was in his mind, took steps to reassure him. The Overture to 'Masaniello' was laid on the shelf for a time, by the side of the music to 'Egmont,' though Bennett ultimately conducted both works. A resolution was carried that no programme should in future be finally passed without his having seen it, and the Directors changed their hours of meeting to the morning of the rehearsals, so that he could have easy communication with them. His 'suggestions' also seem to have been re-considered; for a critique on the third concert mentioned that 'Bach's fine *suite* of movements was an innovation, and a welcome one. It was famously executed, and keenly relished by the connoisseurs. Professor Bennett seems to have registered a vow that the great John Sebastian shall be familiarised in this country. All musicians will respect him for his zeal in a cause so sacred to art.'

So Bennett said no more of resignation, and during the long series of years that he continued to act for the

---

[1] Bennett, therefore, had probably suggested an invitation to Joachim who had not been heard in London for some years. Joachim, however, did not reappear at the Philharmonic till the next year, 1858.

Society nothing further occurred to disturb the harmonious relations between the Directors and himself. He did not try again to influence the choice of music, but the orthodox Philharmonic programmes of the day were almost entirely made up of the works of those composers with whom he was most in sympathy. There were certain operatic Overtures occasionally introduced which he did not like for performance at the Philharmonic, but he made no further appeal on the subject. The orchestra which he conducted had received far the greater part of its training at the Italian Opera. Bennett would say, 'When they dash into one of their favourite Overtures in their operatic style, at the end of my rehearsal, any effect I have been trying to make on them through the morning is scattered to the winds.' It was not altogether that he demurred to the compositions. There were Overtures of Mozart which he disliked conducting with his Italian Opera players almost as much as 'Masaniello' or 'Zampa.'

In the midst of growing public responsibilities, he did not forget old pledges, and though the demands upon his time were rapidly increasing, he could still discover hours in which to work as a volunteer in the service of music. The Bach Society, since the production of the St Matthew 'Passion' in 1854, had continued its winter practices but had given no public performance. The interest of non-performing members had vanished. The Society welcomed the co-operation of students and choristers, from whom, however, no contributions to its funds could be expected. Towards the end of 1857 the Treasurer reported a debt of £75, and an income for the current year of £14 collected from 150 nominal subscribers. Bennett was already preparing for a reproduction of 'The Passion' on a larger scale than before; but the Committee, considering their financial prospects hopeless, called a general meeting in December to raise the question of immediate dissolution. This crisis was happily averted, and early in 1858 Dr Steggall, the honorary secretary, issued a circular announcing that 'Professor Bennett has undertaken the performance of the "Passions-Musik" on the 23rd of March *entirely upon his own responsibility*, and has decided to present to the Society any surplus as an acknowledgment of the promised co-operation of a great majority of the members.'

Many fresh recruits enlisted. The chorus, according to *The Illustrated News*, was 300 strong. At the final rehearsals a quite remarkable enthusiasm was displayed as the beauty of the still unfamiliar music shone through the mist of difficulty. The chorus had now the advantage of singing from printed parts, which Messrs Leader and Cock had published at Bennett's request. St Martin's Hall, which John Hullah used for his singing-school, and also for concerts intended to popularise good music, was the *locale* chosen for the Bach performance. It was thought, and, as it proved, rightly thought, that the 'Passions-Musik' was more likely to find immediate favour with a non-critical and unprejudiced public. The prices of seats were fixed at five shillings, half-a-crown, and one shilling. Mrs Bennett took control of the business arrangements, and was able to dispose of half the number of seats by her own exertions. Though no attempt was made to attract a fashionable audience, a happy idea struck Bennett, about a week before the concert, that there was one amateur of high rank who would surely be interested in the production of a German masterpiece. Members of the Royal Family did not often attend concerts. An annual visit to the Philharmonic was all that was customary. Bennett summoned up courage to write to the Prince Consort. He had a good case to present and no doubt pleaded well; but as he could not be sanguine of the result, he told no one what he had done. In referring to the matter later, he would say, 'I went out and posted the letter myself.' A few hours brought the reply: 'Major-General Grey presents his compliments to Professor Bennett and is commanded to inform him that H.R.H. the Prince Consort will have much pleasure in attending the performance of Bach's Grosse Passions-Musik at St Martin's Hall on Tuesday evening next.

'Buckingham Palace, March 17, 1858.'

Bach's birthday, March 21, fell this year on a Sunday. The 23rd was therefore chosen instead, and *The Musical World* relates that on that evening 'an immense concourse flocked to St Martin's Hall, numbers being unable to obtain admission;' and again, that 'a crowd, gathered from all ranks of society, were rushing to the Hall with as much zeal as is evinced by a holiday-mob on a boxing-night.' These circumstances were noticed because they caused surprise where Bach's music was concerned.

Bennett had been to Buckingham Palace in the afternoon, and had been instructed that the Prince would come for the commencement of the concert. His Royal Highness duly arrived, accompanied by the Duchess of Sutherland, and Bennett was quite touched by a graceful apology which he made between the parts for having been *five minutes* late! The Prince followed the music with close attention from a full score, probably lent him by the Earl of Cawdor, a patron of the Bach Society, who sat beside him. Whenever he lifted his eyes from the book, his face revealed so fascinating, so individual an expression of interest and enjoyment, that no one who watched him from the chorus that night would ever cease to regard him as the ideal amateur of music. Both the Prince and Lord Cawdor afterwards gave solid proof of their appreciation. The Earl had valuable scores of Bach's works in his library, and after the concert he sent some of them to Bennett as a present. The Prince, a year later, returned the invitation, and the Bach Society gave the St Matthew 'Passion' at Windsor Castle.

In the preface to the English edition of the work (published in 1862), Bennett refers to this performance in 1858 as being the first given in England, and there seems to have been at the time an understanding between the critics and himself that the two earlier performances in 1854 were to be remembered as mere preliminary trials. The rendering in 1858 was at least sufficiently accurate and effective to satisfy the critics. It was recorded, as if specially noteworthy, that the attention of a vast audience was completely held, and that no one left the room till the last bar had been heard.

Next day, Bennett's pupils found him in a grateful mood, and there was reason for it. Comparison between what was written in 1854, and again in 1858, shows that this memorable evening of the latter year saw a great change of opinion as to the possibility—and that had been the chief point at issue—of Bach's choral music finding a home in this country. When Mrs Bennett made up her accounts, she found that £186. 14s. 6d. had been received, and £153. 17s. 2d. spent. Bennett's bank-book shows that he had the pleasure, within a week's time, of sending the Bach Society a cheque for £32. 17s. 4d.

The same day that he did this, another pleasing thing happened. His position at the Philharmonic had, of course, brought him into notice as a conductor. In the winter of 1857—58 he had been summoned to Manchester to conduct some Lancashire Festival Concerts, and now came a letter from Mr Kitson of Leeds, offering him the conductorship of a Festival to be held in the autumn, in connection with the opening of a new Town Hall by Queen Victoria. No musical office could be more desired than the conductorship of one of these great meetings, and the invitation was doubly welcome as it was quite unexpected.

The Committee in making their final choice had decided to invite Bennett rather than Costa. Since much was said in those days of the preference shown to foreign musicians, it is interesting to know that in this case an Englishman was preferred because he was an Englishman, whilst a further sentiment, arising from the fact that he was born in Yorkshire, helped to turn the scale. The historians of 'The Leeds Festivals' describe Bennett's letter of reply to the invitation as one calculated to go to the hearts of all Yorkshiremen. Repeating what he had written under similar circumstances to the Philharmonic Directors, he made a point of saying that he imposed none of those preliminary conditions now becoming the fashion with conductors, but that he trusted entirely to the hearty co-operation of the managers in his efforts. Being asked to name his terms he did so, but wrote that he had no experience to guide him, and the Committee then voted a much higher remuneration than he had asked for. The Festival was fixed for September, and in the meantime he was asked to assist in the engagement of the performers. The following quaint appeal, on behalf of a few local aspirants, reached him through Mr R. S. Burton, the Chorus-master:

'H. M. presents his kind respects and would be glad to

receive an engagement for the Festival, and one for his daughter, and I hope you will give one to Billy P——, and one to Billy W—— Tenor singer. Billy P—— is a Bass singer. I have found them useful at many times, anybody knows them. P—— has had a copy of Rossini's Stater Mater a long time. I cannot give you any reference to myself. I sing Tenor when I cannot get a job for the fiddle. Excuse an old stager.

Yours,
H. M.

'N.B.—If you will give us a job, I will have them up to the mark.'

The preference shown by the Leeds Committee to a fellow-countryman was counterbalanced by something which occurred in London at the same time, and which seemed to cast a slight on British musicians in the very Academy where their feelings ought to have been least liable to injury. Bennett was quite the patriot, but in musical international politics he favoured free-trade. The reader will have seen that, far from grumbling, as many others did, at the incursion of foreign artists, he used what influence he had to encourage their coming when he thought it would lead to the expansion of our musical knowledge in the right directions. 'The visits of illustrious musicians to England' was the subject of one of his lectures delivered at the London Institution and elsewhere, and it is remembered what interest he took in dilating upon this theme, 'reflecting,' as he wrote, 'with pride and pleasure on our country's reception and appreciation of these great men.' Among the musicians of foreign birth who made England their home, or who visited it, during his life-time, he numbered many of his best-valued artistic associates, many of his most intimate friends. He was, however, now in the front of the English musical profession, and when necessity arose, which happily it did but rarely, he could fight to guard his own position, and champion the interests of those he represented.

The Earl of Westmorland, when he founded the Royal Academy of Music in 1822, saw 'the disadvantages which the English laboured under in their professional career, the many drawbacks they had to contend against and the struggles which checked their progress.' Thirty-six years had not entirely removed the drawbacks and disadvantages. Any encouragement which could be given to English musicians would still have been welcome. It is therefore all the more strange that the founder of the Academy should have cast the following slight upon his own foundation. In the season of 1858, Lord Westmorland planned a concert, as a means of raising funds for the Academy, to be given in the new St James's Hall. Queen Victoria promised to honour it with her presence, so that there was every prospect of a wide patronage, and of the prime object being realized. Here then might be seen a rare opportunity of displaying before the Court and an influential public the fruits of so many years' work at the Academy. If past and present students had been allowed to combine in a spirited movement, material could certainly have been found for an interesting concert. There happened, for instance, to be lying at the moment in Tenterden Street a MS. Overture just sent over from Germany by a recent student of the Academy, a work in which Davison found 'an independent way of thinking which in one so young looked well.' If Arthur Sullivan could have been granted a hearing on this occasion, some credit would surely have accrued to the Institution in which he had so lately been studying. But Lord Westmorland, when arranging his concert, started by entirely ignoring the Academy, except, of course, as the recipient of charity. He placed a Mass of his own composition as the chief item of the programme. To this no objection would or could have been raised, had he not, apparently in order to give *éclat* to the production of his Mass, secured the services of the staff of the Royal Italian Opera with Costa as conductor of the orchestra. Bennett cordially hated the dominating influence of the Italian Opera as checking the progress of music in other directions, and, of course, the introduction of Costa, who had nothing to do with the Academy, was to him intolerable. It was not enough for him that Lucas, the regular conductor of Academy concerts, had acquiesced in the arrangement. He felt obliged to protest against the reflection which he saw cast on the Academy Professors as a body. He wrote to Cipriani Potter, the Principal,

explained his views in a letter which Potter considered
'very pithy,' and asked him to convey to Lord Westmorland
his resignation as a teacher, and, what was more serious,
a request that his name should be erased from the list of
Associates of the Academy. Then Lord Westmorland,
who appears to have concluded that Bennett had expected
to conduct the concert himself, sent him two messages:
one, through Lucas, asking him to name a work of his own
to be placed on the programme—a proposal which came
too late to be regarded as anything but an afterthought;
and the second through Potter who had been ordered to
write *verbatim* what Lord Westmorland had said to him
in conversation. This message was to the effect that the
resignation could not be accepted; but when it contained
such expressions as, 'Surely he cannot have the pretension,'
and again, 'at a concert composed of the first foreign
artists,' it only gave emphasis to Bennett's exact objections.
He stood firm. The press took the same view that he
did. *The Times* and other newspapers commented severely
upon Lord Westmorland's concert-scheme, and considered
Bennett's resignation as the proper and necessary sequel.
He could ill be spared at the Academy. Everyone felt
that. His name, if only as a pianoforte-teacher, stood
very high. Potter had, for many years, assigned him the
best pupils on the male side. But the Principal also valued
his old pupil's personal influence, and liked to have him
by his side. In 1853 Potter had got Lord Westmorland
to make a post for Bennett as 'Inspector of Musical
Discipline,' and when in 1857 Bennett had found himself
too busy to sit any longer on a 'Board of Professors,'
Potter had written, 'In my opinion, the charm of our
Board has vanished.' Potter now wrote:—'You may well
imagine how much I am grieved with your decision, since
it must be the forerunner of other important events, as
well as lead to changes which can never be congenial to
my feelings. * * * I am persuaded that my Lord's act was
more to gratify his own vanity than with any intention of
insulting the Professors of the Institution. I perfectly
sympathise with your feelings on the subject of "The
Grand Concert," and hope nothing will ever destroy the
mutual good feelings between us.'

Again Potter wrote:—'I wish I could persuade you to

alter your decision, to waive your feelings on the subject, which you might do without giving up the principle (in which I fully concur). You would be acting most kindly to the Institution: as the old, the present, and the future students will naturally look to you in case anything happens to me, or that I wish to relinquish my duties, and will all flock around you and expect you to respond to their wishes.'

Lord Westmorland had expressed himself to Potter as 'surprised' at Bennett's attitude. When his messages brought no result, he himself wrote two letters urging Bennett to call upon him. One letter is as follows:—

CAVENDISH SQUARE,
May 25, 1858.

MY DEAR BENNETT,

I am very sorry your engagements at Cambridge prevented your coming to me to-day, but as I am very anxious to see you, I leave it to you to respond to my anxiety and to come when you can. I am always at home until one o'clock.

Yours very sincerely,
WESTMORLAND.

By avoiding or postponing an interview with Lord Westmorland, Bennett acted with discretion, and with a just regard to the debt which he, in common with other English musicians, owed to the Founder of The Royal Academy of Music. The circumstances to which he objected were past remedy, while their further discussion would involve the danger of painful and useless conflict with one whose age and position demanded all possible consideration. Bennett did not make his protest by an open rupture with Lord Westmorland, though others, later, seemed to conclude that the protest had taken that form. He made it by withdrawing his name from an Institution which submitted too patiently, as he thought, to a severe slight. Though fully appreciating foreign alliances, he showed English musicians, at this juncture, that there was one, at least, of their number, who would jealously guard national interests. When the Earl of Westmorland passed away, eighteen months later, Bennett was invited to return to the Academy. He did not, however, consider that Lord Westmorland's death gave a timely opportunity or a sufficient reason for withdrawing his protest. Sir George Macfarren has written that Bennett's old friends at the Academy repeatedly urged him, as time went on, to rejoin the staff of Professors; but, that they could neither persuade him to listen to their solicitations, nor elicit from him any reason for his continuing to hold aloof. His connection with the Academy was severed for eight years.

CHAPTER XIX.

LEEDS FESTIVAL. 'THE MAY QUEEN.'

1858.
æt. 42.

For the approaching Leeds Festival Bennett had been asked to furnish a new composition. Up to this time of his life he had received no commission to write a Festival work. The libretto of a *Pastoral* entitled 'May Day,' written by H. F. Chorley, had long been in his hands. He now proposed to make use of it for Leeds. In reopening the subject with the librettist, to whom some explanation of the delay was obviously necessary, he appears to have referred to discouragement which he had met with as a composer, for Chorley, in his reply, wrote: 'It amuses me that you should use the word disheartening to me. Only I suppose that musicians imagine that those who furnish them with ideas for works come into the world to be disheartened. However this "May Day" business—solicited from me *nine years ago* when I was in no humour to attempt creation, is perhaps as royal a case of neglect and want of consideration as could be cited.'

Bennett had not neglected the libretto on first receipt of it. The discoloured music-sheets on which one of the earlier numbers in the score is written show that the number was penned many years before the rest of the work, while a musical phrase in this movement proves that he had fixed, when writing it, on an already composed Overture as a Prelude to the *Pastoral* and as a source from which he would gather musical material for it. Moreover, his marginal notes on the original libretto show that he had approached the work as a whole by determining, in advance, the tonality of the several movements. His failure to continue may have been due to dilatoriness, or possibly he did not care very much for the libretto; but his plea of discouragement may also be taken into account. If any one person more than another had contributed to such feeling that person was Chorley himself. It may be imagined that the neglect of his libretto had something to do with the adverse tone which that critic had long adopted in *The Athenæum* when writing of Bennett as a composer or in any other capacity. On the other hand such constant attacks made against the musician's character as an artist might well have damped any further interest in setting Chorley's text. Fortunately their renewed negotiations, lasting until the *Pastoral* was published and well started on its career, were conducted in a conciliatory spirit. Chorley pointed out one difficulty which delay had created. Macfarren, with the librettist Oxenford, had lately produced a Cantata with the same title, 'May Day.' The two librettists, however, had treated the subject very differently, and when Chorley had altered his title to 'The May Queen,' the two works were no longer likely to be confused.

Bennett at this time expressed a doubt to his wife of his ability to write an extended composition. 'It is so long,' he said, 'since I did anything of the kind.' Mrs Bennett insisted on an early close to the summer-term's work. Here a little incident occurring at the time interrupts for a moment the story of 'The May Queen.' On Saturday, July 3, Bennett was in Cambridge with Joachim as his guest at 'The Bull,' the hotel at which he always stayed throughout the years of his Professorship. It happened to be the 'Commencement' week, the town was full of visitors, and he suddenly conceived the idea of giving an impromptu concert with the aid of his friend, who had not been in England for some years, and was almost a stranger in Cambridge. At 5 o'clock he set printers to work, and circulated an announcement the same evening. On Monday afternoon the concert of music for violin and pianoforte took place, 105 tickets were sold, and £21. 10s. was handed to Addenbrooke's Hospital. Thus did the great violinist generously render his first service to the University which in later years has been proud to count him as a member. On July 15 the Bennetts repaired to Eastbourne, quartering themselves at 'The Gilbert Arms,' an old-fashioned hostelry

THE GILBERT ARMS, EASTBOURNE
From a water-colour drawing by W. Chalmers Masters

where they had already spent a short summer holiday the year before. In a remote corner of the rambling building there was a secluded room, and in a bow-window overlooking a large walled-in garden, Bennett placed his table and set to work. Direct from the house there were four ways in which he could start on the short walks which he liked constantly to take while composing: a path across the fields to 'Mill-Gap,' on the way to Willingdon; the two shady avenues towards Old Eastbourne and Southbourne; and the road, then bordered by wheat and clover fields, leading to the sea. Opposite the house was the small railway-station with a telegraph office, to which he kept running across to transact Leeds Festival business. In due course he had written all his music except a Chorus with Soprano solo, to the not very inspiring words, 'With a laugh as we go round.' As this movement concerned the chief character in the piece it was important, but Bennett failed for some time to get any idea for it that suited him. One day, at his invitation, his wife prepared herself to take a walk with him, and was surprised, after they had gone a few yards from the house, by his suddenly turning round and saying, 'We can go back now, the May Queen is finished.'

At the end of August he went to the Birmingham Festival to hear some of the music which he was himself to conduct the following week, and on September 5 he was in Leeds at the house of Walker Joy, one of the chief promoters of the Festival, with whom he now had the pleasure of starting a most congenial friendship. The new Town Hall was opened by Her Majesty on the 7th, and the Festival commenced next day with a fine performance of 'Elijah,' which, in the opinion of *The Times*, followed Mendelssohn's own readings more closely than any that had been given in England since his death. A selection from Bach's St Matthew 'Passion' was another feature of the Festival. 'The May Queen' was produced at the first evening concert. The solos were sung by Madame Clara Novello, Miss Palmer[1], Sims Reeves and Weiss. Davison wrote that the general execution of the work was by no means faultless; this, probably, because the composer would not like to apportion much of the rehearsal-time to his own

---

[1] In the absence of Miss Dolby whose name appears on the programme.

music. In referring to the occasion many years later, Bennett said, 'The May Queen went off very well at Leeds, but there was nothing out of the way about its reception.'

The Leeds Festival was reckoned a great success. The acoustic properties of the new Hall and the magnificent chorus were subjects of general congratulation; but the English conductor also won some laurels. It was the first important occasion on which he had appeared as an Oratorio conductor, and of course he had to submit to comparison with Costa. The historians of 'The Leeds Festivals' remember that in such comparison there was a 'divergence of opinion.' There were many at Leeds, as at the Philharmonic, who gave the palm to Bennett for his readings whether of Oratorio or of Symphony. On the other hand, as a 'chef d'orchestre,' Costa, with his vast experience and consummate mastery held a well-nigh impregnable position. It is then no little evidence of Bennett's remarkable natural capacity, that, limited as his chances were of displaying it, he should have been found comparable to Costa at all. Dando, the violinist, who was closely associated both with Costa and with Bennett in almost all their musical undertakings, and who had great respect for both, when talking of them as conductors—without, of course, referring to the Italian Opera—used to say, 'My ideal would be reached, if they could be combined, Costa beating the time, and Bennett telling him how to do it.'

Bennett was duly appointed Conductor, when another Leeds Festival was expected in 1861, and he was invited to supply a new sacred work for the occasion. He was summoned to Leeds early in that year to confer with the Committee, and the scheme of the Festival was well advanced, when differences arose between the local Choral Societies which proved impossible to adjust, and which prevented the organization of a chorus. The meeting, therefore, had to be abandoned, to the great disappointment of Bennett. The Festivals were not resumed till 1874. By that time he had long retired from conducting, and was within a few months of his death; but he had always looked back to his connection with Leeds as a happy one, nor has that connection been forgotten in the place itself, where room for his works has been found, from time to time, on the programmes of later Festivals. The bâton with which he conducted in 1858 was preserved as a relic by his friend, Walker Joy, and is now in the possession of Mr Fred. R. Spark, the Honorary Secretary of the Festivals.

'The May Queen,' after its production at Leeds, was soon published. It was heard in London in December at two concerts in St Martin's Hall under the direction of John Hullah. On the first day of the New Year (1859) it was sung at Windsor Castle. Later in the same year Bennett himself conducted it at the Philharmonic. At the rehearsal for this performance, Sims Reeves being unable to attend, Bennett sent for one of his Cambridge friends, Mr A. D. Coleridge, Fellow of King's College, who remembers the pleasure of singing with Clara Novello and the Philharmonic orchestra. Bennett also conducted performances at Liverpool and Cambridge. The *Pastoral* was given in Edinburgh by Mr C. J. Hargitt, in Belfast, and before long almost everywhere. 'It is as individual,' Chorley wrote to Bennett, 'as it is graceful and delicate.' Yet its refinement did not prevent the appreciation by uncultured listeners, and it had a long run at 'The Canterbury Music Hall' in the Borough. Amateur vocal societies greeted it with enthusiasm. Many such societies in the provinces who had been content up to that time with miscellaneous programmes of detached pieces, would certainly look back to 'The May Queen' as the first work on an extended scale—with the exception, perhaps, of Locke's music to *Macbeth*—which they had undertaken. It seemed at the time to be suitable alike to the grand concert-hall and the village school-room. Finally, its appearance and its reception attracted many others to compete in the same field. It acted as a great incentive to modest achievement. Yet the countless Cantatas which immediately followed in its wake, however welcome and useful they may have been, certainly accentuated the absolute merit and unique character of 'The May Queen.'

Bennett's friends now seized the opportunity which this success gave them, and urged him to continue writing. 'Great pressure,' Mrs Bennett afterwards said, 'was put upon him after the Leeds Festival.' He had shown his ability to gain the ear of a larger class of music-lovers than that to which his previous compositions had appealed. A livelihood by writing, perhaps even wealth, were thought by his advisers to lie within his reach. But the inducements, such as Chorley, for one, with good intent, put before him, did not attract him. They had indeed a contrary effect; for either by natural instinct, or by some simple principles which he had adopted early in life for the guidance of his career, he put a very restricted value on worldly fame or popularity; and, again, though his refusal to consider composition as a possible source of income may have been due to a certain timidity which he showed in dealing with worldly concerns, yet, apart from that, there was a positive shrinking from coupling art with money in his thoughts. Some years after this, Davison brought him a message from one of the great music-publishers. Well acquainted, no doubt, with Bennett's views, he delivered it with some hesitation, but the gist of it was that Bennett might name his own terms if he would wholly devote himself to composition. Davison did not seem surprised when Bennett at once changed the subject. Next morning, when one of his family, who had been present the night before, referred to the matter, he said, apparently with some effort, 'Nothing shall induce me to place myself in the hands of men of business.' As to writing works in succession to 'The May Queen,' repetition in the same groove is not always successful, and, except in the case of the greatest men, does not always add to, though it often detracts from an already gained reputation. His own publishers planned, as best they could, a method of sounding him on the subject of another Cantata. They engaged one of the most eminent librettists of the day to prepare a new libretto. It was written. Lamborn Cock took it down to Eastbourne in the summer of 1859 and showed it to Bennett in the little room where 'The May Queen' had been composed the year before. There were others looking on with some anxiety to see whether it might interest him. He took it up, glanced for a few moments at the first page, and without a word, or without any look which could betray what was passing in his mind, gently laid it down on the table and quietly walked out of the room.

CHAPTER XX.

THE CHORALE BOOK FOR ENGLAND.
1859—1862.
æt. 43—46.

GREAT interest had been aroused in this country by the appearance, in 1855 and 1858, of two volumes, entitled *Lyra Germanica*. They contained translations, by Miss Catherine Winkworth, of German hymns. In February, 1859, Messrs Longmans announced that a musical edition of this work, 'containing some of the fine old German Chorales, would shortly be completed, under the superintendence of Professor Sterndale Bennett.' It may be said that Bennett had already taken one step in this direction, by editing in short score for the pianoforte the Chorales from the St Matthew 'Passion.' By the end of the summer of 1859, his share in the work proposed by Messrs Longmans, as far as he had seen his way to deal with it, was ready for publication. He had confined himself to the use of J. Sebastian Bach's versions of the Chorales. Miss Winkworth, in her translations of the hymns, had very frequently departed from the original metres; but Bennett had been able to select about fifty examples in which words and music could be blended with strict regard to historic association. The collection would no doubt have proved interesting, and by its means another step would have been taken on the road of introducing Bach to this country, in which, as has been seen, Bennett was profoundly interested.

The unsatisfactory state into which the music of the Lutheran Church had been allowed to fall in Germany had in recent years necessitated a reformation. A conference had been held at Eisenach in 1853, and, with the object of establishing uniformity, a new musical service-book had been ordered, and had been printed in 1855. The subject of Church music had therefore been brought prominently to the minds of German musicians. Mr Otto Goldschmidt, who took up his residence in England in 1858, had conceived the idea, which seemed justified by the deep impression caused by the *Lyra Germanica*, that German hymnology might be widely acceptable for congregational use in the Church of England. Mr Goldschmidt, having set his heart on devoting himself to this cause, was disappointed to find that another was before him. Bennett, his senior by several years, was one whose position in the musical world he had, in his own student days at Leipzig, learnt to regard with the highest respect. Now, therefore, he neither saw his way to carrying out his project independently, nor to approaching Bennett with a view of combining. However, a third party, who sympathised with Mr Goldschmidt, took an opportunity of sounding Bennett privately, when he found him only too glad that the work he had been doing should assume a larger form with a wider object, and that he should gain the help of one willing and able to devote more time than he could himself spare. The task, for its thorough performance, demanded great research, and research which, apart from the question of time, lay more naturally within reach of a musician of German nationality.

The partnership between Mr Goldschmidt and Bennett over this work dated from an interview at Messrs Longmans in November, 1859; their own meetings began in the first days of the New Year, 1860; and exactly three years elapsed before the publication of *The Chorale Book for England*. The first eighteen months were spent in seeking the sources of the melodies, and obtaining them in their purest and most original form. Mr Goldschmidt went to Germany to consult authorities, collected a large library of reference, made the work, for the time being, his chief occupation, and prepared everything for discussion with his colleague. Bennett gave up so much of his time and passed so many hours, in the midst of his other engagements, in Mr Goldschmidt's study at Wimbledon—a study which, he would tell his pupils, was carpeted with Chorale books open for reference—that towards the end of eighteen months Mrs Bennett took fright and spoke of the impossibility of his continuing this work for an indefinite time. It was therefore proposed that the two editors should spend the summer vacation of 1861 together. Mr Goldschmidt went with his family to Eastbourne, and by continuous work lasting several weeks the harmonization of the melodies, and the musical portion of the work generally, made rapid advance. Later, Miss Winkworth proved a most generous coadjutor. She had known all along that her translations would in places require alteration to suit the music, and had agreed to attempt it; but her task grew, and did not end till she had translated quite afresh a very considerable number of the hymns.

Of Bennett's work on *The Chorale Book*, Mr Goldschmidt thus spoke in 1882 at a meeting of The Musical Association of London:—

'This much I would wish to impress upon the meeting, that, although it was probably the busiest time of his life, when his hours and minutes were precious in a mundane sense, he most readily and without the least stint or grudge of objection, sacrificed hours and hours month after month to compile a work from which no great credit could be added to his name or fame, and did so simply from the love of what he thought beautiful and pure. And certainly his love for that kind of music was very great. I can hardly say whether the study of Sebastian Bach led him to his great love for those simple strains, or whether the chorales led him to an increased love for Sebastian Bach, but never have I come across any one who, with so great a knowledge of his art, was able to enter so precisely, so readily and yet so intellectually into the simplicity of the ancient modes and tones, and into those simple strains which he helped to bring home to England in the Chorale Book.'

The book when issued was welcomed, and had a good circulation which, after more than forty years have passed, has not entirely ceased. As a complete collection, it was brought into use in but few churches; but it is a storehouse of beautiful things, and so much of it has been drawn upon by the compilers of Hymn-books for the Established Church and other religious denominations, that the original object of the editors has gone far towards accomplishment.

CHAPTER XXI.

HIS POSITION AT THE PHILHARMONIC ASSURED. WITHDRAWAL OF THE SOCIETY'S ORCHESTRA.

1859—1861.
æt. 43—45.

IN the course of these years, when pianoforte-teaching and public engagements ever continued to make full demands upon Bennett's energy, whilst hymnology filled up the crevices of his time, there was no lack of exceptional incidents to vary the theme of his ordinary life. Before passing to those incidents, it may be mentioned that, in the autumn of 1859, he left Russell Place, which had been his home for fourteen years, and migrated to Bayswater, where he remained, though not always in the same house, for an equal period. He first bought one of the smaller houses in Inverness Terrace[1], the purchase-money representing his savings up to the time.

He had now been conducting at the Philharmonic for four years (1856—59). The members of the band had, from the very beginning, made it clear that his appointment pleased them, and that they meant to support him. He had not allowed himself to count upon their favour as a certainty. In earlier life when, as one of the Directors of the Society, he had been behind the scenes, he had observed conductors failing to obtain the good-will of the players. Confidential references to this appear in his letters to Mendelssohn. Certain musicians in the Philharmonic orchestra stood high in their profession by virtue of other qualifications than that of orchestral playing. They were among the most prominent members, not only of the orchestra, but also of the

---

[1] Then no. 50, now no. 47. On the west side, the 4th house northwards from Inverness Place.

Society. Until such time as a restrictive law was passed, they were favourites for the office of Directors, in which capacity they rose superior to the conductor, taking part in his election and choosing the music that he had to conduct. They had a voice, too, in engaging their colleagues in the orchestra. It followed that they were leaders of musical opinion within the ranks, and that a conductor whose musicianship and personality were not acceptable to such authorities would have a poor chance of success. It will now be understood why Bennett, on the occasion of his first rehearsal in 1856, set less store on a loud ovation than he did on some generous and assuring words spoken to him by a few individuals, one at least of whom might reasonably have expected the conductorship for himself. As a result, he went home able to tell his wife that doubts which he had previously confided to her were already dispelled. Nor did he, later, ever find occasion to speak in any but the most grateful terms of the orchestra's attitude towards him.

The Society's approval, and the continuance of that approval, were shown in a direct way. The Members reserved to themselves for some little time the right of expressing their opinion, and for four years he successfully stood the test of an election at their general meeting. He had set at rest the fears formerly felt by some that no one save Costa could surmount the difficulties of the situation, and the Members, as if acknowledging that the question of the conductorship was permanently settled, now replaced in the hands of the seven Directors the duty of nomination, which, prior to Bennett's appointment, had rested with them. The sufficiently prosperous condition of the Society at this time was in more ways than one due to Bennett's presence. No musician in this country had more absolutely devoted himself to the cause of classical music, or had secured a larger following among those amateurs who belonged to the same party in musical politics. Such a following might not have crowded any large arena, but it certainly made some accountable addition to the Philharmonic audience. His past and present pupils were always well represented wherever he appeared in public, and the Society's concert-room during his *régime* presented one feature of exceptional interest from an educational point of view. Many benches were reserved for the long rows of young girls who were brought there to supplement the instruction which he gave them at their schools.

At the time of his appointment in 1856, the Society, being in straitened circumstances, had reduced the number of concerts given each year from eight to six, thus escaping a pecuniary loss which invariably attended the two concerts given before the commencement of the London season. This retrenchment had not been made without some sacrifice of pride, nor without foreseeing that it would open the way for hostile comments on the Society's decline. A few successful years now made it possible to remove this outstanding reproach, and at the end of 1860, when Bennett had conducted for five seasons, it was resolved to announce the full number of concerts for the year 1861. He underlined the news in a letter written to one of his children in November: 'We are to have *Eight Philharmonic Concerts* next year, so my prospects are busy, what with Leeds and other things.' Little time, however, was allowed for exulting over this happy restoration. Serious trouble was at hand; the well-being of the Philharmonic was not desired by everybody; and the month of December revealed a transaction which stirred up grave suspicions. The Society's concerts were given on Monday evenings. About two-thirds of the orchestra, forty-two out of a total of sixty-six, also played at the Royal Italian Opera. When the Directors sent out the usual letters to engage their orchestra for 1861, these forty-two players replied that they were unable to accept, because they had found in their Opera-engagements a new clause, which bound them to attend at the theatre, if required, on an additional night, viz. Monday. Now, of course, it would have been absurd to expect a great institution like the Royal Italian Opera, with such enormous stakes at risk, to forego, out of consideration for others or from sentimental regard to tradition, any real chance of promoting its own interests. But Monday had never been an Opera night, and it was not believed in Hanover Square that the Managers had any *bonâ fide* intention of making it one, whereas the use of the band on that evening had long been regarded as a prescriptive right of the Philharmonic. The Directors, and Bennett with them, felt convinced that this new proceeding was a malicious act of antagonism on the part of Costa, who conducted at Covent Garden. If they were right, it does not follow that the act was directed against Bennett or, rather, against him alone, because there had been a quarrel between Costa and Anderson, the leading Director, of a more recent date, and of a much more serious kind than that between Costa and Bennett. An incident, with similar circumstances, had occurred a year or two before, when the chorus of the Sacred Harmonic Society, over which Costa presided, had suddenly withdrawn its aid a few days before the annual performance of 'The Messiah' by the Royal Society of Musicians, leaving Bennett, who was the conductor for the latter Society, and Anderson, who as treasurer was its chief officer, very little time to collect another chorus of 500 voices.

Whatever may have been the object or origin of such acts—the opinion held by those whom they affected is all that the writer can vouch for—the Philharmonic Directors were, in any case, now confronted with a difficult dilemma. They must either lose two-thirds of their orchestra, or they must change their night of performance. In neither direction were they likely to escape injury. On the one hand, the members of the old orchestra were the established favourites of concert-goers. Some of them seemed to enjoy a unique position, holding, as it were, the monopoly, granted by public opinion, of performance on their particular instruments. The substitution of other players, however competent, would jar upon the feelings of the Public, who ever expect, and did so no less in the days of small concert-rooms, to enjoy their music amidst accustomed surroundings. Mrs S. C. Hall, the authoress, wrote at this time: 'The members of the old Philharmonic are more like a band of brothers; you know exactly where to look for the old familiar faces.' Certainly, where music is concerned, such sentiment cannot be disregarded, and the Directors could not face so conspicuous a change of *personnel* without much misgiving. On the other hand, to abandon the Monday night, which had been their own since the Society's foundation, was a step from which they no less recoiled. Here, again, the subscribers might be greatly disturbed. The retention of the Monday night would no doubt tell in favour of rival Societies. The New Philharmonic and The Musical Society of London, who gave their concerts later in the week, would still have at their command the old band with its unrivalled prestige. But the interference with their night by those who, as they believed, did not want it for themselves, was the main grievance of the Philharmonic authorities, and to alter it would be an admission of defeat. The Directors, therefore, decided to keep their cherished Monday, to engage a new band, and to make themselves, once for all, independent of Covent Garden.

The difficulty of supplying the places of those players who, much against their will, were obliged to submit to the new conditions laid down at the Opera, was not insuperable. At a no very remote time, it would have been said that there was only one available orchestra in London. In the days when Bennett gave concerts for which he wished to employ a band, he, like others, only knew of one place to find it. Its headquarters during the season were at the Opera-House, and its engagement occasioned trouble and uncertainty, which some concert-givers would doubtless have spared themselves if there had been any alternative. The exigencies of Opera-rehearsals, the doubt as to the time they would last, gave the players little freedom to promise their services for the afternoon. Costa's favour could alone make the fulfilment of such promise a certainty. He did not readily extend that favour to concerts conducted by others than himself, though he had the power to stretch a point when he had the wish. It has already been seen how a concert of Bennett's, which Mendelssohn conducted in 1844, was nearly wrecked by the late arrival of the band. On the other hand, William Dorrell would often relate how he had called upon Costa in 1842 with the object of preferring two requests. He was about to give a Morning concert. He had invited his friend Bennett to conduct it; but in doing this, he had left the beaten track; for though Bennett had just appeared as one of the Philharmonic conductors, he was young, according to the notion of the time, for such a position, and the conducting of orchestral concerts had so far been a privilege of seniors. Dorrell now asked Costa whether he would permit him to engage the band. The situation was awkward; for why, to begin with, should Costa go out of his way to accept for his band an invitation from which he was himself excluded? The refusal Dorrell met with was so prompt and decisive, that he was quite disconcerted, and he could not venture for some little time to put his second question. At length he told Costa that he was wishing to secure the services of his brother, Raphael Costa, as a singer at the concert. Now Costa, being very fond of his younger brother, and desirous of his advancement, did not conceal the pleasure this proposal gave him, for his face at once relaxed from its previous sternness. He then chatted on very pleasantly with his visitor, and as the latter was leaving the room without having mustered up courage to revert to the chief object of his visit, Costa held his hand, saying: 'Good-bye, Mr Dorrell—*and*—I will see that you have the orchestra.' This story is not told as against Costa. On the contrary, it is a pleasure to present him in the character of a good brother. It was told by Dorrell simply as an illustration of the difficulty in obtaining the *one* band.

The time, however, came when this single orchestra could no longer supply every need. Then it was suddenly discovered that London, or London with a little help from the Continent, was equal to the emergency. The secession of great singers from Her Majesty's Theatre in 1847, and the establishment of a rival Opera at Covent Garden, for which Costa and the hitherto sole orchestra were secured, necessitated the formation of a new band for the old House. This second force, on its appearance, caused considerable surprise; first, by the mere fact of its existence, and, secondly, by the efficiency which, under Balfe's direction, it soon displayed. Jullien's monster concerts gave, in their turn, further proof of the increasing number of clever executants, native and foreign, who were residing in London. Nevertheless, as the years went on, nothing occurred outside the confines of the theatrical world to disturb the general impression that the famous old orchestra stood by itself. It continued to be seen and heard at all the sacred and secular performances of prime importance throughout the country. As far as regarded the class of music presented at the Philharmonic, it was the only organization which possessed, through long experience, the already acquired knowledge so indispensable in the days of long concerts and comparatively short rehearsals. Thus, when the Society was bereft of its assistance, any new combination, however abundant the materials from which its elements might be selected, must, for the special purpose intended, be an entirely untried one. The Directors took infinite pains in filling the vacancies, and in this business they certainly allowed Bennett, who was full of anxiety as to the result, to take an active part. It was afterwards assumed, on a rough estimate, that the new orchestra at the Philharmonic was identical with that of Her Majesty's Theatre, but the Directors were not satisfied to follow so simple a course. They took a wide survey of possibilities. Even two Opera-Houses no longer accounted for all the good stringed-instrument players in London. A three-months' engagement at the theatre, with protracted rehearsals and very late hours, disturbed any plan for continuous work throughout the year in other directions. Some preferred to emancipate themselves, and to follow the regular life of a professor of music, teaching the pianoforte, playing the organ, and of course giving lessons to, or leading quartets for, the few amateur stringed-instrument players of the day. These men were open to concert-engagements, and could not be left out of count in the formation of an orchestra. Then, again, there were a few whose prominence as soloists had absolved them from orchestral-playing, but who, it was thought, might be willing to make an exception in favour of the Philharmonic. If the Directors could have had free choice of the talent to be found at Her Majesty's Theatre and elsewhere, their path would have been a smooth one; but there is such a thing as a Table of Precedence in an orchestra, and they accordingly found themselves baulked at every turn by conflicting claims. Of the former orchestra, twenty-four members remained, representing the contingent which had always been drawn from Her Majesty's private band. These naturally looked for promotion under a fresh arrangement. The negotiations spread over many weeks, and demanded delicate diplomacy. It is well remembered how much time was spent over finding the best possible successors to Lucas and Howell, who, as leaders of the basses, had for years been in the front of every orchestral scene, just as Lindley and Dragonetti had been in the previous generation. Bennett worried himself immensely over the question whether he could approach his friend Piatti, without hurting the *amour propre* of one who had long ceased to play in orchestras. There was a prolonged search for a first double-bass player, till at last A. J. Rowland, who had settled at Southampton as an organist and pianoforte-teacher, agreed to come up for the rehearsals and concerts, and did so as long as Bennett held the conductorship. In process of time, gentle persuasion brought performers to see that they could not all occupy front places, and upon agreement that a few of the more eminent should sit at the chief desks in rotation, the combination was adjusted, and Hogarth, the Secretary and Historian of the Society, has recorded that 'when the concerts of the 1861 season commenced it was unanimously admitted that the Philharmonic orchestra had suffered no loss of the qualities by which it had gained its high and European reputation.' Bennett, when anticipating this change, said to one of his pupils that the prospect troubled him, and that he would have to begin his work all over again. He did not scruple to mention, at the same time, the name of the man to whom he imputed the injury. The severance of a friendly association with the old orchestra was bound to be painful, but from a musical standpoint he became reconciled to the change. He discovered, for one thing, that he could more easily influence those who had no preconceived and firmly-rooted notions. He had now to deal with some who, though fine executants, were conscious of their inexperience of classical music. These were glad to learn from him, and to submit themselves to the guidance of a conductor always so considerate for their feelings. To give a particular case, a member of the band, who was known to be one of the most skilful performers in Europe on his particular instrument, would often consult Bennett on the interpretation of passages, and the latter would speak most sympathetically of the delightful humility with which this man, who could by his solo-playing astonish crowds, came to him to be privately coached in a passage of accompaniment to Schumann's Pianoforte Concerto, admitting that he could not, by himself, master the rhythm.

This new band worked with Bennett most loyally for six years. Critics, other than Hogarth, did not allow that it was equal to the old one. Davison, who was never quite in accord with the Philharmonic, and who did not go far out of his way in order to write anything in its favour, sometimes disappointed Bennett very much by little things he wrote or did not write about the orchestra. On one occasion, however, he paid the conductor a pretty and well appreciated compliment by saying: 'I can't make out, Bennett, why it is, that though the other Societies have the best band, the Symphonies always go best at the Philharmonic.'

CHAPTER XXII.

THE INTERNATIONAL EXHIBITION OF 1862.

1861—1862.

æt. 45, 46.

BENNETT was still engaged on the Chorale Book, when certain forthcoming events demanded his services as a composer. By a strange coincidence, a Chorale of his own was the first thing asked for.

INTERNATIONAL EXHIBITION, 1862.
July 17th, 1861.

SIR,
 I am directed by Her Majesty's Commissioners for the Exhibition of 1862 to inform you, that at the opening of the Exhibition on the 1st of May, it is their wish to have four new musical compositions, each by a different composer, representing France, Germany, Italy and England.

Her Majesty's Commissioners, having regard to the position which your name occupies in connection with the music of this country, desire me to enquire whether you would kindly represent her on this occasion.

The Commissioners do not wish to have the copyright of the Music, but only the permission to have it performed on the occasion of the opening; and they are of course prepared to pay the expenses of copying the music.

The Class of Music contemplated is:

(1) An Anthem, of about the same length as Handel's Coronation Anthem.
(2) A Chorale—for voices only.
(3) A Triumphal March.
(4) A March for Wind Instruments only.

The Commissioners would ask you to undertake the composition of the Air for the Chorale, the words of which they hope will be furnished by the Poet Laureate. All means of adequate execution will be provided to the best of their resources; and they will feel obliged by an early answer to this letter.

The Commissioners in working out this part of their plans have applied to Mons. Meyerbeer to represent Germany, Mons. Auber to represent France, and Signor Verdi to represent Italy.

I have the honour to be,
Sir,
Your obedient servant,
F. R. SANDFORD (*Secretary*).

W. Sterndale Bennett, Esq.

There was an air of novelty about this scheme. At a grand international festival, music was to be introduced, not as a mere handmaid to ceremony, but for its own sake, and with a prominent place assigned to it beside other arts which it was an object of the Exhibition to display. Here might be imagined a sign that respect for music was increasing in this country among those who were not necessarily concerned in cultivating it themselves. The plan was far in advance of anything that had been thought of at the time of the 1851 Exhibition, and it gave great satisfaction to all those who had the interests of music at heart. Bennett was evidently pleased to receive the invitation, though he felt the responsibility of the task. 'I thought Balfe would be asked,' he quietly said; and, after that, he scarcely spoke about the subject, except, as will be seen, in reference to Costa, who had been appointed to conduct the music. When, later on, any pleasure he felt was spoilt by attendant circumstances, and when a universal excitement was aroused on his behalf, he showed remarkable restraint, and allowed few words to escape his lips.

In November, 1861, Tennyson sent him a message to the effect that he had written something, that he felt nervous about it, and would like to talk it over with him.

Thereupon Bennett went to the chambers in the Temple where Tennyson was stopping with a friend. He was fascinated by the quaint occupation in which he discovered the poet completely absorbed, viz. that of drying tobacco on the hobs of the grate; he thought, as a listener, that the reading of the poem was curiously monotonous; but when, before leaving, he ventured to confide his own anxiety and spoke of public criticism as sitting at his elbow when he tried to compose, then the words of sympathy which followed, and Tennyson's assurance that he himself knew that feeling only too well, went to his heart.

When Bennett made a study of the words, he thought them too elaborate to be set to a simple Chorale and to be sung entirely by unaccompanied voices, according to the original wish of the Commissioners. Indeed, with regard to one section of the Ode, he felt doubtful how it would yield to his musical treatment at all. When, in the course of composition, he found it manageable, then he was relieved, and would afterwards playfully say that he had set 'The Exhibition Catalogue' to music; for the nineteen lines in question contained the poet's enumeration of the 'marvels' gathered within 'the long laborious miles of Palace.' To illustrate such a poem Bennett desired an orchestral accompaniment. An orchestra was to be used by the other composers, so he asked and was granted permission to employ it. This was settled in December. In the same month, the death of the Prince Consort occurring, the Poet Laureate made a very important addition to his Ode, and of this he wrote to Bennett:—

FARRINGFORD, FRESHWATER,
I. OF W.
Jan. 13*th*, 1862.

MY DEAR SIR,

I wish you would come down and see me, you know you promised to come, pray do.

As to the inauguration poem—when our good Prince left us, I thought it was absolutely necessary to notice his loss and therefore inserted four lines. Afterwards I heard that the Queen did not wish any allusion made to Her loss—so I would not trouble you with the lines. Now I hear (none of my instigating) that Lord Granville showed them to H. M. and she wished them to be included.

Pray come if you can, you start by 11 o'clock train from Waterloo and take your ticket for Lymington—then in half-an-hour the boat crosses.

Yours always,
A. TENNYSON.

The additional lines, the first of which is now so well-known through its constant quotation in references to the Prince Consort, were:—

> 'O silent Father of our Kings to be,
> Mourn'd in this golden hour of jubilee,
> For this, for all, we weep our thanks to Thee!'

together with another new line—

> 'The world compelling plan was Thine'—

with which to open the next section of the poem.

The first message from Tennyson, which had taken Bennett to the Temple, and the above letter, which resulted in a short visit to Farringford, show the poet anxious to confer with the musician; but for what purpose, beyond that of conveying to him his own emphasis of the words by reciting them in his presence, is not clear. Bennett mentioned in one of his letters to the Commissioners that there were still many things on which he must consult Mr Tennyson before parting with the MS. of his music. Tennyson, perhaps, invited him to suggest difficulties which particular words might present. Bennett did make some suggestions of that kind, because he afterwards said that he had found Tennyson very inflexible about changes. One change at least was made. In the original MS., which lies in Bennett's album, the Ode opens with the line, 'Up-lift a hundred voices full and sweet,' and it was at Bennett's request that Tennyson substituted the word 'thousand' for 'hundred.' Certainly, his association at this time with the Poet Laureate, ending, as it did, with a charming letter from Mrs Tennyson when the music was published, remained as one of his few pleasing recollections of this Exhibition. In the following year, 1863, when Tennyson wrote his Ode of Welcome to the Princess Alexandra (now

Her Majesty), Bennett hoped to renew such a connection. He at once asked and obtained the poet's permission to set the Ode to music. Unfortunately, however, another composer, without waiting to obtain the same permission, hastily set the words in the form of a popular song, and this upset Bennett's project.

In the third week of January, 1862, the composer had the complete poem for the Exhibition in his hands, and it was about this time that he was overheard to strike up on the pianoforte, with that decision and finished effect which made such a delightful impression on those privileged to hear his music for the first time, the unaccompanied Chorale with which the Ode was to open. Mrs Bennett, who was one of the listeners outside his room, and who failed at the moment to recognize the evident connection between his strains and the words of the Ode, would not believe that he had made so early a start with the work; but this was so, and as it still wanted fifteen weeks to the first of May, no anxiety was felt at home about his being ready in time. Five weeks later, however, a needless and irritating pressure was put upon him to produce his score. This was quite unfair, because it must have been very well known that the poet had taken his full share of the period available for the joint-work.

Bennett had assumed that the time had now come for bygones to be bygones between Costa and himself. He took for granted, and expressed himself pleased to think, that Costa was going to conduct his work. The letters which next arrived did nothing to disturb that impression. They could only tend to confirm it. Thus, the Secretary to the Commissioners wrote on February 20 :—

'Costa called here to-day and was anxious to know whether I had received your contribution to the musical part of the opening Ceremony. I told him that I was expecting to hear from you *very soon*.' The Secretary wrote again, on March 3 :—'I have just had Costa here, very uneasy as to the Music for the opening. When may I hope to have your part of the work?' Bennett replied on March 5 :—'You need not be uneasy with respect to my contribution, which I shall soon have the pleasure to hand over to you. You are perhaps aware that the Ode is on a much larger scale than was first suggested to me as to be illustrated by a Chorale, and the composition has given me much thought—added to which Mr Tennyson has since the death of the Prince Consort put in some extra lines in the middle of his work which, much as I admire them, has caused a reconstruction of much of the music. I will not be later than ten days or a fortnight, and I should be glad to wait upon Mr Costa in the meantime, if he wishes to see me—being very glad that he has undertaken the care of my humble work.'

The last paragraph in this letter appears to have caused a little delay. The Commissioners now discovered, perhaps through forwarding Bennett's message to Costa, that there was a flaw in their preliminary arrangements. Bennett heard nothing further for ten days. Then the Secretary wrote:—'When you are *ready*, as I hope you will be *soon*, will you kindly communicate with Mr Bowley, of the Sacred Harmonic Society, in whose hands all the working arrangements of the musical part of the opening ceremony are placed. He will be able to settle as to the rehearsals for which you may wish, the arrangement being, as I believe you are aware, that you should conduct your own composition.'

Bennett replied :—

March 19th, 1862.

MY DEAR SIR,

I have already learnt from Mr Bowley the probable arrangement for rehearsals, &c., and will take care to be quite ready although it is still necessary for me to consult Mr Tennyson upon several points before parting with my MS.

Allow me to say that I have never had the idea that I was expected to conduct my work at the opening ceremonial; this you will readily see from my letter of the 6th inst. wherein I expressed my satisfaction that Mr Costa would take charge of my work. I also offered in that same letter to wait upon Mr Costa and talk the work over with him. It disappoints me then to find no reply to this intended courtesy on my part. I certainly should consider that my position should entitle me to have direct communication with the chief Director of the music, and feel assured that you as the organ of Her Majesty's Commissioners can wish me nothing less.

I must now most respectfully and distinctly decline to conduct my work on the occasion of the opening of the Exhibition, as by so doing I should place myself in a very false position with the public, who would certainly wonder that I should interfere with Mr Costa's duties.

Believe me, My dear Sir,
Yours very faithfully,
WILLIAM STERNDALE BENNETT.

F. R. Sandford, Esq.

Sir Wentworth Dilke, one of the Commissioners, now courteously offered to call upon Bennett at any time convenient. He came, and then explained that Costa, when engaged as conductor eight months before, had made it a condition of his services being available, that he should not be expected to conduct any work by Bennett in the event of the latter being asked to furnish one. Now, the Commissioners, when inviting Bennett to compose, had stated that 'all adequate means of execution would be provided;' but they had either forgotten to arrange for the work being conducted, or if they had made any such arrangement, had neglected to make Bennett acquainted with it. It was not usual in those days for a composer, when his works were played, to take the bâton from the regularly appointed conductor. The foreign representatives had not been invited to do so, and Bennett had nearly finished his composition before he became aware that any exceptional circumstances were to attend its production.

The Commissioners, however, from this point, threw the onus of an omission, the importance of which they pretended to ignore, on to Bennett's shoulders, and he was now asked to conduct his music himself or to name some one to take 'his place.' But it was not *his* place, and he would have nothing to do with supplying it.

April 4, 1862.

MY DEAR SIR,

According to my former note I do most distinctly yet respectfully decline to conduct my own composition at the opening of the Exhibition, nor do I feel it at all within my province to name any gentleman to supply the place of Mr Costa in that which he declines to undertake. Of course I cannot help feeling disappointed that it should be proposed to present my work in a different manner to the works of other Composers invited to write for the occasion.

I remain, Dear Sir,
Yours very faithfully,
WILLIAM STERNDALE BENNETT.

F. R. Sandford, Esq.

A few days passed, and then only three weeks remained before the Opening ceremony. Bennett's music was finished and he understood that it was being printed. On April 10, the Secretary wrote:—

'I am directed by Her Majesty's Commissioners to say that they cannot take the responsibility of naming a conductor for your music. They must therefore request you to name one, as you refuse to conduct it yourself. It will otherwise be impossible for the music to be performed, Mr Costa having as you are aware declined. The Commissioners are prepared to invite any one you name.'

This letter caused some consternation in Bennett's household. He himself showed no sign of being disturbed by it, and he wrote the following reply:—

April 11, 1862.

MY DEAR SIR,

I cannot on any consideration undertake to name a conductor of my music in the place of Mr Costa, and as your letter of yesterday leads me to infer what the decision of Her Majesty's Commissioners will be in that case, I have only to say that I shall bow to their decision with the utmost respect.

Believe me, My dear Sir,
Faithfully yours,
WILLIAM STERNDALE BENNETT.

Before the Commissioners thus threatened a withdrawal of the work, it would appear that their musical advisers or agents had already been scheming in that direction. On March 15, Bennett had been asked to communicate, as soon as his work was complete, with the Secretary of the Sacred Harmonic Society. This was in view of arranging rehearsals, and of sending the vocal parts, for preliminary practice, into the provinces, whence 1400 of the chorus singers were to be drafted. When Lamborn Cock, Bennett's publisher, towards the end of March, was starting to engrave the parts, the Secretary of the Sacred Harmonic Society called upon him and urged that the said Society should be entrusted with the engraving, as they had at their command resources which would ensure a maximum of speed. Lamborn Cock naturally liked to manage Bennett's affairs himself. He therefore demurred, but he was pressed to give way, and at length, though with much reluctance, parted with the manuscript. A fortnight passed. Then, within three or four days of the music being actually required, the score was returned to Lamborn Cock, without explanation, and without a single note of it having been stamped. When a protest was made, the Secretary of the Sacred Harmonic Society said that he had received instructions not to print the work, as it was not going to be performed. It then proved exceedingly difficult to get it ready for rehearsals, but this was done by Lamborn Cock's strenuous exertions, so that there should be no excuse for its non-performance on the ground of its not being ready in time.

When it became generally known that the Ode was in jeopardy, the Press took the matter up with great vehemence. A storm was brewing. The Commissioners, at last, had the thing shown to them in a new light, and they approached Bennett again. The Secretary wrote on April 15:—

'I am desired by H. M. Commissioners to say, in answer to your letter of the 12th inst., that though they are at a loss to understand why you will neither conduct your own work or name any person except Mr Costa to act for you, they are so unwilling that it should not be performed that they have decided on suggesting two names to you and asking you to select one—M. Sainton and Mr Mellon.'

Bennett consistently declined to take part in such selection, and the matter was finally settled by the Commissioners themselves appointing a conductor. The Secretary wrote on April 23:—'I have the pleasure, by desire of H. M. Commissioners, to forward you copy of a letter just received from Mr Sainton, whom they have asked to conduct your Cantata.'

From the rehearsal on April 29, at Exeter Hall, Bennett absented himself. Feeling was running very high, and he disliked anything like a demonstration. At this very rehearsal, when Costa observed a few members of the chorus leaving the Hall, and called out in a brusque tone, 'Turn those women back,' he was vigorously hissed by those who habitually submitted to his rule without a murmur. Davison came to Bennett's house the same evening, upbraided him for not being present to support Sainton in a rather trying position, and obtained from him a promise of attendance at the final rehearsal in the Exhibition Building next morning. Bennett accordingly went, and any soreness of feeling that remained was greatly soothed by the marked courtesy which Lord Granville, the President of the Commissioners, showed him on the occasion. His reception by the performers, who numbered 2400, was so extraordinary, that Meyerbeer, who must have been well-versed in such proceedings, was quite astonished and turned to Davison for an explanation. The incident was thus reported in *The Times*:—'After the Ode had been gone through once, a general cry for "Bennett" was raised, and the Professor, at length making his appearance was led into the orchestra by M. Sainton. The greeting he received was such as he will possibly never forget. We remember nothing more hearty, nothing more spontaneous. There was one universal burst of cheering, accompanied by waving of hats and handkerchiefs, the thousand ladies of the chorus being conspicuous in their manifestations of enthusiasm. About the extraordinary popularity of Professor Bennett, if there had ever been a doubt, this would have dispelled it.'

Next day the Exhibition opened. The Prince Consort's

death had been the cause of general and deep depression. The absence of the Royal Family on this occasion with the mournful reason for it, gave to the proceedings a dull and perfunctory character which nothing could be expected to brighten. At the same time all the music specially written— as far as the public were allowed to hear it; for alas! Verdi's contribution had been rejected by the Commissioners, in spite of his willing response to their request—was much admired. The English choral work was thought to stand out in bold relief between the brilliant orchestral pieces by Auber and Meyerbeer. Reserved seats for those officially connected with the Exhibition and their friends were numerous. Bennett had no place assigned to him. He listened to his music, as well as he could, standing at the back of the crowd. He had felt a special desire to judge of its effect, because in view of a monster performance in a building sure to present acoustical disadvantages, he had deliberately aimed for simplicity and breadth of treatment when preparing his score. His wife, now a great invalid, stood by his side, participating for the last time in anything that publicly concerned her husband's artistic life.

The Ode was published, and numerous performances of it were given both in London and the provinces. It had a 'run' at 'The Philharmonic'—not the classic temple in Hanover Square, but a Music Hall in Islington—where it was reverently sung by a choir of some twenty voices to the accompaniment of a pianoforte and harmonium. It was interesting to watch the attentive faces of the audience, who nightly encored the Ode and listened to a repetition of the last movement.

The Commissioners, for their treatment of Bennett, and Costa for the condition he had made with them, were attacked on all sides with great severity. The incidents were discussed at full length not only in musical journals, or in the columns specially devoted to music in daily papers, but as matters of some national concern. *Punch* made several caustic references, showing himself specially bitter against Costa. One of the references headed 'Amiable Excuses' ran thus:—

'We don't think that STERNDALE BENNETT has a right to complain that Mr COSTA will not conduct him at the

Inauguration. Costa sometimes does not even know how to conduct himself. Besides he perhaps wanted to show, by making the exception, that he was not an *omnibus* conductor —in spite of what might have been inferred, from his manners touching this matter.'

The Daily Telegraph chose the circumstances as the subject of a leading article, this probably being an early if not the first instance of a musical matter finding such place in an English newspaper. After referring to the position which Costa enjoyed in this country and the generous treatment that he had always met with at the hands of England and the English people, the writer[1] of the article added:—

'Suddenly he [Costa] turns round upon us and won't play Professor Bennett's music, or wave the bâton to a note of his cantata. Fêted and feasted for years and years on English soil, he has interposed his contemptible private bickerings on this solemn occasion. The spoiled child of the easy English public, he slaps its sensibilities in the face upon this exigency. The man whom we have made something from nothing, famous from obscure, selects the moment when we show him our greatest favour, to show us his greatest arrogance. M. Costa, it is ill done of you! it is ungratefully done! it is done unlike an artist and the interpreter of art! It is enough to cure us of the mania for foreign music so profitable to you and to your fellows. It is almost enough, though the idea will be as horrible to you as a discord, to make us ask henceforward whether England can do without M. Costa, since M. Costa can so easily affront England!'

This was hard-hitting, but it was no more than an expression of the general feeling at the time. The day after the article appeared, Costa wrote a letter to the Commissioners taking for his text the first word, 'suddenly,' of the passage quoted above. He was justified according to the strict letter of the law in throwing the responsibility of what had happened on those who had engaged him. However discreditable the public might consider the condition that he had made with regard to their compatriot's music, after all, the discredit really rested with those who had accepted that condition. The Commissioners, however, now made their

---

[1] Presumed, at the time, to be Campbell (afterwards Sir Campbell) Clarke.

position far worse by introducing Bennett into their reply to Costa, thereby trying again, as they had all along tried, to make him the scapegoat for their own mistakes. Costa published his correspondence with them in the newspapers:—

59 ECCLESTON SQUARE, April 26, 1862.

DEAR SIR—My attention has been called to several statements in the public newspapers, reflecting upon me as to the performance of Dr Bennett's music at the opening of the Exhibition; and as it appears to be the object of the writers to induce the belief that I have through caprice or some other unworthy motive, created embarrassment by 'suddenly' declining to conduct Dr Bennett's composition, and virtually violated an engagement previously made between me and Her Majesty's Commissioners, I must request that you will favour me by recalling to the recollection of the Commissioners that, at the very outset, when I was first consulted on the subject of the musical arrangements, early in July last, I made it a distinct condition of my services being available, that I should not be expected to conduct any work of Dr Bennett, if he should be invited to furnish one for performance on the occasion of the opening, as I must, for reasons which were explained to the Commissioners, positively decline, with their complete assent, to do so.

Under these circumstances, I shall esteem it as a favour if the Commissioners will relieve me from the imputation now cast upon me, by admitting the facts to be as I have stated above.—Believe me, dear Sir, &c., &c.

M. COSTA.

F. R. Sandford, Esq., &c., &c.

EXHIBITION BUILDINGS, April 28, 1862.

DEAR SIR—In reply to your letter of Saturday, Her Majesty's Commissioners desire me to express their regret that you should have experienced any annoyance from the unfounded reports to which you refer, and to state that your letter gives a perfectly correct account of the condition which you laid down with respect to any work by Dr Bennett at the opening of the Exhibition, when you kindly undertook to direct the musical arrangements for that occasion.

I am to add that Dr Bennett, when applied to by Her Majesty's Commissioners, declined either to conduct his own chorale, or to name any one whom he would wish to do so, or finally to state whether he would prefer that his work should be entrusted to Mr Alfred Mellon or to M. Sainton, when the Commissioners offered to invite either of these gentlemen to fill his place in the orchestra.

Under these circumstances, the Commissioners, knowing the confidence that you place in Mr Sainton, and the position which he fills in your staff, invited him to conduct Dr Bennett's work; and they have much satisfaction in thinking that it is now in the hands of one so well qualified to do justice to its merits.

I am, dear Sir, &c., &c.,

F. R. SANDFORD.

Michael Costa, Esq., &c., &c.

The Daily News thus commented on the above letters:—

'* * * Mr Costa certainly shows that there has been no ambiguity or vacillation on his part. As early as last July he announced his intention not to conduct any music of Dr Bennett's, and he has consistently adhered to it. This, as we read his letter, is all the merit he claims.

'Mr Sandford, on behalf of the Commissioners, accepts and confirms Mr Costa's representations, and adds an explanation which does not seem to be called for by anything in Mr Costa's note, but is apparently put in for the benefit of the Commissioners themselves. The Commissioners are anxious to make it known that having made a secret arrangement to the prejudice of Dr Bennett, they subsequently tried to make him a party to the arrangement. It cannot, we think, surprise any one that Dr Bennett declined their invitation to name a conductor and left the responsibility on the right shoulders.'

When the Commissioners' letter to Costa appeared in print on April 29, Bennett immediately went off to see their Secretary. He, too, had now some questions to ask. A few days later, he was requested to send his questions in writing. This he did, adding:—'I put these questions in a formal manner according to the wish of Her Majesty's Commissioners. The answers to them are necessary to me, as I find the public have derived an erroneous impression, prejudicial to me, from your letter to Mr Costa which he published in *The Times* of the 29th ult. My feelings were certainly not considered in that letter, as I have really done nothing more nor less than the Commissioners invited me to do, and am in no way responsible for anything disagreeable which has happened.'

The Commissioners did not reply to Bennett's questions with the same alacrity that they had shown in the case of Costa. They did not give to the one the same chance, if he was wishing to take it, as they gave to the other, of publishing a pair of letters while public interest was still rife. Until Bennett pressed them for a reply, they did not answer him at all. Three weeks after his interview with the Secretary, he received the following halting apology:—

EXHIBITION BUILDING,
May, 1862[1].

DEAR SIR,

In reply to the enquiries contained in your letter of the 6th inst. I am directed by Her Majesty's Commissioners to state that they regret that it would appear that you were not made acquainted with the condition, under which Mr Costa had accepted the post of conductor of the musical performances, when you were invited to compose a chorale for the opening ceremony—and that it would seem that until the day named by you, you did not receive any intimation that you would be expected to conduct your own piece, although a statement to that effect appeared in some of the public journals in the month of July, 1861.

I am, Dear Sir,
Yours very truly,
F. R. SANDFORD.

Professor Sterndale Bennett.

[1] The letter does not give the day of the month, but Mrs Bennett endorsed it as received on May 20.

CHAPTER XXIII.

A YEAR OF CONTRASTING IMPORTS.
INSTALLATION OF THE CHANCELLOR AT CAMBRIDGE.
JUBILEE OF THE PHILHARMONIC SOCIETY.
DOMESTIC BEREAVEMENT.

1862.
æt. 46.

THE year 1862 was very interesting to those who desired Bennett's advance towards a still wider recognition. Up to this time—he was in his 47th year—he had only received one commission to write music for an important public occasion, viz. for the Leeds Festival in 1858. It was contrary to his nature to canvass for opportunities of publicity as a composer, and he had not been drawn out by the invitation of others, to prepare works wanted at fixed times. But the calls which now came to him, and the readiness with which he responded to them, led his friends to hope that such calls might for the future reach him more frequently, so that the act of composition might be less at his own discretion than in the past. This hope, however, was not realized. He only received in later years one other such invitation. Therefore the time now passing remained, in this respect, exceptional. It had another feature, which marks it as a serious period of his life. The season of 1862 provided him with a very closely-knit series of engagements. From March 3, the date of the first Philharmonic rehearsal, until the beginning of August, his time was measured by minutes rather than by hours. This was a dispensation by which his mind was relieved from the full pressure of a more painful burden. A cloud of sorrow was gathering above his hearth, and as he worked, he was all the while conscious that the year, before its close, must prove the saddest he had known.

While finishing his music for the Exhibition, he was constantly superintending rehearsals of the St Matthew 'Passion' for a performance on May 24. That performance, as compared with those previously given, gained much through the masterful rendering of the Tenor part by Sims Reeves. The singer found here an opportunity of displaying his genius and his highly cultivated musicianship to an extent which surprised many who thought themselves already well-acquainted with his powers. In view of the same occasion, Bennett saw through the press, and wrote a Preface for his English edition of Bach's work[1]. Proofs of 'The Chorale Book for England' were at the same time passing to and fro between Mr Otto Goldschmidt and himself. He conducted the eight ordinary concerts at the Philharmonic, with an extra one given to celebrate the Society's Jubilee. He also conducted the annual performance for the benefit of the Royal Society of Musicians, a concert for the Society of Female Musicians, and the Grand Matinée given by Mrs Anderson on her retirement. His old pupils valued his assistance at their concerts, and he liked to give it; so this year he conducted his Exhibition Ode for W. G. Cusins, and played, with Joachim, Bach's Sonata in E major for Harold Thomas. In the course of the same season, business called him to Cambridge on nine days. The musical arrangements for the Installation of a new Chancellor of the University, which included a performance in the Senate House and a concert in the Guildhall, were entirely in his hands, and it is well-remembered that the engagement of eminent singers and of an efficient orchestra for two days in Cambridge, during the height of the London season, gave him much personal trouble, and involved late visits to the Opera House after his day's work was done. As a judge of musical instruments at the Exhibition he attended many meetings. He gave much consideration to composition. An Ode for the Installation at Cambridge followed closely upon that which he wrote for the Exhibition. The Jubilee of the Philharmonic Society claimed another work from his pen. Though with all this

---

[1] For later proceedings of Bach Society, see Note, Appendix A.

his usual time-table was no little disturbed, he managed, in the twenty weeks between the dates named above, to teach the pianoforte for exactly 600 hours. The reader is asked to excuse the details. They may help to upset a tradition, the result of false report, that 'Sterndale Bennett was such a lazy man.'

The Duke of Devonshire was elected to succeed the Prince Consort as Chancellor of the University of Cambridge. The preparations for his Installation brought Bennett into a close and delightful association with Charles Kingsley, whose acquaintance he had first made in 1848 at Queen's College, Harley Street, and whom, since 1856, he had occasionally met in Cambridge. It was now Bennett's province to set music to the Ode which Professor[1] Kingsley, at the request of the University, had undertaken to write for the ceremony of Installation. The obligation of furnishing music for poetry which a composer does not choose himself, and which he must accept without demur, is no light one. That Bennett, on the one or two occasions when he had to face this duty, should feel some anxiety is not to be wondered at. But it might cause surprise, and it came as a surprise to himself, that a distinguished poet of that time should look round the question, and try to consider it from the musician's point of view as well as from his own. Extracts from Charles Kingsley's letters to Bennett will show his careful consideration for the composer, his unconventional idea that the work should, as far as practicable, be the work of two minds acting conjointly and concurrently, and his generous wish to bend his thoughts in any direction suggested by his fellow-worker. Bennett was soon relieved of any preliminary fear as to the form or character which the Ode might take. He was not asked to find pompous strains. Charles Kingsley shrank from what he called the 'high-felutin[2]' panegyrics of earlier Odes. Poetry and Music had no need to remind the members of the University, on the day they welcomed their Chancellor, of the almost unparalleled Academic distinctions which he, as Mr Cavendish, had gained at Cambridge. Bennett found the ideas, the metres, and the words of his colleague quite

---

[1] Regius Professor of Modern History.
[2] This expression, on its first introduction, was variously spelt.

congenial to his own modes of expression, while the letters which came with them from Eversley Rectory were very inspiriting. He later said that if anything would induce him to write an Opera, it would be the possibility of another partnership with Charles Kingsley.

On March 5, Professor Kingsley wrote:—

'* * * I believe it better to find the music first and set the words to them, as dear Tom Moore did, and that I should like to have done. But as you can understand my words; and I cannot understand your music—unless I had you at my elbow to render it as you had conceived it—which is unfortunately impossible—I fear that I must write, and you must set to music afterwards.

'But if you, on thinking it over, have any clear and strong conception which you would wish embodied; I would come up to you, or—which I should much enjoy—you could come down and visit me; and you would find me most glad to do what I am told—which most poets are not.

'Mind, I am not a poet; and therefore I do not demand absolute right to have my thoughts stand exactly as I put them, as poets do now-a-days. If you choose to enter into partnership with me—(and I think that so we might do something worthy) I can give to the firm an ear practised in all sorts of metres and in the meaning thereof—having made *Time* a study, which I have often hoped to reduce to a science. I can give the power of finding a sonorous word or vowel whenever you want one; and, I hope sense worthy of us and our audience. But Poetry in its present meaning of fancy I possess in a very small degree. I can sing (in words not with voice): but I cannot write poetry.

'Will you, then, kindly tell me your conception of what we ought to say, and I will tell you mine after a few days thought. * * *'

Bennett could think very little about the Installation till the Exhibition was off his mind. A few days before the Opening ceremony on May 1, he completed his duty to the Commissioners by correcting the instrumental parts of his Ode for the final rehearsals. He then turned his attention to the next composition, and went to Eversley Rectory on April 26 for a consultation with his colleague. He returned to London a day or two later much refreshed by the excursion. When trying to relate to his family the incidents of a walk through the village, the look of wonder on his face told more clearly than words, how deeply he had been impressed while observing the cordial relations that existed, and while listening to the interesting conversations that passed, between the parishioners of Eversley and their Rector. He probably promised to send, on his return home, some suggestions for the Ode.

On May 14, Charles Kingsley wrote:—'Are you still alive? Have you had a fit after the brilliant success of your May-day Ode; or has Costa pistolled you in despair of harming you by any less direct means? If not, dont you think you can subvenire misero, and tell me what I am to do for you about the Ode? Did you receive that first scene, and the letter I sent with it? Pray give me the order for so many yards of bad verse, and you shall have them: but give it soon, for I am going fishing, * * * and can easily finish the Ode when the trout wont rise.'

Bennett did make at least one suggestion for his own sake. Water-music was a favourite theme with him, and he asked if the river might be introduced on the scene. Charles Kingsley adopted this idea, extended it by carrying on the river to the sea, and thereby wrote one of the most striking sections of the Ode. On May 16 he wrote to Bennett:—'Your welcome letter passed mine on the road, and here is the first result.

'Will this make a water-song? I have put it into quatrains; and made it end with the words with which it began, to make it complete. If it wont, send it back and I'll do something else. Of course leave out the 4 last lines of 3, or anything else you like; for—"Anything for a quiet life" is my motto at this moment. I am writing a fairy tale, your ode, a sermon; seeing after the parish, and going a fishing all at once—so where the quiet life is to come I dont quite see.'

The Installation was fixed for June 10. On May 26, Bennett left his pupils, went to Brighton, and returned home on the 30th, with the music written for the opening Chorus. On the same day he received the last instalment of the words. Charles Kingsley wrote:—'I may alter the last six lines but not in *metre* only in words. So that your music will do for it quite as well.' The last six lines referred to ran thus[1]:—

> *Solo, allegrissimo, by the poet*
>
> 'So here's a ford and to my rotten old Spruce
> I wonder now how it's for finished in time;
> And I think you're on marvellous luck say poor fellows,
> To have found so much wind in my musical bellows,
> But for none a duke upon earth would I pen it
> If 'twere not for the sake of my friend Skendale Bennett'

The composer, however, could not as yet echo the poet's joyous tone. In the next week (June 1—7), when the Philharmonic concert on Monday evening was over, Bennett gave nearly all his time to composition. The Ode comprised five Choral numbers, two Airs, and four long Recitatives. He voluntarily interpolated an orchestral movement. On the morning of Monday, June 9, he went up to Cambridge as the guest of the Master of St John's. On arriving at the Master's Lodge, he at once retired to his room, wrote a Tenor Song—a lament for the Prince Consort—and engaged a copyist to prepare the band-parts. The Ode was then complete, and ready for the rehearsal in the afternoon. In the evening he conducted a grand concert in the Guild Hall with the London orchestra and the singers engaged for the Installation.

Next morning when he appeared in the Senate House in his figured-silk robes, and took his place in the gallery to conduct the orchestra, he received an embarrassing ovation. The undergraduates were quite in their element when expressing their opinion on the Costa and Bennett controversy. They hailed their Professor of Music with an uproar of shouting and applause of so long a duration, that Bennett, who hated being conspicuous, became very dis-

[1] This facsimile reduces the size of the handwriting.

concerted. Mdlle Titiens, who sat by his side, observing this, but not understanding University etiquette, asked him why he did not 'turn round and bow and have done with it.' At length 'Groans for Costa' having been called for, and given with keen relish, the Chancellor's procession entered to the strains of the March from 'Athalie.' The music to the Ode was full of melody, and Bennett was warmly congratulated by the Cambridge connoisseurs. The poet fully shared the honours, though, to the great disappointment of all, he modestly absented himself. Bennett wrote to him without delay to tell him of the 'Three ringing cheers for Professor Kingsley.'

Bennett intended to publish the music. He reserved a numbered place for it in the catalogue of his compositions, and he corresponded for some little time with Charles Kingsley on the subject. A Minuet, suggested by the lines

'Alma Mater * * * *
* * * * * * * *
Like stately matron gay
Gladly leads the dance adown,'

was issued as a pianoforte Duet, and a Part-Song for male voices, 'Health to courage firm and high,' reached the stage of being engraved; but he took no further steps. The Minuet, with a Trio added to it, was later placed in his Symphony in G minor.

A few days after his return from Cambridge, his wife had an alarming attack of illness. A physician had been consulted early in the year, and had then said that she was suffering from heart-disease at an advanced stage. Her husband's anxiety on her account had been intense, and this more acute seizure, now occurring, caused a delay in his setting to work on another composition which he had been asked to write. The Philharmonic Society was to celebrate its Jubilee by a grand extra concert at St James's Hall on July 14. On this night the subscribers were to come as invited guests. Mdlle Titiens, Santley, Joachim and Piatti promised their assistance. The veteran pianist, Mrs Anderson, was to make it the occasion of her last appearance in public. Madame Jenny Lind-Goldschmidt, as a personal tribute to Bennett, postponed an intended journey to Stockholm, in order to take part in the concert.

The band was to be largely augmented to give effect to music in a room which, though already in use for Chamber-music, was regarded by many as too large even for orchestral performances. A long programme of thirteen items was drawn up. Extra rehearsals were necessary, and, in the preparation for so important an event there was, of course, plenty to occupy the Conductor.

But Bennett, according to promise, had the further duty of writing a new work for the occasion. In the first days of July, he began a descriptive orchestral piece (afterwards styled 'Fantasie-Overture'), taking Moore's 'Paradise and the Peri' for its subject. He did not feel sure that he could write it there and then, but he was determined to keep his promise, and said that if he could not get on with that particular work he would lay it aside in time to write at least a Festal March. He used every spare hour, and was obliged to give up a few days' teaching. Mrs Bennett was at this time entirely confined to her room. He wrote much of the Overture at a table placed by the side of her couch. The music is certainly not far off from being the most beautiful he ever conceived. Maybe, the circumstances of the time lent themselves to that result. A bystander one day watched a great tear slowly collecting in his eye until it suddenly dropped on his score whilst he continued to write. He calculated the hours at his disposal with accuracy. His manuscript is subscribed, 'July 14th, 7 a.m.' Then the engravers completed the orchestral parts in time for a long rehearsal of the Overture and other works, over which he presided later in the day. What remained of the afternoon sufficed for him to give two pianoforte lessons, and the same evening he conducted the Jubilee Concert which lasted till midnight. That was a long and arduous day for a so-called 'lazy man.'

The end of the season found him in the possession of a silver salver presented by the Philharmonic Society, and of an equally beautiful gift which had been subscribed for in Cambridge as a thoughtful return for his trouble in arranging the Installation Concert. The Duke of Devonshire, in due course, wrote a full expression of thanks for the music to the Installation Ode, and according to established precedent enclosed a handsome 'honorarium.' Bennett would have been justified in expecting, though he never mentioned the subject, that the Commissioners of the Exhibition might find time to append their signatures to some document acknowledging what he had done for them. They did, however, direct their Secretary to act for them, and he accordingly wrote a short and polite note of eight lines.

Bennett remained in London till the middle of August to make up arrears of lessons. Then, as his wife seemed a little better, he was advised to take her to Eastbourne. Thence she wrote on August 18. 'Dear Sterndale's holiday is a dull one, but he will not allow this, and says he enjoys the rest and being able to nurse me.' In the middle of September, it became doubtful whether she could ever return home, but an invalid carriage was obtained, and a very anxious journey accomplished. At the end of the month Bennett wrote to his Aunt:—

'We are very much obliged to you for your kind letter. My poor Wife is indeed in a very bad state, but we are safe at home again which is a very great comfort. My wife's mother is with us, which allows me to follow my usual life, feeling I have some one responsible at home when I am obliged to leave the house. Nevertheless, my life is one of great anxiety. I nurse[1] till nearly five o'clock in the morning, and leave home before half-past eight, and am obliged to remain out many hours. If you could fix a day to come up and see us, my wife would be delighted to see you, as she often talks of you. We have the best advice, and I sincerely trust things may be alleviated, but you will see a great invalid when you see my poor wife. * * * How many will miss her when she is taken!'

Mrs Bennett died on October 17, in her thirty-eighth year. For more than eighteen years of married life, she had, without neglecting any family or domestic duty, assiduously yet very unobtrusively done all in her power to help her husband forward in his professional career. It was her habit to spend hour after hour every day, during his prolonged absences from home, in arranging and supplementing what he himself did. She conducted a large

---

[1] This was *actual* nursing; the patient requiring to be carefully supported in order to obtain any continuous sleep.

correspondence, and interviewed the ever increasing stream of former pupils and other visitors who came for his advice or assistance. She so completely identified herself with his concerns, the charm of her personality so clearly reflected his own, her disposition was so generous and helpful, that few failed to accept her in place of her husband, or to take from her the counsel that they could not get from him. She attracted the confidence of influential persons whose path she crossed when managing her husband's affairs, and thereby her own influence was strengthened. She worked zealously for charitable objects. She also did much to aid young people, musical or otherwise, on their first start in life, establishing what Bennett used to call her 'agency.' She had correspondents amongst her husband's friends in Germany, who looked for her help and returned their help to her, in such negotiations. Full of sympathy, full of anxiety for others, when failing health, long before her death, clearly asserted itself, no persuasion of others could induce her to put on one side, while any strength remained, even the slightest of those duties which she had always, with so great a thoroughness, discharged. The words, 'How many will miss her when she is taken!' which Bennett wrote to his Aunt, and again the words 'Many knew and loved her' which he placed on her tombstone, were used, with concise expression but comprehensive meaning, and were used by a man who, at a time of great grief, could think of others as well as of himself. But it may be added that though loved for her own sake, her well-known devotion to her husband, and her partnership in his laborious pursuits gave an independent cause for the wide respect she gained. A letter of condolence from the Philharmonic Society will illustrate the general feeling of Bennett's professional brethren about her, and about the loss they well knew he would sustain by her death.

LONDON, *Nov. 15th*, 1862.

DEAR PROFESSOR BENNETT,

We the Directors of the Philharmonic Society for the last and the present year desire to join, as your sincere and affectionate friends, in expressing our deep sympathy with you in the great calamity with which you have been afflicted, the loss of your excellent wife. We all know how long and happy your union has been, and how much your happiness was the fruit of her amiable character, good sense, and beautiful performance of every duty, and we can therefore understand how strongly you must feel so sad a bereavement.

But we also know that you will bear it like a man and a Christian, that you will not mourn like those who are without hope, and that you will (if possible) redouble your exertions for the sake of those dear pledges whom she has left to your care and protection.

Trusting that you will not regard this expression of our feelings as an intrusion on the sacredness of your sorrow,

We are with every respect and esteem,
Your most sincere friends,
G. F. ANDERSON.
[&c., &c., &c.]

Bennett's Aunt at Cambridge, though proud of her nephew on his own account, said with emphasis in her old age, and long after he had passed away :—' It was his *marriage* that was the making of him.' He himself would have made no reservation, either by word or by thought, to that opinion. After his wife's death he sealed up, as a sacred symbol of his indebtedness, the 'teaching-book' in which her last entries were made, and then wrote on the first page of a new one, ' May I never forget all the help and affection I have ever received from the best and dearest of wives.'

CHAPTER XXIV.

HE FACES SORROW.
A SYMPHONY IN G MINOR.
VISIT TO LEIPZIG.
THE PROFESSORSHIP OF MUSIC AT EDINBURGH.
HE RESIGNS THE PHILHARMONIC CONDUCTORSHIP.

1862—1866.
æt. 46—50.

BENNETT bravely faced the altered position in which his wife's death placed him. He sought solace in a determined effort to make her presence felt, and to keep his memory of her as a pervading influence of his life. He spoke of her constantly, at first with effort, but soon naturally and without reserve. He resolved, as he said, to remain grateful for a happy past. He felt additional responsibility as a parent, and though it could not be possible to increase the affection he had always shown to his children, he now gave much thought to the plans for their education, increased the insurances on his life, and, as far as he could, the hours of his work, so that during the next two or three years, notwithstanding the loss of his wife's services, he managed to increase his income. He was his own housekeeper during those years. He parted with his daughter, then very young, and placed her for her education in a clergyman's family at Oxford, but it so happened that, nearly to the end of his life, one or other of his three children in turn resided with him, and his wife's mother, Mrs Wood, usually visited him for six months of each year. The arrangements of his house had always been a hobby with him, nor did he find minor domestic duties beneath his notice. He strove to keep everything in the same order in which his wife had left it. Faithful servants were always found anxious to study the wants of a gentle and considerate master.

Though his house could no longer be the rendezvous for

many, his intimate friends vied one with another in showing him attention. Madame Lind-Goldschmidt, in a letter inviting himself and his children to spend a quiet Christmas at Wimbledon in 1862, wrote:—'I have all[1] since your great sorrow came upon you had a great desire to see you and shake hands with you, but—as I have not been able to be out for these last seven weeks—I have not had my desire fulfilled. But I have often and warmly thought of you! it is but *natural* that I should so feel towards you for more than one reason, for a nature like yours has a deep attraction for me; add now to this the kind delicacy with which you have treated my husband these three years—your cooperation with him in a work that so profoundly touches the most religious and musical chords of my soul, and you will find the key to the whole of my sincere regard and friendship for you. Therefore, I ask if you would not let me have this longed-for shake of hands on Xmas eve or on Xmas day.'

The writer possesses a memento, touching by its simplicity, of the friendship between Madame Lind-Goldschmidt and his father. When Bennett was at Ashford in Derbyshire, in 1860, he entered the village shop, and, before speaking about his own forefathers to the old man who kept the shop, made a purchase of a bundle of rather large lead-pencils. These proved to be of very good quality, and he afterwards used them for teaching purposes, making each pencil last out a year. At the end of the year he would present the remaining stump to one of his family, or to some intimate friend as a kind of humorous keepsake. One of the first must have been given to Madame Goldschmidt. She may, perhaps, have asked for the funny little souvenir, and so have given him the idea of presenting the same to others in later years. After her death the pencil was found amongst her things wrapped in paper on which she had written in Swedish, 'Dr Bennett's pencil, which he used when at work on *The Chorale Book*.'

On removing to Inverness Terrace in 1859, Bennett made the acquaintance of a neighbour, Mr Robert Case, a member of the London Stock Exchange. Mr Case had spent the greater part of his life in Liverpool, where, as an amateur of music, he had mixed with some of the first

---

[1] *sic*; a word may have been omitted.

artists of the day. He understood Bennett's position as a musician, and was already an admirer of his music. The kindness shown by Mr and Mrs Case during Mrs Bennett's illness was unremitting, and Bennett now found in their friendship great present comfort and the beginning of much future happiness. Of older family friends, the Ferraris also lived near, and never ceased to show their affection, while his schoolfellow, William Dorrell, and his publisher, Lamborn Cock, spent their Sundays with him and often accompanied him on the weekly visit to his wife's grave.

In February, 1863, the 'Athenæum,' under their well-known Rule II[1], paid honour to music and to Bennett by electing him a member. This was a recognition which a musician could value in the interests of his art, as well as on his own account, and Bennett had good reason to be proud of it. Mr George Richmond, R.A., who proposed Bennett's name to the Committee, wrote to him after the election:—
'It was very near my heart that our Club should be enriched by a musician, and it was fortunate that I was able to point to one whose reputation none can doubt, for it is more than probable that among the twenty-four members of the Committee, not one would be fully capable of estimating the claims of a great musician. I frankly disclaimed that power myself, so that you are indebted for your election by the Committee simply to your great reputation as an Artist, and if I may be permitted to say so much, to your high character as a gentleman.'

The year 1863 passed without any incident that could disturb Bennett in a time of sadness. The season brought its usual round of duties but none of an exceptional kind. The death of the Prince Consort, and the necessarily retired life of Her Majesty, shed for some time a certain sombreness on all public proceedings. The Philharmonic Society, however, welcomed a new Patroness in the Princess of Wales, who, with the Prince, attended two consecutive concerts. A second visit in one season was unusual, but it was understood at the time that the Royal party paid it expressly to hear Beethoven's music to *Egmont*. This was the work which had been the cause of disagreement between the Directors and Bennett some years before. The

[1] Under Rule II, the Committee of the Club annually invite *nine* men of distinction to become members without the usual Ballot.

present production was due to the influence of the late Prince Consort, who, before his death, had named it as a work he should desire to hear at the next concert of the Society which he might attend. The words, 'By Special Desire,' heading the programme, had, therefore, on this occasion, something beyond their conventional meaning.

In noticing the concerts of this season, *The Times* made several references to the progress of the new orchestra, giving the Conductor the credit of having 'created' it. The following passage concisely expresses the difficulty which the Philharmonic had encountered when their old orchestra was withdrawn :—'Professor Sterndale Bennett deserves infinite credit for the manner in which he has disciplined what, two years ago, was, for the major part, little better than an army of raw recruits.' On May 25, Bennett took the orchestra to Cambridge and conducted a 'University Subscription Concert.' The success of the concert given the year before at the time of the Installation had raised a hope that a similar one might become an annual occurrence. It was found, however, that the time was not ripe, and no subscription adequate for such a purpose was forthcoming in the University and town. The failure of the experiment was a great disappointment to Bennett, as also to his friend and ever staunch supporter, the Rev. T. P. Hudson[1], Fellow and Tutor of Trinity College, who was for many years justly regarded as the chief representative of Music among the resident members of the University.

The summer found Bennett on the Rhine, reviving old memories, and with his thoughts reverting to Leipzig. A visit there would involve writing new music. He could not go empty-handed. Soon after his return from the holiday on the Rhine, he began to play on the pianoforte the opening section of an orchestral movement in G minor, the first phrase of which he called 'the waves of life.' This became the principal movement of a Symphony which he soon afterwards completed. The tone of the movement reflects the seriousness of the days in which he first conceived it. Some of his sacred Anthems belong to the same period.

In the early months of 1864, he wrote and delivered a

---

[1] Afterwards, through change of name, Canon Pemberton.

second course of four lectures at the London Institution, taking for his subject, 'The music for the theatre composed by natives of Belgium, Italy, France and Germany.' These lectures, as well as an earlier course in 1858, were much appreciated, and in subsequent years he was often pressed to appear again in the same place. He took great pains over the selection of musical illustrations. He wrote concisely and clearly. His voice was singularly expressive, and he had an excellent delivery. He always rehearsed his lectures by reading them aloud to his friend George Hogarth. His opinions, however, on music and musicians were given with his habitual restraint, and for that reason the lectures, which he left in manuscript, are unsatisfying. They give the impression that he often checked himself just as he was on the verge of letting out something very interesting. There are sentences scratched out which confirm this impression. In conversation about music, he often gave similar disappointment.

While writing this course of lectures, he was also engaged with Mr Otto Goldschmidt in editing, at the request of Messrs Longmans, a collection of English Hymns and Hymn Tunes to be published as an Appendix to *The Chorale Book for England*. As the Philharmonic season advanced, he decided to complete the above-mentioned orchestral work in G minor. The Directors arranged for its performance at the last concert of the year on June 27. In his teaching-book, he accounts for lessons missed during the week before the concert by writing: 'This was a bad week, as I wrote the whole of my G minor Symphony in it.' This was nearly true as regards music-paper and penmanship, but not so as regards the composition itself. To the first movement he had certainly given much previous thought, and though, towards the end of the time at his disposal, he discarded a very taking second subject in favour of another which he said was 'more workable,' the movement was complete in his head and already *sketched* on paper, as the subscribed date on the score proves, eight days before the concert. An engagement then took him to Cambridge. On his return, he was met at King's Cross, and he then said that he had just composed a last movement in the train and could write it out when he got home. The rhythm derived from the motion of the train may be fancied when listening to the music, but he said that a rustic fair was in his mind, and that some pathetic bars, in which the oboe is prominent, portrayed a disconsolate maid who had lost her lover in the crowd. For a middle movement he made use of a Minuet from the Cambridge Installation Ode, to which he now added a Trio for the brass instruments. In the days of small concert-rooms these instruments, when used in combination with others, were played in very subdued tones. When Bennett was considering the effect of his new Trio, he said in advance:—'It will surprise the audience to find that there is a full brass band in the orchestra.' He connected his three movements together by short 'Intermezzi,' and in that form the work was played at the Philharmonic. He had not intended to call it a Symphony, and had written to Davison begging him not to describe it as such in any preliminary announcement in *The Musical World*. He added, 'It is little more than a long Overture on a Symphony plan.' After the rehearsal George Hogarth strongly urged that it should bear the more important title on the concert-programme. 'It is a Symphony,' he said, 'and a very fine one too.' Bennett did not seem to care to argue the point, and gave way. The concert at which it was played was a brilliant one. The Prince of Wales was present and warmly congratulated the Conductor on his composition. The Princess of Wales witnessed the highly successful debût in London of her young compatriot, Mr Fritz Hartvigson. Joachim produced a new Violin Concerto of his own composition. Bennett naturally treasured the following letter —it lies in his album—from his old master.

> 3 CRAVEN HILL, HYDE PARK,
> *June* 29, 1864.
>
> DEAR BENNETT,
> I must congratulate you on your transcendent success last Monday, not more than you deserved. I was perfectly charmed with your Symphony, for the beauty of *Composition* as well as the truly happy *instrumentation*. I thought it went admirably; no doubt we shall hear it again early next season with another movement.
>
> I remain,
> Ever yours sincerely,
> CIPRIANI POTTER.

A Grateful Society

The Directors of the Philharmonic wrote their thanks for his 'beautiful' Symphony, and for his 'liberal and generous conduct with regard to it.' They perpetuated their appreciations by engraving them on a silver claret-jug. At their first meeting in the following autumn they resolved to ask him to compose another work of the same kind. This he declined to do, probably feeling that his name had already sufficiently appeared on the programmes of concerts which he himself conducted. What he wrote on the subject may be gathered from the Secretary's reply.

Dec. 14th, 1864.

My dear Sir,

Your letter of the 8th inst. was duly laid before the Directors of the Philharmonic Society, who have desired me to express their satisfaction at your acceptance of the office of conductor for the ensuing season, and their deep sense of your generous devotion to the Society in refusing remuneration for the two usually unprofitable concerts before Easter. The Directors fully appreciate the delicacy of the motive which, unfortunately for art, has actuated you in declining to bring out a new Symphony of your own during the season, and cannot but consent, however reluctantly, to abandon for the present the idea of inducing you to enrich the world of music with another contribution from your pen. They feel, however, that they are not justified, in the interests of the Society which they represent, in acceding to your request that no work of yours shall be performed during the season, and, indeed, it is out of their power to give any pledge to that effect.

I remain,
&c., &c.,
Campbell Clarke (Secretary).

Professor Sterndale Bennett.

Bennett was now planning his intended visit to Germany, and was in correspondence with his old friend, Ferdinand David, the Concert-Meister at Leipzig.

LONDON, 50 INVERNESS TERRACE,
November 22nd, 1864.

LIEBER DAVID,

Do not think me ungrateful that I have not written sooner in answer to your most kind letter. I have been confused in my plans. My music-publishers have dissolved their firm and I have been very anxious to know how I could get my symphony (Orchester-stimmen) ready for Leipzig, and also I have some work at Cambridge which will keep me in England until the end of the year.

Aber! I want to see you very much and all my Leipzig friends, and I could come (I hope and believe) the second week in January, and in the holidays will make the little corrections in the symphony which I wish to make, and send you the Partitur and Orchester-stimmen before then.

I dream always about seeing dear old Leipzig again. I hope it may be. I dreamt the other night that I had arrived in the middle of one of your rehearsals, but I could not find you before the dream was over. You will find me an *old* man, but *true* to you and all my dear friends in Saxony. If I cannot come, will you still play my Symphony? It is a very small work, but it would be a great happiness to me to hear it played by your orchestra.

And now let me thank you *vom Herzen* for your kind 'Einladung.' Tell Madame David how much it will delight me to come and abide at your house. I hope you will forgive me for not having written before. I hope the Directors will be so kind as to give my Symphony *after* Christmas. I will write again soon. Please say everything kind to Madame David for me, and hoping to see you in January,

I am, dear David,

Ever your friend,

WILLIAM STERNDALE BENNETT.

Everything good to
Schleinitz, Kistner, &c.

Bennett started from London on January 6, 1865, and reached Leipzig on the 10th. Many of his friends there had not seen him for twenty-three years. Their reception of him is fixed in the memory of the writer, who had the privilege of accompanying him, because it was so different from what he had been expecting to see. The meeting with David, for instance, at the railway station would have given no idea of warmth of feeling on either side had it not later been realized that suppression of feeling was at the moment necessary to both. David immediately took refuge in talking about Bennett's music, and between the railway platform and the cab it was agreed that a final bar must be repeated, and that the title 'Allegro, Menuetto, and Rondo Finale,' was preferable to that of Symphony. Other friends as they one by one met him, seemed to eye him with a gentle and affectionate curiosity, but words of greeting did not come easily. His presence among them touched a tender chord. They associated him with a broken past. They had never seen him before, save by the side of a man whom they had lost. An almost silent hour at the house of Conrad Schleinitz, during which manuscripts of Mendelssohn were being reverently handled by their owner, by David, and by Bennett, was singularly impressive. Then some idea could be formed of the blank that the death of Mendelssohn had left in the lives of these men.

At the rehearsal in the Gewandhaus, Bennett, as a distinguished visitor, was greeted, according to a pretty old custom, by a fanfare of trumpets, and at the concert, when he appeared to conduct his work, the audience received him with the applause which they strictly reserved as a compliment to the well-known. He had not been over-confident about the fate of his music. 'It is a different matter here to what it is in London,' he said in the train as he was nearing Leipzig. Nevertheless, he thought this Symphony one of his best works. Both at the Philharmonic and at the Gewandhaus, the arrangement of seats enabled any one who wished to do so to watch faces and get some idea of the effect music was making on an audience. Of applause, Bennett always got his full share, but there were other signs at the early performances of this work that it was very effective and gave genuine pleasure. Whether the composer heightened the effectiveness, when he later added a fourth (slow) movement, has been questioned.

He passed six days full of interest at the Davids' delightful house in Quer-Strasse. He attended a Ball given by Madame Brockhaus; played Sonatas with David to Julius Kistner, then a confirmed invalid; made the acquaintance of Capellmeister Reinecke (who three years later spent a month with him in Bayswater); and paid a flying visit to Dresden, where he found Julius Rietz. The Students of the Conservatorium had prepared a concert for him with a programme selected from his own works. On the last day, Herr Carl Voigt, who had so often entertained him in earlier times, invited a large party to meet him at mid-day dinner. In the afternoon, Moscheles contributed to the amusement by his grotesque tricks on the pianoforte, and then the whole company followed Bennett to the railway station, where a crowd of other well-wishers had assembled with the object of giving him a good send-off. He stopped at Cologne, passed a few hours with the genial Ferdinand Hiller, and heard a performance of 'Joshua.' The playing and singing was rather spiritless, and Bennett said in explanation, 'Ah, yes, but they don't understand Handel here.' The Directors of the Gewandhaus, 'in grateful remembrance of his presence in Leipzig,' sent him the complete edition of Beethoven's works which had just been issued by Messrs Breitkopf and Haertel. In the inscription which the donors placed in the books, they paid a well-conceived tribute to the Englishman by styling him 'the zealous fosterer of German music.'

In the autumn of 1865, the house in Inverness Terrace, in which he had lived very comfortably for six years, was, perforce, taken from him by the Metropolitan Railway Company. Houses in Bayswater were difficult to find at the time, and he had no choice but to buy one larger than he required in Queensborough Terrace. The removal caused a good deal of trouble and expense. If this had not happened, he might have considered a fresh scheme of life which was suggested to him a few weeks after he had settled down in his new home. It is some evidence of his success as Professor at Cambridge, or at least of the respect in which his name was held there, that he should now be approached by another University at the suggestion of a distinguished Cambridge mathematician. Professor

Donaldson, after holding the chair of music at Edinburgh for twenty years[1], had just died. The Professorship was of greater value than any similar musical post in England, and was now sought for by many eminent musicians. Professor Tait, a Cambridge man who held a chair of Mathematics in Edinburgh, sounded Bennett on the subject, and then Sir David Brewster, Principal of the University, wrote:

UNIVERSITY OF EDINBURGH,
October 6th, 1865.

SIR,
  I was about to take the liberty of writing to you to ask your opinion of some of the leading candidates for the chair of music in Edinburgh—confidentially, of course, and for the guidance of myself and other patrons, when I received a letter from Professor Tait stating that you would 'delight in the honour of being Professor of Music in Edinburgh.'

Professor Tait will no doubt write to you again on the subject, but in the meantime you would oblige me by letting me know if you would accept the chair if offered to you.

I am, Sir,
Ever yours most truly,
D. BREWSTER.

LONDON, October 19th, 1865.

SIR,
  Allow me to say that I feel highly gratified that you should have taken the trouble to write to me in regard to the vacant chair at Edinburgh.

I certainly did write to my friend Professor Tait that I should delight in the honour of being Professor of Music in the University of Edinburgh, but I added at the same time a broad reason for my not coming forward as a candidate, that I feared the risk of failure.

Not believing for a moment that the chair could be obtained otherwise than by open competition, I failed to think of many smaller impediments to any change of my professional life. Since the receipt of your kind note,

---

[1] H. H. Pierson, who obtained the Chair when Donaldson and Bennett stood for it in 1844, resigned in the following year and Donaldson succeeded him.

I have tried to come to some decision on the matter, and with great reluctance say, that even should the University pay me the high compliment of offering me the chair, I should from many private and professional reasons, which I cannot at present control, be obliged to decline it.

Any service which I can offer to you, according to the commencement of your note, is most heartily given. I have the consolation of thinking, that in losing the chance of becoming Professor of Music in Edinburgh, I am not interfering with the hopes of many among the candidates for whom I have the warmest esteem.

I am, Sir,

Most truly yours,

WILLIAM STERNDALE BENNETT.

Sir David Brewster,
Principal of the University of Edinburgh.

UNIVERSITY OF EDINBURGH.

SIR,

Professor Tait and I much regret your decision, though we are not surprised at it.

You would oblige us greatly if you could give us an opinion, which of course will be confidential, of the principal candidates for our chair. * * *

I am, Sir,

Ever most truly yours,

D. BREWSTER.

W. Sterndale Bennett, Esq.

A move from London to Edinburgh would have been a bold stroke on Bennett's part. The idea of it was attractive, because he was at this time desiring to escape from that side of his work which entailed appearance on concert-platforms, but at the same time, to remain on active service in any other direction that presented itself. He had long ago fixed a time-limit to his duty as a conductor. He would often say that he did not intend to resign his place at the Philharmonic till he had held it longer than any of his predecessors. When he said this he mentioned no names, but, as a matter of fact, only one predecessor had remained any length of time. Costa conducted for nine years. When Bennett finished his tenth season in 1865, he said that his period of office was complete, and that he felt justified in retiring. The Directors took his resignation sadly. He had not the heart to resist their entreaties, so he compromised by agreeing to conduct for one more season.

Bennett's retirement from the concert-room coincided closely, in point of time, with the general acceptance by this country of the music of Robert Schumann. In this connection something may be said about Bennett's attitude or, rather, his supposed attitude towards that composer. In days when the taste for Schumann's music was so rapidly developing here, there was a natural curiosity to discover how far his English friend shared the enthusiasm. As a result, Bennett's friends, acquaintances and pupils appear to have agreed unanimously that he felt little or no love for Schumann's music. This opinion, however, when the present writer has seen or heard it expressed, has been based upon what Bennett could not be got to say rather than upon any definite statements that he made. Silence may be construed into disapproval, but with no certainty in Bennett's case. He was under no obligation to satisfy curiosity, and was, when under cross-examination, a most unwilling witness. Schumann happened to be the modern composer about whom he was most persistently approached, but enquiries would have found him, at least in his later years, no less reticent about other contemporaries. A like caution in earlier life was the probable origin of an erroneous statement that he lacked appreciation for Chopin, a composer for whose music he undoubtedly had a genuine, though, may be, not an unbounded admiration[1]. If he spoke or wrote about art, he used, as a rule, strictly temperate expressions—not such expressions as would appeal to enthusiasts in the hey-day of a new and fascinating cult. On the other hand, his sayings in praise of music or of musical performance often betokened, to those who understood his manner, an intense warmth of feeling, while their brevity and directness served as a guarantee for their abso-

[1] See note in Appendix A.

lute sincerity. Mendelssohn was one of those who recognised this and valued not alone his appreciations but also his occasional reservations. When therefore Bennett, in his letters to Schumann, wrote that he had been playing the 'Etudes Symphoniques' 'a great deal and with much enjoyment;' when he quoted the bar of 'very great beauty' which he was repeating 'a hundred times a day;' when he wrote from Leipzig, 'I have seen here for the first time your Fantaisie Stücke and they greatly delight me;' when he found the Davidsbündler 'very charming;' and when, many years later, he wrote to Madame Schumann, 'What a beautiful work is the Peri;' he meant each word he said. His tongue or pen might at times refuse to express his feelings, but they never expressed anything he did not feel, and the above words need no discount because they were addressed to the composer himself or to his wife. After all then, even if he were unable, probably on some technical grounds, to assign to Schumann a place among the greatest masters of music, the recent discovery of these letters brings something to set against the idea that Bennett could feel no love for Schumann's music. As for the silence of his later life, there was one circumstance which, in relation to Schumann, specially tied his tongue. In the years when he was expected to speak, there were few persons who could keep Mendelssohn's name out of any conversation about Schumann. Bennett, as the intimate friend of both, recoiled from disputants who could say little in favour of the one save at the expense of the other. This fact, of itself, goes far to explain why Bennett's precise estimate of Schumann as a composer was and must remain a sealed letter.

When occasion arose, Bennett took his part in the performance of Schumann's music with all the affectionate interest that might be expected. After the first year of his Philharmonic conductorship, he abandoned, for a reason already given, any attempt to influence the Directors in their choice of music. Therefore while he could claim no further credit for the introduction of new or unknown works, he had, on the other hand, nothing to do with their exclusion. The cold reception of the 'Paradise and the Peri' in 1856 may have deterred the Directors from attempting other works by the same composer, though in this respect Schumann did not stand alone. The scant time for rehearsal was a strong bar to the satisfactory introduction of new music, and especially of music in an unfamiliar style. From 1856 Schumann's name was seldom, if ever, seen on Philharmonic programmes, until in 1864 his Symphony in C major was brought forward. *The Times* then wrote: 'Professor Bennett took infinite pains with the Symphony, it was magnificently played, and favourably received by a large number of the audience.' In 1865, Madame Schumann revisited England, after some years' absence, and played her husband's Concerto in A minor at the Philharmonic. Her visit gave great impetus to the appreciation of Schumann's music, and *The Times*, when reviewing the musical events of the next year (1866), remarked that Robert Schumann had been the 'sensation' composer of that year with the directors of concerts. The Philharmonic took a prominent part in this movement. The 'Paradise and the Peri' was again produced under Bennett's direction, and at the last concert of the season Alfred Jaell played the A minor Concerto so delightfully, that the audience was moved to an exceptional display of approval. This was the last Concerto that Bennett conducted. *The Times*, in a critique on the concert, wrote: 'Professor Bennett received a loud and unanimous call at the end, and his reappearance provoked an enthusiastic demonstration, the feeling of which was in a great measure derived from the announcement that the learned and popular Professor is about to retire from the conductorship of the Society.'

The record of Bennett's career as a conductor needs no peroration. Tradition gives him no position on this side of his work comparable to that which it gives him as a pianist. He was not called to the regular exercise of a conductor's duties till he was forty years of age, and the six or eight Philharmonic concerts which he then annually conducted for eleven years could not nearly represent the amount of work associated with the notion of a great *chef d'orchestre*. Nevertheless, he went to the Philharmonic with a knowledge of and a feeling for the music with which he had to deal, of an order higher than could be claimed for other conductors who were doing similar work elsewhere in London at exactly the same time. This advantage may have lost its full effect, because a musician of high ideals who aimed for the nicer subtleties of interpretation, had in those days a limited chance of riveting his refinements upon an orchestra which he only met once a fortnight, for a few months of each year, at rehearsals which were not much longer than the corresponding concerts. In any case, however, few denied Bennett very high rank, while many assigned him the foremost place among contemporary conductors of classical music in this country.

The following passage is taken from an obituary notice of Bennett in *The Daily Telegraph* :—

'How far his reign [at the Philharmonic] was a success, and in what degree he brought to the discharge of his duties the mingled strength and delicacy of a perfect *chef d'orchestre*, are questions which, if propounded, would receive a variety of answers. True it is, assuredly, that in nice perception of a composer's meaning, and in sympathetic appreciation of the methods by which it was conveyed, few conductors could equal Sterndale Bennett. He may have lacked—nay, he *did* lack—the firmness, energy, and power of command that enable a *chef d'orchestre* to animate every subordinate with his own spirit ; but, assuming that these merits could not be found united, he at least possessed the more essential.'

What the Philharmonic Society itself thought of him, after his work of eleven years, is thus recorded on their minutes. The Directors met in November, 1866, when they drafted a long resolution, containing a proposal that if he would remain, they would appoint an assistant-conductor to relieve him from any part of the work that he would name, and a request that he would allow them to announce that 'at the earnest solicitations of the Directors Professor Bennett had undertaken to conduct the concerts of the ensuing season.' But Bennett did not revoke his decision. Indeed, before he conducted his last concert in 1866, he had accepted another appointment which substituted new work for old.

PART V

REPAYMENT OF A DEBT TO ALMA MATER

CHAPTER XXV.

THE ROYAL ACADEMY OF MUSIC.
BENNETT IS APPOINTED PRINCIPAL.

1866—1867.

æt. 50, 51.

IN his last years, Bennett became so closely associated with the Royal Academy of Music, and the connection so materially affected the circumstances of his life, that no account of him can be complete which does not borrow freely from the history of the Academy itself. It fell to his lot to save the place from annihilation, to guard and to guide it, with much discretion, during a critical period of its existence, and by a devotion and self-sacrifice the extent of which no one at the time can have realized, to repay fully the debt he owed to the home of his early life. A long effort, which severely taxed his powers of mind and body, was at last crowned with a success for which he alone paid the penalty. Nothing in his life better deserves record than the self-denying way in which he ended it.

It was in December, 1864, that the question was first broached of his returning to the Academy as its Principal. Charles Lucas, who had succeeded Potter in 1859, was, by reason of failing health, meditating retirement. Bennett's replies to one of the Directors who approached him on the subject show that he was not then eager for the appointment. He wrote: 'I have yet sufficient interest in the R. A. M. to be of any service I can, and at any rate to entertain any proposal you think fit to make me, altho' I say this without committing myself to a promise.' He wrote again: 'I could not answer your letter without much more thought. * * *

You had better not consider me in your plans, but let me help you as far as possible, when I have time to think.'

The fortunes of the Academy were at a low ebb. The interest which Lord Westmorland had been able to excite forty years before had now all but vanished, and with it most of the subscriptions on which so much had depended. Poverty had affected the educational results of the Institution, a fact which was openly admitted by its own members. Lists of pupils, and the subsequent achievements of many, prove that at no period were there wanting some students of exceptional promise; but as the funds from which assistance could be given when needed diminished, such students became fewer, whilst others had to be admitted for the sake of their fees, without regard to their ability. Many were withdrawn who could not afford to complete their course, and could not, therefore, bring credit on their teachers. The numbers had decreased. Foreign *Conservatoires* were attracting, and rival schools had been started in London. It would have taken a bold man to believe that in the office of Principal, where he would be allowed no voice in the general management of the Institution, he could do much towards its revival.

On the other hand, the Academy had recently met with one stroke of good fortune. This particular circumstance was destined to affect Bennett very considerably. In 1863, a Board of Professors, on which Lucas and G. A. Macfarren were the most prominent members, drew up a petition for State aid, and submitted it to the Directors. The Professors had nothing whatever to do with matters outside their class-rooms, and such a proceeding, under Lord Westmorland's rule, would have been regarded as an intolerable liberty. The present Directors, however, approved of this petition, and it was forwarded to Mr Gladstone, then Chancellor of the Exchequer, with the result that a Grant of £500 was placed on the estimates for 1864. The understanding was that this money should be spent on the rent of the Academy house. Government support of music was a startling novelty; the Academy's success in obtaining it attracted notice; and those who had been long wishing to establish a national school of music on another site thought the time had come to bestir themselves.

Early in 1865, the Society of Arts, at the suggestion of Mr (afterwards Sir) Henry Cole, who had since 1852 been Secretary of the Science and Art Department at South Kensington, formed a special committee of its members to enquire into and to compare the state of musical education at home and abroad. This enquiry, which was spread over nearly a year, was exhaustive. Many musical experts, including representatives of the Academy, were examined. One of the chief questions raised was whether a national school of music should be started *de novo*, or whether the Academy should be adopted as the basis of a larger Institution. The majority of those examined were in favour of the latter course; but the representatives of the Academy, in giving their evidence, harped, more than it was wise of them to do, on their own drawbacks and defects, thus playing into the hands of one or two very hostile witnesses who spoke of the Institution as 'rotten' and as 'an old coat past patching.' The evidence, as a whole, might well give to unbiased judges the impression that there was little of the Academy worth preserving except its name. Even this last point was thought open to question, and witnesses were asked whether they deemed it advisable for the new Institution to adopt the title of the old one. Now though the Academy might be regarded as 'moribund,' the term applied to it a little later by Mr Cole himself, there was one very potent reason for incorporating it, at least nominally, in any new scheme. It had a Royal Charter, the Royal Family had always been its Patrons, and the Prince of Wales, in allowing his name to be used as President of this Committee of enquiry, had stipulated that nothing should be done hostile to the Royal Academy of Music. Mr Cole, during the enquiry, expressed the opinion that the system now proposed by him for a general Institution of musical education was compatible with the existing Charter of the Academy, and that it would be more desirable to enlarge the action of that Institution than to form a new one. 'I think,' he added, 'as we have an Academy with a Royal Charter, and the Queen as its Patron, and many noblemen connected with it, it would be an ungracious act to attempt to entirely supersede the present Institution, until its revival was utterly hopeless. I for one should not be disposed to take any part adverse to the Royal Academy of Music.'

Before the end of the year (1865) Mr Cole was in correspondence with Sir George Clerk, the Chairman of the Academy Committee, about a removal of the Institution to South Kensington. The proposal was to give temporary accommodation at the South Kensington Museum for three years, during which time subscriptions might be raised for a special building, or the promise obtained of a permanent home in the projected Albert Hall of Arts and Sciences. The reception of the Academy at Kensington required the sanction of the Commissioners of the 1851 Exhibition, as also of the Lords of the Committee of the Privy Council of Education. On February 7, 1866, Mr Cole obtained Lord Granville's consent, and on February 24 the Academy made formal application for the accommodation. It was agreed that some changes were to be made in the working of the Institution, and Sir George Clerk promised that any changes suggested should be made, as far as the limited means at the disposal of the Directors would allow.

Much was said during the Society of Arts' enquiry about the appointment of a Musical Director for the new or enlarged school, and about the necessary qualifications of such an official. In February, 1866, Mr Cole obtained Sir George Clerk's authority to offer the Principalship to Costa. This shows that Mr Cole was, at the time, regarding the removal of the Academy to Kensington as a foregone conclusion; for, otherwise, he would scarcely have concerned himself with the choice of its officials. Costa accepted the post, naming £1200 a year and a residence as his terms. This negotiation appears to have been quite confidential between those who conducted it. The poverty of the Academy can be taken as sufficient reason for its failure. The Directors then approached Mr Otto Goldschmidt, who had for nearly three years been working for them as a Professor of the pianoforte; but he, instead of considering the Principalship for himself, urged its being offered to Bennett. The latter, after withdrawing from the Academy in 1858, had listened to none of the requests sent him to rejoin the staff, and the overtures made to him in 1864 with regard to the Principalship had come to nothing. The Directors were now in no mood to apply to him again, but Mr Goldschmidt pressed his point, urged them to allow him to interview Bennett on the subject, and at last obtained their consent to his doing so. For a man in Bennett's position the Principalship could scarcely be regarded as a *preferment*. No immediate honour or substantial emolument could attach to it. But the invitation was not such an appeal *ad misericordiam* as that which had reached him fifteen months before. The removal to South Kensington was now counted on as a certainty. The development of the Academy into a more important Institution might follow, so that there was some prospect of the office now offered becoming in due time a desirable one. Meanwhile, the duties as at present proposed did not threaten the disturbance of other important work or of the private teaching on which the security of his livelihood depended. The Academy could not afford to ask for much of his time. He was to set aside, for regular attendance, six hours a week to be spent in supervising musical arrangements and in giving some instruction. His presence at concerts and examinations would also be necessary. A fixed salary of £150 a year, in addition to fees for class-teaching, was all that could be offered to him at the outset. The scheme, as regards hours, would have been imperfect, had not the Directors supplemented it by introducing a Vice-Principalship. This office Mr Otto Goldschmidt consented to fill. The Vice-Principal in the absence of the Principal would act as his representative, and one or other of them would be on the spot at stated times every day. The arrangement promised to be feasible, and Bennett, in accepting the appointment, saw no reason either for grave consideration, or on the other hand, for any congratulatory excitement. He expected that his work would be of a quiet kind, while a public position which involved no concert-room appearances struck him as being a good substitute for the Philharmonic conductorship. It would have been unwise at the time of life which he had reached—his fiftieth birthday occurred in the week during which he was considering the Academy's offer—and after years of continuous toil, to accept an additional duty if it promised excessive strain. He foresaw nothing of the kind. On the contrary, he had already begun to talk of a time soon coming, when, if he could not be independent, he might at least reduce his work, and have more freedom in the choice of his occupations. For three or four years he must still go on at high pressure, but chiefly for the sake of his family, as a letter written just then to Southampton will explain:—

THE ATHENÆUM, *Feb. 15th*, 1866.

MY DEAR SIR,

Accept my best thanks for your kind invitation to visit you in Easter week.

How much I should like to see your house and your pictures and the many other attractions which you offer me; but alas! I am in harness *ever*. My two boys, one at Oxford the other at Cambridge, come and meet me in London at the only breathing-time allowed in my incessant work. It was very kind of you to send me your Hartley Institute lecture, which I have read through with great interest, and have forwarded to my brother-in-law, a young clergyman who takes immense interest in the subject. What a labour it must have been to you.

Dear old Southampton, I was married there—to one of the best creatures God ever made—I am getting old now, looking forward with earnest hope to seeing her again.

If you ever come to London come and find me out at my new abode 38 Queensborough Terrace Kensington Gardens Bayswater

Ever y^r truly obliged

WILLIAM STERNDALE BENNETT.

In May, the Lords of the Committee of the Privy Council on Education gave their consent to the reception of the Academy at Kensington, on condition that the contemplated changes in the working of the Institution should be satisfactory to the Lord President when explained to him. The same Lords had named two special conditions: first, that they themselves were to have no financial responsibility; and secondly, that the Academy was to offer scholarships of such amount as would correspond to the rental value of the premises assigned to it. Indirectly,

interest in the subject —
What a labour it must
have been to you —

Dear old Southampton,
I was married there — &
one of the best creatures
God ever made — I am
getting old now, looking
forward with earnest hope
to seeing her again —
If you ever come to London
come and find me out
at my ~~present~~ new
abode 38 Queensborough Terrace
              Kensington Gardens
     Ever y.r truly Obl.g.d B[?]
  William Tindale Bennett

therefore, rent was to be paid, and this was a hard bargain, because the Lords of the Council had ascertained, that the Lords of the Treasury saw no objection to the removal, but would, if it took place, withdraw the £500 per annum which had been granted as *a provision for rent*. If, however, the Academy was ever to find itself included in the grand schemes floating in the air, this was no time for hesitation; so the Directors, on the chance of indefinite future advantage, passed a resolution on May 31 (1866), 'that the offer of accommodation at South Kensington be accepted.'

Room could be found at the Kensington Museum for *eighty-four* students. Mr Kellow Pye, a Director of the Academy[1], now drafted a scheme in which it was promised that *twelve* of these students should be educated as free scholars. It was decided that the present thirty-seven Professors, an unwieldy body in relation to the proposed number of students, should all receive notice that their services might no longer be required. Suggestions which had been made by Mr Cole and others before the Society of Arts were adopted. Local examinations were to be held in the provinces to secure a wide choice of candidates for scholarships. A three-years' course of instruction was to be the shortest on which a certificate could be granted. Some provision was to be made for the training of Church musicians and military bandmasters. The musical executive was to include a Principal, Vice-Principal, and Chief Professors of the most important branches of study, and small salaries beyond tuition fees were to be assigned to these Chief Professors. The Academy was making itself responsible for as much as it dared, and for quite as much as could have been expected by the Kensington authorities, who of course knew that the institution was not endowed, while their own condition with regard to free scholars would limit the number of paying students to *seventy-two*.

On June 8, Lucas resigned the office of Principal, giving as his reason that precarious health unfitted him for carry-

[1] The Earl of Wilton, the President, Sir George Clerk, Bart., Chairman of the Committee of Management, and Mr Pye were almost the only members of the Governing Body who showed active interest at this time in the affairs of the Academy.

ing out the new measures incident on the removal to Kensington.

At a Directors' meeting on June 22, it was moved by Lord Wrottesley, and seconded by Mr K. J. Pye, that Dr Sterndale Bennett be appointed Principal, and Mr Otto Goldschmidt Vice-Principal. Madame Jenny Lind-Goldschmidt, when announcing her husband's appointment to a friend, wrote:—'I could only bear to see him under Bennett, and B. is certainly the only man in England who ought to raise that institution from its present decay.' Twenty years later, Sir George Macfarren said to the Academy students:—'With the renown that Bennett had gained as a student and with the interest that gathered round him as Principal, his holding the highest position at the Academy proved to be the most propitious event for its welfare that has ever occurred.'

The new officers were engaged to enter upon their duties in September, but preliminaries demanded their immediate attention. They had to draw up a report, to be submitted to the Privy Council, of their new scheme of work, and, in connection with this, they had before them the delicate task of reconstructing the Staff of Professors. All went well for a month, and an appointment was made for July 25, when the Principal and Vice-Principal were to go with some of the Directors to inspect the accommodation at the South Kensington Museum.

Then the first blow fell:—

July 24, 1866.

MY DEAR BENNETT,

The appointment for to-morrow for South Kensington is put off by Mr Cole.

Yours ever,

K. J. PYE.

The appointment was cancelled only in so far as Bennett and Mr Goldschmidt were concerned. Mr Cole on the day named did receive Lord Wilton and Sir George Clerk, who once more expressed themselves willing to make any change in the working of the Academy which the Duke of Buckingham, as President of the Council, might desire. The Duke received the Directors on July 31, when the removal was further discussed. Great was the surprise and disappointment at the Academy, a few days later, when Lord Wilton received from the Duke the following announcement:—

'I regret to state that the means to secure the efficiency of the Academy do not appear sufficient to secure permanence and success for the altered system. There is every desire to afford temporary accommodation at South Kensington Museum as soon as circumstances may permit it, but it would lead to serious inconvenience and misapprehension if the Academy were established even temporarily at the Museum until the permanence of the new system and organisation had been really secured. Such a course would inevitably give rise to a public impression that Government had become responsible for the management of the Academy.'

The Directors did not understand this. The original offer would have had no meaning unless Mr Cole had stated the authority on which he made it, and had been able to explain the immediate improvements which the institution, its poverty being considered, would be expected to make in its arrangements. It was thought that an agreement had been arrived at, and that the removal had only waited for the *formal* sanction of the President of the Council. Sir George Clerk now wrote to Mr Pye of 'the *change* of determination on the part of the Privy Council,' and wished to learn the reasons of it. Both Lord Wilton and Sir George Clerk, when they saw later that nothing further was to be done in the matter, felt aggrieved, as will presently appear.

Bennett had no means of finding out what had occurred by way of hindrance. The postponement of the appointment for him to see the rooms at Kensington, without any explanation following, was of itself an injury to his feelings. In the last conversation which he ever had with Sir George Macfarren he still spoke of it, although he was then referring to the treatment of the Academy rather than of himself. A probable explanation of the sudden check to the negotiations is to be found in a fact which is stated in the Life of Sir Henry Cole. It appears that Lord Granville, acting for the Commissioners of the 1851 Exhibition, had consented to Mr Cole's plan of receiving the Academy at Kensington, but had only done so on the condition that Costa was to be appointed Principal; and therefore it can be assumed that the appointment of Bennett had much to do with, if it did not entirely account for, the apparent *change* of front which Sir George Clerk did not understand. If this was so, it also follows that it would not be easy to explain the circumstances to Bennett, and they never came to his knowledge. That his appointment did not meet the views of the promoters of a new institution, is confirmed by a broad hint given by the Society of Arts, who, in forwarding to the Academy Directors, a month after Bennett had been made Principal, the Report of their enquiry, solicited special attention to 'Paragraph 12,' which paragraph urged the necessity of appointing a musical director of 'proved administrative ability.'

Bennett was afterwards accused of obstructing schemes for placing the Academy at Kensington. In the beginning, at any rate, this was not the case. On the contrary, the removal being now uncertain, the prospects which had induced him to accept office were altered, and both he and Mr Goldschmidt drew back. The Directors, however, believing at first that the removal was only postponed, arranged with their landlord for a quarterly tenancy, and at length prevailing on the new Principal and Vice-Principal to stand by them, decided to re-open at Tenterden Street in September. The Directors continued their meetings and correspondence throughout August. Bennett almost entirely missed his summer holiday. He remained in town till the middle of August, while for the rest of the month—according to a memorandum of his own—he was only 'off and on at Eastbourne.' Mr Otto Goldschmidt remembered long days spent this summer at the Academy with Kellow Pye and Bennett, and how difficult it was to get the Principal to attend to anything in the shape of lunch. One evening as they were leaving, the 'posters' were just announcing the formation of a new Conservative Ministry. The fresh list of the Academy Professors was not quite complete at the time, and Bennett, as he shook hands with Mr Goldschmidt, laughed and said: 'Well, Good-bye, we will go on forming *our* ministry to-morrow.' He could not foretell that the change of Government would prove no laughing matter to the Academy or to himself.

The new prospectus, when drawn up, contained the names of many eminent native and foreign musicians. It ought surely to have commanded the confidence of those who continued to talk, from time to time, of adopting the Academy. While new names were introduced, old associations were duly regarded. Lucas, the retiring Principal, accepted an invitation to remain as a teacher. Bennett happily invented an office for his old master, Cipriani Potter, prevailing upon him to regard himself as the 'Honorary Visitor' of the Institution. In accordance with this idea, Potter, for the last six years of his life, regularly attended the students' concerts, sitting at Bennett's side, while—as the writer has been told—the young people in the orchestra would whisper to each other that they were in the presence of a friend of Beethoven.

At the Academy itself, Bennett's appointment, whatever may have been thought of it elsewhere, was unanimously approved. All rallied round him, as Potter had predicted in a letter already quoted. He would himself tell a tale of the confidence placed in him by one of the humbler officials, an eccentric caretaker whose oddities of speech and manner did not escape Bennett's ready powers of mimicry. Benjamin Badman had, in earlier years, ingratiated himself with Bennett by bringing him cups of tea during afternoon lessons, and had gone so far as to entrust him, and him alone, with the secret of his surname. Not long after Bennett's election to the Principalship, and at a time when the Directors had decided to close the Academy, he met the old retainer in the vestibule and said to him, 'Well, Benjamin, we're all going to be ruined.' But Benjamin replied, 'No, no, Mr Bennett, if you'll stick by us, *we'll* pull it through.'

The opening of the winter session under the new arrangements, in September, 1866, found the Directors, or, to speak more precisely *three* of them, busily continuing their efforts to gain external aid, as extracts from their correspondence will show. Bennett, as Principal, had no actual part in this; nor did he, for some little time to come, allow himself to take much interest in schemes of doubtful issue. After the first check in the Kensington negotiations, his feeling was that the Academy had been slighted, his confidence in its ever being adopted was shaken, and he trusted to efficiency within the walls of the Institution as giving surer promise of future prosperity than indefinite proposals of outside help. It was no time for day-dreams. There was plenty at hand to do, work which could be done with certainty of thereby improving the existing state of things. Here is an illustration of the simple course he set himself to pursue. Soon after his election the Directors summoned him to one of their meetings. They were rather in the clouds at the time, with a panorama before their eyes of glittering castles in which they hoped they might reside. Bennett startled them by begging them to vote, 'that the Committee-Room[1] be cleaned, the ceiling whitewashed and an estimate obtained for a cheap papering of the walls.' There was a freshness in the idea. The Academy had not for years paid attention to such details. The Directors laughed, but agreed.

Removal to other premises was, however, now their chief thought. The following is an epitome of their correspondence.

Oct. 1, 1866. Sir George Clerk is anxious for the Academy to be established in the basement of Burlington House.

Oct. 3. Sir G. C. has been led by Mr Cole to believe that the Commissioners of the Great Exhibition would give assistance.

Oct. 24. Sir G. C. thinks that Mr Cole should make some distinct proposition, and should be told that he had caused an increased expenditure at the Academy by holding out hopes of external aid.

Nov. 29. Lord Wilton thinks that the Academy has been placed in an unmerited position.

Dec. 3. Sir G. C. thinks that the idea of Burlington House must be given up, the philosophers dreading the

---

[1] The room in which parents and other visitors were received. Mr Otto Goldschmidt told the writer that the house had been allowed to drift into a most disreputable state.

proximity of the R. A. M. as Babbage does the barrel-organ.

Dec. 24. Sir G. C. thinks that Mr Cole should give notice whether there is any prospect of accommodation at South Kensington.

Jan. 17, 1867. Directors write to the Commissioners of the 1851 Exhibition asking for £10,000.

Jan. 21. Lord Derby replies that a site might be given, but not money.

Jan. 28. Sir G. C. thinks it would be well to see Mr Cole and get something definite out of him.

Feb. 14. Sir G. C. thinks that all Mr Cole's fine promises will produce very little.

April 4. The Directors write to the Exhibition Commissioners, and would be glad to have some definite proposition from them whereby progress might be made for the establishment of the R.A.M. on their estate.

May 9. The Commissioners, in reply, suggest that the R.A.M. should continue negotiations with the Committee of the Royal Albert Hall.

May 20. Sir G. C. begins to despair of getting any assistance through Mr Cole, from the Commissioners of the Exhibition or from the Treasury, and thinks it may be absolutely necessary to close the Academy before the vested capital is quite exhausted.

May 31. Mr Kellow Pye writes a Memorial (adopted by the Directors) to be sent to Mr Disraeli, who had replaced Mr Gladstone as Chancellor of the Exchequer, setting forth the claims of the Academy and asking for the present grant of £500 per annum to be increased to £2000.

The result of this last venture was not known for five months. Meanwhile an Academical year of spirited musical work was drawing to a close. The memorandum-books kept by Bennett and Mr Goldschmidt, in which from day to day, at their alternate attendances, they made their reports to each other, furnish evidence not only of how well they worked together but also of the enthusiasm of the other Professors and their pupils. The Directors, at the end of the summer term, went out of their way to address to the Staff a grateful acknowledgment of their services, and specially referred to the Principal and Vice-Principal having consented to retain their offices notwithstanding the failure of the Kensington scheme. Mr Goldschmidt, as one of his duties, had taken control of the students' orchestral and choral practices. On July 24 he conducted a very interesting Prize concert, at which the pupils both as composers and executants showed to good effect. A special feature of this concert was a revival of Handel's 'Ode for St Cecilia's Day' which Mr Goldschmidt had lately introduced into Germany at the Lower Rhine Festival. Musically speaking, the house in Tenterden Street was already brightening, and the doings of the Academy, for the first time for many years, received favourable notice from the Press.

On July 26, Bennett was at Eastbourne, looking pale and worn. He had enjoyed no proper holiday for two years; nor could he take one now, for he had to complete a sacred work which was to be performed at the approaching Birmingham Festival.

CHAPTER XXVI.

CAMBRIDGE PROFESSORSHIP.
'THE WOMAN OF SAMARIA.'

1867.
æt. 51.

THE year 1867 brought from Cambridge gratifying recognition of Bennett's services. He had held his Professorship for eleven years. Among the amateurs who had gathered round him at the time of his election, some had now risen to high positions in the University, and wished to use their influence in placing the proceedings of the musical faculty on a more settled footing, and also in doing something for the Professor himself. As the first result of this movement, the following letter came from the Vice-Chancellor:—

CHRIST'S COLLEGE, CAMBRIDGE.
May 11, 1867.

MY DEAR PROFESSOR,

It has been pointed out to me some little time ago, to my great surprise, that no fee or pecuniary consideration was assigned by the University to the Professor of Music.

As the Professor has duties to perform of a laborious kind in regard to degrees in Music, I think such an anomaly should be rectified, and I would wish, with your permission, to submit a proposition to the University on the subject, not that I wish to mix you up in any way with the proposition, for I think it is an act of justice which ought on general grounds to be done.

Very truly yours,
JAMES CARTMELL.

Musical degrees were in more than usual evidence during the May-term in which the above was written. Two of the chief resident musicians, J. L. Hopkins, organist of Trinity, and G. M. Garrett, organist of St John's, were both proceeding to the degree of Doctor, which had so far been granted only once during Bennett's Professorship. The performances of the important exercises required for the senior degree aroused a great deal of interest, and the College chapels on both occasions were densely crowded. It was Bennett's duty to conduct the compositions in the presence of the Vice-Chancellor and other University officials.

Pending the decision as to the emoluments of the Professorship, a rare distinction was conferred upon him by the University. The holding of a Professorship did not give complete membership of the University, and it was now proposed to grant him the status of a member of the Senate, and accordingly the Vice-Chancellor wrote to offer him the M.A. degree. This was conferring, so to speak, the freedom of the University. A large party of his London musical friends, including Cipriani Potter, were present in the Senate-House when he took the degree. Bennett greatly appreciated the spirit of this friendly act on the part of the University. When others congratulated him upon it as an *honour* he would at once correct that idea, saying, 'No, it was not an *honorary* but a *complete* degree,' by which he meant that the membership of the Senate was the main point. The Public Orator in his Latin speech on the occasion made graceful references to Bennett's musicianship, but he gave the real explanation of the award in this particular case when he spoke of the Professor's 'diligent and effectual performance of his honorary duties.'

A Syndicate was appointed to report on the 'Proceedings in Music.' This appears to have been the first time that the University gave any serious consideration to the subject. The Report, when issued at the end of a year, did not go very far beyond confirming the course which Bennett had hitherto pursued, but the personal examination of candidates was now established by authority; 'after much deliberation,' it was found desirable to dispense with the *performance* of the Bachelors' Exercises; and it was ruled that the 'solemn canticum' could not be construed as referring alone to sacred music, but that secular compositions could be submitted by the candidates. The University was not as yet prepared to disturb the arrangement by which the Doctor's degree could be granted without that of Bachelor having previously been taken. The Syndicate suggested that the Professor should be asked to give lectures before the University, and recommended that a stipend of £100 a year should be assigned 'as long as Professor Bennett held the chair,' because they considered 'that his services could not with propriety remain any longer unrequited.'

As in Cambridge, so also at the Philharmonic, the work of eleven years was gratefully remembered. Though Bennett was no longer Conductor of the concerts he was a member of the Society, and remained its faithful ally. The Directors begged him to do something for them, in the season succeeding his resignation, to show the public that he was still in friendly accord with them. His Symphony in G minor was to be played in course of the season, and they asked to be allowed to announce that he would add a slow movement to the work for the occasion. This he did, developing the piece from a song which he had recently composed, but had laid aside, owing to some difficulty about the words. The opening lines of the first verse,

> 'Tell me where, ye summer breezes,
> Are the friends that passed away,

may perhaps be taken as a motto for the slow movement of the Symphony. He now assigned the melody to the violas. He went to the Hanover Square Rooms to hear the movement rehearsed under Cusins, who had succeeded him as Conductor, and listened from the end of the room; but so little fuss did he make over the performance of his own music that he did not criticise at the time. Afterwards, he said at home that the violas had not given enough prominence to their part. A hint, on such a point, might, one would think, have been given on the spot, but whatever he might have done when younger (as, e.g., in the case of 'Parisina,') it had long ceased to be his way to influence the playing of his own works.

Composition on a larger scale was now occupying his thoughts. In October, 1864, he had been asked to prepare a sacred or secular work for the Birmingham Festival of 1867. His first reply begged time for consideration. A work for Birmingham, of all places, could not be easily promised. Since the time of Mendelssohn, few composers had entered the lists. In 1851, an attempt was made, and was later renewed, to induce Meyerbeer to come forward. He entertained the proposal, wrote about the difficulty of finding a subject, and decided that if he did compose a work, it should be a short one to take up only one part of a programme. This intention, though Meyerbeer did not carry it out, might have been quoted as a precedent, when Bennett was later blamed for not contributing an Oratorio of the standard length.

To satisfy the requirements of a grand occasion, and at the same time to tread modestly in the domain of the great masters of sacred music, would present a great difficulty to Bennett. It was therefore no dilatoriness, but rather a justifiable hesitation, that caused sixteen months to pass before he accepted the invitation. In February, 1866, he wrote to Colonel Oliver Mason, the Secretary of the Festivals:—'If blessed with health, the only condition I make with your Committee, it will give me great pleasure to produce a new work at your next Festival. I have found it impossible to resist the invitation which has through yourself been given so kindly and thoughtfully upon all points.' The original invitation, although it made no direct reference to Costa as conductor of the Festival, was so worded as to anticipate any difficulty that Bennett might feel on that ground. The production of the work was to be entirely under his own direction and control, and he was begged to give careful consideration to a request which was 'made with all sincerity. * * * '

Before accepting, he had found in the Scriptural episode of 'The Woman of Samaria' a subject which he thought suitable for his musical treatment. If he wished to write a reflective and devotional rather than a dramatic work, his choice was surely a good one. There was one powerful attraction in it. Sustained conversations in which our Lord takes part are so rarely recorded in the New Testament, that few musical works except the great 'Passion' oratorios have been written, in which His presence and teaching form the great feature. Before Bennett began his composition, he said to a former pupil, 'I have had the subject in my mind for a long time, and think I can manage it, for it will not require grand Choruses.' If the solemn utterances of our Lord could be set, the most serious part of the composer's work would be accomplished. Bennett's contemporaries, in the result, acknowledged his power of treating the sacred text with impressive reverence[1].

A year before the Festival, his publishers engaged an eminent writer to prepare the book of words. The librettist had interviews and correspondence with the composer, but gave little practical assistance. After some delay, when he found that Bennett had himself made three successive editions of a libretto, he expressed his approval of the result, and retired. No offence was given or taken by either party, but Bennett was disappointed, for he had relied upon obtaining some help. It was fortunate, however, that he had not entirely done so. When the Academy closed in the summer of 1867, and he settled down at Eastbourne on July 26, twenty-eight days of hard work lay before him. Some of the most important numbers of the score were already written, the subject was well in his mind, and by the time of the London rehearsal on August 16, all the music for orchestra and chorus, except a final Fugue, was engraved. The rest of his time was ample for completing the other portions of his work. A manifest anxiety which burdened him during the first few days at Eastbourne, quickly disappeared as the music began to engross him. He showed no signs of haste, spent much time in the open air, retired early to rest, and in the first hours of the summer mornings would work recumbently, though always up and about in good time. One morning, when called, he was wide awake and seemed in very good spirits, but begged for a little respite, saying, 'I am getting on with my Fugue.'

The Birmingham Committee had appointed Cusins to conduct the work. This arrangement was most agreeable

---

[1] Vide, specially, W. S. Rockstro's article on 'Oratorio' in the first edition of Grove's *Dictionary of Music and Musicians*.

to Bennett. Cusins had been one of his most favourite pupils and was very delighted, as he told the present writer at the time, to have the opportunity of rendering this particular service. Cusins went to Eastbourne to go through the music, and Bennett did not think it necessary to attend the London rehearsals, but he went to Birmingham in time for the final rehearsal on August 26. All care seemed to have been taken for his reception. When Costa had finished his share in the morning's work, he called for Cusins and leaving the orchestra retired to the President's gallery, from which he listened to Bennett's music with earnest attention. 'I suppose you remember,' writes Mr Stockley, the Birmingham Chorus-master, 'that your father at the rehearsal was heartily summoned to the orchestra by band and chorus, although with characteristic modesty he wished to remain in the body of the hall.'

The performance of 'The Woman of Samaria' took place on the morning of August 28. The deep impression it made on the audience could be observed, and was duly noticed by the press. Without the power, or may-be without the desire, of exciting listeners to a high pitch of enthusiasm, Bennett could cast a spell and rivet attention, and on this day his hold was complete. The sea of faces upturned towards the President, Earl Beauchamp, at the end of almost every number made it no easy task for him to decide what should be repeated. The soloists were Mdlle Titiens, Madame Sainton-Dolby, W. H. Cummings, and Santley. Madame Sainton caused a great sensation by her singing of the contralto Air, 'O Lord, Thou hast searched me out.' Bennett had composed this song on his journey from Eastbourne to London on the previous Saturday morning. On his arrival in Birmingham next day he at once took it to Madame Sainton. She received him rather coldly, as she had naturally wished to see the music sooner. When, however, she had sung the song to his accompaniment, she was so affected by it, that she could not help embracing him. Both he and Cusins returned to 'The Stork Hotel' much touched by her display of sympathy. At the performance, this number, as also the tenor Air, 'His salvation is nigh them that fear Him,' sung by Mr W. H. Cummings, and a six-part Chorus, 'Therefore they shall come and sing,' which Bennett had borrowed from his early Oratorio 'Zion,' were redemanded by the President. 'At the conclusion of the performance, rules and regulations to the contrary notwithstanding, loud applause broke out from every part of the hall, in response to which Dr Bennett at length appeared for a moment at the top of the stairs, and then vanished with characteristic alacrity.' Although several critics more or less disapproved of Bennett's choice of subject, they all, save one, wrote most appreciatively of his music, and this the same writers or their successors were still doing twenty-one years later, when 'The Woman of Samaria' came of age at a Hereford Festival.

A small party of Bennett's intimate friends went down to Birmingham for the day, expressly to hear the new work. Charles Lucas was one of them. As he had been concerned, nineteen years before, with the unfortunate quarrel between Costa and Bennett, he now desired to seize a chance, which the present proximity of the two men seemed to give, of effecting a reconciliation. After the performance of 'The Woman of Samaria,' he went to the artists' room and begged Costa to shake hands with Bennett. The only reply was, 'Lucas, remember 1848.' Costa looked exceedingly angry when he was making ready to go up and conduct the rest of the morning's programme, and the writer has been told that the mere mention of Bennett's name in his presence was sufficient to produce that effect. He remained consistent to the end. At the time of Bennett's death, he would not listen to Sir George Macfarren's earnest appeal that he should sign a petition for an interment in Westminster Abbey. He delegated the bâton to Sainton, when the 'Dead March' was played 'in memoriam' at a concert of the Sacred Harmonic Society. Time, which hardened Costa, softened Bennett. On one occasion, the latter was being pressed by others to express some opinion on Costa. At last, he said, 'He is an implacable man,' and there he stopped. As a rule, if any conversation to Costa's disadvantage went on in his hearing, he would only join by harking back to the early days when they had frequently met at the house of the Seguins, and he would often close such a conversation with the set phrase, 'All I know is that when I was young, I used to think he wrote very pretty music.' He certainly did not allow those who lived with him to inherit from *himself* any animosity against his foe. Whether Costa's hostility to Bennett was based entirely on the incident of 'Parisina' in 1848, is open to some doubt. Weist Hill, the first Director of the Guildhall School of Music, but previously a leading member of Costa's orchestra, told one of Bennett's former pupils, that he *knew* the malign influences which had been at work to keep Costa and Bennett apart.

CHAPTER XXVII.

A CRISIS AT THE ROYAL ACADEMY OF MUSIC.

1867—68.

æt. 51, 52.

AFTER the Birmingham Festival, Bennett was able to indulge in a fortnight's holiday. This he much enjoyed, spending the time with his daughter at Eastbourne and Brighton. Mr W. C. Stockley, the Birmingham Chorusmaster, came across him in Eastbourne, and found him very grateful for the fine performance of 'The Woman of Samaria.' This holiday, though none too long, was opportune. It was a breathing-space between the fulfilment of a duty as a composer and the arrival of trouble from another source.

When the Academy re-opened in September, 1867, the Directors were expecting an answer to their petition for increased aid from the Government. In a circular sent by them to the Professors during the vacation they stated, that while they had feared the necessity of closing the institution, a deputation to the Chancellor of the Exchequer had met with a reception so favourable as to lead them to expect the larger Grant. Their hope, however, was not realized. In October the news came that the present allowance of £500, instead of being increased, would be withdrawn. The Lords of the Treasury wrote in explanation that they were about to consider what steps should be taken 'to establish a cheap system of musical instruction under some department of the Government.' Since advice on a musical question would probably reach Mr Gladstone and Mr Disraeli from different sources, it is conjectured that the change of Ministry had turned the scale in favour of those who regarded the Academy as a stumbling-block in the way of new schemes. The Academy authorities only saw one issue, as regarded themselves, of Mr Disraeli's decision. Lord Wilton considered it 'the death-blow to the Academy.' Sir George Clerk wrote, 'The Academy must be closed without delay.' The Directors met on Nov. 20, and, though too few of them were present to form a quorum, resolved, 'that in consequence of the Treasury letter, the Academy would be closed in March [1868], and that a letter should be addressed to the Queen placing the Charter at Her Majesty's disposal.' A few days later, Lord Wilton wrote to a fellow-Director: 'If anything could be more annoying than, under the present greatly improved position of the Royal Academy of Music, to be obliged to close the institution, it is the circumstance of the want of interest or necessary absence of the Directors at such an important crisis in its affairs rendering it incumbent upon those few who were present to take the responsibility of action in the matter.'

At this extremity, Bennett came to the rescue. He had been invited to attend the Directors' meeting. A few days after that meeting, he wrote:—

38 QUEENSBOROUGH TERRACE.
November 24, 1867.

MY DEAR PYE,

As a very old friend I cannot disguise from you that I feel myself to have been in the wrong position at the Directors' meeting on Wednesday. When I was invited to meet the Directors, according to the Secretary's note of some three weeks since, I certainly thought it probable that I should be asked to take part in the discussion whether the Academy should close or not. Instead of that, I was called into the Committee-room when the deliberations were over, to have the bare fact announced that the Academy was to be given up. I am still of opinion, though I stood alone at the meeting, that the Academy could be kept going on until July, so as to give further time for reflection. It is a consolation to me that even the smallest opportunity occurred to allow me to raise my voice in favour of the old place. Your activity and zeal I know full well, and you will not believe this personal. I have been obliged to write, to get the thing out of my mind, as far as I can.

  Believe me, My dear Pye,
    Ever yours sincerely,
      WILLIAM STERNDALE BENNETT.

Bennett could not get the thing out of his mind. He saw and seized a chance of saving the Academy. The Directors, of themselves, were really powerless to avert its doom. With them it was a simple question of how long funds would last out. Bennett called the Professors together, and found them ready to follow his lead by offering their services for the summer term, without regard to remuneration, if the Directors would consent to *postpone* the closing from March to July. The Directors demurred to accepting the Professors' offer. They knew that there was a strong feeling among some members of the staff, that the Academy should be entirely under professional control. Lord Wilton thought that if the Professors were allowed to take any share of financial responsibility, the management must to some extent pass into their hands. He thought this would not answer, while at the same time he doubted whether it lay within the power of the Directors to allow such a change. Bennett then suggested to the students that they should send up a petition for a respite. The Directors had already been troubled about the injury which the students might suffer from an abrupt dispersal. The case of those who had been elected to the new scholarships—initiated, by the way, to satisfy the demands of the South Kensington authorities—was very hard to deal with. The Directors found the students' petition irresistible, and, at a meeting on Feb. 15, 1868, they resolved that, in consequence of the proposal of the Professors, and the interest shown by the students in the Institution, the R. A. M. would be continued till July. This same meeting had, in another respect, a rather important bearing on the future of the Academy. It has not yet been necessary, for the purpose of this narrative, to refer to the constitution of the Academy's Governing Body. Its management had lapsed into the hands of a few individuals, who have so far, been mentioned by name, or called Directors. But the actual management of the Academy was vested in a Committee, a Committee which might or might not be selected from the Directors, but which, as a matter of fact, had been almost invariably so selected. The Committee was, in fact, though perhaps not intended to be so by the Charter, a sub-committee of the Directors. In the Charter, the office of Chairman of the Committee had been reserved to Lord Westmorland for his life, and it was as Chairman that he found the power of ruling the Institution with an almost absolute sway. The Presidency of the Directors, which he did not hold, had more the nature of a titular distinction. When he died, in 1859, Sir George Clerk, Bart., who had been connected with the Academy since its earliest days, and who had acted as deputy during Lord Westmorland's long absences as Ambassador, succeeded him as Chairman. Tradition gives Lord Westmorland the credit of having managed the Academy with a personal interest so keen, as to discourage others, when he was on the spot, from rendering him any assistance. At any rate, whatever the reason may have been, the Committee had gradually dwindled away, and at the time to which this story relates was scarcely existent. Sir George Clerk died just before this meeting in Feb. 1868. Two active officials remained. Lord Wilton was already President of the Directors, and Mr Kellow Pye naturally took the vacant Chairmanship. A Committee was wanted, but where was it to be found? Sir George Clerk had tried his hardest, but had admitted his inability, to obtain fresh members. At this meeting, the Principal, Vice-Principal, and two other Professors to be nominated by them were placed on the Committee of Management. The introduction of the professional element was a new departure[1], but, for the time being, seemed imperative.

The intention to close the Academy still held good. The dissolution was merely *postponed* from March to July. The Directors had sent away the Charter. Bennett was

---

[1] Mr Kellow Pye, previously mentioned in this book as a *musician*, had, early in life, left the musical profession.

able to get privately from a high legal authority an opinion upon the right of the Directors to surrender the Charter. The opinion was that, according to the terms of the Charter itself, the 'Subscribing-members' constituted the Corporation, and that the Academy could not be dissolved if any one member dissented. But the Charter was returned to the Directors for another reason. It could only be annulled by Act of Parliament. This would involve cost, and the Academy had laid nothing by to pay its own funeral expenses. Sir Henry Cole (as appears in his Biography) described this as an unsuccessful attempt on the part of the Directors 'to clear the way for new action.' But the Directors, as their correspondence shows, thought themselves *forced* to close the Academy. They did not surrender to oblige opponents. The *attempt* at a clearance must be credited to Mr Disraeli's advisers.

The Directors made use of the further time, which the postponement gave them, to appeal again to the Chancellor of the Exchequer. An unfavourable reply reached them in April, and they then called a general meeting of the Subscribing-members. They, too, had taken counsel's opinion and had found that they could not act by themselves. Sir John Pakington (afterwards Lord Hampton), as one of the Directors of the Academy, presided at this meeting on May 2. He then said; 'In this report the Directors have placed in a few words the whole situation. The insufficiency of funds for its support leaves us no alternative but to close the Royal Academy of Music.' Sir John Pakington, who was at the time a Cabinet Minister, had probably been able to convince the Directors that there was no hope of a renewal of the Grant by the present Government. When he left the chair, a supplementary meeting was held. Bennett, smarting under a sense of injury, and imagining that the Ministry were really about to propose a system of *cheap* musical education, threw aside all reserve, made a long and telling speech, referred to the treatment of the Academy at the time of his election as 'a deception,' ridiculed the idea of setting up 'a gigantic school of music in Hyde Park' with Mr Cole as the 'national music-master,' and prophesied a sure future for the Academy, if his hearers would but agree that it *should* exist. He carried the meeting with him. Mr George Wood moved the appointment of a special committee to consider the means for continuing the Academy, and to communicate the result to the Directors. Several sums of £50 were subscribed in the room.

The various reasons for withdrawing the Grant, which were given by the Lords of the Treasury in correspondence with the Directors, as well as in answer to questions put in the House of Commons, were never twice alike. The impossibility of getting any satisfactory explanation, or of finding what influence hostile to the Academy was at work, severely tried Bennett's patience. He had no experience of the intricacies of diplomacy and statecraft. Even a small argument was not to his taste. On one occasion, when asked to explain an admired modulation in a composition of his own, he is said to have avoided discussion by taking down a box from a shelf and saying, 'Try one of these cigars.' Meetings, speech-making, letter-writing on important subjects, were not to his liking, and it would take a great deal to rouse him to controversy; but he now entered upon a campaign from which, though it worried him terribly, he did not flinch. He wrote at great length to *The Times*; he sent letter after letter to the Treasury; he demanded, but very respectfully, an explanation from the Prime Minister of his statement in the House, that 'after *examination* the Academy had been found in an unsatisfactory condition' and pressed for a withdrawal, which after much persistence he obtained, of what he considered a groundless imputation on the Professors of the Academy. This was but the beginning of a kind of work which came to him quite unexpectedly, when he was well on in life without having acquired any habitual facility for it. There was a great deal more of it in store for him. He did it conscientiously, and it lay within his powers to do it very well, but not without a great expenditure of time and thought. Exceeding caution regulated its performance, and kept him always on his guard. Having once taken up the Academy he gave his heart and soul to it. Its grievances and troubles became his own personal grievances and troubles, and they greatly affected so sensitive a man.

The special Committee appointed at the meeting of

May 2 found, without much difficulty, new Directors, including the Earl of Dudley as President. On June 27, the majority of the old Directors, after taking part in the election of their successors, retired.

For reasons which were not published, the Academy now lost the services of Mr Otto Goldschmidt. It was known that the creation of the Vice-Principalship, a new office carrying authority over others, had not been regarded with favour by some prominent members of the staff, and without full support and allegiance the duties of the office may at length have appeared impracticable. The letters passing between Bennett and Mr Goldschmidt at the time show, that though there was some difference of opinion between them on an important question relating to the functions of the 'Chief Professors,' this at any rate caused no breach in their friendly relations. Mr Goldschmidt's last act was to conduct the Prize Concert in July. Lord Dudley, the new President, who attended the concert, took the opportunity of begging the Vice-Principal to reconsider his decision, but without result. Bennett had previously suggested that he should at least retain the conductorship of the orchestra, but this was scarcely to be expected. The students, when parting from Mr Goldschmidt, showed their gratitude by presenting him with a handsome silver testimonial.

Mr Kellow Pye, at the same time, vacated the Chairmanship of the Committee. Bennett could not persuade him to the contrary. Mr Pye had recently written to a friend: 'The case of the R. A. M. is now quite hopeless, and I should hardly think the Professors will persevere in their attempt to carry it on without external aid.' The other lay-members of the Committee followed Mr Pye's lead, and their places were almost entirely filled by Professors. As a result of this the Principal was elected Chairman, and Bennett thus became the chief manager of the Academy, in relation not only to music but to general business. The current of events had carried him rapidly into a position very different from anything which he had anticipated when he accepted the Principalship two years before, but he did not look back.

CHAPTER XXVIII.

CAMBRIDGE LOCAL EXAMINATIONS.
ADDITIONS TO 'THE WOMAN OF SAMARIA.'
ASSOCIATIONS WITH GERMANY. UPPINGHAM SCHOOL.

1868.
æt. 52.

WHEN the Cambridge Local Examinations were instituted in 1858, the 'Grammar of Music' was introduced as an optional subject. Any fresh sign of music being respected as a serious study by educational authorities was gratifying to an English musician. Whether school-boys would be found willing to take up such a subject must at first have seemed uncertain. Bennett was interested in the experiment. He was asked to examine, and did so for sixteen years.

Ten years earlier, in 1848, when Queen's College, Harley Street, was founded, he had started Harmony-classes there, being possibly the first person to teach the subject in this country to classes of young ladies not intending to become professional musicians. He wrote, at this time, portions of a Text-book on Harmony; also, and with more completeness, 'A Companion to the Harmony Book.' In the latter, with the view of impressing on the mind of students the individuality of each chord and of each inversion, he culled, from the works of great musicians, examples of their use which, to quote some of his own words, he thought 'bold,' 'beautiful,' 'happy,' 'telling,' 'charming,' 'fresh,' or 'independent' 'master-strokes.' Though he did not complete these books, he may have used them in manuscript for teaching; and at any rate he carried them to a further point than the pupils of the College are likely to have reached. The young ladies did not absorb much Harmony. After some years, when he passed on this work to others, he admitted that the results had been most discouraging. Difficulty in realizing the sound of written notes may at first have come to him as a surprise. In other ladies' schools with which he was connected he would urge and sometimes induce the Principals to engage a teacher of Harmony, so that his own pianoforte pupils might be instructed in the Theory. When their exercises were brought for his occasional inspection, he would say, 'It looks very nice on paper, but I hope they have got it in their heads.'

The boys' papers, on their first arrival at Cambridge were, as might be expected, very poorly done; and this remained the case for a few years. Bennett, however, paid great attention to them, without stint of time. As years passed, and improvement gradually came, he was much pleased. The arrival, at length, of a paper perfect in every detail, was an event which so delighted him, that he often referred to it, and still had it on his mind when he again crossed the path of the successful boy[1] some years later. He would look forward to the week at Christmas time which he gave to this examination. It was a change for him, and he would mention it in letters, as one of the events of an approaching holiday. He would linger over a harmony-exercise of a few bars and become so absorbed in it, that when ten or fifteen minutes had passed, it would be necessary to disturb him and to tell him that he must get on. Then he would say, 'Yes, yes, give him his marks'; for he liked some one by his side to register the results, not himself caring for arithmetical details. He was, however, always anxious to hear the total of the addition, and very sympathetic if it nearly, but not quite reached the prescribed minimum.

The week thus spent, and a few days at Brighton represented, in these years, the usual extent of his Christmas holidays. In January, 1868, the Brighton days were occupied in beginning an additional Chorus, 'Therefore with joy shall ye draw water,' for 'The Woman of Samaria.'

[1] Richard Pendlebury, afterwards Senior Wrangler, and Fellow of St John's College, Cambridge.

This Chorus he finished on his return to London. Lamborn Cock, who was now publishing the work, was also arranging for two performances of it at St James's Hall in February and March, in order to introduce it to a London audience. For the first of these, Bennett had the new Chorus ready. On the eve of the rehearsal he wrote the unaccompanied Quartet, 'God is a Spirit.' Dr W. H. Cummings, who took part in the Quartet, has said that when the copied parts were handed to the singers on the platform, the ink was not yet dry.

A lady, who just at this time was taking lessons from Bennett, asked him if his surroundings influenced him when composing. 'I do not know,' he replied, 'but I get an idea sometimes while staring at a brick wall.' A small sitting-room at the back of his house in Queensborough Terrace, had its window facing the side wall of the next house, and the table stood in front of the window. He never had any room of his own which he styled a 'study,' and when composing he was so absorbed that others could sit near him or go quietly in and out without his minding. When he was writing 'God is a Spirit,' one of his family, on opening the door to enter the room, was struck with his appearance. He was not at the time facing the brick wall. His head used to turn round, with a very gradual movement, when music was in it, as if he were listening for a distant sound; and at this moment had reached the full extent of its swing, and he was looking, with a very beautiful expression on his face, directly towards the door. His large eyes were, therefore, full on the intruder, who was only a few feet from him, and feared that interruption had been caused. But this was not so. He was not conscious of any one's presence, and when his head had finished its short period of rest, it gently took its backward swing, and the hand began to move on the music-paper.

To set the seal of approval on a sacred work written for a Festival, a performance of it by the Sacred Harmonic Society was in those days generally looked for; but that Society, being one of Costa's strongholds, was not likely to favour Bennett. 'The Woman of Samaria' had to be content with the two performances mentioned above, another by the National Choral Society under G. W. Martin, and a fine rendering at the Crystal Palace under August Manns, to start it on its way. It soon found its place with provincial choral societies, and excerpts were adopted as Anthems.

Bennett's work for the past two years or more had been well-nigh incessant. So-called holidays had been disturbed by Academy business, or closely devoted to composition. His anxiety as to the fate of the Institution which he was so bent on preserving had become intense. This had not been without effect upon his health and happiness; but so cheerful was he by nature, so inclined towards the bright side of things, so patient by long habit, that no murmur escaped his lips. A note written in the luncheon-hour of a long day spent with pupils gives as much as he would ever say about the hardness of his life. The note will serve another purpose by presenting him in the character of a parent.

SOUTHGATE,
June 10, 1868.

MY DEAR JEMMY,

I must write you a few lines to send you my best love and congratulations on your majority to-morrow. It will be a day of great interest to me and I shall think of you very much. What interest would your dear lost mother not have taken in such a day! I must try that you do not suffer too much by her loss.

If you had not been such good children to me, I hardly know how I could have got through the last two or three years, and now things look a little brighter.

Ever your fond father,
WILLIAM STERNDALE BENNETT.

Among the pleasures of his life, the recollection of Leipzig ever remained one of the greatest. His short stay there in 1865, and the proof he then received of his friends' continued affection, increased, as far as that was possible, his grateful feelings. Julius Kistner, whom he had found an incurable invalid, wrote to him a few months afterwards: '*Remembrance* that is the last help in my misfortune, and so I often think of the happy hours in which I saw you.'

Retrospect became the chief feature in Bennett's love for Germany. His house, in his later years, was no rendezvous for musicians coming with musical purposes. After he resigned the Philharmonic conductorship, he had no longer any fixed opportunities of coming into contact with foreign artists of a younger generation who visited this country. Those, however, who had known him earlier, still regarded him as the chief worker, amongst English musicians, in the cause of German art; and he was never happier than when a letter of introduction from Germany brought to his doors some young foreigner, to whom he could render service. Of his own contemporaries, Ferdinand Hiller, with whom he had, in earlier life, only a slight acquaintance, came to England more frequently in these later years, and lost no chance of cultivating his friendship. Hiller afterwards wrote: 'As a man, Bennett was extremely simple, unaffected, open, honourable, good-tempered, cheerful and sociable. German musicians found in him a truly heart-felt welcome.' Bennett, when young, expressed, in writing, his contempt for those English artists who, after a tour on the continent, aped foreign manners, and even pretended to forget the pronunciation of their own language. But, from old associations, he retained a love for the sound of the German tongue, thoroughly enjoyed to speak with it himself, and when in the society of Germans to show himself, as far as possible, the German. He would amuse them and himself by comparing the customs of their country and his own, would take care that some attempt should be made to introduce German dishes on his dinner-table, or would order such English ones as would give his foreign visitors a new experience. Many a laugh would go round at his loyal effort to show a keen relish for *Sauer-kraut*, and he would watch with lively interest the faces of those who suspiciously tasted *mint-sauce* for the first time.

Before his departure for Leipzig in 1865, the Rev. Edward Thring, Headmaster of Uppingham, commissioned him to find some one to take charge of the music at that school. Bennett referred this matter to Ferdinand David, who mentioned his own son. Mr Paul David accepted the appointment, and from that time became a frequent visitor, during the school holidays, at Bennett's house in London.

In the summer of 1868, Ferdinand David was expected in England on a visit to his son, and it was arranged that he should spend part of the time in Queensborough Terrace.

ATHENAEUM,
July 5, 1868.

MY DEAR DAVID,

I am looking forward with great pleasure to your visit to us. I also hope it is certain you will bring your *two* daughters with you. We have plenty of *zimmer*. Let me know when you come. Cannot you persuade Schleinitz to come with you? He must bring the score of the 'Meerestille' with him, that will keep him well, if he leaves out the middle movement[1]. I have plenty of room for him. Write soon.

Ever your friend,
WILLIAM STERNDALE BENNETT.

Bennett postponed his Eastbourne holiday and remained at home in the beginning of August to receive David, his daughter, and Mr and Mrs Paul David of Uppingham. This was a rare treat for him. It was no unusual thing for him to have intimate friends staying in his house, but as a rule he could himself see little of them. He now said that he could not remember ever spending a whole week in his own house entirely free from work and under circumstances of greater enjoyment. He always asked German visitors to go with him to Cambridge, taking much pride in showing them an English University. He had occasionally been vexed when his persuasion had failed, and when he had been unable to convince one or other of such visitors that they would find something different from the many Universities they had seen in their own country. David's appreciation of Cambridge entirely satisfied him. He would afterwards relate how upon entering King's College Chapel, David was so taken aback by the beauty of the interior, that he seated himself and, after a few minutes silence, said with great seriousness: 'Bennett, you must let

---

[1] Schleinitz probably possessed the *original* score of Mendelssohn's Overture which would account for the reference.

me stay here, I must see nothing after *this*.' Bennett's own love for the Chapel was so intense that his companion could not have touched a more responsive chord. This was his last reminiscence of Ferdinand David, who was on the point of leaving Cambridge for Uppingham. They never met again. The following affectionate letter illustrates the warm place which Bennett had retained in the hearts of his German friends.

EISENACH, *Aug.* 24, 1868.

MY DEAR BENNETT,

I got back here happily eight days ago, and must now no longer delay to thank you a thousand times for all the love and goodness which you have shown to myself and my daughter. Never shall I forget it, and happy shall I be if any opportunity arises to show my gratitude.

But you will be tired with my German feelings, and I will try to say the rest in my bad English. * * * Here in Eisenach I found my wife pretty well. She is quite gerührt über Ihre Gute für mich und meine Tochter. I always think with the greatest pleasure of my stay with you in England. I understand the country and everything much better than before and I am returned a great admirer of your country, your countrymen, your institutions and of everything. That day in Cambridge was one of the most interesting to me, and very often I read in that book which you were kind enough to leave for me.

Good-bye, dear Bennett. God bless you in every respect.

Believe me, for ever,

Your friend,

FERDINAND DAVID.

My wife sends her
herzlichste Grüsse dem guten Bennett.

Bennett took great interest in Mr Paul David's work at Uppingham. He went down twice every year to examine the music of the school. As time went on he was specially pleased at the progress made in instrumental music, which was beyond what he had thought possible at a public school. 'I can account for their chorus-singing,' he would say when he returned home, 'but to learn an instrument is a different thing, and the results of teaching the violin and pianoforte surprise me.' Mr Thring made him very welcome and acquired a sympathetic regard for him. When speaking of him and of his hard life to the present writer, he said, 'I wish I were King of England, so that I might do something for your father.' After Bennett's death he wrote: 'I honour myself in remembering that your honoured father was friendly to me and I feel privileged to bear witness to the greatness of his pure and gentle character. There was no true place for him in England, and while I am glad for the sake of others that the nation has given him some of his due now he is gone, I cannot but feel how little it makes amends for the "weariness of the journey," and I mourn that England has no place left for men who put their life-work first and turning neither for fame nor money, aim with high hearts to bring out truth. Such was your father.' Mr Thring and Mr Paul David paid tribute to Bennett's memory by saying, when he died, that they would have no more music-examinations, as they did not wish to see any one else in his place.

CHAPTER XXIX.

GOVERNMENT GRANT RESTORED TO THE R.A. OF MUSIC.
THE R.A. OF MUSIC AND THE SOCIETY OF ARTS.

1868—69.
æt. 52, 53.

In September, 1868, when Bennett entered upon the third year of his Principalship at the Academy, with the duties of Chairman of the Committee of Management now added, the new Committee reported 'that the Professors' sacrifice of their fees during the summer term had cleared the institution from debt, that the Principal had altogether resigned his salary, and that new donations and subscriptions had been received.' On the other hand, the Directors' determination to close the institution in the previous summer, had made it difficult to admit new pupils in the earlier part of the year, and the number of students, which had risen in 1867, had again decreased. No one, at this time, who watched from outside, had any belief that the institution would survive the crisis.

The year 1869 opened with a graceful display of good feeling towards Bennett in his native town. At a meeting held in Sheffield during the previous autumn, it was resolved to invite him to spend a few days amongst his friends and former pupils resident in the town. The invitation bore many signatures; he accepted it; and went down for five days in January as the guest of William Howard, his father's friend, whose house had sheltered him as an orphan fifty years before. As an episode of the visit, a complimentary concert was carefully prepared. The programme, drawn from his own music, included 'The Woman of

Samaria,' and the P.F. Concerto in F minor played by his pupil, Miss M. H. Parkes. The conductor, Walter Ibbotson, and the organist, Percival Phillips, had both been his pupils at the Academy. The orchestra, led by H. J. Freemantle, included several members of Halle's Manchester band. The Concert Hall was specially decorated for the occasion, and when the guest of the evening, accompanied by Mr Howard, entered, the audience rose *en masse* and gave their fellow-townsman a Yorkshire ovation. This was not the last occasion on which his connection with Sheffield received recognition. When he was knighted his friends and admirers in the town sent him a handsome address of congratulation. After his death they subscribed liberally for a marble bust, the work of M. Malempré, which they presented to the Cutlers' Hall, and which was unveiled by Stirling Howard, son of William Howard, in December, 1875.

Now, in 1869, came a turn of the tide in the fortunes of the Royal Academy of Music. The policy of 'waiting' and of defying discouragement proved sound. The fall of the Conservative Government, in December 1868, gave an opportunity of re-opening the question of the Grant, and Bennett appealed to the new Prime Minister, Mr Gladstone, who had, as Chancellor of the Exchequer, first bestowed the Grant five years before.

11 CARLTON HOUSE TERRACE,
March 5, 1869.

SIR,
    I have not neglected the subject of your letter which reached me some time back, and a further enquiry shall be made into the circumstances by the Chancellor of the Exchequer.
            I have the honour to be,
                Your obedient servant,
                    W. E. GLADSTONE.
Dr Sterndale Bennett.

The Chancellor of the Exchequer had, apparently, no difficulty in judging the circumstances which had prompted the withdrawal of the Grant. The above letter was immediately followed by another announcing that the £500, as an allowance for rent, would be replaced on the estimates.

The good news, when received at the Academy, gave occasion not so much for open rejoicing as for solemn thanksgiving. The stigma, which the withdrawal of the Grant had cast upon the Institution, was at length removed, and the machinations of unknown foes had been overturned. The £500 came back with a greatly increased value. No event connected with Bennett's later life was more satisfying to him than the restoration of this Grant. As Chairman of the Committee, he himself received the order, annually sent, for the money. The last time it reached him was a few days before his death. It was one of the last things he handled, and he showed a somewhat painful reluctance to relax his grasp of the paper. A custom of the Academy was to ask some lady to distribute the prizes to the students at their summer concert. From the time the Grant was restored, Bennett always asked Mrs Gladstone to preside on these occasions, and she very kindly consented for some years in succession. This gave her an opportunity of hearing the pupils' performances, as also the Principal's Report and the announcement which he was now annually able to make of a continuous increase in the number of students. Mrs Gladstone's constant appearance on these days was much appreciated. She showed lively interest, and took her part in the ceremony with charming grace. Moreover, there was a general feeling that her presence symbolized a link between the Academy and the statesman who had befriended it.

History now repeated itself. The Academy was again enjoying the patronage of the Government, and the promoters of a new scheme thereupon renewed their overtures. The musical Committee of the Society of Arts had just recommenced its sittings, and Mr Cole still found the desire remaining in influential quarters that a new Institution should be a development of the old one. The Society of Arts now proposed that the Academy should join them in a petition for state-aid towards a music-school on a large scale. The Academy, having so recently secured what it wanted from Government, wisely shrank from asking for anything further. The experience of eighteen months ago was dead against such a course. One of Mr Disraeli's various explanations for having withdrawn the Grant, indeed by far the best he gave, was, that if the Directors required, as they told him they did, £2000 a year for the upkeep of their Institution, £500 could be of no use to them. Since, however, a new or enlarged school was now, again, being confidently talked of, the Academy was obliged to give careful consideration to the Society of Arts' proposal, and for four months Bennett was in doubt as to the attitude he ought to take.

Sir John Pakington, who had remained on the Directorate of the Academy when most of the old Directors had retired in 1867, and who was also on the Council of the Society of Arts, undertook to negotiate between the two Committees. The following memorandum dated April 24, 1869, was sent by Bennett to be read at an Academy meeting which he was unable to attend.

'On receiving the documents from Sir John Pakington (all of which I send), I sent to know when I could see him. The appointment was made for the same day at 12 o'clock. I was with Sir John Pakington for nearly an hour. It appears he had had two interviews with the Society of Arts' Committee, and at the first meeting, according to Sir John's impression, they did not seem aware that the grant of £500 had been restored to us, but at the second they were in possession of the fact.

'I asked Sir John whether he would be surprised if the result of the petition would be to annihilate the old Institution and rear a new one. He then said that he would be both surprised and indignant, for his only idea was that the Committee of the Society of Arts would help to make the present Institution the nucleus of a larger one. I, however, renewed my suspicions. Sir John told me to dismiss them. He behaved with the greatest courtesy throughout, and I thanked him in the name of the Committee. His note to me of the same day [April 22] will show that he did not leave the matter resting and found out the best arrangement for us to make with regard to calling a meeting of the Directors. In the meantime no harm can take place.'

The Directors of the Academy met in June and July. They resolved to postpone their decision about the proposed joint-petition until the autumn and to ask for a conference with the Society of Arts at that time. Mr Cole wrote of finding Bennett and Lord Dudley, the President of the Academy, so opposed to union with the Society of Arts that the prospects of any successful issue grew smaller and smaller. They were certainly opposed to, and in the end declined, union over this particular venture. To sign the petition, drafted by the Society of Arts, which exhibited the present Institution as failing to satisfy the requirements of a national school of music, was in their opinion decidedly impolitic. They could not again place in jeopardy the recovered support of the Government. How could they count on its continuance, if they appended their names to a petition which prayed for a Grant towards 'a *proper* Academy'?

When the Society of Arts sent in their petition to the Government, it was backed by another one emanating from a private Institution entitled 'The London Academy of Music.' This second appeal urged the foundation of a 'Government School of Music and National Opera.' The suggestion of the Opera ensured the signatures of many leading operatic artists, so that the document was likely to carry weight. The foundation of a Government School would scarcely benefit 'The London Academy of Music,' but the downfall of 'The Royal Academy of Music' might do so, and therefore the prime object of this petition seemed to disclose itself in a paragraph which advised the Government that any further help to the Royal Academy of Music would prove 'equally discreditable to the country, and wasteful of its funds.'

It was well for the Academy that it did not participate in these movements. They were unsuccessful, and the old Institution did not risk the loss of the only assistance which the Treasury was prepared to give to higher musical education. With a Royal Charter, Royal Patronage, prestige attaching to Government recognition, now also with an increasing number of students to bring fresh spirit to its work and to help its finances, the Academy was in a fairly strong position. The Institution was not too proud to hope for further assistance from outside, but could wait until such time as that assistance might come in a more definite shape than had yet been the case. The main duty of the Academy was, in Bennett's opinion, to concern itself with the present.

CHAPTER XXX.

COMPOSITIONS.
SOME CIRCUMSTANCES OF HIS PRIVATE LIFE.

1869—1870.
æt. 53, 54.

In May, 1869, Bennett was associated with an important ceremony at Cambridge. St John's College, of which he was a member, was holding high festival on the occasion of the consecration of a new Chapel, and had gathered within its walls some thousand of its own alumni and distinguished visitors including the Chancellor of the University. Bennett had been asked by Dr Bateson, the Master of St John's, to write the Anthem for the Consecration Service. After ascertaining that his doing this would be agreeable to Dr Garrett, the Organist of the College, he gladly consented. He wrote at considerable length to words selected by Dr Bateson and himself. The Anthem, 'Now, my God, let I beseech Thee,' with its grave and reverent measures, was valued as a very appropriate accessory to an event which saw the result of much self-sacrifice on the part of many members of the Foundation and which was regarded by them as one of deep solemnity. The day, however, was also celebrated with much outward rejoicing.

The members of the College Musical Society, with the assistance of London artists, gave a concert in the Guildhall, which was attended by the Chancellor and other guests of the College. Bennett, with Carl Reinecke of Leipzig sitting by his side, showed a wide-awake interest in the proceedings. At a supper-party later, he congratulated the undergraduate performers on the soothing effect of their strains, and upon the number of Bishops whom he had watched gradually sinking, under its influence, into slumber.

Except for one short Præludium, in B flat, written at the request of a favourite pupil, Harold Thomas, for performance at a concert, Bennett had not, for many years, added to his pianoforte music. So long ago as the beginning of 1856 he was contemplating a series of pieces illustrative of the months of the year. He chose mottoes from the poets, also pictorial illustrations which were engraved as vignettes for the title-pages, and probably set himself the task of writing one number each month as that year went on. He finished 'January' and 'February'; but in March he was elected to the Cambridge Professorship, and the conductorship of the Philharmonic immediately followed. He abandoned playing in public, and, possibly as a natural consequence, ceased for some years to write for the pianoforte. By the summer of 1869, however, he had made some advance with the principal (the 2nd) movement of a Sonata, which he christened 'The Maid of Orleans.' The writer remembers a day at Eastbourne in that year, when he was shown a passage beginning at the 53rd bar, and in their walk the same afternoon father and son sang together several times, as a piece of fun suggested by Bennett, the two parts written in contrary motion. But this movement took some time to complete. In nothing that he wrote could he have taken more interest, yet he seemed quite content to let the music, as it came to him, regulate its own progress. About the publication of his works he showed the same caution as ever. In this year he had quite a long correspondence with his German publishers about printing the score of his seven-year-old Overture, 'Paradise and the Peri.' He kept his Symphony in G minor in manuscript till it had reached the same age. As another instance of caution, he would, in his later life, get his London publisher, in the case of smaller works, to engrave them, so that he might see how they looked in print, and he would then keep them to himself in that form. If he lent them to his friends for private performance, they would find the words 'Proof as MS.' stamped upon the copies. One of these was an eight-part

Motet, 'In Thee, O Lord, do I put my trust,' which now ranks as one of the best of his vocal compositions. He wrote the two movements of this Motet in 1856 and 1857. The first of them was engraved in 1864. He asked his friend, Dr Steggall, to arrange for its being sung in Lincoln's Inn Chapel, that he might judge of its effect. He often, later, played the movements to himself on the pianoforte, but they did not reach the stage of publication in his lifetime.

The years following his appointment at the Academy—where he had anticipated no excitement or disturbance of his affairs—not only brought a burden of responsibility in connection with its management, but also a great change in his private circumstances. His habit had been, after his wife's death, to add up at the end of each year the income derived from teaching. This reached its maximum in the year preceding his election to the Principalship. It then began to decrease, but there was to be a payment from the Academy as a set-off. After he resigned his stipend as Principal, and ceased to place any fixed limit on the time spent in performing his duties, there was at once a great shrinkage of his income. At the end of 1869, after making his calculation, he added, as was his wont, his few words of thanks to the Almighty; but the figures were in front of him, and he must have noticed how serious matters were becoming. He seems, however, to have wished to banish from his mind the sacrifice he was making; for he never added up his income again. The cheques which he received from the Academy, in return for all the work he did there, were drawn, term after term, for six-and-a-half guineas. This sum must have represented some reduced fees for the teaching of composition. The other Professors, after voluntarily allowing their fees to be taxed for a term or two in 1868, had then been paid in full, but Bennett must have declined to receive, or perhaps, as Chairman, to award himself the higher fee. Balancing what he received against what he lost through decrease of other work, the writer has carefully calculated that during the eight years from the time of his election to the Principalship in 1866 to the time when he was again assigned a salary in 1874, his position at the Academy cost him an annual average sum equivalent to twenty-seven per cent. on the income he was making when he accepted the appointment. In January, 1870, he wrote to his Aunt at Cambridge on the subject of some family obligation for which they had made themselves jointly responsible. He then mentioned his difficulties, but without referring to, and perhaps without thinking of, the Academy as being the cause of them. 'I do not tell you these things,' he wrote, 'to make you unhappy, but to show you what a critical time of my life this is.'

In the same January his daughter was happily married to Mr Thomas Case, then Fellow of Brasenose College, Oxford, and the second son of Mr Robert Case. Since leaving school in 1865, she had worked very hard for her father, and, especially as a secretary, had made herself almost indispensable. 'She is just like her mother,' was his favourite phrase about her. Her new home was at Oxford, but fortunately he was still able to see her for long spells of time. University terms were short, and she with her husband spent vacations in Bayswater, where their parents continued to reside as close neighbours. Nevertheless, letters written soon after her marriage show how seriously Bennett felt the loss of her assistance. He determined to take a decided step towards lessening his anxieties. Immediately behind the house in Queensborough Terrace lay a cottage, which happened to be vacant, in Porchester Terrace. He let his own house furnished, and moved into this cottage. He could not leave his Penates, even temporarily, without a pang; but the change enabled him to continue his costly work at the Academy without further pecuniary troubles. Moreover, the cottage with its garden just large enough to contain a pear tree and a fine mulberry tree was a pretty place. Madame Clara Novello had at one time occupied it.

A letter to his friend, Alfred G. Price, of Gloucester, with whom he spent a few days at Easter, was written from his new home.

18, PORCHESTER TERRACE,
April 29, 1870.

MY DEAR PRICE,

I ought sooner to have thanked you for all the pleasure my visit to you at Gloucester gave me. I had a very pleasant journey home, stayed an hour in Porchester Terrace, and then on to Brighton, where I arrived at 6 p.m. I set to work at my overture and sent it off to Leipzig. Of all the Cathedral towns I know, Gloucester seems to me the most cheerful and happy. Places like Ely, Winchester, Salisbury, &c. seem to me like *Malines* where old Dussek was organist for three years. How about the Raven and Edgar Poe? I think if I had the chance of getting a real piping-bullfinch free of expense, I would break a pane of glass and welcome the intruder. Seriously speaking, I think some family in Gloucester would be glad to welcome the renegade. Why not advertise? I send the sketch of the Bench. With best regards and many thanks for my treat last week.

   Sincerely yours,
    William Sterndale Bennett.

P.S. I am now writing under the shadow of my pear-tree, the blossom just saying 'Adieu' for the season.

CHAPTER XXXI.

BENNETT WITH THE ACADEMY STUDENTS.

1866—1874.
æt. 50—58.

MANY of Bennett's friends who were outside the Academy circle, and who studied his interests rather than those of that Institution, thought it a great pity that he should cling to a position the drawbacks of which were so apparent, while the advantages were so vague. Pecuniary sacrifice on his part was not the only point they considered. A School so slenderly endowed, and of necessity rather mean, at the time, in its visible equipments, could not, by any stretch of imagination, be regarded as on a par with the Institutions of London where other arts and sciences, more fortunate than music, were fostered. Bennett's connection with the place could not raise his already acquired standing among the men of his time. Those near him regretted that he should wear himself out over an undertaking which seemed to them unlikely to bear any fruit within his life-time at all commensurate with his labours. He, however, knew what he was doing. He had accepted a commission, and was evidently bent on executing it, without counting the cost or looking for a return. He turned away from all hints that he ought to consider himself, whether those hints came from without or from within. A letter, written to a colleague who was wishing to be relieved from teaching at the Academy, gives a slight but pertinent reference to the subject :—

Responsibility as Chairman

2 ADELAIDE TERRACE, EASTBOURNE,
August 3, 1870.

MY DEAR DORRELL,

I received your letter, as you will believe, with great regret. We can ill afford to lose the services of an old and sincere friend and fellow-worker at this time, just as everything seems as promising as at any period since 1822. You have often heard me say that I should like to escape from my heavy duties and anxieties at the Academy, but I have never had the courage to do so, although my health and pocket would point to that course. Now, my dear old friend, I have often been lucky in staving off disasters to the old place (I take no merit for the same), and firstly I will beg you to reconsider your present resolution and stay with us *for one year at least*. If that cannot be, then I sincerely beg that you will not give up your pupils, until they have finished their course. * * * I wish you would come down for a day or two and have a long talk. I only got here yesterday.

Ever most sincerely yours,
WILLIAM STERNDALE BENNETT.

As to the future of the Academy, there was one paramount anxiety which burdened Bennett's mind for at least seven years. This was caused by the harassing uncertainty of the relationship which the Institution would be allowed to have with the projected School of Music at Kensington. The protracted negotiations with the promoters of the new scheme greatly increased his responsibility as Chairman of the Committee of Management. It was in that capacity that he represented the Academy in those negotiations. Meanwhile, he never lost sight of his duties in his other office as Principal. Let it be granted that, up to the time of his election, he had given no proof to the world at large of the 'administrative ability' on which the Committee of the Society of Arts, with Costa in their eye, had laid so much stress. These pages do not desire to claim for Bennett distinction as a man of business. Suffice it to say, that when he was put to the proof he did, as Chairman, administer the affairs of the Academy with discretion, and with some advantage to its financial position;

while, in the office of Principal his characteristics and his long experience in a special direction were found of great value. Respect for his musicianship, combined with a trust in the simplicity of his motives, brought hearty allegiance from his colleagues on the Staff. One or other of them may have imagined him too timid when it seemed his province to adjust their differences; too prone to wait and to try the effect of pouring oil on troubled waters; too deaf to discords. But the Academy was passing through a crisis. The Principal's 'peace-loving and peace-promoting propensities were invaluable[1]' at a time when the survival of the House greatly depended upon the union of its inmates. 'Where he could not satisfy he at least soothed[1].' Sir George Macfarren wrote, in special reference to Bennett's dealings with the Professors: 'He had a peculiar power of drawing the love of those with whom he had commerce; it is true he shrank from the utterance of harsh words, and evaded on all occasions the performance of functions that would be painful to those to whom they would have been directed; but this, far less than a sympathetic manner, a positive more than a negative quality, rendered him the centre of affection.'

But Bennett had another qualification, of a very positive kind, for presiding over a place of education. He had spent the greater part of his previous life in teaching and influencing young people, in studying their characters and dispositions, in sympathizing with their successes or disappointments. Simple discourses which he committed to writing and delivered in schoolrooms, when he wished to say something to his pupils of rather deeper import than what they could read in a musical Grammar, give a clue to the serious view he took of his calling. His private pupils have spontaneously acknowledged the strong influence for good which he, using music as the means to an end, spread among them. The Academy students were not slow to appreciate their Principal. One of them wrote, soon after his death: 'His interest in the progress and careers of the students was unfailing[1].' The numbers never rose so high in his time as to make individual attention on his part impossible, though he lived to write of the Academy as

[1] *Fraser's Magazine*, July, 1875.

growing 'very large,' and ever making greater demands upon his time. He did not limit himself to the supervision of studies. He talked to the students of their future, of the various openings in the musical profession, and of the direction in which, according to their special abilities, they might look for success. He had seen plenty of difficulty and distress, especially amongst orchestral players, in days when concert-engagements were scarce, and when amateur pupils, except for pianoforte and singing, were all but unknown. For many years of his life he seldom went to church without having first listened to some tale of distress on the only morning that he could be found at home. As late as the time of his Principalship, he still demurred, save in case of very marked ability, to students taking as their chief study any orchestral instrument, even were it the violin. His evidence before the Society of Arts in 1865 showed him opposed to the idea of training large numbers for the profession. The supply, he thought, might soon exceed the demand. Though he had himself received a free education, he doubted the expediency of giving much encouragement by scholarships such as Mr Cole was proposing. He thought that fees, fixed as high as practicable, would provide a safeguard against an overcrowded profession. As Principal of the Academy, he steadfastly held the view that an educational establishment should feel some responsibility in respect to the worldly prospects of its pupils.

He had a fatherly concern for the health of the students, and would watch for any signs of overstrain. At entrance examinations, even when additional pupils were badly wanted, he would consider the question of admission in the interests of the candidate. He would say to parents: 'She seems nervous, and not strong enough; take her back into the country and let her go on quietly with her present teacher for another year'; and this would be said in the presence of other Professors who thought a clever pupil was being lost. 'There is a story told of how he found a very small boy crying over the intricacies of chromatic chords and enharmonic modulations. "Ah," said he, "I see what you want, my little fellow, it is pudding!" and he took him straight to his own house where he was regaled for a fortnight, and perhaps got a little assistance in his musical difficulties[1].'

The monthly concerts gave him special opportunity of observing the results of work, students being encouraged to take part in these at a comparatively early stage of their course. 'No concert ever took place without his presence, so quiet and undemonstrative, and yet felt so distinctly throughout the room as to make the uppermost thought in every performer's mind as he or she ascended the platform, "Will Sir Sterndale like this?" No Academy student in Sir Sterndale Bennett's time will ever forget him as he appeared month after month at these concerts. They will be able to recall all their lives the slight spare figure, the attitude of motionless attention, and the deeply-knitted brow, which gave his face an expression of displeasure but which they understood to denote only the concentration of thought with which he listened to each performance. The moment the sonata or song was over, his face would relax, often into a smile of satisfaction, for though rigid and unflinching as regards the music to be performed at these concerts, as to the performance of it he was always ready to be pleased if possible[1].'

His class for composition, to which he devoted a few hours every week, kept him in close touch with many of the senior students. He had been reluctant to undertake this class, but Mr Otto Goldschmidt, at the time of their joint election, had urged the necessity of his taking some share in definite teaching, and he had given way. Mr C. H. Couldery, who was in the class, remembers his saying that though he had often been offered more than his usual terms as an inducement to take a private pupil in composition, he had refused, because he so disliked the idea of teaching the subject. He had, at various times, taken a few professional pupils for composition; of whom may be mentioned, Edward Bache, Charles Steggall, W. S. Rockstro, and W. G. Cusins; but he generally advised applicants for lessons to study under Macfarren or Molique, who both made a speciality of teaching the subject. He gave some lessons in Knightsbridge Barracks

[1] *Fraser's Magazine*, July, 1875.

to Hon. Seymour Egerton (afterwards Earl of Wilton), the conductor of the amateur orchestral society known as 'The Wandering Minstrels.' This is remembered, because at one of the lessons he took exception to a horn-passage, as being too difficult, in the score submitted to him; and he afterwards liked to relate how his clever pupil, who could play all the instruments in the orchestra, there and then took down a horn hanging on the wall and played the passage admirably. At the request of Mr Gambier Parry, he gave some private lessons to his son, and of the son's gifts he spoke warmly to others at the time; but though Sir Hubert Parry remembers him as 'extremely kind and sympathetic,' he found him 'too sensitive to criticize.' A similar view was taken about the same time (i.e. in the early days of Bennett's class at the Academy), by Mr W. Crowther Alwyn, who, in response to certain questions submitted to him by the writer, has kindly supplied the following reminiscences:

'From the time of my entering the Academy in March, 1867, to the time of my leaving it at the end of July, 1869, I was Sir Sterndale's pupil for composition. I have a most vivid recollection of the time and of himself. Shakespeare, Kemp, Couldery, Wingham and Joseph Parry were my fellow-pupils. He paid close attention to the compositions brought to him, generally reading them through at the table, but sometimes asking us to play them, and occasionally playing portions of them himself. When reading them through he became wholly absorbed, few words escaping him,—I remember that some of the fingers of his right hand habitually covered his mouth,—and there appeared to be an atmosphere about him that debarred you from asking questions or made you feel that questions would be unwelcome. When we played our compositions he did not seem so absorbed, and I can remember watching him as he was listening with great animation and evident delight to the first movement of a sonata by Shakespeare, and saying to himself, "charming," "beautiful." I can recall how tenderly anxious he was that we should not play our compositions as if we were ashamed of them. He encouraged us to discuss one another's works in his presence, and, speaking for myself, I was more sensitive to the criticisms of my fellow-students than to any he made. In fact, his comments were few, briefly expressed, and, at least in my own case, he did not correct or suggest much. On rare occasions he would leave his seat, and standing with his back to the fireplace would unbend, talking to us and answering our questions. Then he would send down to the library for music,—I remember thinking what a quantity he knew,—and point out passages which haunted his mind on account of their surpassing beauty. Of such examples, I remember three bars (52nd–54th) from the Andante in Beethoven's G major Concerto; four bars (53rd–56th) from the Adagio in Beethoven's Sonata (Op. 106); and a passage in Mendelssohn's Capriccio in A mi. (Op. 33, No. 1), beginning in the 51st bar from the end. "Such things," he would say, "everybody ought to know by heart."

'To gauge the actual progress made at the time in composition, or to estimate how far such progress was due to his influence is impossible. Students possessing such temperament as to be susceptible of and capable of being infected by his own qualities could scarcely fail to be influenced thereby in their work. Intercourse with him stimulated and heightened the ideal and made you more sensitive to and appreciative of beauty, but it did so because he was what he was; no apparent effort of his own had anything to do with it. And, indeed, in my memory, questions of composition teaching or progress in composition fade away to nothing in comparison with the impression produced upon me by the man himself. I cannot connect him, as I knew him, with such words as "system" and "detail." He appeared to me to stand very high, and mists may have shut out the view of things below.

'We were very much struck at the readiness with which at first sight he played our scores on the piano, grasping their form and contents and exhibiting an apparent *familiarity* with them, in spite of our defective and, in some cases, almost illegible manuscripts. When at times we could not refrain from some expressions of wonder at his unparalleled facility in reading at sight, he would say, "Ah, but I have lost the power now. When I was younger, I did not fear anything."

'I remember him [1867—1869] as a serious, reserved

man with bright moments but rarely more than plaintively gay, whose life was apparently saddened by sorrow, or harassed by anxiety. I can recall the remarkable smile with which he used to greet us, the peculiarly gentle manner with which he always treated us. Occasionally, he would go so far as to enter into private conversation, and would speak of something out of the ordinary course which had happened in his own family, but at all times there seemed a long bridge between him and myself which I could not cross, notwithstanding the strong attraction towards him. There was an indefinable fascination, a delicacy, a refinement about him that was palpable and akin to the refreshment derived from intercourse with another nationality.

'Soon after leaving the Academy, I asked him to let me continue my studies under him as a private pupil, and received the following reply:—

ATHENAEUM,
November 13, 1869.

MY DEAR ALWYN,

How glad I shall be to have you as my pupil again but I don't know how to manage it unless you come into my class at the Academy. Could not this be managed? We begin now at 10 o'clock. I don't think I should like to teach composition except in a class, where so many things crop up (musically) to talk about.

Ever yours sincerely,
WILLIAM STERNDALE BENNETT.'

Those students who remained in the class for several years or who entered it at a later date, vouch for Bennett's *definite* instruction in composition. When he could no longer avoid this branch of work, he settled down to it, and became very interested. This was noticed in his own house, where, as a rule, he said little about pupils or teaching. As time went on, he would talk of his composition-class in a happy vein, and as if he was pleasurably surprised at the occupation proving so congenial. He would mention his young composers by name, and evidently enjoyed his musical and personal association with them.

Mr William Shakespeare writes: 'I have never ceased

to think of Sir Sterndale as a most *excellent* and *thorough* teacher of composition. His insistence on the study of *form* on the part of his pupils made his teaching so useful in after years. He was much more particular than any other Professor I have met as to the necessity of acquiring *continuity of matter, character* in the first subject, *contrast* between the two subjects, the middle development or working, the necessity of holding as precious the key of the composition, the avoidance of the repetition of keys. Our dear master was most particular, passed nothing by, corrected much himself, clearly expressed suggestions for improvement, cutting down or lengthening the work. I remember we were always reminded of the study and analysis of the classics. He was strict, but kind and encouraging, troubled when we were idle, a little cold and severe at times, yet so loving and noble that we all revered him. I had no special opportunity of seeing him read at first sight other than by the extraordinary way he would play *our* attempts at composition on the pianoforte.'

Among the pupils of Bennett's later life, none showed him greater devotion or remembered him with more reverent affection than the late Thomas Wingham, for many years Director of the music at The Oratory, Brompton. Already well advanced in musical studies when he entered the Academy, he at once found a place in Bennett's class, and in it he remained for no less than seven years. His Symphonies and other orchestral works were in due course performed, and they attracted considerable attention in the best musical circles. Shortly before his own death, he gave this account of his master's teaching:—

'As far as I can state them, Sir Sterndale's methods were as follows. Careful study and analysis of the works of the great masters. He recommended pupils always to take some work as a model till they had a complete mastery of the subject of "form." He would frequently send down to the library for some work and make one of the pupils play it and then explain its plan and what points of interest were specially worth noticing. When pupils were more advanced he would allow them more freedom, but even then would recommend them to study and even copy out and learn from memory large portions of the scores of the great composers. He once required me to learn an intricate portion of Mozart's G minor Symphony and to write it out from memory in his presence. He impressed upon us the importance of the opening of a composition. He used to say that a work ought to be known by its very first chord and would give any number of examples from Mozart, Beethoven, etc. He was particular about points of imitation, canon, etc., and again *inversion*. "Remember," he used to say, "that by *inversion* you not only add greatly to the interest of your composition, but you double its length." Then he gave us great assistance in the choice of subjects, pointing out what would make effective contrasts, what could or could not be worked, and what could be combined.'

These young men meeting Bennett week by week, year after year, were permitted to discover that he was not *always* a serious man. They heard, and have retained the echo of his laugh, and even became familiar with his humorous stories. Mr Louis N. Parker, the eminent dramatist, who began life as a musician and received his musical education at the Academy, speaks of mirthful moments in composition hours. He remembers that on one occasion when he arrived without his work and explained that he had left it in the train, Bennett did not readily pass the matter over, but continued for some time to make tender enquiries after 'The District Railway Sonata.' Mr Parker has given the following picture of Bennett as he appeared in his latter days to one of his latest pupils:—

'There was a door labelled "Committee Room" on the first landing of the Academy House, which, in the early days of my sojourn there, I, in common with other junior students, regarded with profound veneration. Through it we saw our seniors passing twice a week on their way to evolve masterpieces under the eye of the Principal, and the sight was one which aroused feelings of the bitterest envy. To this day I have no idea how I ultimately got into the class. I leave it to others to hint that my promotion was due to transcendent merit. In my own opinion it was due to cheek. But, somehow I got in, and I think when I was safely installed, I became duly humble and duly grateful, and did my best to make myself as inconspicuous as possible. Now, you must imagine a long table covered with an official green baize; at the head sits Sir Sterndale; on each side his pupils: Joseph Parry, Eaton Faning, Roberts, the handsome and accomplished Arthur Jackson (a lovable fellow destined to an early death while still a student), Stephen Kemp, Tobias Matthay, and last, but not least, Thomas Wingham, who, by reason of his undoubted genius, of the authority he exerted and the noble example he set, was regarded as the doyen of the students of his time. Over this group Sir Sterndale presided with a certain indefinable grace and dignity which marked him as a being set apart, as, in short, a great man. The recollection of him is as clearly before me now while I write, as though I was speaking of yesterday and not of—Ah! do not ask me how many years ago. A spare man, not tall, yet giving some impression of height by the proportion of his build and by the extraordinary impressiveness of his head. Graceful hair, black streaked with grey. A fair broad forehead with a certain feel of strain about it, as though there were constant neuralgia. Dark, piercing, yet kindly eyes with a merry twinkle and sympathetic and humorous wrinkles in the corners. The great beauty of the face lay in the finely chiselled mouth. A touch of pain and sadness about that too, but wonderfully sensitive lips, mobile to every impression, and now and again melting into a smile which lighted up the whole face and made you love the man without a word spoken. The influence of his mere external personality over the impressionable young artists who surrounded him is indescribable. I believe there was not one of us who would not gladly have died for him, who did not worship him and look up to him as a being set apart. To me, at any rate, he seemed holy, beautiful, adorable. It was enough to sit and watch him, to watch his hand with its graceful, sensitive fingers drumming on the table-cloth, to watch his face, as he studied the score submitted to him by some student, light up when he came to some passage less than usually stupid and jejune.

'How did he teach? I think he taught chiefly by personal influence, by the outflow of his exquisite mind. You lost certain things when you came before Bennett by the mere fact of being in the same room with him. Vulgarity, for instance, and roughness. You felt you were in the presence of a man, who, without any cant about art with a capital A, did really and truly move in a higher sphere than the ordinary man, and that here was a man for whom the best was not too good. He taught, again, by examples drawn from the great masters of old. His memory was a storehouse of all music, and the range of his knowledge embraced every composer from Palestrina to Weber and Spohr. If a student brought him something which touched a responsive chord in his imagination, which was good enough to be considered actual music as distinguished from a mere exercise, he shirked no trouble in analyzing it, in pointing out its merits to us others who had brought up our club-footed sonatas and wooden-legged fugues. Then he would often make the contents of such a work the basis of his reference to the classics. "Play me," he would say to one of us, "such and such a passage from Weber," or "Show me what Beethoven would have done in such a case"; and we were expected to remember the points in question. If we did not, then he himself would go to the piano and play them, and one led to another in a wonderful series of illustrations until the possibilities of that particular modulation, imitation or enharmonic change were completely exhausted. I fear we often led him by judicious wiliness and exaggerated ignorance to go to the piano; for, to hear him play, to watch those delicate fingers coaxing music out of the instrument, to see his face light up, as now Mozart, now Haydn, now Beethoven, now Gluck, now some half-forgotten worthy such as Scarlatti or Buononcini forced his way into his memory, was an experience never to be forgotten.

'He had, with all his tender gentleness, a power of irony about him, which inspired one with wholesome terror. He had only to look at you in a certain way, and for the rest of that day you felt you had ceased to exist. He had an excellent wit, and a gift of kindly and yet scathing satire. Many a time have I wished myself unborn as he has recalled the original authors of my most treasured melodies. But his most cutting things were always said so kindly that they never discouraged you, but, on the contrary, spurred you on to try again. When by some fortunate chance there happened to be anything good in your work, a passage, a bar, even a single chord, his praise was so generous, that the glow at your heart very much more than counteracted any chill his sarcasm may have previously left there.

'As the Head and Director of a public Institution his manner was absolutely perfection. His charm conquered all hearts; yet his dignity, not assumed, not arrogated, but inherent, gave him a personal supremacy to which all alike bowed. I have met many men in the course of much wandering. I have never met one who impressed me so peculiarly at first sight as a great man, or whose every word and movement seemed so completely in harmony with an exquisite mind and a lofty soul.'

CHAPTER XXXII.

HONOURS AND REWARDS.

1870—1872.
æt. 54—56.

STERNDALE BENNETT received in due course a fair share of this world's honours. There is no desire here to lay stress on the titular distinctions of a man who may be deemed worthy of remembrance by his plain names. But some of the recognitions that reached him may still possess an interest because they were granted to music in his person for the first time. They were among the signs that the art was growing in esteem, and regaining a position of dignity, which at some time or another it had forfeited. The works and letters of great writers such as Macaulay and Thackeray convey the impression that the brilliant vocalists and pianists who represented Music in Society failed to present the art in a favourable light to reflecting minds. If the improved attitude which was now to be observed, came through the efforts of musicians themselves, then credit may be claimed for a band of workers, of whom Bennett himself was not the least conspicuous figure. Many of his contemporaries, towards the end of his life, expressed the opinion that both by what he had done, as well as by what he had not done, he had helped to raise the status of music and of the musical profession in England.

His election in 1863 by the Committee of the Athenæum as the representative of a so far excluded art, has already been mentioned. Another circumstance which attracted some attention a little later was the appearance of his name on the list of guests at the annual banquet of the Royal Academy of Arts. This may appear at first sight an incident of no exceptional importance, but it meant a great deal to an English musician who had longed to see music placed in his own country, as he had seen it placed in Germany, on an equality with other arts. A compliment of similar significance followed a few years after. In 1870 the Marquess of Salisbury was elected Chancellor of the University of Oxford. A new Chancellor, at the first 'Commemoration' after his election, himself nominates the recipients of honorary degrees, and Bennett was one of fifty to whom he offered the degree of D.C.L. in June. Bennett's name appeared last on the printed list. Thus it may be inferred that music was the last thing considered; but at any rate it was admitted, and admitted for the first time in connection with an honour reserved for the highest forms of distinguished attainment. The Chancellor must have been convinced by the reception accorded to the musician in the Theatre that his act was generally appreciated. 'Finally,' wrote *The Daily News*, 'William Sterndale Bennett, Professor of Music in the University of Cambridge, was rapturously hailed as "a priest of Apollo and the Muses."' Canon Liddon received the great ovation of the day, but according to *The Morning Post* and other papers, 'Mr Sterndale Bennett appeared to rank next in popularity.'

After passing an uneventful year at his cottage in Porchester Terrace, there came a sudden change, and Bennett found himself beset with excitements of a kind quite new to him. One afternoon in March 1871, when he was teaching in a school at Clapham, a special messenger, who had enquired for him at Porchester Terrace, arrived with a letter from Mr Gladstone offering him the honour of knighthood and requesting his presence at Windsor next morning. The offer came so suddenly and unexpectedly, without the connection which any special event might have given, that he had some hesitation in believing it genuine. 'It was a relief to me,' he afterwards said, 'as I entered Paddington Station to catch sight of Benedict on the platform. Then I felt it was all right, and Mr Gladstone soon came forward and spoke to me.' Another friend of

Bennett's, W. Boxall, R.A., Director of the National Gallery, had also been summoned, and on arrival at Windsor it was found that Dr Elvey, organist of St George's Chapel, was to share the honours. Costa had been knighted two years earlier, Goss was similarly honoured a year later, and this generous bestowal of distinction was regarded not so much as a mark of favour shown to individual musicians, but rather as a proof of Queen Victoria's desire to encourage and advance the musical profession in England. It may be added that Her Majesty had already, early in her reign, conferred this honour on Sir Henry Bishop, and that up to the time now referred to he was the only musician who had thus been distinguished by a British Sovereign[1].

When Bennett was next in Cambridge, he entered King's College Chapel during Service time. As the congregation issued from the Choir, at the conclusion of the Service, and as Dr Okes, the Provost, was nearing the door of egress, he saw Bennett standing aside in the opposite corner of the Ante-chapel. He left the head of his procession and crossed over to congratulate 'Sir Sterndale.' There was no more dignified or ceremonious man in Cambridge than Dr Okes, and Bennett was surprised at this departure, on his part, from official routine, saying of it afterwards, 'He actually came right across the Chapel to speak to me.' Dr Okes would see in Bennett the chorister who had become the knight. He chose a time and place, under ordinary circumstances inappropriate, to insinuate, in the presence of many who would observe and understand his graceful act, the special significance which Bennett's promotion had within those walls. Dr Okes survived Bennett, and showed further interest in the latter's early connection with the College, by kind correspondence with the writer and by personally hunting up the particulars of the choristership. He found out that the boy had been admitted two months before the statutable age of eight, and the laxity of this proceeding, though fifty-seven years had intervened, seemed to trouble the mind of the strict disciplinarian.

Simultaneously with knighthood Bennett gained another

[1] Sir John Stevenson and Sir George Smart were knighted by the Lord Lieutenant of Ireland.

reward, of a very different kind though it came quite as unexpectedly. It was merely a sum of money, in return for past work, not a very large sum, and not of itself requiring any special notice here. But the incident of this payment,—the writer is alone responsible for calling it a reward,—has suggested the telling of the whole tale to which it was the conclusion; the tale, that is, of Bennett's career as a composer from the commercial point of view. The connection between money and his musical compositions seems only twice in his life to have been brought prominently to his notice, and at neither of these times by his own act. The first occasion came when his early publisher Coventry failed, about the year 1850; and the second came in 1871, when Messrs Lamborn Cock & Co., owing to some change in their business arrangements, desired to settle a cross account which had been running between their firm and Bennett for some twenty years. When Coventry failed, Bennett's published works, twenty-eight in number, were put up to auction and sold in one lot to Messrs Leader and Cock for £503. It may be said, in passing, that this was considered a high price at the time, and that, though Coventry had a varied catalogue of saleable works, those of Bennett, in proportion to their number, realised more than those of any other composer save Mendelssohn. In connection with this sale a complication arose. Coventry had borrowed money on the security of Bennett's works, but had so borrowed from an intimate friend who was not a business man and who had probably made no enquiry as to the publisher's legal claim to them. Certainly in the case of most of these works, probably in the case of all, there were no deeds of assignment from the composer to the publisher. Coventry, however, was able to state that he had paid Bennett for the first thirteen of the twenty-eight works. With regard to the first eight, he was unable to mention the price paid for each, but said that he had paid £80 or more *in toto*. His memory may have exaggerated the true sum, for his statement places a higher value on the music than on that which he next published, though there is nothing in the nature of the works themselves to account for the difference. He was able to name the separate prices paid for the next five pieces, so that the total amount given for them, viz., £31. 10s., may be accepted as accurate. At the time of Coventry's sale, Bennett had received no payment for the remaining fifteen of the twenty-eight works, and, as there were no legal assignments of them, he was advised that they were his own property. Why he did not claim them is not known. Perhaps, had he done so, he would have placed his old friend Coventry, from whom he had received much personal kindness, in an awkward position. He consented to assign the works to the new purchasers. It is the deed of that assignment which recites the chief of the particulars given above. Bennett cannot have taken this step without compunction. It is noticeable that he delayed signing the deed for three or four years. Long afterwards, when speaking of the first set of Six Songs, he said in a regretful tone: 'Ah, I was obliged to give those away, they ought really to be mine.' Accepting Coventry's figures, it follows that when Bennett had reached his thirty-fifth year and had published twenty-eight works, which represent in number about two-thirds of his complete publications, he had only received £111. 10s. for the copyrights.

With his next publishers, Messrs Leader and Cock[1], he fared better. He left it to them to assign prices, and they did it liberally according to the valuation of the day set upon the class of music he wrote. The accounts kept were cross ones, including, on the one side, music which he bought for his pupils or himself, and, on the other, sales of tickets for his concerts, fees for his editions of Bach, Beethoven, Mendelssohn, etc. and for his own compositions. These accounts were only made up at long intervals through the course of twenty years. There was no appreciable balance on either side of them, and for that reason, perhaps, no actual settlement was considered necessary. It is probable that in his wife's life-time Bennett never even looked at them. In 1871, a *resumé* of the whole account, which he had not asked for, was sent to him. It is not surprising to find in this *resumé* that two or three of his pieces were accidentally omitted. He would not himself be likely to notice it after a long lapse of time. One or two Anthems, published in his life-time, he gave away

[1] Afterwards Messrs Lamborn Cock & Co.

to Collections of such works. In this final account—he saw no further one—he was credited with the following amounts :—

	£	s.
For 7 Pianoforte Pieces	41	5
2 Sacred Duets	10	10
6 Songs (2nd Set)	47	5
Preludes and Lessons	150	
'The May Queen'	315	
Exhibition Ode	50	
Overture, 'Paradise and the Peri'	25	
Symphony in G mi.	25	
Anthem, 'Now, my God'	25	
Part-Song, 'Sweet Stream'	10	10
'Woman of Samaria'	500	
	£1199	10
Add Coventry's payments	111	10
	£1311	0

He also received money for his compositions from Kistner of Leipzig, and perhaps also from a Paris publisher who printed several of his pianoforte pieces. All his instrumental works that were published in England (except two early Concertos), as well as his twelve songs and 'The May Queen,' were also published in Germany, but he preserved no accounts of the payments made. A quotation from a letter will illustrate him when dealing, as a composer, with business. Here, again, was the case of a cross account about which nothing had been said for some years. He wrote to Julius Kistner in 1847 :—' You write about my account with the firm of your good departed brother. I do not know how he arranged this. You will know the money he gave me and the compositions he received, and I beg you will balance the account and let me know if I am still your debtor. Since I was last in Leipzig I have sent Rondo Piacevole, Scherzo, Trio, and before I left I gave him the Six Songs and the Suite de Pieces, but make the reckoning just as you please. We never made any specific arrangement together. I have never received any money from him without giving a receipt, and you will therefore know how much he has given me and what my compositions have been worth.'

Enough has been said to show how little attention Bennett can have paid to this one side of money-earning. When the account from Messrs Lamborn Cock & Co. reached him in 1871, he was completely surprised to find that there was a balance of nearly six hundred pounds in his favour. Had he given any previous thought to the matter, he might have foreseen that, as he had long given up providing music for his pupils, except at one or two schools, the account would gradually turn in his favour. He was exceedingly pleased. The prize came opportunely. A good Providence, may be, had held it in reserve, and awarded it to this non-mercantile musician at a time of his life when it seemed to be wanted.

Immediately after he was knighted, the Royal Society of Musicians invited him to preside at their annual Festival dinner. The Secretary, in a circular addressed to the Patrons of the Society, drew attention to the fact that the Chair had never before been occupied by a musician. No other Society so comprehensively represented the national profession of music, and British musicians could not, at the time, have devised a more signal way of acknowledging Bennett as the head of that profession. He performed what was to him a novel and therefore trying duty with success but not without effort.

ATHENÆUM,
April 29, 1871.

MY DEAR J.,
I have been very unwell all the week about the dinner business, but it is all now well over. It was considered a success. Look at *The Times* if you can. In great haste,

Ever your affectionate father,

W. S. B.

For the next three months he found it difficult to keep pace with the flattering consequences of his new distinction. Levées, garden-parties at Buckingham Palace and Marlborough House, other social functions too important to disregard, entangled themselves with lectures at Cambridge, examinations at the London University,

Uppingham and Queen's College, and the already fixed engagements which the London season always imposed on the substratum of heavy work at the Academy and with private pupils. The personal attentions now paid to him were gratifying, but they taxed his time. He referred to them, in a letter to his Aunt, as 'the crust which must be taken with the crumb'; and at the end of July, he wrote to his son, 'I am so tired,' a species of remark in which he had, so far, seldom indulged. Early in August he was at Eastbourne, with his daughter, her husband, and a little grandson who joined the sea-side party for the first time. A fortnight later he had recovered himself, and was on his way, in high spirits, to the Beethoven Festival at Bonn. On this, his last visit to Germany, as on the first visit in 1836, Davison, whom he now very rarely met in London, was his travelling companion. Mrs Davison with her two sons and Bennett's son-in-law and son were also of the party, and they were no little astonished, as two long days in a railway carriage passed on, at the continuous unflagging merriment with which the two old friends infected one another. Ferdinand Hiller conducted the Bonn Festival. He welcomed Bennett with great cordiality. One night, when a large company was assembled for supper at a Club which had been placed at the disposal of the Festival Committee, Hiller, having Bennett at his side, made a graceful little speech, bidding a number of young students who were sitting near him to take a good look, while they had the chance, at the great English musician. At this Festival Bennett met the Danish composer, Niels Gade, whose connection with Leipzig had been similar to his own, but who had never been there exactly at the same time. Another composer who was present, in whose music Bennett had taken great interest when writing lectures on 'The Opera,' and whom he had great pleasure in now seeing, was the learned M. Gevaert of Brussels.

The honour conferred upon him by the Queen was the subject of much rejoicing at the Academy. The students, with generous impulse, straightway purchased a grand silver cup, and presented it to their Principal with all due formality. Sir George Macfarren afterwards wrote of the lasting impression which Bennett's words of reply to

Mr Stephen B. Kemp, the senior scholar, must have made upon his hearers; words 'so graceful, so modest, and so encouraging to the students, who could all, he said, surely meet with such success as had fallen to his lot.' The Professors followed suit, called a meeting, and decided to open a subscription-list with a view of perpetuating Bennett's memory by founding a scholarship, at the Academy, to bear his name. The presentation of a parchment, on which the list of subscribers was enrolled, was made the occasion of a public ceremonial, and on April 19th, 1872, a few days after his fifty-sixth birthday, Bennett was called upon to face a large concourse of people who met in St James's Hall to pay him honour. The Philharmonic orchestra offered tribute to their former conductor by playing his Overture, 'The Naiads.' Henry Leslie brought his famous choir, which filled the balcony at the back of the Hall and sang two of Bennett's Part-songs. One of them, 'Sweet Stream that glides through yonder Glade,' had been recently written for a concert at Buckingham Palace. The Attorney-General, Sir John Coleridge, presided over the meeting and was surrounded 'by the most eminent native and foreign musicians in London at the time.'

It was a trying ordeal for Bennett. He not only had to endure, while his career was being described by the speakers, a conspicuous personal prominence on the day itself, but the proceedings were so exceptional that they naturally attracted great attention, and in the course of the week he became the subject of much written comment. His reputation bore the test to which, in this day of reckoning, it was put. It is impossible not to observe some feeling of disappointment, among those who commented upon him, that a man, universally acknowledged as one of the foremost on the roll of British composers, should not have written more music and should not have produced, in later life, more works on a large scale. But it was not as a composer alone that Bennett had gained his position in England, and the respect of his musical brethren. His character and principles as an artist stood for a great example. 'He has aimed at the highest,' said Macfarren at this meeting, 'not only in his musical works, but in his life,' and none who

[1] Afterwards, Lord Coleridge, Lord Chief Justice.

spoke or wrote of him at this time failed to emphasize the fact that his days had been spent in furthering the highest interests of his art in his native land. Sir John Coleridge, who knew Bennett personally, spoke of 'a long and laborious career,' and added:—'Whether we are musicians or not, we can all admire the simple, unpretending and manly character of our friend. We can all congratulate him that the Queen has thought fit to confer dignity upon a man who dignifies and adorns the noble profession which he practises.'

CHAPTER XXXIII.

COMPOSITIONS. THE ROYAL ACADEMY OF MUSIC AND THE ALBERT HALL.

1872—1873.
æt. 56.

In the season of 1872, Bennett finished an Overture which had been in his mind for the past year or two. This Overture was the first instalment of an intention to set music to the *Ajax* of Sophocles. A translation of the Choruses had been sent to him, many years before, by the Rev. Herbert Snow[1], then Assistant-master at Eton. He had disappointed some of his Cambridge friends, by his hesitation in undertaking a work the idea of which had originated from themselves. He had lately been pressed by them to reconsider the matter, and having written the Overture he desired its immediate performance, in order to prove to those interested in the matter that he had made a start with the work. The 'Prelude'—as he called it—to *Ajax* was accordingly given at the Philharmonic. It was finished a fortnight before the performance, but certain excitements such as that caused by the 'Testimonial' meeting, and fresh agitations with regard to the future of the Academy, had tired him very much, and he was unable to attend either the rehearsal or the performance of his new work. When it was played, after his death, at the Crystal Palace, Sir A. Manns spoke of it warmly as 'a real inspiration,' but on its first hearing it created no visible impression. *The Times* considered that it was too short to be played as a concert-piece. Bennett, on hearing that it had been coldly received at the Philharmonic rehearsal, seemed a little upset.

[1] Now the Rev. H. Kynaston, D.D., Canon of Durham.

When asked if he thought the music was on a level with his other Overtures, he said, 'Yes, I'm quite sure of that'; but he was conscious that others did not, at the time, think the same. As soon as he found himself at Eastbourne in the beginning of August, he said, 'Now I must finish my Sonata. I want something to show to them at the Academy when I go back.' Disappointment about one work acted as the incentive to another. The Sonata in question was 'The Maid of Orleans.' He did not finish it, as he hoped to do, in that same holiday; but he completed the principal movement, prefaced it with an introductory movement of a pastoral character, and wrote on August 24, 'I shall, I hope, send the first two movements of my Sonata to London to-morrow.' The slow movement, which depicts the Maid of Orleans 'In Prison,' was added early in September, while he was staying for a few days with his son at Sherborne in Dorsetshire, but the Finale, his holiday being over, moved slowly. Six months now came during which the Royal Academy of Music monopolized his thoughts.

The condition of affairs at the Academy had been steadily improving. At the end of 1869, the Committee had reported a balance beyond expenditure of a substantial sum. By the end of 1870 this margin had been more than doubled, while in the same year the number of students rose to 121, comparing favourably with the number 66 at the end of 1868. By the spring of 1872 the total reached 176. The Institution had now attained its fiftieth year and could celebrate a Jubilee with rejoicing, and with gratitude for increasing prosperity. The Society of Arts again came forward. The fresh negotiations which they now opened with the Academy had an additional importance owing to the fact that the Duke of Edinburgh had joined their musical Committee and was taking active interest in their suggestions upon musical education. Representatives of the Society and of the Academy met at Clarence House, the Duke's residence, on July 1, 1872. On July 3, the Academy gave a Jubilee dinner at Willis's Rooms, where Mr Cole announced in the course of the evening that scholarships to the value of £5000 could be offered to the Academy, 'if it remodelled its administration.' The present administrators of the Institution, who were Mr Cole's hosts, did not understand their guest's remark, nor was it subsequently explained to them. On July 9, the Duke of Edinburgh came with Mr Cole to inspect the Academy House in Tenterden Street. On July 17, the Duke met the Academy Committee at the Royal Albert Hall. 'Accommodation' was there shown, which Mr Cole said could be placed rent-free at the disposal of the Academy. This offer required grave consideration, and remained under discussion till the following spring. The accommodation was part of a vacuum between the circular exterior and elliptical interior of the building. The Academy was now asked to erect, within this space, the required class-rooms, and to defray the expense of their erection. The Trustees of the Albert Hall explained that they were in a state of great impecuniosity, and had not a shilling to spend. To be housed in a fine and finely situated public building was a prospect not without strong attraction to the Academy. Sir George Macfarren, referring to the circumstance many years later, wrote: 'It was a glittering proposal.' Moreover, if the offer was not accepted the Academy would perhaps sacrifice their chance of being connected with the projected music-school at Kensington.

The empty shell was to be rent-free, but then, as a consequence, the Treasury would withdraw the Grant which had been expressly assigned for the payment of rent. The removal, therefore, would be of no pecuniary advantage; while the countenance of the Government, which gave much prestige to the Academy, would be lost, or, at the best, exchanged for the uncertain patronage of others who had not yet matured their own plans for musical education, and who were unable to state definitely the conditions under which they would make the Academy the centre of their future scheme. The term 'promoters of the new scheme' has been adopted to serve the purposes of this narrative; but except in the case of Sir Henry Cole, whose great interest was throughout apparent, the term has little reference to known individuals. The Society of Arts, the Conservative Ministry when in office, the Commissioners of the 1851 Exhibition, the Trustees of the Albert Hall, might all in turn advise, or give hopes of assistance to musical education; but throughout the negotiations described in these pages no Committee was formed to carry a new scheme through, no organized body appeared with whom the authorities of the Academy could deal securely and from whom they could obtain pledges for the future. 'I do not know where I am;' Bennett would privately say, 'if the Prince of Wales would come forward, I should have no more hesitation.'

It was noticed, that when Bennett presided over the Academy Committee, he did not himself take a prominent part in the debates. If, at the end of a discussion, he gave any opinion, he would express it in very few words. His colleagues, however, had such faith in his judgment that they were generally content to accept what he said, even though his reasons were not forthcoming. Sir George Macfarren remembered that there was much curiosity at the Academy, while the negotiations about the Albert Hall were pending, to know what was passing in Bennett's mind. Up to the time of the final conference, he was very reserved, and gave no sign of the attitude he was likely to take. Representatives of the Society of Arts, of the Albert Hall, and of the Academy met at Clarence House on March 8, 1873. As the meeting drew to a close, something was said about the expense which the Academy would be likely to incur in erecting the class-rooms. The representatives of the Albert Hall estimated this at about £2000. The proposed structural alterations implied a building operation of an exceptional kind, and some one, on the part of the Academy, suggested that this estimate might easily be exceeded. The cost of removal and re-furnishing had also to be provided for. The Academy had known all along that this expense was a necessary condition of the scheme, and made no serious objection to it; but the introduction of the subject at this meeting gave Bennett the chance of raising a question which had so far not been considered. 'If we incur this expense,' he said, 'what guarantee can we have of security of tenure?' Mr Cole at once replied, 'We can give no guarantee'; upon which Bennett as quickly added, 'Then, I fear, we must decline the offer.'

The raising of the required money might have given

the Academy no trouble, but Mr Cole's reply to Bennett's question put a new complexion on the whole matter. The Academy authorities could not abandon their at present improving position, could not risk any fraction of their independence, could not surrender the privilege of Government recognition, for the sake of a new arrangement, which, however alluring it might at first sight appear, was known to be terminable at any moment by the other party. As Bennett was leaving Clarence House after the meeting, Mr (later, Sir) Charles Freake said to him, 'Sir, you will live to repent this.' The Academy authorities, however, notwithstanding some disappointment, agreed that Bennett was right. A fortnight later, the Directors passed a resolution 'approving the course adopted by their special Committee in declining the proposition to go to the Albert Hall.'

CHAPTER XXXIV.

SOME PERSONAL CHARACTERISTICS.

BEFORE presenting the closing scenes of Bennett's life, an attempt will be made to recall some personal characteristics which have failed to find a place in the foregoing narrative, to add something about his tastes and occupations other than musical, and even something about the few amusements allowed to so busy a man.

On March 8, 1873, the day of the important Conference at Clarence House mentioned in the last chapter, he wrote to his son:—'I am sorry I have not written to you before. One thing is decided, that we do not go to the Albert Hall—(I mean the Royal Academy of Music) so I am freed from meetings of that kind for the present. *We* declined. * * * I am pretty well and have a lunch here to-morrow expecting Joachim, Millais, Barlow, Case, at one-thirty. * * *'

Three of the guests mentioned in this letter were concerned in the production of a portrait of Bennett which was being finished just at this time. The portrait owes its existence to the generous heart of Mr Robert Case and to his devoted regard for his friend's musicianship and personality. When at Mr Case's house, where he was as much at home as in his own, Bennett, in these later years, would often seat himself voluntarily at the pianoforte and play short pieces, —a certain Mazurka of Chopin is remembered as a constant item of his little programme. One evening towards the end of 1872 when he was thus engaged, Oldham Barlow, the engraver, was watching him, and whispered to his host, 'There ought to be a portrait of him.' Mr Case seized the idea; he was a man of prompt decision; and before the music ceased he had commissioned Barlow to speak to Millais on the subject. The great artist consented to paint the portrait for Mr Case, and Bennett referred to its completion in a letter, dated March 16, 1873, to his daughter, 'Just a line to say we (Charlie and I) are quite well. I have been at home all day, the weather being so bad, also altering the Exhibition Ode, the piano part only, for a small shilling copy. All Tom's[1] corrections have been made in "The Woman of Samaria." The Sonata has made some little progress but is not yet finished. The Academy business of moving to the Albert Hall has taken much of my time and thought. My picture is nearly finished and I believe my last sitting takes place to-morrow.'

The portrait appeared at the Exhibition of the Royal Academy of Arts in 1873. It represents Bennett, towards the close of his fifty-seventh year, arrayed in robes he seldom wore, seated at a table and looking up from the occupation, in his case certainly a rare one, of reading the score of a composition of his own. The Doctor of Music's gown was introduced as an afterthought, the artist finding a difficulty as he proceeded owing to Bennett's head being, in his opinion, large in proportion to the spare figure. The chair, which is in keeping with the idea of showing him as a University Professor, did not belong to Bennett; but the engraving of 'The Apotheosis of Handel,' the inkstand, the original score of 'The May Queen' lying open before him, and a printed copy of 'The Woman of Samaria,' which appeared in the picture, were chosen and sent by his eldest son, in response to the artist's wish that accessories should, as far as possible, have a real connection with the person portrayed.

The original picture, now the inherited possession of Mr Robert Case's son[1], the President of Corpus Christi College, Oxford, gives a marvellously satisfying resemblance. Bennett himself is there, in the serious mood habitual to him as a musician. The attitude, in its every detail, is one in which he was constantly to be seen. Oldham Barlow, who first suggested the portrait, himself en-

---

[1] Bennett's son-in-law.

graved it. He took infinite pains to preserve the likeness, and no doubt did so with all the accuracy which the art he practised could reach. A reproduction of his work has been adopted for the frontispiece of this book[1].

A few facts may supplement what pictures already tell. Bennett was five feet seven inches in height. His head, as Millais noticed, was certainly on a large scale in relation to his whole figure. This would account, as Mr Louis N. Parker has suggested above, and as Miss Bettina Walker has also suggested in her reminiscences, for his appearing at times taller than he was, or at any rate for his actual height escaping notice. His hair was black, his eyes of a deep blue colour. His complexion was clear, and had warmth of colour, but no floridness. He looked his best in the height of summer. The thermometer could never be too high for him, and he thrived beneath a burning sun which, though it tanned him but little, acted as a tonic and gave him the maximum of health. On the other hand, when he came before the public as an artist, his face was remarkable for its extreme pallor.

His large eyes often attracted attention by reason of the intense and prolonged earnestness of their gaze. In a summer holiday of 1861, he was daily playing Bach's first Prelude, restudying, with a solicitude that could not fail to excite curiosity, a piece of music which he must have known since boyhood, and must have taught to countless pupils. He did not only play it, but from time to time sat peering into particular bars of the printed music, as if considering the exact shade of tone which he would choose for each note. Davison told the writer that Bennett's unwearying industry, as a young man, over minute details, was one of the secrets of the individuality of his playing, and that the result was alone sufficient to differentiate him from many eminent pianists of his time. In another holiday, some years later, he was often watched, while he sat motionless at his pianoforte absorbed in the silent examination of one and the same page of a slow movement by Mendelssohn.

---

[1] The original picture does not lend willingly to photography, a process under which it parts with many of its details and seems, even as a likeness of Bennett, to sacrifice its superiority over the engraving. The eminent engraver's version of the portrait can be reproduced with precision.

On such occasions, the appearance of his wide-opened eyes, with their strongly fastened but eagerly searching look, would fascinate a bystander however familiar with him he might be.

When recalling the personality of a pianist, hands and fingers claim their share of the remembrance. The keyboard of a pianoforte was perhaps the last place at which to observe any peculiarity in the contour of Bennett's hands. There they only showed themselves as exactly fitted for the work they were doing, and as a perfectly adjusted constituent of the instrument's mechanism. It was, rather, when they were otherwise employed, that something uncommon about their general appearance caught the eye. The separate parts of the hands were shown with distinctness when he was performing little feats and tricks for mere amusement. The hand, with the fingers open, gave the impression of being a large one. The fingers were long, so too, perhaps, was the hand; but the back of the hand, when he doubled the fingers under it, at once looked surprisingly small. It was almost triangular in shape, and, probably as a result of physical training, scarcely any flesh was visible beyond the bones that bounded the sides. The fingers were slender, as a ring which he wore on the third finger, but which few men could wear on the fourth, remains to prove. The fingers, however, by their agile movements, by their capacity of wide extension, and by the clear articulation of their joints, gave at all times a striking look to the hand as a whole and, through occupying a large space, no doubt deceived the eye as regards actual size. The finger-tips by reason probably of continued pressure had become flat and broad, as if the flesh of the upper finger joints had been drawn up and collected into the form of padded cushions nearly coinciding in breadth with the white keys of a pianoforte. This alteration did not reach the stage of unsightliness, but it did bring him one special discomfort which gave evidence of its reality and extent. When he was obliged to wear kid gloves, a pair large enough to admit his fingers lay quite loosely over his hand and wrists. Sir Arthur Sullivan, as a boy, took lessons on the pianoforte from him, and recollected in after-life that his attention had often been distracted from his work, because he could not help looking at his master's hands, and wondering what amount of practice it had taken to induce such a result.

The fingers were very strong. Miss Bettina Walker wrote of him in this connection:—'He often said, that when the *fingers* are tired, it is a sign that one has practised well; and he constantly warned me from letting any other part of my body become engaged in the work—It took, he said, "from the strength that ought to be in the fingers."' In one of the little feats above mentioned he clearly, though unintentionally, exhibited his own possession of this strength; also the power he had of regulating that strength so that each of the five fingers should have an equal share of it; and, further, he gave evidence of how close a counterpart the left hand, whenever he wished it to be so, was of the right. This last quality would doubtless have great value on some sides of pianoforte playing. Sir George Macfarren, in a 'Memorial' lecture upon Bennett, specially referred to the fact of his two hands having possessed, to a very exceptional extent, equality of effectiveness.

When his mind was not absorbed with music or with other serious thoughts he was full of vivacity. Rapidity of bodily movement was natural to him, and had in it no appearance of hurry or precipitancy. His visible alertness was in correspondence with the no less certain quickness of his mind, though in nearly all he did, whether of major or minor importance, control was noticeable. He excited the surprise of others by the apparent suddenness of some of his physical acts and mental impressions. His comprehensiveness of sight was in evidence to those who witnessed him instantly transfer to the pianoforte unfamiliar pages of a manuscript score. He showed something of the same gift of sight in other ways. His household marvelled at the celerity with which he could survey his house and its contents, as he passed through it when he came in for a few moments from his work. The house in Queensborough Terrace was a high one; his book-cases were on landings, as well as in most of the rooms. If an inmate when reading a book, heard his carriage drive up, he or she would know that very few moments would elapse before Bennett would be enquiring for the particular volume. This, though a frequent incident, continued to cause surprise, and to baffle average understanding.

As an example of what may be called his instantaneousness, Thomas Sparrow, an amateur pianist and for some years his pupil, was one day playing at high speed a passage consisting of a close cluster of semiquavers. Bennett, sitting quietly by his side, said, 'Play it again'; and then the pupil, before he was conscious of any time elapsing, found one of his fingers held, as in a vice, on a false note, while Bennett was ejaculating, 'I've got it now.' Sparrow, when relating this some thirty years afterwards, said, that it had always remained as a miracle to him, how Bennett could have thrown his hand from a position of rest and caught the erring finger, on one particular note out of so many, in such a flash of time. A companion story was told by Kellow Pye, a man who was himself noted for activity and for quickness of musical perceptions. Bennett visited him at Exeter when they were both young men, and one afternoon they approached the Cathedral during the time of Service. The customary arrangement of baize-covered doors guarded the entrance. As Pye touched the handle of the outer door, he being as yet unconscious of any sound within the building, Bennett startled him by saying, 'What a curious key to have a Service in.' The organ had recently been tuned to a high pitch and therefore a Service of Attwood's which, after entering, they found was in progress, did sound in an extreme key, but Pye told the writer fifty years later, that Bennett's instantaneous impression, which came before the door was open more than an inch, had always lingered in his mind as something inexplicable.

Much used to be said by those who had known Bennett in his early life about his wonderful memory, perhaps, however, only shown in any remarkable way in relation to music. The great quantity of music which he recollected surprised, as has already been seen, the pupils of his later days. One striking instance of his power of recollection will suffice here. Shortly before his death, he was conversing with W. H. Holmes, the pianist, in a class-room at the Academy. Holmes had known him in his boyhood, had taught him for seven years, had always followed his career with affectionate and admiring interest and naturally thought that after a friendship of nearly fifty years his knowledge of him was complete. But there was still a little margin for fresh experience. At this interview he was fairly astonished,—so he told the writer a few years later, —when Bennett sat down to the pianoforte and played long extracts from a MS. Concerto of his (Holmes's) composition, which he could not possibly have heard more than once, and that many, many years before.

Of Bennett's mental activity in other directions than music, or of any results arising from it, there is nothing very definite to say. His own views on such a subject act as a caution to its discussion here. He would not have forbidden the statement that his early training lay, rather exclusively, in a single direction; but he would strongly have resented any credit being placed to his account, for the subsequent attainment of more varied knowledge. He inveighed against the free use of expressions like 'self-improvement' or 'culture,' thinking that such matters should go without saying, and that the mention of them savoured of conceit. He sternly rebuked a young man who, when applying for an appointment, accounted for time that had elapsed since leaving college, by writing that he had employed it in continuing his studies. 'You must never mention such a thing,' he exclaimed, 'everybody does that.' A man, in his opinion, might pride himself on what he had learnt from others, but must court no acknowledgment of what he had added himself. 'Self-educated men,' he would say, 'are too often vain men.' He had a very marked respect for eminent scholastic learning approached by the stepping-stones of an early liberal education. He was nurtured in the atmosphere of a University, where he would start by hearing of, and by, no doubt, admiring heroes of learning. Even amongst his own playmates there were Cambridge-bred boys destined for a college career. With these he continued to associate when he went home from the Academy for his holidays, and at length saw them taking a share in the coveted honours of a University. This connection with Cambridge accounted for and intensified an after-regret that his own education could not have been of a more liberal kind. His reverence for great scholars seemed, at times of his later life, to be excessive, considering his own distinction. This was noticed, and even thought to be a pity, by some of his Cambridge friends. He did not, however, openly show any thirst for knowledge, nor did he attempt by any settled course of study to become a scholar in the sense in which he read the word. He wrote from Germany, in 1842, to his future wife:—'You must know very well what an Academy education is, and I often wish that I knew less of music and more of other things. However, I try to make up by experience and by coming out in the world for the want of a first-rate education.' As a comment upon what he thus wrote about himself, it may be noted, that a first-rate education, such as he meant, was not in his young days attainable in England by many. It must not be assumed that there was, in this respect, any disability peculiar to a young musician. Bennett always remained grateful for the benefits he had received at the Royal Academy of Music. Towards the end of his life, he said at a public meeting, 'I can never repay the debt I owe to the old place.' Within its walls he had not only been taught music, but he had come under the daily personal influence of men of fine character, of great mental ability, of wide and varied interests. During the ten years of his residence as a student, he enjoyed educational advantages probably of a higher type and certainly of a much longer duration than those which fell to the lot of most English youths of that period. With intellect and taste cultivated by a deep study of his own art, and with appealing graces of manner and disposition, he lacked nothing afterwards at any time to make him congenial and companionable to men whose education had been on different lines to his own. If his early training had been too much in one special direction; if his thoughts were centred, as there can be little doubt they were, upon music, he seldom betrayed this in his intercourse with others. It was the occasion of no little remark that in the course of general conversation he not only refrained from introducing music or musical events as a topic, but, in his own house at least, discouraged others from doing so. A fellow-artist once remarked that he thought it would be possible to stay in Sterndale Bennett's house for several days without discovering that he was a musician. One day some musical matter was being discussed at his table. When the time came at which he might be expected to say something, he smiled at the young German lady sitting by his side, who had just come to England well instructed in his artistic position, and astonished her by saying, 'Ah, you see, *I* am *not* musical.' G. Augustus Sala was dining at Bennett's house on an evening when the party was chiefly composed of musicians. In the course of the dinner, he said to his host and another guest, 'I like sitting between you two men, because you talk of other things than music.'

Bennett accumulated a well-assorted library, and one which might be considered large for a man who, during the greater part of his life, could not spare much time for reading. When he first took a house and was apportioning under different heads a modest sum of money,—this is told by an old pocket-book,—he wrote down £30 for additions to the contents of his book-shelves as against £5 for the furnishing of his kitchen. Henry G. Bohn, the publisher, who made his acquaintance about the year 1848, admired his choice of books, and would often afterwards send him presentation copies of such publications of his own as had exceptional interest. With the highly cultivated and genial George Hogarth, a friend of Sir Walter Scott and the father-in-law of Charles Dickens, Bennett lived on terms of the closest intimacy, and with him he delighted to converse on literary subjects. Hogarth would examine the book-shelves, and when the regret was expressed, 'I have so little time,' would console by saying, 'Ah, but you have the books, and there is much to be learnt on their mere title-pages.'

Bennett had a good knowledge of English poetry, and, though a little shy of showing it, would enjoy a quiet talk over one of his favourite poets with his neighbour in the Combination-room of a College or in his own house with some literary friend of wider reading than his own. At a late period of his life he had—probably it had always been his habit to have—a few books, or one book, to which he would remain constant for many months together. He could, for instance, be seen evening after evening, month after month, reading *The Deserted Village*; apparently studying it as a work of art with all the earnestness which he had applied to Bach's first Prelude. At night-time, long and tiring as the day might have been, he sat up in his chair with his back straightened—for he never lounged—and, if reading, would hold his book on a level with his eyes, forgetting the pipe which he had meant to smoke. There is a letter to him from E. S. Dallas, a critic on the staff of *The Times*, answering an enquiry on the authenticity of some lines in *The Traveller*, which gives the idea that Bennett, as far as he went, aimed at thoroughness in his literary pursuits. Cowper and Gray he read in the same constant way as he did Goldsmith. Byron, Moore, and Burns he had studied in earlier life, and they lent their inspiration to some of his music; but his interest in poetry was independent of musical considerations. He did not think, and he lived at a time when it had scarcely been discovered, that important works of great poets could be illustrated by a musical setting of their actual words. As a teacher of composition, he went so far as to recommend students to postpone the use of words and to acquire the habit of gaining their musical ideas without reliance on the suggestions which words might give.

Of the fine arts he was no professed critic. It is curious, in relation to his views on music, that he thought classical architecture cold and was little touched by its beauty; though he would say of the two great churches in the High Street at Oxford that when he saw them side by side he could not help preferring the classical one. He covered the walls of his house with pictures and engravings. In their possession he took a delight which was always manifest though seldom expressed in words. Amongst his books a prime favourite, and one he constantly read or consulted, was Sir Joshua Reynolds' *Lectures on Painting*. In proportion to his means, he allowed himself a generous indulgence in his various tastes as a collector; and this was the more possible, because those pleasures of a more transient kind which contented him involved little expense. The value of his musical library, considering the price of music at the time he bought it, probably tallied very nearly with what he received during his life-time for his own compositions. The general charm of his personal possessions was enhanced by their ever graceful arrangement, which did not bend to convention, but showed a refreshing individuality. The appearance of his rooms would often prompt his visitors to speak their admiration. A few days after his death his friend Davison, going through the passages of his house stopped before one of the pictures and said with great feeling, 'He was a man who always loved to have beautiful things about him.' Of the distinguished artists of his time, Bennett knew the Landseers, and set great store on a charming water-colour sketch that Sir Edwin had painted in his album. He was on intimate terms with Mulready and Creswick. Charles Kemble, the actor, was often at his house in Russell Place.

He is reported, on good authority, to have said at the Academy in his last days, 'I do not like books.' These words seemed to contradict what has been said above, but they reappeared without any context which might explain them. Even in the same house and at about the same time he took a keen personal interest in forming a small library to provide profitable employment for students while waiting for music lessons. He did, however, make reservation about the *use* of books. Thus, as a teacher of music, he cautioned pupils against an excessive reliance on theoretical text-books, suggesting to them, in illustration of his meaning, that they should try to reduce the rules of Harmony within the compass of a card or sheet of notepaper. Then again, he often said, and said it as if it were a conception of his own, though of course it is not original, 'I believe there can be too much reading and too little thinking.' Sometimes he would say this against himself in reference to his own newspaper reading, which he thought he had allowed to grow into an excessive indulgence to the detriment of forming independent opinions. Long hours in his carriage gave the opportunity for this reading and especially for the study of a favourite subject.

Up to middle life he took a keen interest in politics, inclining to the Liberal side. This recalls his valued friendship with Wyndham Goold, an Irish landowner and M.P. for the county of Limerick, who first came to him early in 1847 for letters of introduction to Leipzig whither he was going in order to place his young friend, Arthur

O'Leary, in the Conservatorium. Bennett was already in the good graces of Mr Goold's sisters, the Countess of Dunraven and Lady Gore Booth, whom he described to Mendelssohn as 'two of our best amateurs.' Wyndham Goold, himself a most attractive and lovable man, was immediately drawn towards Bennett, and thenceforward when Parliament brought him to town, he spent much time at Russell Place, in no formal way, but catching his busy friend when he could, and seeking his intimate companionship. He became a fresh medium of communication between Bennett and Leipzig, for he continued to visit that place, and was so appreciated there, that the remembrance of him was treasured in German families long after his death[1]. He liked to hear Bennett play Bach's Fugues, but he also liked to draw him out upon politics. He corresponded with him, and, if the one letter preserved is a sample of the others, the political situations of the day were the chief subjects of the correspondence. He once told Mr Arthur O'Leary that he had been surprised at Bennett's interesting and seemingly original views on politics, and that he had been puzzled as to how they had been acquired. Bennett would not be likely to satisfy enquiries on that point. Those who knew him later used to hear him enunciate quaint and fresh-sounding theories on a variety of subjects, which marked him as a man of curious thought or observation; but he was a little irritating sometimes when he declined to state the premises by which he had arrived at his opinion. However, by one of his theories—as he himself called them—he would often start lively conversations at his own table, which it would amuse him to listen to, but in which he would take no part. He did not care to argue. It was noticed that with regard to music he did not try to give or want to hear verbal explanations of uncommon effects. He probably felt that beauty lost some of its charm in the process of analysis. This same disposition of mind was shown when he went, as he much liked to do, to conjuring entertainments. He wanted to preserve the idea of the mystery of the thing; and it spoilt his simple enjoyment to hear any suggestion

---

[1] Mr Wyndham Goold died very suddenly in 1855, just as he was on the eve of starting to see a relative who was on service in the Crimea.

about the ways in which the tricks were done. His concern for politics was shown in later life, though not by a declared adherence to any particular party. On one occasion he went the length of becoming an electioneering agent in Liberal as against Radical interests. He put off his pupils, and volunteered to conduct Colonel Romilly, a candidate for Marylebone, round the many organ and pianoforte factories in that borough. A strong opinion which he held on one subject is well remembered, because it led him to adopt an adverse and, as some thought, a too restrictive view of a great public character. The 'peace-loving and peace-promoting propensities' which were noticed in his management of the Royal Academy of Music, were not inconsistent with abhorrence of the doctrine of 'peace-at-*any*-price.' He would, in consequence, listen to no word of praise or defence of John Bright as a statesman. About this extreme attitude, his friend Mr Robert Case, a warm admirer of Bright on general grounds, often teased him in a good-humoured way, and Bennett in the same spirit habitually closed his strict censure of the politician with a laugh, whilst exclaiming, 'Well, at any rate I could not sit at the same table with him.' Bennett, however, had to eat these words. In the last years of his life he annually dined with the Attorney-General, Sir John (afterwards Lord Chief Justice) Coleridge. Coming home from one of these dinners, he called in at the house of the Cases, and, with a demure look upon his face, asked them to guess who had been his *vis-à-vis* at the dinner-table. The riddle was instantly answered, and this peaceful meeting with John Bright was for some time a subject of much raillery between Bennett's friends and himself.

He had but a scanty chance of amusing himself in the day-time, and yet his amusements lay rather without than within doors. They were much the same as he might have enjoyed when a boy or even when a child, though, one might be inclined to say, in some respects a *peculiar* boy or child. Sir George Macfarren has noticed this in the following reminiscence: 'Always as a youth he had the sense of humour which characterises every person of genius, and this never left him; he was always quickest to perceive a jest, and never unready with a pertinent saying; but he

had some notions of fun which few but himself could enjoy.'
He found great pleasure in watching the movements and
noting the characteristics of his fellow-creatures. When
living in Bayswater, if he took a walk, he did not stroll into
the Kensington Gardens, which were close at hand, but
went off to Praed Street or the Edgware Road, where he
could see more of the activity of life; for a walk in London
was a rare treat which he must make the most of. His
attention would be attracted by minor incidents which the
ordinary passer-by would leave unnoticed, and about which
a companion, if he happened to have one, could not share
or understand his curiosity. He took advantage of its
being permissible in a busy thoroughfare to watch without
discourtesy what people in the humbler class of life are
doing and to hear what they are saying. He would thus
collect miscellanea which he retained in his memory and
which furnished him with a fund of lively anecdote, the
interest of which he could heighten by his ready mimicry.
He would join a knot of spectators, listening eagerly to
their comments on what was happening, and sometimes
putting in a word himself. He would become so interested
in proceedings which did not immediately concern him, as
to involve himself in them, and to interfere if he saw wrong
being done. On more than one occasion he nearly got
himself into trouble thereby. He was followed home one
day and threatened by some hawkers of wretched German
prints, because they had overheard him advising a likely
purchaser that better English pictures could be bought at
the price. He said afterwards that he could not stand
by and see a poor person throwing away money on such
rubbish. On the cricket-ground at Eastbourne he publicly,
and with great dignity, rebuked a professional cricketer
whose career he had for some time watched with pleasure.
The man had lost his temper at the umpire's decision, and
used bad language on his return to the pavilion. Bennett
had no official connection with the club authorising him to
do this. His action made him very conspicuous, and the
issue of it seemed for a few moments very doubtful; but his
manner of doing it happened to meet with general approval.
The delinquent accepted the reproof, and Bennett said
later, 'I couldn't help myself, because I like the fellow.'

For the last seventeen years of his life he spent his longer holidays at Eastbourne, and those who passed them with him had a better chance in that place than elsewhere of observing his choice of amusements. He never missed a cricket-match, and on the old ground near the railway station he passed many happy days. Where his interest exactly lay was never discovered, but probably he had in boyhood caught something of that enthusiasm for cricket for which the town of Cambridge was always noted. No competent critic of the game watched it more intently than he did. He was always very anxious for the success of the Players, whose cause he espoused as against the Gentlemen, maintaining that the best result ought to be produced when livelihood was at stake. Dr W. G. Grace, who had already at that time made his mark, was a great thorn in his side as an upset to his theory. As a spectator he showed much nervousness at exciting moments, so that he almost invariably missed any final issue; in fact, the least shock, as when the bat touched the ball, would generally cause his eyes to blink, nor could he keep them open to see if a catch were held or not, but would say under his breath, 'What's that?' or 'What happened?' He would, when in London, drive off to 'Lord's,' if he ever got the chance, for the sake of seeing even a quarter-of-an-hour's play, but this happened very seldom, as the cricket-season came at the busiest time of his year.

An annual event at Eastbourne which he anticipated with boyish delight was the arrival of a circus. The caravans generally reached the town in the night; he would be on the spot early in the morning, and would stand for some hours outside the paling of the field, watching the company as they pitched their camp, cooked their meals, watered their horses, and set up the circus-tent. No companion had the patience to remain by his side, but periodical visits in the course of the morning would find him rooted to the same spot, his face still beaming with pleasure and interest. He said that he admired the unceasing industry of the people and their methodical plan of work, and therein, no doubt, was one cause of his fascination. When he lived in Queensborough Terrace, house-building was in progress there. If an expected pupil failed to appear, he would go out and stand in a fixed position on the pavement, for three-quarters of an hour, looking up at the bricklaying, and following with his eyes the workmen as they ascended and descended the ladders. On returning to the house, he would show some special knowledge of the processes and materials, of the different grades of the work and the etiquette attached to them by the men.

His usual morning walk at Eastbourne was through the town; in the afternoon he turned towards the country, sometimes going long distances. On Sundays he often went to the Churches of Willingdon, East Dean, Jevington, or Westham near Pevensey, for the morning Service. He went little by the sea, but he always turned that way on the days of an exceptionally high tide. He would be in the crowd on the Grand Parade, to share the excitement and amusement caused by the adventurous spirits who hazarded a run round a narrow part of the esplanade at the risk of being deluged by one of the greater waves. In his morning walk he would look in at the shops, not always as a purchaser, but to chat with some characteristic person. He usually spent half-an-hour in the confectioner's shop at the junction of the Terminus and Sea Side Roads, not to eat anything, but because he was amused by the independent manner in which Mrs Morris, the proprietress, treated her customers. The cares of business often ruffled Mrs Morris's temper, but he could always propitiate her, and both herself and her daughter came to appreciate his morning call and to miss him much when he died. Another friend, of humbler rank, was Philadelphia Hollebone, an aged vendor of vegetables, who lived in the village of Willingdon and drove her donkey-cart into the town every day. Bennett had no business dealings with her, but often conversed with her on his morning round, and would repeat her quaint sayings on his return to his lodgings. No one, however, had realized the extent of this curious friendship until a day of his later life when a companion joined him for an afternoon walk. He was at first preoccupied, appeared to be composing, and his mood was gloomy. He emerged on the high road above Old Eastbourne without having so far uttered a word. Suddenly he woke, his face lighted up, and pointing with his stick, he cried out, 'There she is, there she is!' He had espied 'Philly,' as the old dame was called, on the road before him, driving home to Willingdon. He quickly overtook her, and the pleasure of meeting was mutual. They chatted to each other with ease, and with a pretty courtesy on both sides, till they reached her cottage, where Bennett proved to be quite at home. Philly sat down to rest in her high-backed chair, whilst he showed his companion all the arrangements of her little dwelling, opening cupboards, lifting the lids of lockers, and explaining in her hearing where she kept her cooking-utensils and her food, and how by certain methods of economy she managed to make ends meet. The hostess, smiling and chuckling, watched him with great delight, nodding from time to time in approval of his statements. She did not appear to know exactly who he was, nor did she call him by name; her manner precluded any idea that she was beholden to him for charities; it was evidently the man himself that made her so happy, and as he led the way out of the cottage, she said to his companion, 'Dear, dear, what a merry fellow he is.'

Bennett found good and true friends in all sorts and conditions of life. Nor must it be forgotten that he owed much to the companionship of the dogs who in turn became members of his household. One of these, a half-bred pug, came to him in 1858, and it can be said with certainty that the faithful creature did much, a few years later, to help his master through a time of sadness. 'Pug' was full of character and intelligence, and, though he led an independent and nomadic life, spared a great deal of time for his master, generally accompanying him on his long drives into the country, and invariably keeping himself free from other engagements on the particular days reserved for teaching at Southgate. He was much liked by Bennett's friends, he paid his calls upon them with a polite regularity, and always knew where to find a late dinner—for he was a bit of a gourmet—when there happened to be none at his own house. There was, however, one of his master's best friends of whom he lived in terror. When Bennett came home from a concert, Pug would rush to the front door to meet him; but if Joachim, with violin-case in hand, also appeared on the threshold, he instantly turned tail and made a bolt for the kitchen. After supper, Joachim would go to the top of the kitchen-stairs and begin to play, while poor Pug's pathetic howls would respond from the furthermost recesses of the basement. But the criticism was acute in more senses than one, for Pug paid very little attention to violinists of a less exalted order. The king of them could alone make him crouch. Bennett had two portraits of his favourite painted, one for himself and another as a wedding-present for one of his maidservants. He was very grieved when Pug died, but other dogs came and did their best to fill the vacant place. There were times in his later life when these little companions cheered many an hour which would otherwise have been a solitary one.

CHAPTER XXXV.

LAST DAYS.

1873—1875.
æt. 57, 58.

IN February 1873, Bennett reappeared as a conductor. Somewhat to the surprise of his friends, he accepted an invitation from Mr W. Kuhe to direct a performance of 'The Woman of Samaria' at the Brighton Festival. This was the sole occasion on which he conducted an important rendering of the work. Then, again, on May 20, he took a share in directing a Festival Service, for the benefit of the Choir Benevolent Fund, in the Chapel of King's College, Cambridge. A week later he again went to Cambridge, though this time not without effort. 'I have been so bewildered with one thing or another,' he wrote a few days before, when mentioning the coming engagement to one of his family. However, he kept his promise, and conducted 'The May Queen' for the University Musical Society. The concert had a special claim to his presence. The Society was enjoying a fresh and vigorous existence under the inspiriting guidance of Mr C. V. (now Sir Charles) Stanford, and on this particular evening a notable departure was made by the introduction, for the first time, of ladies into the chorus. The occasion has a second interest here, because it proved to be Bennett's farewell to the concert-stage. On the same spot he had given his first concert a little more than forty years before.

After spending two years at the cottage in Porchester Terrace, Bennett had returned, in March 1872, to his house in Queensborough Terrace; but in the summer of 1873 he was able to let it on lease, and found another in St John's

Wood Road, of smaller size, but large enough to hold his principal belongings. The house was on two floors, detached, well set back from the road, with a good-sized garden behind, amply stocked with shrubs and fruit-trees. Everything wanted in way of renovation, both of house and furniture, was attended to, all was cheerful and comfortable, and on his return from Eastbourne, in September 1873, he settled down very happily in his new home.

His anxiety as to the external policy of the Academy, which had lasted for seven years, was now off his mind. He had the satisfaction of seeing the Institution supporting itself and rising in repute. His association with it promised, for the future, to bring him nothing but pleasure. Of other occupations, if he found it were desirable to reduce them or alter them he could afford to do so, for he had no longer anyone entirely dependent upon him. In January 1874, the Academy Committee, when he was absent from a meeting, voted that a salary of £300 per annum should be assigned to the Principalship, and this would add to his resources without increasing his work. By the ready assistance of Mr H. R. Eyers, a young Professor, who had for the past few years acted as Private Secretary to the Principal, he was able to keep pace with the growing details of official business. He had reached the threshold of that quieter and less burdensome life which he had often spoken of and had hoped might be in store for him.

By this time, however, his friends were beginning to realize that his strength had been too severely taxed by the work and the cares of the past years, that his health had gone almost beyond hope of recovery, while at times it could not escape notice that his mental powers were to a certain extent already affected. He was, in fact, a worn-out man; but so elastic was his temperament and so often was he still found merry and entertaining in his ways and conversation, that he could himself, from time to time, allay the fears that others had on his account. Though he was now nominally living alone, many intimate friends kept in close touch with him. Mr Robert Case's youngest son, George, would come over from Inverness Terrace, and stay for weeks together at the St John's Wood house to bear him company. His daughter and sons were able to spend long holidays with him, and the visits from Oxford of his little grandsons, for the elder of whom he invented games in the garden, and for whose future use he wrote a Sonatina, were a great delight to him.

'Macfarren and I,' he would say, 'have now found a subject which does not lead to argument—we talk about our grandchildren.' Sir George Macfarren was a keen debater, which Bennett was not. Their dispositions were in many respects strongly contrasted, but their early personal attachment remained firm to the end. Bennett came home to St John's Wood one day much touched by the generosity of something that Macfarren had said in one of their last conversations on the door-steps of the Academy. Possibly Bennett had been talking of his own career. 'Well, Bennett,' was Macfarren's remark, 'you are the one of us all who has done nothing you need repent.' At the 'Testimonial' Meeting in St James's Hall, Bennett had said, 'I thank my old school-fellow, Mr Macfarren, for the kind manner in which he has expressed himself to-day, not for the first time, not for the twentieth—I can't count up the number of times in which he has so spoken of me.' After Bennett's death, Sir George Macfarren, whether as Professor at Cambridge, or as Principal of the Academy—in both these capacities he followed Bennett—never lost any opportunity of paying graceful tribute to the memory of his brother-musician.

Before the year 1873 had ended, Bennett had the satisfaction of knowing that his new Sonata, 'The Maid of Orleans,' was making its way. It was first played by Miss Channell, at a concert given by Madame Rebecca Jewell. Madame Arabella Goddard[1], to whom the composer dedicated it, was, at the time, on a tour through the Colonies; but Charles Hallé, Lindsay Sloper, Dr Hans von Bülow, and Mr Franklin Taylor produced it at important concerts. In December, Bennett wrote to his son: 'I shall look forward to seeing you on the 17th. I am pretty well and in good spirits. Shall be glad when the holidays come. They have printed 1150 copies of the Sonata.'

---

[1] For twenty-one years, Madame A. Goddard (Mrs J. W. Davison) had been playing Bennett's pianoforte-music with the greatest constancy.

Hallé, Hans von Bülow, and Mr Franklin Taylor all came to St John's Wood to play the Sonata to the composer before they performed it. This, of course, gave him great pleasure. Mr George Case remembers that on the occasion of Dr von Bülow's visit, Bennett first played a few bars of each movement, and then the visitor took his seat. The latter had scarcely started playing when he raised his hands off the keys and with a surprised look said to Bennett, 'However can you manage to play on this piano?' The pianoforte, though in excellent preservation, was twenty-two years old, and had the very deep and resisting touch of the Broadwood Grands of its day, which touch Bennett himself liked for his own playing. The black keys, moreover, were narrower than in later instruments. It was certainly a very difficult pianoforte to play on, and Dr von Bülow was not the first great pianist from abroad who had found it so. Bennett had preserved it, by using it moderately, and by annually giving it a long period of rest. It was his habit, during the London season, when it would have been liable to harder usage, to send it into retreat at Broadwood's and to have a new one as a temporary substitute.

At Christmas time, 1873, he was at Eastbourne for a fortnight. The old inn 'The Gilbert Arms,' where he had stayed during his earliest visits to the place, was about to be destroyed, and as a memento he secured the bow-window of his favourite room, built a summer-house, expressly for the window, at the bottom of his garden at St John's Wood, and in this summer-house he spent many of his last hours. He had sat in the same bow-window when he was composing 'The May Queen.' Since his death, house, garden, and summer-house have all vanished; for they stood exactly over the cutting made by the Great Central Railway.

In February 1874, Mr Henry Guy sang, at the Monday Popular Concerts, two songs, 'Maiden Mine,' and 'Dancing Lightly,' which Bennett had written to words furnished him by his son-in-law, Mr Thomas Case. He was, at this time, still hoping to complete the music to *Ajax* for the next series of Philharmonic Concerts, but those who watched him saw that he was no longer capable of so great an effort. He went through his daily work by the force of long habit, but in a somewhat mechanical way. Yet he still wished, as of old, to add voluntary services to fixed duties. Thus he spared five days in March and spent them in Cambridge, where he had undertaken the general direction of a concert though no share as a performer. The musical circle in the University gave this concert, with the valuable co-operation of Joachim, in aid of a fund for raising a memorial to Sebastian Bach in Eisenach, and with such a movement Bennett was, of course, proud to be associated. This final reference to his connection with Cambridge affords an opportunity which he himself would most certainly have wished to see taken, of acknowledging how much he owed, during the later years of his Professorship, to the personal kindness and attention always so affectionately shown to him by the late Gerard Francis Cobb of Trinity College. Another Fellow of Trinity, Mr Sedley Taylor, was also a friendly ally. He delivered lectures on Acoustics at The Royal Academy of Music during Bennett's Principalship and dedicated to him his well-known treatise, 'Sound and Music.'

In the summer of 1874, at Eastbourne, working little by little, Bennett extended to a considerable length a Funeral March, which he had begun in the previous year, for the projected music to *Ajax*. 'How long do you think I may make it?' he would say; for he had in his mind the remembrance of the Duke of Wellington's funeral in 1852, and he wanted to produce the effect of fresh bands striking up, as the sounds of others died away in passing. He finished the orchestral music, up to the point at which the chorus was to enter, and set the words:—

> "But come, all ye who would attend
> The last departure of a friend,
> Hither in solemn procession throng
> Bearing the solemn bier along,
> Following the dead for a little way
> Out of the light of the glaring day
> To the threshold of Pluto's gloomy portals;
> Following him whose virtues were known
> Through life to his faithful friends alone,
> Who was always the bravest and best of mortals."

This was a 'swan-song' of beautiful chords and progressions; but the subject was gloomy for one who may have felt that he himself had not long to live. Quietly, and with apparent resignation, he said in the garden of his Eastbourne lodging, 'The night has come, when I cannot work.'

He visited his daughter at Oxford twice in September, and then began his work at the Academy, writing thence on Sept. 28 :

> My dear Dolly,
>
> We had an extremely pleasant and short journey to London. I went straight off to the Academy and did nearly two hours work in opening letters and examining new students. My visit to Oxford did me good, I am quite sure, and I thank Tom and yourself for your kindness to me. The Academy did not receive the letter which you wrote for me yesterday to Mr Eyers—this was by accident, and I was all the better pleased to be there five minutes before my usual time.
>
> With kind love to you all,
> Ever your affectionate father,
> William Sterndale Bennett.

In December, Bennett, on hearing that the Hanover Square Rooms were to be used no longer for music, but in future for the coffee-room of a club, expressed a wish that the Academy students should give the last concert there. A special performance was accordingly arranged for Dec. 19. One of the students afterwards wrote of Bennett's connection with this occasion :—

'His conservative spirit made him grieve over the loss of the Hanover Square Rooms, sacred with musical traditions of the past * * * The very last concert in the Rooms was given by the students of the Royal Academy of Music just before Christmas 1874, and strangely enough it was the last concert he ever attended. Many who were present noticed that he had a sad far-away look that night. Possibly the idea was in his mind that such changes could not affect him long. Twice during that evening he left the concert-room expressing his intention of going home, and each time returned, as if he did not know how to tear himself away though he felt unequal to remaining[1].'

[1] *Fraser's Magazine*, July 1875.

He continued to take a few pupils up to Christmas, and began with them again through the first three weeks of January 1875. On the other hand he was evidently unable to examine, when he tried to do so, the compositions which had been sent by candidates for musical degrees. Dr Garrett, of Cambridge, afterwards wrote of a visit which he paid him on Jan. 12. 'I was with him the whole afternoon. He was very weak, but cheerful, and the afternoon being very fine and warm, he would take me out in his garden to show me the bow-window from his old Eastbourne lodging with which he had been presented when the house was destroyed. He talked hopefully too, of the future he was never to see, and was most kind and delightful.'

On Thursday, Jan. 21, he attended the entrance examination at the Academy. On Saturday the 23rd, he took two private pupils in the morning, but declined Mr Robert Case's proposal to drive him to the Crystal Palace, where his Symphony in G minor was to be played. On occasional excursions to Sydenham, where he would like to go, if there was a concert on the anniversary of Mendelssohn's death, or if he could hear a Symphony of Schumann's, he had always preferred to go by road, passing through the beautiful village of Dulwich; but he did not allow himself the treat on this afternoon. He had another engagement.

Of this, the Rev. Thomas Darling wrote, a fortnight later, to *The Guardian*: 'It was his wont to finish his week's labour by giving a free lesson to three girls from the Clergy Orphan School, the house of which lay hard by his own dwelling place in St John's Wood. The lesson thus given on Saturday Jan. 23, proved to be the last act in his vocation and ministry.' This was again mentioned by Dean Stanley, from the pulpit of Westminster Abbey, as a fitting close to his life's work.

The next morning, Sunday, when he was called, he said he should not get up just yet. This sounded unusual; but it was only as the day wore on, and he showed no sign of moving that a fear about him began to be felt. In the dread of a complete failure of mental power, those near him had lost sight of the possibility of the less painful solution of his trouble coming so soon. His family were seriously considering a plan of his living in his daughter's house at

Oxford. They had overcome the difficulty involved in proposing it to him, and he had not shown himself so unwilling to retire as they had expected. But from the time, on this Sunday evening, when medical assistance was summoned, it was known that recovery was impossible and that the end was imminent. Death laid a gentle hand upon him. There was no apparent pain or discomfort, and, after lingering a week, he passed peacefully away, dying of disease of the brain, shortly after noon on February 1, within ten weeks of completing his fifty-ninth year. 'The sad tidings,'—thus wrote his former pupil, Mr O'Leary, —'soon reached the Academy, where the classes were in full activity. The message went from room to room, quelling all sounds of study, until as if with a dying cadence from afar, all was stilled in death-like hush.'

A meeting of the Academy Committee was at once held, to consider what steps should be taken to pay the last tribute of respect. A petition was prepared, which the Duke of Edinburgh was the first to sign, and to which the names of many distinguished persons, including representatives of science, art and literature, were appended, asking the Dean of Westminster to grant interment in the Abbey, 'as a fitting tribute to the genius and worth of a gifted Englishman who was unquestionably at the head of the musical profession in the country, and on more public grounds as a just recognition of the Art of which he was so distinguished an ornament.' A similar step was taken at Cambridge, and in reply to a private letter from Professor Kennedy, Dean Stanley wrote:—

DEANERY, WESTMINSTER,
Feb. 3, 1875.

MY DEAR CANON,

The request—preferred from various quarters—to bury Sir Sterndale Bennett in the Abbey has already been granted. The funeral will probably be on Saturday.

Yours sincerely,

A. P. STANLEY.

It is a great pleasure to think that he was not only so eminent a musician, but so good a man.

The Royal Academy of Music, the Royal Society of Musicians, and the Philharmonic Society joined in making the arrangements for the Funeral, which took place at noon on Feb. 6. As the time approached, Hanover Square was lined with carriages, among them those sent by the Queen and the Royal Family, awaiting the arrival of the hearse from St John's Wood. Not the least solemn episode of the day, probably conceived by the tender-hearted Macfarren, was the resting of Bennett's remains for a few silent moments at the door of the Academy, before starting on the last stage of the journey. The Abbey was crowded with so large a congregation, that Dean Stanley afterwards said he had seen no such gathering, on a like occasion, save at Lord Palmerston's funeral. Twelve pall-bearers were chosen from among those who had been his fellow-students, and the coffin was followed by representatives of the University of Cambridge, including the Vice-Chancellor, the Master of St John's, and the Precentor of King's; by the Earl of Dudley as President of the Royal Academy of Music with the Directors and Professors of that Institution; by a deputation from the Royal Society of Musicians led by the veteran Sir John Goss; by the Directors of the Philharmonic and other musical Societies, and by members of the German Athenæum. Among the wreaths placed upon the coffin was one sent from the University of Edinburgh as if in remembrance of how nearly, twice in his life, Bennett had been within reach of a connection with that University.

The music was, according to precedent, that of Purcell, Croft, and Handel, but one piece of Bennett's own composition was added. James Turle, the Abbey Organist, was assisted by Dr Steggall, Dr Stainer, E. J. Hopkins, George Cooper, and J. Hopkins of Rochester. The Abbey Choir was augmented by contingents from St Paul's, the Temple, the Chapel Royal, the Chapel of Lincoln's Inn, and then numbered fifty-four singers. The Quartet 'God is a Spirit,' from 'The Woman of Samaria,' was sung by Master Beckham, Messrs Foster, Carter, and Lawler, the full choir entering on the repetition of the first subject. 'That is *Music*,' whispered Arthur Sullivan to his neighbour Davison, as the strains of the Quartet died away. 'It was hard enough to bear I can tell you,'—so wrote Dr Garrett to the Rev. J. R. Lunn,—'and when in the middle of the service, unexpectedly, the soothing strains of his own "God is a Spirit" were heard (most exquisitely rendered), there were few dry eyes. It was almost too much to see the flower-covered coffin before us, and remember that we should see his face no more. I confess it broke me down utterly, but no one was much better, and many of his old friends and colleagues were deeply affected.' 'Crowded as was the Abbey,' Sir George Macfarren said to the Academy students a few years later, 'there could not have been a tearless eye among the many hundreds who congregated to pay the tribute of love and admiration to the friend and the artist.' The grave, the site of which was chosen by Dean Stanley, is in the North Choir Aisle, just below one side of the Organ, and in close proximity to the graves of Purcell and Croft.

The funeral sermon was preached next day by Dr Woodford, Bishop of Ely.

'Yesterday,' he said, 'the great Under-Congregation of the Dead within these walls received an additional member upon whom the thoughts of many present will fall.* * * There was laid in the grave, side by side with another great musician whose solemn strains welcomed his brother home, one of high name and honour, not only in this country, but beyond the sea. His was one of those lives which it does good to note, a life beginning in obscurity, ending in a wide repute. The chorister-boy of King's Chapel, Cambridge, advancing to the Professorship of Music in that University, gathering round him, as he grew in years, the esteem of the whole earth, and laid to rest at last amidst those whom this country has for centuries delighted to ennoble, he reads a lesson which we can never too often learn—how to those who do not waste the life which God gives, or dissipate or leave uncultured the inspirations which He has breathed into them, there is assigned, even in this world, a sure reward.

'I rejoice that it has fallen to me to speak thus of one so distinguished in the University which it is the boast of my diocese to contain within its borders. Let me say but one word more. I have nothing to tell of the inner spiritual life of him who was yesterday laid in the grave. But this fact is in the common possession of all: he was the professor of one of the sublimest sciences—a science, perhaps more than any other, in its noblest developments, the offspring of the Christian civilization. * * * That science, like literature and painting and sculpture, may be made to serve ignoble uses, to fan the flame of passion, to minister to dissipation and excess. As far as I know, the great musician whom we lament, in whatsoever he wrote, maintained to the full the moral dignity of his Art, and so is to be numbered amongst those who use God's gifts of this nature in such wise as to promote His glory, and vindicate their nature as indeed divine.'

The North Choir Aisle
WESTMINSTER ABBEY

APPENDIX A.

FOUR NOTES.

(1) *Annals of the Bach Society.*

Oct. 27, 1849.	The Society instituted; see p. 203, (where, by a much-regretted mistake, the date is given as Oct. 29).
March 21, 1850.	First 'Trial' of music; see p. 206.
July 29, 1850.	Centenary Performance; see pp. 206, 207.
June 1851.	Bach's six Motets published in London; see p. 207.
March 22, 1852.	Performance of Motets, Concertos &c., in the Concert-rooms in Store St; see p. 232.
April 6, 1854.	1st performance in London of the 'Passions-Musik' (St Matthew); see pp. 232–234.
Nov. 28, 1854.	2nd performance of the same; see p. 235.
March 23, 1858.	3rd " " " ; see pp. 276–278.
April 23, 1859.	'Passions-Musik' (St Matthew) at Windsor; see p. 278.
June 21, 1859.	Bach Concert, miscellaneous, vocal and instrumental.
July 24, 1860.	Bach Concert (with 11 movements of Mass, B minor).
June 13, 1861.	1st performance of 'Christmas Oratorio,' Parts I and II.
March 1862.	English edition of Bach's 'Passions-Musik' (St Matthew) published; see p. 319.
May 24, 1862.	4th performance, in London, of the same; see p. 319.

Apart from public performances, for which the Society was not founded, and for which its financial schemes had made no provision, the Bach Society, from 1850–62, gave regular opportunity, for six months of each year, for the practice of Bach's choral music. This is certified by a minute-book and by correspondence preserved by the Hon. Sec., the late Dr Steggall. The Society was formally dissolved on March 21, 1870, by which time it had accomplished the object for which it was founded, and could see the growing results of its pioneering labour. The library was presented to the R.A. of Music.

(2) *Bennett placed among the opponents of Chopin.*

On the authority of his friend the late Mr A. J. Hipkins, Bennett has gained an unenviable, and it is here thought an undeserved niche in so important a work as the *Life of Chopin* by Professor Niecks. Mr Hipkins's memory of the attitude taken by the musicians and amateurs towards Chopin's music appears to refer to a period starting in 1848 and lasting for several years. Professor Niecks wrote: 'Mr Hipkins told me that he had to struggle for years to gain adherents to Chopin's music while enduring "the good-natured banter of Sterndale Bennett and J. W. Davison."' These words might be construed as no very grave accusation; but the particular pages on which they occur take a serious view of the musical aspect of London in 1848. It seems hard upon Bennett that he should be mentioned in close connection with 'hostilities' against music of a high purpose, when his own 'battle' in life was from first to last waged from the opposite side and merely against the frivolities of his time.

The reminiscence given by Mr Hipkins was not brought to the notice of the present writer till long after its appearance, and when it was late in the day to collect rebutting evidence. Mr Hipkins may, in his early days, have been misled, when he found his own enthusiasm disappointed by Bennett's more guarded expression, or parried by his 'good-humoured banter.' Further, he might fail to notice that Bennett was out of sympathy not with Chopin, but with many pianists of the Paris school, who while they were ready to introduce that composer to England, introduced him among the composers of Fantasias rather than by the side of classical writers. For that reason Bennett would not at first be much associated with the phalanx of Chopin's admirers.

Bennett did not choose pianoforte-music as the title of any lecture. He has left no mention of Chopin in writing. It is admitted that he never played his music at his own Chamber-concerts; but it has been shown in the proper place, that he did not make solos for the pianoforte a special feature of those concerts. Moreover, a pianist, in public performance, is not expected necessarily to extend his repertoire in all directions.

Fortunately it is still possible to refer to his work as a pianoforte-*teacher*; to follow a thread of evidence, slender but fairly continuous, now stretching back some sixty-five years; and to gain thereby some knowledge of service rendered to Chopin, knowledge suggestive of that service having been considerable. An analysis of music distributed to pupils in 1839 and 1840 has been given on p. 94. Chopin's name does not occur in it. The next available reference is to the teaching-books kept by Mrs Bennett from the beginning of 1845. For the first six months she entered in these books, not only the lessons, but also such music as was supplied to the pupils direct from the house. She has thus left a proof that at least as early as Jan. 24, 1845 (*i.e.* more than three years before Chopin's visit to England, the event which appears as the starting-point of Mr Hipkins's reminiscence) her husband was teaching Chopin's music. Of the pieces entered during the six months, Chopin contributed 8 per cent., with a ratio, to the pieces on the same list by Beethoven, of 5 : 9. The next information comes from Mr Arthur O'Leary, who in the early fifties studied the pianoforte in Bennett's class at the Academy, and who remembers that Chopin's *Études* were prescribed for all pupils who joined that class. Writing of a little later time, 1858, or thereabouts, Miss Bettina Walker mentions that she studied music of Chopin under Bennett. She formed, in the process, the impression that her teacher had no such love for Chopin as for certain other great masters. Her impression was probably quite correct. Nobody who knew Bennett would for one moment have imagined that his appreciation of Chopin approached his appreciation, *e.g.* of Beethoven. But another pupil, the late Miss M. H. Parkes of Sheffield, gained by the same means as Miss Walker an impression of a different kind, an absolute rather than a relative impression. Miss Parkes, who before studying under Bennett had been a pupil of Dr Wesley at Winchester, became an accomplished pianist, and as a lady of great character and general attainment her opinion should have the same weight, at least, as that of Miss Bettina Walker. Miss Parkes wrote in 1902:—

'My lessons with your father were from the autumn of 1866 until Easter 1868. * * * Once he said, "Madame Clara Schumann has been playing Chopin's Polonaise in A flat to everybody's admiration. You had better study it and bring it at your next lesson." At that time, not being very familiar with Chopin's music, I made a mistake and got the Andante Spianato and Polonaise in E flat instead. Bennett, however, said, "That was not the one I meant, but play it all the same," and greatly he seemed to enjoy the dreamy Andante with its lovely peasant dance, often playing scraps of the slow part of the Polonaise himself with the most loving touch, and remarking on the fairylike beauty of— shall I call them?—the *grace-notes*. Every lesson for the rest of the term I finished by playing that "Andante Spianato and Polonaise" of which the master never seemed to weary. Towards the last I was invited to play at a concert of an important German Sangverein in London, and on my asking what piece I should select, he answered, "The Andante Spianato and Polonaise in E flat, by all means." Thanks to Bennett's careful tuition, I gained an encore at the end of my performance of it. So please do not allow people to say your father disliked Chopin's music, because it is *not* true.'

Miss Parkes's memory of the 'loving touch' will recall to others the grace and the warmth with which he played, and played so constantly, in his last days, one of Chopin's Mazurkas.

Lastly, an account (dated 1872) for 295 pieces of music, by 29 composers most of whom are of the highest rank, supplied by a music-shop in one term to a large school, has escaped destruction, and shows Bennett teaching Chopin's music to the end of his life. When the 29 composers mentioned on this account are arranged in order, according to the number of pieces which Bennett selected from each composer, Chopin stands sixth on the list.

Counting from the date, given above, of Mrs Bennett's first entry, Jan. 24, 1845, to the date of the last lessons which Bennett gave, Jan. 23, 1875, the result shows that he taught Chopin's music, probably as soon as any other teacher in this country, and after that, almost certainly without cessation, for thirty years. The writer claims for him that he was *a supporter* rather than *an opponent* of Chopin's interests.

(3) *On the order in which Schumann reviewed some of Bennett's works.*

Of the more important works which Bennett wrote and published between 1838 and 1842, Schumann reviewed at great length and with much favour: in 1839, the Overture 'The Wood-nymphs;' in 1840, the Concerto in F mi. Op. 19; and in 1842, the 'Suite de Pièces' Op. 24. In the last of these critiques he wrote: 'Bennett's works have continued to increase in originality.' If by the side of this there is anything which might suggest the absence of complete satisfaction, Schumann only expresses it by urging Bennett to write more music, and to aim, on the strength of what he has already done, at achievements on a grander scale. Since this Suite was the latest important work by Bennett that Schumann reviewed, it might be assumed that the great critic, up to the time that he abandoned criticism, was content with Bennett's progress and fairly hopeful for his future. It is, however, necessary to notice that in 1843 he reviewed the Caprice with orchestra, Op. 22, and apparently did so as if he thought it was a new work, whereas it was by that time five years old and older than any of the three works mentioned above. No wonder, therefore, that Schumann failed to trace in it the continued development of originality which he desired, and that he should even have thought it showed a decline of inventive power. If this Caprice had reached him in its proper chronological order he would not have handed down the unfortunate impression that he was, in the end, a little disappointed about Bennett's advance as a composer.

(4) *The production, in 1856, of Schumann's 'Paradise and The Peri' by the Philharmonic Society.*

As this performance failed to create a favourable impression of Schumann as a composer, and as the failure appears to have retarded the acceptance of his music as a whole, it seems only fair to those who took part in the performance, as well as to those who judged Schumann by that performance, to observe that there were physical reasons sufficient of themselves to render success on the particular evening well-nigh hopeless. The limits of the Hanover Square Rooms were stretched beyond endurance. The body of the Hall, together with the Royal balcony (divided into three Boxes) which Queen Victoria did not use, could seat, with little margin allowed for comfort, 600 persons. This can be seen on a plan of the concert-room, now before the writer, with the seats numbered and reserved for a Philharmonic concert. In the 1856 season, the Members, Associates and Subscribers numbered 604, and would therefore by themselves fill the room. On very attractive occasions, such *e.g.* as some of the appearances of Mendelssohn, 100 extra tickets are said to have been sold. There is a newspaper report of one Philharmonic concert which estimates the audience at 800, but if this was near the truth, many must have been content to stand in corridors and on stairs. The night on which the 'Paradise and the Peri' was produced under the aegis of Royalty, and with the assistance of the greatest and most attractive singer of the age, saw, according to every account, one of these overcrowded gatherings. The advent of the Royal Family with their Royal visitors, who came in an unusually large party, necessitated ample room being reserved for themselves and their attendants in front of the orchestra, and considerably reduced the space otherwise available for the audience. On the orchestra matters were as bad, and had more immediate effect. The stage, with its organ, looked well-filled when occupied by the band alone. When 80 chorus-singers were added, and six Soloists occupied seats in front, inches had to be counted before the stringed-instrument players could use their bows. The immediate proximity of Royalty naturally caused a certain restriction on the ease of performance. The conductor was not allowed to take up his usual position, and awkwardly faced his forces at the 'half-turn.' The Philharmonic Society had often performed choral works, but seldom any that lasted over more than one part of a concert. The performers of the 'Paradise and the Peri' underwent a species of martyrdom for three long hours. Mr Otto Goldschmidt remembered that Madame Lind-Goldschmidt sang the part of the *Peri* under great personal discomfort. There was no method of ventilation in the Hanover Square Rooms other than by the opening of large sash-windows, a proceeding which was, of course, always violently resented by a section of the audience. The critic Davison, in his denouncement of the 'Paradise and the Peri' outdid himself in the direction of forcible expression, but he was not beyond bounds when he wrote of the poor audience being, as the oppressive evening wore on, half of them suffocated and the other half asleep.

Appendix

APPENDIX B.

LIST OF WORKS

arranged, as nearly as can be determined, in the order in which they were written. Titles of *published* works are given in capitals. References are given to the pages where the works are mentioned in this book.

OPUS

    Fairy Chorus, 'Now no more in dells we sleep,' for Solo, Chorus and Orchestra; 1828; see p. 16.

    Canons, Chants, Fugues, &c. Academy Exercises; approved specimens, dated 1829—32, entered in a note-book; see pp. 16, 19, 21.

    String-Quartet, G mi.; 1831; see p. 22.

    Canzonetta (Metastasio), 'Ch'io speri! padre amato,' with accompt. for P.F. and Horn.

    Symphony for Orch., E flat; finished Ap. 6, 1832; see p. 26.

1 CONCERTO, P.F. and Orch., D mi.; 1832; see pp. 27—30, 157.

    Symphony for Orch., No. 2, D mi.; 1832—33; see p. 28.

    Overture to 'The Tempest;' Dec. 29—31, 1832; see p. 28.

4 CONCERTO, P.F. and Orch., No. 2, E flat; July 6—Nov. 4, 1833; see pp. 32, 37.

    Overture, without title, D mi.; perhaps first intended for opening movement of a 3rd Symphony; Oct. 1—12, 1833.

    Symphony for Orch., No. 4, A ma.; 1833—34; see p. 34.

2 CAPRICCIO, for P.F.; written, according to Sir G. Macfarren, early in 1834; see p. 36.

    Overture to 'The Merry Wives of Windsor;' May, 1834; see p. 36.

    CANZONET, 'In radiant loveliness,' with Orch.; June, 1834; see p. 36.

    SONG, 'Gentle Zephyr;' 1834; see p. 36.

9 CONCERTO, P.F. and Orch., No. 3, C mi.; Aug.—Oct. 31, 1834; see pp. 36, 37, 40, 41, 54, 56, 158, 224, 225, 247, 248.

3 OVERTURE to 'PARISINA;' March, 1835; see pp. 37, 45, 59, 189—192, 194, 224.

    Concerto for 2 P.F.s, 1 movement only, written jointly with G. A. Macfarren, whose memory dated it *about* May, 1835; see p. 39.

OPUS
- 11 SIX STUDIES, in form of Capriccios, for P.F.; according to Davison and Macfarren, 4th Study in F. mi. written some time before the others, probably therefore in 1834; 1st, 3rd, 5th, 6th early in 1835; 2nd, E ma., in summer of 1835; see pp. 36, 39.

    SONG, 'Resignation,' probably 1835, for *The Sacred Melodist*, published Jan. 1, 1836; unknown to present writer when he made the statement on p. 36, l. 36.
- 10 THREE MUSICAL SKETCHES, 'The Lake, The Millstream and the Fountain,' for P.F.; probably 1835; see pp. 39—41, 118, 148, 202, 215.
- 8 SESTET, P.F. and Strings, F sharp mi.; begun, probably in summer of 1835, while staying at Southernhay, Exeter, with K. J. Pye, who preserved a MS. of 36 bars headed *Concerto*. Last movement subscribed Dec. 1835; see pp. 39, 164, 165.

    Dramatic Overture, score not filled up; 1836; see p. 40.

    Concerto, P.F. and Orch., No. 4, F. mi.; first movement headed Feb. 12, 1836; third movement subscribed 'Sketched April 13, score filled up May 4, 1836;' see pp. 40, 42, 69, 75, 76.
- 12 THREE IMPROMPTUS, for P.F.; according to Davison, soon after May, 1836; see pp. 47, 52, 109.

    N.B. *The foregoing works were written before Bennett left the R.A. of Music in July*, 1836.
- 15 OVERTURE, 'THE NAIADS;' finished Sept. 1836; see pp. 41, 44, 45, 57, 58, 62, 63, 67, 88, 162, 189, 202, 415.

    N.B. *Bennett went to Leipzig, for the first time, Oct.* 1836.
- 13 SONATA for P.F., F mi.; begun, according to Davison, in London; first movement, in MS. at Leipzig, dated (?finished) Jan. 24, 1837. Work completed about March 28, 1837; see p. 60.
- 14 THREE ROMANCES for P.F.; No. 1, uncertain; No. 2, Ap. 10, 1837; No. 3, Leipzig, May 3, 1837; see p. 61.
- 16 FANTAISIE for P.F., A ma., 4 movements; Leipzig, 1837; see p. 61.
- 22 CAPRICE, P.F. and Orch., E ma.; first played on May 25, 1838; see pp. 46, 69, 70, 72, 118, 122, 224, 453.
- 19 CONCERTO, P.F. and Orch., No. 5, but published as No. 4, written in England, before leaving for Leipzig in Oct. 1838; see pp. 42, 70, 72, 75—79, 88, 127—129, 131, 141, 167, 453.
- 20 OVERTURE, 'THE WOOD-NYMPHS,' Leipzig, Nov. 1838; see pp. 72, 76, 86—88, 109, 190, 453.
- 18 ALLEGRO GRAZIOSO for P.F.; Leipzig, Dec. 16, 17, 1838; see pp. 72, 118.
- 17 THREE DIVERSIONS, Duets for P.F.; Leipzig, Xmas 1838; see pp. 72, 78.

    Chorale, Voices and Orch., May 19, 1839.
- 26 CHAMBER TRIO for P.F., Vln, and V.Cello, A ma., London, 1839; see pp. 104, 146, 211, 412.

    GENEVIEVE for P.F., London, Nov. 10, 1839; see p. 100.

    SONG, 'The Better Land,' advertised under 'New Music,' Nov. 1839.

    SONG, 'Stay, my Charmer,' date unknown, but not likely to be *later* than 1839; published posthumously.

Appendix

OPUS

WALTZ, Album piece for P.F., in 6-8 time, given, for publication in *The Harmonist*, to J. W. Davison, who, as he told the writer, entitled it 'Waltz.'

Oratorio, 'Zion.' Orchestral Introduction, Adagio, Assai Moderato; Chorus, 'Ah, sinful nation;' Aria (Bass), 'If ye be willing and obedient;' Chorus, 'Oh Jerusalem, wash thine heart from wickedness;' Recit. (Tenor), 'Make ye mention to the nations;' Chorus, 'Hear, O earth, behold I will bring evil upon the people;' Aria (Tenor), 'The Lion is come up from the thicket;' Chorus, 'Flee, save your lives' [Score not filled up]; Chorus, 'And her gates shall lament;' Chorus, 'Therefore they shall come and sing;' Air (Soprano), 'I will love Thee;' Chorus, 'Trust ye in the Lord.'

The MS. Score, closely written, numbers 112 pages. The Oratorio was begun in 1839; see pp. 98, 99, 146.

PSALM TUNE, *Boulcote*, 'To my complaint, O Lord my God,' for Hackett's *National Psalmist*; March 22, 1839.

Fandango for P.F., written in G. A. Macfarren's Album; June 22, 1840.

24 SUITE DE PIÈCES for P.F., 6 nos.; Mrs Anderson accepted their dedication, and consented to hear Bennett play them, in a letter of Nov. 28, 1841; see pp. 118, 129, 130, 138, 146, 148, 175, 453.

23 SIX SONGS, 1st Set: (1) 'Musing on the roaring ocean;' (2) 'May Dew,' probably written at Leipzig, 1842; (3) 'Forget me not;' (4) 'To Chloe in sickness;' (5) 'The Past;' (6) 'Gentle Zephyr,' written in 1834, and first published as a separate Song. The set published 1842; see pp. 36, 104, 127, 195, 411, 412.

25 RONDO PIACEVOLE for P.F.; summer of 1842; see pp. 145, 146, 215, 412.

Concert-Stück or Concerto, P.F. and Orch., No. 6, A mi., begun in 1841; the earliest score now known is headed London, 1843, with Finale subscribed June 2, 1843; advertised in 1844 to be published as Op. 27. He made another edition in 1848; see pp. 125, 150, 151, 194.

OVERTURE, 'MARIE DU BOIS;' 1843; another edition, ultimately used for 'The May Queen,' 1844; see pp. 151, 163, 166.

29 TWO CHARACTERISTIC STUDIES, L'Amabile e L'Appassionata, for P.F.; published as above in 1848; probably *both* written and printed earlier; W. C. Macfarren in his edition of Bennett's works traces them to the *Études de Perfectionnement*, a collection of Moscheles. They are not in the first edition (1841) of that collection, but possibly in a subsequent one. Bennett played the first Study in 1844.

27 SCHERZO for P.F., mentioned in letter to Kistner, Oct. 6, 1845.

28 (No. 1) INTRODUZIONE E PASTORALE for P.F., received at British Museum, May 3, 1846.

PART SONG, 'Come, live with me;' for Hullah's *Part-Music*; probably 1846; reviewed in *Athenæum*, Jan. 1847.

N.B. *For some explanation of slender output noticeable at about this time, see pp. 166, 174. In June, 1847, Bennett finished, for the Handel*

OPUS

Society, an edition of '*Acis and Galatea,*' on which he had worked with great interest and care.

30 SIX SACRED DUETS, composed expressly for the Misses Williams, who sang No. 1 at the Hereford Festival in 1849: (1) 'Remember now thy Creator,' April, 1848; (2) 'Do no Evil,' 1849; (3) 'And who is he that will harm you?' Thanksgiving Day, 1849; (4) 'Cast thy bread upon the waters,' perhaps 1850, first appeared in Haycraft's *Sacred Harmony*, 1851. The intended set of *six* not completed; see pp. 194, 412.

31 TEMA E VARIAZIONI for P.F.; advertised under 'New Music,' April, 1850.

28 (No. 2) RONDINO for P.F. Not received at British Museum, unknown at Stationers' Hall; without evidence to contrary, various facts suggest 1850—51.

33 PRELUDES AND LESSONS for P.F., in all major and minor keys. Several of these were also issued as separate pieces; 1851—53; see pp. 223, 412.

32 SONATA DUO, P.F. and V.cello, finished March 16, 1852; see pp. 194, 211, 212.

28 (No. 3) CAPRICCIO for P.F., Easter, 1853. Op. 28 was dedicated to Miss Catherine Jameson, daughter of Professor Jameson who supported Bennett at Edinburgh in 1844; see p. 161.

PSALM TUNES, 'Day of Wrath,' for Dawson's *Psalmody*, Nov. 1853; *Russell Place*, 'Praise the Lord Who reigns above,' for Rev. P. Maurice's *Psalmody*, Jan. 1854.

38 TOCCATA for P.F., Jan. 13, 1854; see p. 235.

MINUETTO ESPRESSIVO for P.F.; received at British Museum, Aug. 16, 1854; arranged for full orchestra by Ferd. Praeger.

34 RONDEAU, 'PAS TRISTE, PAS GAI,' for P.F., Nov. 1854.

35 SIX SONGS, 2nd Set: (1) 'Indian love,' (2) 'Winter's gone,' both sung, first time, by Mrs Lockey, March 13, 1855; (3) 'Dawn, gentle flower,' dated Oct. 1853; (4) 'Castle Gordon;' (5) 'As lonesome through the woods I stray;' (6) 'Sing, maiden, sing.' The set was completed in 1855. No. 4 had been published separately by Coventry some years before; see pp. 195, 412.

ANTHEM, 'Remember now thy Creator;' consisting of the Duet, Op. 30, No. 1, with an added Chorus, dated Brussels, Aug. 1855.

37 RONDEAU À LA POLONAISE for P.F., first published in a *Musical Album* of Messrs Payne, Leipzig. Bennett mentions the invitation to write it, in a letter of Nov. 4, 1855.

'JANUARY,' 'FEBRUARY,' for P.F.; 1856; published posthumously; see p. 390.

ANTHEM, 'Lord, who shall dwell in Thy tabernacle?;' 1856; posthumously published, but with omission of a portion which he had used in a later work; see pp. 257, 267.

MOTET, 'In Thee, O Lord, do I put my trust,' 8 voices, 1st movement begun at Cambridge, Aug. 1856, subscribed London, Oct. 1856; 2nd movement, Hampstead, 1857; published posthumously; see pp. 26, 267, 268, 390, 391.

OPUS
39 'THE MAY QUEEN,' A Pastoral, for Soli, Chorus and Orch.; 1858; see pp. 194, 285—290, 412, 423, 440, 443.

N.B. *From 1859 to 1862, Bennett gave much time to Hymnology; see pp.* 291—293, 319.

ANTHEM, for St Thomas's Day, 'Oh that I knew where I might find Him;' contributed to Vol. I of Ouseley's *Anthems for certain Seasons and Festivals of the Church of England*; published 1861.

SONG, 'Maiden Mine,' Eastbourne, 1861, lost, and the music rewritten, Eastbourne, Aug. 1866. The present words adapted later, published posthumously; see p. 443.

Song, 'Tell me where, ye summer breezes,' written, lost and rewritten at same dates as the preceding one; see p. 363.

40 ODE, Chorus and Orch., for Opening of Exhibition, 1862; see pp. 303—317, 319, 321, 412.

Ode, Soli, Chorus and Orch. for Installation of Chancellor at Cambridge: (1) Orchestral Introduction and Chorus, 'Hence awhile, severer Muses;' (2) Recit. (Tenor), 'So go, for in your places;' (3) Minuetto; (4) Song (Sopr.), 'Then let the young be glad;' (5) Part Song, 'Health to courage firm and high!' (6) Recit. (Sopr.), 'Yet stay awhile, severer Muses, stay;' (7) 'Come, Euterpe, wake thy choir;' (8) Recit. (Tenor), 'Then let the young be gay;' (9) Air (Tenor), 'Can we forget one friend?' (10) Chorus, 'Severer Muses, linger yet;' (11) Recit. (Sopr.), 'Nay, let us take what God shall send;' (12) 'So shall Alma Mater see;' see pp. 320—324, 334.

42 FANTASIA-OVERTURE, 'PARADISE AND THE PERI,' 1862; see pp. 325, 390, 393, 412.

PRAELUDIUM for P.F., B flat, May or June, 1863.

ANTHEMS: (1) 'Great is our Lord,' for a Meeting of Choirs in Southwell Minster, May, 1863, published posthumously; (2) 'The fool hath said in his heart, There is no God,' for Novello's 31 *Anthems by modern composers*, published April, 1864.

HYMN TUNES: (1) 'God Who madest earth and heaven;' (2) 'Holy, Holy, Holy;' both for a Supplement to *The Chorale Book for England*; 1864.

43 SYMPHONY for Orch., G mi.; Allegro; Menuetto e Trio; Rondo Finale, 1864; Romanza added in 1867; see pp. 332—337, 363, 390, 412, 446.

HYMN TUNE, 'Peace be to this habitation,' Christmas morning, 1866, published posthumously.

44 'THE WOMAN OF SAMARIA,' Sacred Cantata, 1867; see pp. 364—367, 378, 384, 423, 440, 448.

44 CHORUS and QUARTET, added to above, 1868; see pp. 377, 378.

SACRED SONG, 'Lord to Thee our song we raise,' 4 female voices, for the Inauguration Ceremonial of British Orphan Asylum, Slough, June 24, 1868.

ANTHEM, 'Now, my God, let, I beseech Thee;' May, 1869; see pp. 389, 412.

OPUS

ORGAN VOLUNTARY, Adagio à 4 voci, published in *The Village Organist*, Jan. 1870.

Introit, 'The Lord bless thee and keep thee,' for the wedding of J. Lamborn Cock, 1870.

HYMN TUNES: (1) *Inverness*, 'From all Thy Saints in warfare,' for Dr Steggall's *Hymns for the Church of England*, Aug. 1870; (2) 'The radiant morn hath passed away,' for Dr E. G. Monk's *The Anglican Hymn Book*, Aug. 13, 1870.

PART SONG, 'Sweet Stream that glides,' 1871; see pp. 412, 415.

SONATINA for P.F., C ma., Aug. 1871; see p. 442.

HYMN TUNES: (1) 'Courage my sorely tempted heart;' first set to words dated Nov. 1871; published posthumously; (2) 'Jesu, solace of my soul,' for *The Hymnary* of Messrs Novello, Jan. 1, 1872.

Prelude to *Ajax* for Orch.; finished June, 1872; see p. 417.

46 SONATA, 'THE MAID OF ORLEANS,' for P.F.; 1869—73; see pp. 390, 418, 442, 443.

TWO SONGS: (1) 'Dancing lightly comes the summer;' see p. 443; (2) 'Sunset,' also belonging to his later years; both published posthumously.

Part-Song, 'Of all the arts,' for a concert given by the Fitzwilliam Musical Society, Cambridge, on Dec. 1, 1873.

Funeral March, Orch. with Chorus, for the music to *Ajax*, 1873—74; see p. 444.

Bennett left little unfinished music. Belonging to his earlier life, there remain: Some movements of a String-Quartet; part of an Evening Service; and a small parcel of music-sheets which give the beginnings of a few songs or themes for instrumental pieces. From about the year 1850 he used a quire or two of music-paper stitched together in a paper-cover, and in such books (one of which he lost) he entered most of his minor compositions, but no fragments. For the last nine years of his life he adopted as constant companions two bound octavo musical note-books, brought to him from Germany by his friend Gerard F. Cobb, of Cambridge. Acquiring a fresh habit—so it seems to have been in his case—he did make use of these as *sketch*-books. Many pages were written with pencil, probably in his carriage. Besides fragmentary sketches for works afterwards published, they contain part of a *Te Deum*, the opening of a Soprano solo which he intended to add to 'The Woman of Samaria,' and some subjects for movements of other Sonatinas which he thought of joining to the one written in 1871.

Appendix

APPENDIX C.

PUBLISHED WORKS IN THE ORDER OF OPUS-NUMBERS.

1	P.F. Concerto, D mi.	25	'Rondo Piacevole,' P.F.
2	Capriccio P.F.	26	Chamber Trio, P.F., Vln., V.cello.
3	Overture to 'Parisina.'	27	Scherzo, P.F.
4	P.F. Concerto, No. 2, E flat.	28	Introduzione e Pastorale, Rondino, Capriccio, P.F.
5, 6, 7	Vacant[1].	29	Two Studies, 'L'Amabile' e 'L'Appassionata,' P.F.
8	Sestet P.F. and Strings.	30	Four Sacred Duets.
9	P.F. Concerto, No. 3, C mi.	31	Tema e Variazioni, P.F.
10	Three Musical Sketches, P.F.	32	Sonata Duo, P.F. and V.cello.
11	Six Studies, P.F.	33	Preludes and Lessons, P.F.
12	Three Impromptus, P.F.	34	Rondeau, 'Pas Triste, Pas Gai,' P.F.
13	Sonata, F mi., P.F.	35	Six Songs. 2nd set.
14	Three Romances, P.F.	36	Vacant[3].
15	Overture, 'The Naiads.'	37	Rondeau à la Polonaise, P.F.
16	Fantaisie, A ma., P.F.	38	Toccata, P.F.
17	Three Diversions, P.F. Duets.	39	Pastoral, 'The May Queen.'
18	'Allegro Grazioso,' P.F.	40	Ode for 1862 Exhibition.
19	P.F. Concerto, No. 4, F mi.	41	Vacant[4].
20	Overture 'The Wood-nymphs.'	42	Overture, 'Paradise and The Peri.'
21	Vacant[2].	43	Symphony, G mi.
22	Caprice, E ma., P.F. and orch.	44	'The Woman of Samaria.'
23	Six Songs. 1st set.	45	Vacant[5].
24	'Suite de Pièces,' P.F.	46	Sonata, 'The Maid of Orleans,' P.F.

[1] In view of publishing other works of his Academy period.
[2] Possibly for his unfinished Oratorio.
[3] The German publishers placed the 'Minuetto Espressivo' (which was not numbered in England) as 35 and the Six Songs (Op. 35 here) as 36. Bennett, by skipping to 37, would resume agreement with the German order.
[4] For Cambridge Installation Ode, one No. of which *was* published (see p. 324).
[5] For music to *Ajax*.

PUBLICATIONS WITHOUT OPUS-NUMBERS.

For P.F.: Romance 'Genevieve;' Waltz, see p. 456; Minuetto Espressivo; 'January' and 'February;' Præludium in B flat; Sonatina.

For Organ: Adagio à 4 voci.

Vocal: Canzonet 'In radiant loveliness;' Songs: 'Resignation,' 'The Better Land,' 'Stay, my Charmer,' 'Maiden mine,' 'Dancing lightly comes the summer,' 'Sunset;' Part-songs: 'Come live with me,' 'Sweet Stream that glides,' 'Of all the arts.'

A Motet (8 voices), 6 Anthems, A Sacred Song (4 female voices), and 12 Hymns are now published in one volume by Messrs Novello and Co.

DEDICATION OF WORKS.

Opera (2) and (4), to Cipriani Potter; (3) H. Field; (8) C. Coventry; (9) J. B. Cramer; (10) J. W. Davison; (11) G. A. Macfarren; (12) W. P. Beale; (13) Mendelssohn; (16) Schumann; (19) Moscheles; (22) Madame Dulcken; (24) Mrs Anderson; (25) R. Barnett; (26) K. J. Pye; (27) John Suett; (28) Miss C. Jameson; (32) A. Piatti; (46) Madame A. Goddard; *Without Opus Nos.*: Minuetto Espressivo, to J. Turner Hopwood; Præludium, to Harold Thomas; Song 'Maiden Mine,' to Mrs Robert Case; Sonatina, to his grandson, T. B. Case.

APPENDIX D.

TABLE OF COMPOSITIONS ARRANGED IN PERIODS.

PERIOD I. APRIL 1832—APRIL 1836. AGED 16—20.

Orchestra: Unpublished Symphonies and Overtures written while studying under Crotch and Potter; Overture to 'Parisina.' *P.F. and Orchestra:* three published Concertos, D mi., E flat, C mi.; one, F mi., MS.; one for 2 P.F.s, MS. *Chamber Music:* String-Quartet, MS.; Sestet, P.F. and Strings. *P.F. Solos:* Capriccio; 6 Studies; 3 Musical Sketches. *Vocal:* 2 Canzonets; Songs, 'Gentle Zephyr,' 'Resignation.'

PERIOD II. MAY 1836—APRIL 1843. AGED 20—27.

Orchestra: Overtures 'The Naiads;' 'The Wood-nymphs.' *P.F. and Orchestra:* Caprice, E ma.; Concerto No. 4, F mi. *Chamber Music:* Trio, P.F., Vln., V.cello. *P.F. Solos:* 3 Impromptus; Sonata, F mi.; Fantaisie, A ma.; 3 Romances; 'Allegro Grazioso;' 'Genevieve;' Waltz (see p. 456); 'Fandango;' Suite de Pièces; 'Rondo Piacevole.' *P.F. Duets* '3 Diversions.' *Vocal:* Unfinished Oratorio; Songs, 'The Better Land,' 'Stay, my charmer;' 6 Songs (1st set) one of them written in Period I.

PERIOD III. MAY 1843—APRIL 1851. AGED 27—35.

[N.B. *During the early years of married life Bennett paid close attention to securing a position by teaching.*]

Orchestra: Overture 'Marie du Bois' (two editions). *P.F. and Orchestra:* Concert-Stück, or Concerto, No. 6, A mi., MS. (three editions). *P.F. Solos:* 2 Studies, 'L'Amabile e l'Appassionata;' Scherzo; 'Introduzione e Pastorale;' Tema e Variazioni; Rondino, E ma. *Vocal:* Additions to unfinished Oratorio; 4 Sacred Duets; Song, 'Castle Gordon;' Part-song, 'Come live with me.'

PERIOD IV. MAY 1851—APRIL 1859. AGED 35—43.

Orchestra and Voices: 'The May Queen.' *Chamber Music:* Sonata Duo, P.F. and V.cello. *P.F. Solos:* Capriccio, A mi.; Toccata; 'Minuetto Espressivo;' Rondeau, 'Pas Triste, Pas Gai;' 'Rondeau à la Polonaise;' Preludes and Lessons; 'January and February.' *Vocal:* 6 Songs (2nd set), one written in Period III; Anthems, 'Remember now thy Creator' (see p. 458), 'Lord, who shall dwell in Thy tabernacle?' 8-part Motet, 'In Thee, O Lord.'

PERIOD V. MAY 1859—APRIL 1866. AGED 43—50.

[N.B. *For the first three years of this period Bennett devoted much time to German Hymnology.*]

Orchestra and Voices: Ode for 1862 Exhibition; Ode for Cambridge Installation. *Orchestra:* Overture, 'Paradise and The Peri;' Symphony, G mi. *P.F. Solo:* Præludium in B flat. *Anthems:* 'Oh, that I knew where I might find Him;' 'Great is the Lord;' 'The fool hath said in his heart.' Songs: 'Maiden mine,' 'Tell me where, ye summer breezes.'

PERIOD VI. MAY 1866—SEPTEMBER 1874. AGED 50—58.

Orchestra and Voices: 'The Woman of Samaria;' Funeral March, for music to *Ajax*. *Orchestra:* Prelude to *Ajax*. *P.F. Solos:* Sonata, 'The Maid of Orleans;' Sonatina. *Organ:* Adagio à 4 voci; *Vocal:* Anthem, 'Now, my God, let, I beseech Thee;' Sacred Song (4 female voices), 'Lord to Thee our song we raise;' Introit, 'The Lord bless thee, and keep thee;' Part-songs: 'Sweet stream that glides,' 'Of all the arts;' Songs: 'Dancing lightly,' 'Sunset.'

INDEX.

Adelaide, H.M. Queen, 29
Albert, H.R.H. The Prince Consort, 162, 178, 202, 248, 277, 278, 305, 306, 308, 312, 320, 323
Alwyn, Mr W. Crowther, 179, 399–401
Amps, Mr Wm., 266, 268
Anderson, G. F., 163, 190–193, 224, 241, 249, 297
Anderson, Mrs G. F., 113, 118, 224, 319, 324, 462
Antient Concert, The, 133
Armfield, Rev. H. T., 267, 269
Ashford, Derbyshire, 1, 227, 330
Athenaeum (club), The, 18, 331
Attwood, Thos., 18, 25, 31, 37, 40, 41, 47, 48, 251
Ayrton, Wm., 86, 88, 187, 188

Bach, C. P. Emanuel, 33
Bach, J. Sebastian, 92, 120, 130, 140, 267, 275, 424, 444, 451
Bach Society (London), The, 203–208, 232–235, 276–279, 319, 451
Bache, Edward, 398
Badman, Benjamin, 357
Bakewell, Derbyshire, 3, 4, 6
Banister, H. C., 186
Barlow, T. Oldham, A.R.A., 422–424
Barnett, Robert, 110, 112, 203, 213, 226, 227, 462
Bartholomew, W., 207, 248
Bateson, Rev. W. H., D.D., 389
Beale, W. P., 109, 462
Beard, Rev. Arthur, 271
Beethoven, 33, 34, 51, 53, 134, 156, 199
Benecke, one of two brothers, F. W. and V., probably the latter, 60, 62
Benedict, Sir Julius, 408
Bennett, Elizabeth (née Donn), W. S. B.'s mother, 5–7
Bennett, Sir John (Sheriff of London), 166
Bennett, John (W. S. B.'s grandfather), 3, 4, 6, 9, 10, 19, 20, 26, 27, 46
Bennett, Mr Joseph, musical critic, 22
Bennett, Robert (W. S. B.'s father), 3–10

Bennett, Sarah, later Mrs J. Glasscock (W. S. B.'s aunt), 7, 9, 20, 28, 63, 65, 136, 161, 326, 328
Bennett, Mrs Wm. Sterndale (née Wood), 113, 115–128, 136, 143, 144, 149, 157, 159, 160–162, 165, 195, 197, 231, 277, 279, 313, 324–328, 452, 453
Bennett, Wm. Sterndale
  Composer, As a, 16, 17, 21, 24–28, 34, 36, 39–42, 44–46, 60, 61, 69, 70, 72, 78, 79, 85–88, 95–108, 145, 146, 151, 163–165, 175, 194, 211, 212, 256, 257, 267, 268, 285–287, 289, 290, 303–310, 322, 323, 325, 332–334, 363–367, 377, 378, 389–391, 410–413, 417, 418, 442–444, 450, 455–464
  Compositions.—For references to mention, in this book, of particular works, see Appendix B, 455–460
  Composition, As a teacher of, 196, 398–406
  Concerts, Chamber, 110, 147–149, 166, 209–215
  Concerts, Orchestral, 69, 70, 162, 165, 202
  Conductor, As a, 58, 100, 134, 141, 150, 154 note, 170, 171, 228–230, 242–249, 268–270, 274–276, 279, 287–289, 294–302, 319, 323, 325, 331, 332, 335, 337, 342, 344
  Letters of, to, Alwyn, Mr W. Crowther, 401; Anon., 352; Bennett, Sarah (later Mrs Glasscock), 28, 65, 136, 171, 326; Brewster, Sir David, 339; Case, Mrs Thos., his daughter, 423, 445; David, Ferd., 336, 381; Davison, J. W., 44, 49, 77; Dorrell, Wm., 395; 1862 Exhibition, The Commissioners of, 307–310, 316; Kistner, Fr., 98, 100, 102, 104, 151; Kistner, Julius, 412; Leipzig, Concert-Direction of, 229, 230; Lucas, C., opp. p. 190, 192, 193; Maurice, Rev. F. D., 200; Mendelssohn Bartholdy, F., 46, 66, 68, 70, 98, 136, 137, 139, 145, 148, 149, 151, 152, 160, 164, 166, 173;

Philharmonic Society, 275; Philpott, Rt Rev. H., D.D., 263; Price, A. G., 392; Pye, Kellow J., 370; Romilly, Rev. J., 261; Schumann, R., 63, 72, 76, 218; Schumann, Clara, 236, 244; Son, his, 379, 422, 442; Voigt, Carl, 109; Whewell, Rev. W., D.D., 263; Wood, Mary A., later his wife, 115–128, 429
Letters to, from, Bishop, Sir H., 223; Bennett, John, 19; Brewster, Sir D., 339, 340; Cartmell, Rev. James, D.D., 361; Chorley, H. F., 285, 289; Exhibition of 1862, Commissioners of, 303, 307, 308, 310–312, 317; Davison, Mrs, 90; Gladstone, Rt Hon. W. E., 385; Goethe, W. von, 73; Hamilton, Rev. F., 43; Henslow, F. H., 251; Holdsworth, Thos., 83; Horsley, C. E., 250; Kingsley, Rev. Charles, 320–323; Kistner, Fr., 99, 105, 106; Leipzig, Concert-Direction of, 228; Lind-Goldschmidt, Madame, 330; Mendelssohn Bartholdy, F., 48, 66, 98, 138, 142–144, 149, 153, 156, 158, 159, 165, 172; Philharmonic Society, 249, 274, 327, 335; Philpott, Rt Rev. H., D.D., 264; Potter, Cipriani, 282, 334; Richmond, George, R.A., 331; Romilly, Rev. J., 261; Schumann, R., 220; Smart, Sir G., 109; Tennyson, Lord, 305; Westmorland, Earl of, 283
Organ-playing, 35, 36
Pianoforte-playing, First teachers, 10, 15; Debût at R.A.M., 16; Other early performances, 21, 28, 29; Studies under Potter, 32–34; Debût at Philharmonic, 37; Sight-reading, 39; Debût at Gewandhaus, 55–57; 2nd appearance at Gewandhaus, 76–79; Industry as a pianist, 21, 108, 424; Last performance at Gewandhaus, 127–129, 131; Mendelssohn's Lieder ohne Worte, 185–187; Last appearance at the Philharmonic, 187, 188; Playing at his own Chamber-Concerts, 209–215; Opinions on his playing by Wm. Ayrton, 88, 187; H. C. Banister, 186; J. W. Davison, 184, 187, 188, 424; John Field, 21; Otto Goldschmidt, 188, 189; Ferd. Hiller, 78; G. A. Macfarren, 184, 426; Mendelssohn, 56, 154, 157; *Musical Examiner*, 158; Piatti, 212; Pye, K. J., 186; Mr W. Shakespeare, 214; Schumann, 40, 56, 61, 129, 215, 216; His retirement, 215–217, 274
Pianoforte-teaching, 36, 68, 83, 84, 88, 89, 91–94, 174, 195–201, 223, 231, 274, 320, 446
Residences in London, 68, 135, 164, 294, 338, 352, 392, 440

Singing, 18, 251, 252
Violin and Viola playing, 15–17, 18, 21, 26
Berlin, 122–124, 126, 127, 136, 140
Berlioz, H., 235
Billet, A., 202
Birch, Charlotte A., 36, 146
Birmingham, 65, 66, 109, 171, 175, 223, 287, 364–368
Bishop, Sir H., 134, 152, 164, 170, 221–223, 264, 409
Blagrove, H., 66, 157, 210
Bohn, H. G., 430
Bonn, 414
Bowley, J. S., 23, 87, 184
Bowley, R. K., 308
Boxall, Sir Wm., R.A., 409
Breitkopf u. Haertel, 76, 122
Brewster, Sir David, 339
Bright, Rt Hon. John, 434
Brighton, 196, 377, 440
British Musicians, Society of, 37
Brizzi, Scipione, 17, 18
Broadwood, H., 40
Broadwood and Sons, Messrs, 39, 76, 122
Brockhaus, Heinrich, 52, 53, 75
Bülow, Hans von, 442, 443
Bunnett, Dr E., 263
Burghersh, Lord, 12, 14, 29, 30, 113. See also Westmorland, Earl of
Burton, R. S., 186, 279

Cambridge, 4, 9–11, 20, 23, 27, 28, 32, 36, 44, 63, 120, 213, 249–272, 274, 286, 289, 319–325, 332, 338, 361–363, 376, 377, 381, 389, 409, 440, 444, 449
Cartmell, Rev. J., D.D., Master of Christ's College, Cambridge, 361
Case, Mr George, 441, 443
Case, Robert, 330, 422, 423, 434, 446
Case, Professor Thos., President of C.C.C., Oxford, 392, 423, 443
Case, Mr Thos. B., 462
Canterbury Music Hall, 289
Cassel, 74, 114, 116–119
Cawdor, Earl of, 278
Channell, Miss A. A., 442
Chopin, 150, 341, 451–453
Chorale Book for England, 291–293, 319, 333
Chorley, H. F., 194, 285, 286, 289, 290
Clarke, Sir Campbell, 314 note, 335
Clarke Whitfeld, Dr J., 4, 5, 258
Classical P.F. music, republication of, 92, 93
Clementi, 32, 93, 94, 110, 214
Clerk, Sir George, Bart., 350, 353 note, 355, 356, 358, 359, 370, 372
Cobb, Gerard F., 444, 459
Cock, J. Lamborn, 277, 290, 311, 331, 459
Cole, Sir H., K.C.B., 38, 349, 350, 353, 354, 358, 359, 386, 418–421

Coleridge, Mr A. D., 250, 289
Coleridge, Sir John (later Lord), 415, 416, 434
Cooke, Grattan, 13, 15, 110, 111
Cooper, George, 204, 448
Costa, Sir Michael, 96, 162, 166, 169, 170, 189-193, 224, 225, 241, 242, 248, 279, 281, 288, 295, 297-299, 304, 307-317, 322, 324, 341, 350, 356, 364, 366-368, 409
Cotterill, Rev. Thos., 7
Couldery, Mr C. H., 398, 399
Coventry, Charles, 39, 44, 47 note, 63, 64, 92, 93, 95, 109, 110, 148, 151, 410, 411, 462
Cox, Miss Frances, 112
Cox, Frank R., 203
Cramer, J. B., 12, 32, 39, 88, 94, 110, 153, 187, 188, 214, 462
Cramer, François, 29
Creswick, Thos., R.A., 432
Crotch, Dr Wm., 12, 21, 22, 26, 27, 153, 268
Crystal Palace Concerts, 417, 446
Cummings, Dr W. H., 366, 378
Cusins, Sir Wm. G., 226, 227, 319, 363, 365, 366

Dallas, E. S., 431
Dando, J. H. B., 147, 178, 204, 210, 288
Darnall, nr. Sheffield, 7
Darling, Rev. T., 446
David, Ferd., 49, 51, 52, 65-67, 75, 78, 79, 84, 89, 113, 121, 122, 147, 148, 168, 174, 175, 180, 228, 335-338, 380-382
David, Mr Paul (son of above), 121, 380-383
Davison, James W., 18, 19, 24, 26, 33, 34, 36, 39-41, 44, 45, 48, 49, 61, 68, 69, 77, 79, 89, 90, 92, 94, 96, 103, 105, 110, 130, 145, 150, 171, 175, 184, 185, 187-189, 210, 224, 233, 242, 270, 287, 290, 302, 312, 424, 432, 454, 456, 457, 462
Davison, Mrs, née Duncan (mother of above), 89, 90
Devonshire, Duchess of, 3
Devonshire, Dukes of, 7, 320
Dibdin, Charles, 208
Dilke, Sir Wentworth, Bart., 309
Dirichlet, Gustav, 131
Disraeli, Rt Hon. B., 369, 370, 373, 386
Döhler, Theodor, 94
Dolby, Charlotte H., 146, 205, 235, 287. *See also* Sainton, Madame
Donaldson, Professor John, 155, 156, 161, 252, 339
Donn, James (W. S. B.'s maternal grandfather), 5, 46
Dorrell, Wm., 26, 27, 34, 37, 110, 115, 116, 141, 142, 196, 204, 207, 212, 331

Dresden, 126
Dreyschock, Alex., 150
Dudley, Earl of, 375, 387, 447
Dulcken, Madame (née David), 462
Dunraven, Countess of, 433
Dussek, 16, 39, 93, 94, 110, 187, 211
Düsseldorf, 39, 40-42, 46-48, 68, 141, 218-220

Eastbourne, 286, 287, 290, 293, 360, 365, 390
Ecclesall, 7
Edinburgh, 152-155, 158, 161, 289, 339, 340, 448
Edinburgh, H.R.H. The Duke of, 164, 418, 419, 447
Edmonton, 36
Egerton, Hon. Seymour (later Earl of Wilton), 399
Ella, John, 15, 96
Elvey, Sir George, 254, 255, 409
Ernst, H. W., 9 note, 151, 210
Eversley, 321, 322
Ewer and Co., Messrs, 207
Exeter, 93, 427, 456
Exhibition of 1851, 221-223
Exhibition of 1862, 303-317, 319
Eyers, Mr H. R., 441, 445

Faning, Dr Eaton, 404
Fantasia, The P.F., 91, 185
Farringford, 305, 306
Ferrari, Adolfo, 111, 112, 226, 227
Fètis, F. J., 17, 32
Field, Henry (of Bath), 462
Field, John, 21
Filtsch, Charles, 150
Finsbury, 213
Franck, Dr Eduard, 49, 56, 58, 60
Frankfort, 63, 165
Freemantle, H. J., 385
Frege, Madame, 128
Frere, Mrs, 251, 254

Gade, Niels W., 156, 228, 414
Garrett, G. M., Mus. D., 362, 446, 449
Gevaert, F. A., 414
Gewandhaus Concerts, *see* Leipzig
Gifford, Miss, 10
Gladstone, Rt Hon. W. E., 348, 385, 408
Gladstone, Mrs W. E., 386
Gloucester, 202, 392
Goddard, Madame Arabella (Mrs J. W. Davison), 224, 225, 247, 442, 462
Goethe, Madame von, 52, 53, 62
Goethe, W. von, 52, 53, 58-60, 64, 71-73
Goldschmidt, Madame Jenny Lind-, 242-244, 248, 324, 330, 354, 454
Goldschmidt, Otto, 188, 243, 292, 293, 333, 350, 351, 354, 356, 359, 360, 454
Goold, Wyndham, M.P., 433
Gore-Booth, Lady, 433
Goss, Sir John, 204, 213, 262, 409, 448

Index

Governesses' Benevolent Institution, 202
Grace, Dr W. G., 436
Grantchester, nr. Cambridge, 40, 44, 70, 75
Granville, Dr, 18
Greatorex, Thos., 12
Greenwich, 142, 143, 166, 213
Grove, Sir George, C.B., 33, 121
Guy, Mr Henry, 443

Hackett, C. D., 457
Haertel, Dr, 51–53
Haertel, Madame, 52, 122
Hallé, Sir Charles, 9 note, 150, 442, 443
Hamburg, 49, 75, 138, 141
Hamilton, Rev. F., 11, 13, 15, 29, 43
Hampstead, 102, 458
Handel, 3, 10, 27, 33, 55, 97, 98, 130, 133, 149, 177, 179, 183, 213, 251
Hargitt, Mr C. J., 289
Hartvigson, Mr Fritz, 334
Hasper, Dr, 49, 60
Hauptmann, Moritz, 116
Haydn, 6, 16, 23, 51, 93, 94, 130, 133, 209, 214, 269
Haweis, Rev. H. R., 200, 269
Heller, Stephen, 213
Helmore, Rev. Thos., 206
Hendon, 36
Hensel, Madame (née Mendelssohn Bartholdy), 126, 127, 131, 214
Henslow, Frank H., 251
Hereford, 202, 458
Herschel, Sir John, Bart., 252
Hill, Weist, 368
Hiller, Ferd., 78, 187, 214, 338, 380, 414
Hipkins, A. J., 451, 452
Hogarth, George, 241, 248, 301, 302, 333, 334, 430
Holdsworth, Thos., 83, 84, 89, 108, 223
Holland, 235
Hollebone, Philadelphia, 437
Holmes, W. H., 13, 15, 16, 18, 32, 204, 427, 428
Hopkins, E. J., Mus.D., 203, 448
Hopkins, J., 448
Hopkins, J. L., Mus.D., 257, 362
Hopwood, J. Turner, 462
Horsley, C. E., 204, 250, 254
Horsley, W., 12
Howard, Stirling, 385
Howard, William, 384, 385
Hull, 109
Hullah, John, LL.D., 105, 185, 186, 204, 266, 277, 289, 457
Hummel, 21, 94, 211

Ibbotson, Walter, 385
Ipswich, 196
Islington, 313

Jackson, Wm., 101, 197
Jackson, Arthur H., 404
Jaell, Alfred, 343

Jameson, Professor, 161
Jameson, Catherine, 457, 462
Jansen, Gustav, 54 note, 74
Jasper, Fraülein, 74
Jay, John, 108
Jewell, Madame Rebecca, 442
Joachim, Joseph, 157, 210, 275, 286, 319, 324, 422, 438, 439, 444
Johnson, A. C., 44, 70, 136, 142, 156, 161
Johnson, Mrs (mother of above), 136, 158, 161
Johnston, Helen F. H., 205, 207, 208, 257
Joy, Walker, 287

Kalkbrenner, F. W., 94
Kemble, Charles, 432
Kemp, Mr Stephen B., 399, 404, 415
Kennedy, Rev. Prof. B. H., D.D., 447
Kingsley, Rev. Charles, 320–324
Kingsley, Rev. W. T., 250, 251
Kistner, Friedr., 49, 52, 55, 60, 61, 63, 65, 98–100, 102, 104, 105, 108, 114, 121, 137, 138, 140–142, 146, 151, 164, 216
Kistner, Julius, 49, 65, 175, 180, 218, 336, 338, 379, 412
Kitson, Sir James, 279
Klengel, Dr, 34
Klingemann, Carl, 40–42, 48
Kuhe, Mr W., 440
Kynaston (formerly Snow), Rev. Canon H., D.D., 417

Landseer, Sir Edwin, R.A., 432
Leader and Cock, Messrs, 277, 410, 411
Leeds, 279, 280, 285, 287–289, 318
Leipzig, 34, 46–62, 66–68, 70–79, 87, 88, 101, 113, 121, 122, 124–131, 146, 148, 154 note, 166–168, 171–173, 214, 215, 218, 227–232, 235, 335–338, 379, 412
Leslie, Henry, 415
Liddon, Rev. Canon, D.D., 408
Lincoln, H. J., 204
Lind-Goldschmidt, Madame Jenny, see Goldschmidt
Lindpaintner, 225
Lipinsky (or Lipinski), 48
Liszt, 112, 123, 127
Littlehampton, 195
Liverpool, 47, 289
Lloyd, Mr Edward, 271
Lockey, Mrs (née Williams), 458
Loder, Kate, see Thompson, Lady
Logier, J. B., 8
London Institution, 333
London, University of, 413
Longmans, Messrs, 291, 292, 333
Lowe, Miss, 198
Lucas, Charles, 15, 16, 19, 21, 32, 134, 170, 190–193, 224, 225, 281, 282, 300, 347, 348, 353, 357, 367
Lunn, Rev. J. R., 257, 267, 449

Macfarren, Sir George A., 18, 21, 24, 28,

Index

32, 36–39, 79, 112, 184, 227, 245, 247, 284, 286, 348, 354, 355, 367, 396, 398, 414, 415, 419, 434, 442, 447, 449, 455–457, 462
Macfarren, Walter C., 457
Maclise, Daniel, R.A., 164 note
Macmurdie, J., 274
Maidstone, 196
Mainz, 63, 104, 137
Malibran, Maria F. (née Garcia), 47
Malzburg, Madame de, 116, 117, 119
Manchester, 8, 9 note, 47, 279
Manns, Sir August, 379, 417
Mapleson, J. H., 96
Marschner, H. A., 50, 61, 102, 117
Martin, Rev. F., 251
Martin, G. W., 378
Marylebone Literary Institution, 100
Mason, Colonel Oliver, 364
Masson, Miss E., 149
Mathison, Rev. W. C., 251
Matthay, Mr Tobias, 404
Maurice, Rev. F. D., 199, 200
Maurice, Rev. P., 458
May, Oliver, 203
Meerti, Elise, 121, 122
Mellon, Alfred, 312, 316
Mendelssohn Bartholdy, J. L. Felix, 23, 24, 27, 30, 31, 33, 37, 39–42, 46–52, 56–61, 63–68, 70–72, 75, 84, 86–89, 92–95, 97, 98, 109, 117, 120, 122–131, 134–180, 183–188, 195, 201, 211–214, 216–219, 234, 245, 287, 298, 337, 342, 446, 454, 462
Mendelssohn Bartholdy, Cecile (née Jeanrenaud), F. M. B.'s wife, 57, 66, 67, 126, 137, 139, 140, 142, 144, 147, 172, 173, 218
Mendelssohn Bartholdy, Fanny, F. M. B.'s sister, *see* Hensel, Madame
Mendelssohn Bartholdy, Madame, F. M. B.'s mother, 123, 126
Meyerbeer, 131, 304, 312, 313, 364
Millais, Sir J. E., Bart., P.R.A., 422–424
Molique, Bernhard, 139, 207, 210, 250, 398
Monicke, C. H., 49–51, 59–61, 65, 75, 121, 172, 218
Monk, E. J., Mus.D., 460
Montgomery, James, 6 note
Mori, Nicolas, 85
Mori, Frank, son of above, 116, 117
Morris, Mrs, 437
Moscheles, Ignaz, 46, 64, 92, 134, 140, 148, 151, 153, 164, 165, 170, 171, 174, 210, 213, 214, 338, 457, 462
Mozart, 6, 16, 22–26, 33, 50, 51, 55, 69, 92–94, 96, 97, 110, 120, 125, 129, 130, 148, 186–189, 209, 211–213, 245, 251, 276
Mulready, Wm., R.A., 432
Musical Association of London, 188, 293
Musical Society of London, 298

National Choral Society, 378
Neate, Charles, 210
Netherlands, Society for Promotion of Music in the, 235
Neukomm, Chevalier S., 222
Niecks, Professor Frederick, 451
Novelli, A. A., 121
Novello, Madame Clara A. (Countess Gigliucci), 66, 67, 245, 287, 289, 392
Novello, J. A., 48
Nunn, Wm., 10

Okes, Rev. Richard, D.D., 409
O'Leary, Mr Arthur, 128, 188, 189, 227, 432, 433, 447, 452
Orchestral Union, 225
Oury, James, 15
Oxford, 261, 263, 264, 392, 408, 445

Pakington, Sir John, Bart. (later Lord Hampton), 373, 387
Paris, 216, 223
Parker, Mr Louis N., 403–406, 424
Parkes, Marie H., 385, 452, 453
Parry, Sir Hubert, Bart., 399
Parry, John, 112
Parry, Joseph, Mus.D., 399, 404
Pearson (or Pierson), H. H., 121, 161, 339 note
Pemberton (formerly Hudson), Rev. Canon T. P., 332
Pendlebury, Richard, 377 note
Philharmonic Music Hall, 313
Philharmonic Society of London, 37, 40, 70, 85, 86, 88, 123, 132–135, 137–143, 150–152, 156, 158, 161–166, 187–194, 215, 220, 224, 225, 241–249, 274–276, 289, 294–302, 319, 324, 325, 327, 328, 331–335, 340–344, 363, 415, 417, 448
Philharmonic Society, The New, 225, 298
Philharmonic Society of Paris, 235
Phillips, Percival, 385
Phillips, Lovell, 18
Philpott, Rt Rev. H., D.D., 263
Piatti, Alfredo, 194, 210–212, 250, 301, 324, 462
Pickering, J. A., 70–72
Pierson, H. H., *see* Pearson
Pinto, G. F., 39, 110
Portsmouth, 151
Potter, Philip H. Cipriani, 16, 17, 27, 28, 32, 33, 36, 37 note, 65, 85, 92, 110, 134, 139, 153, 204, 213, 214, 222, 231, 247, 281, 282, 283, 334, 347, 357, 362, 462
Pratt, John, 10
Preussers, the, 75, 168, 218, 231
Price, Alfred G., 392
Punch, 204, 224, 313
Pye, Kellow J., 93, 186, 353, 354, 359, 370, 427, 456, 462
Pyne, Louisa (Madame Bodda), 228, 230

470 *Index*

Queen's College, Harley Street, 195, 199, 200, 203, 223, 256, 320, 376
Queisser, Carl T., 51

Rea, William, 171, 214
Reeves, J. Sims, 287, 319
Reinecke, Carl, 338, 389
Reissiger, Carl G., 153
Reuss, Count, 62, 71, 113, 124, 125
Rhine, The, 41, 68, 332
Richmond, 102
Richmond, George, R.A., 331
Rietz, Julius, 228, 338
Robinson, Joseph, 171
Rochlitz, Friedrich J., 74
Rockstro, W. S., 164, 165, 393
Rogers, Robert, 9
Romilly, Colonel, 434
Rotterdam, 63, 235
Rowland, A. J., 301
Royal Academy of Arts, 408
Royal Academy of Music, 12–43, 65, 85, 88, 113, 143, 144, 190, 196, 280–284, 347–360, 369–375, 384–388, 391, 392, 394–406, 414, 415, 418–421, 429, 441, 445–447, 452, 456
Royal Society of Female Musicians, 319
Royal Society of Musicians, 297, 319, 413, 448

Sacred Harmonic Society, 222, 308, 311, 367, 378
Sainton, Prosper, 210, 241, 312, 316
Sainton, Madame, 366. *See also* Dolby, Charlotte A.
Sala, G. Augustus, 430
Salaman, C. K., 196
Salisbury, Marquess of, 408
Salmon, Mrs, 6
Salomon, J. P., 7, 133
Santley, Mr Charles, 324, 366
Scarlatti, Domenico, 130, 149, 214
Schleinitz, Conrad, 66, 67, 147, 168, 232, 336, 381
Schneider, Friedr., 126, 131
Schönberg, Princesses of, 62
Schumann, Madame Clara (née Wieck), 50, 122, 124, 125, 213, 218–221, 236, 237, 244–248, 274
Schumann, Robert A., 40, 49, 51–65, 67, 71–73, 76–78, 85–87, 91, 103, 105, 121, 122, 124, 125, 129, 130, 175, 176, 201, 210, 213–216, 218–221, 236, 243, 244, 246, 248, 269, 301, 341–343, 446, 453, 454, 462
Schumann, Madame Therese, 62, 64
Schuncks, the, 66, 67, 75, 125, 126, 147, 172
Seguins, the, 96, 367
Seymour, C. A., 188
Shakespeare, Mr Wm., 214, 399, 401
Shaw, Mrs Alfred (née Postans), 73, 77, 124, 125

Sheffield, 3, 5–9, 384, 385
Slack, Samuel, 3, 4
Sloper, Lindsay, 442
Smart, Sir George T., 12, 15, 27 note, 69, 109, 134, 153, 204, 221–223, 250, 409 note
Smart, Henry, 204, 206, 207
Smith, Rev. Sydney, 101
Snow (later Kynaston), Rev. H., 417
Southampton, 136, 145, 149, 151, 158, 223, 227, 352
Southgate, 198
Spagnoletti, —, 15
Spark, Mr Fred R., 289
Sparrow, Mr Charles E., 233
Sparrow, Thomas, 427
Spohr, Louis, 23, 74, 86, 87, 114, 116–122, 131, 134, 140, 146, 149–151, 153, 157, 162, 211, 212
Spontini, 122, 131
Stainer, Miss, 233
Stainer, Sir John, 233, 448
Stamaty, Camille M., 49, 51, 64
Stanford, Sir Charles V., 171
Stanford, John, 171
Stanley, Rev. A. P., Dean of Westminster, 446–449
Steggall, Charles, Mus.D., 196, 203, 205–207, 214, 255, 276, 391, 398, 448, 451, 460
Sterndale, John, 7
Sterndale, Wm., 7
Stockley, Mr W. C., 366
Storace, Stephen, 129
Suett, John, 462
Sullivan, Sir Arthur, 97, 425, 448

Tait, Professor P. G., 339, 340
Taubert, W. C. G., 127, 131
Tauchnitz, Dr (later Baron), 53
Taunton, 27
Taylor, Edward, 146
Taylor, Mr Franklin, 442, 443
Taylor, Mr Sedley, 444
Tennyson, Alfred (later Lord), 304–308
Tennyson, Mrs (later Lady), 306
Thacker, Rev. A., 251
Thalberg, Sigismund, 64, 91, 100, 112, 142
Thomas, Harold, 319, 390, 462
Thompson, Lady (née Loder), wife of Sir Henry Thompson, Bart., 113, 224
Thring, Rev. Edward, 380, 383
Tideswell, 3
Titiens, Therese, 324, 366
Turle, James, 448

Verdi, 304, 313
Verhulst, J. J. H., 121, 124, 235
Victoria, H.M. Queen, 248, 279, 287, 305, 331, 409, 448
Vienna, 17, 58, 71, 72 note, 76

Index

Vieuxtemps, Henri, 67, 157, 210
Vince, Rev. S. B., 10, 11
Vocal Concerts, The, 69
Voigt, Carl, 53, 55, 64, 75, 109, 122, 126, 172, 338
Voigt, Madame Henriette, 52, 53, 55, 60, 64, 72, 74

Wageman, Thos., 6, 9, 10
Wagner, Richard, 241, 242, 269
Wales, H.R.H. Prince of (H.M. King Edward VII), 248, 331, 349, 420
Wales, H.R.H. Princess of (H.M. Queen Alexandra), 306, 331
Walker, Bettina, 93, 112, 199 note, 424, 426
Walmisley, Professor T. A., Mus.D., 249, 251, 258–260, 266, 267
Walmisley, T. F., father of above, 259
Wandsworth, 35, 254 note
Watts, W., 156, 160, 161
Weber, Carl M. von, 15, 60, 66, 87, 94, 134, 211, 245
Weimar, 71, 73, 74

Weiss, W. H., 287
Wendler, Dr. 229, 230
Westmorland, Earl of, 281–284, 348, 372. *See also* Burghersh, Lord
Whewell, Rev. Wm., D.D., 250, 254, 256, 258, 263, 267
Wieck, Clara, *see* Schumann, Madame
Williams, the Misses, 458
Willingdon, 287
Wilton, Earl of, 353 note, 355, 358, 359, 370–372
Wimbledon, 292
Winchester, 158
Windsor, 28, 202, 223, 278, 289, 408
Wingham, Thos., 399, 402, 404
Wood, George, 374
Wood, Mary A., *see* Bennett, Mrs W. Sterndale
Wood, Thomas, 250, 254
Woodford, Dr, Bishop of Ely, 449

Yorkshire Choral Concerts, 6

Zwickau, 54, 62, 64

CAMBRIDGE: PRINTED BY JOHN CLAY, M.A. AT THE UNIVERSITY PRESS.

Music and Books published by Travis & Emery Music Bookshop:

Anon.: Hymnarium Sarisburiense, cum Rubricis et Notis Musicis.
Agricola, Johann Friedrich from Tosi: Anleitung zur Singkunst.
Bach, C.P.E.: edited W. Emery: Nekrolog or Obituary Notice of J.S. Bach.
Bateson, Naomi Judith: Alcock of Salisbury
Bathe, William: A Briefe Introduction to the Skill of Song
Bax, Arnold: Symphony #5, Arranged for Piano Four Hands by Walter Emery
Burney, Charles: The Present State of Music in France and Italy
Burney, Charles: The Present State of Music in Germany, The Netherlands ...
Burney, Charles: An Account of the Musical Performances ... Handel
Burney, Karl: Nachricht von Georg Friedrich Handel's Lebensumstanden.
Burns, Robert: The Caledonian Musical Museum ..The Best Scotch Songs. (1810)
Cobbett, W.W.: Cobbett's Cyclopedic Survey of Chamber Music. (2 vols.)
Corrette, Michel: Le Maitre de Clavecin
Crimp, Bryan: Dear Mr. Rosenthal ... Dear Mr. Gaisberg ...
Crimp, Bryan: Solo: The Biography of Solomon
d'Indy, Vincent: Beethoven: Biographie Critique
d'Indy, Vincent: Beethoven: A Critical Biography
d'Indy, Vincent: César Franck (in French)
Fischhof, Joseph: Versuch einer Geschichte des Clavierbaues. (Faksimile 1853).
Frescobaldi, Girolamo: D'Arie Musicali per Cantarsi. Primo & Secondo Libro.
Geminiani, Francesco: The Art of Playing the Violin.
Handel; Purcell; Boyce; Geene et al: Calliope or English Harmony: Volume First.
Häuser: Musikalisches Lexikon. 2 vols in one.
Hawkins, John: A General History of the Science and Practice of Music (5 vols.)
Herbert-Caesari, Edgar: The Science and Sensations of Vocal Tone
Herbert-Caesari, Edgar: Vocal Truth
Hopkins and Rimboult: The Organ. Its History and Construction.
Hunt, John: - see separate list of discographies at the end of these titles
Isaacs, Lewis: Hänsel and Gretel. A Guide to Humperdinck's Opera.
Isaacs, Lewis: Königskinder (Royal Children) A Guide to Humperdinck's Opera.
Kastner: Manuel Général de Musique Militaire
Lacassagne, M. l'Abbé Joseph : Traité Général des élémens du Chant.
Lascelles (née Catley), Anne: The Life of Miss Anne Catley.
Mainwaring, John: Memoirs of the Life of the Late George Frederic Handel
Malcolm, Alexander: A Treaty of Music: Speculative, Practical and Historical
Marx, Adolph Bernhard: Die Kunst des Gesanges, Theoretisch-Practisch
May, Florence: The Life of Brahms
May, Florence: The Girlhood Of Clara Schumann: Clara Wieck And Her Time.
Mellers, Wilfrid: Angels of the Night: Popular Female Singers of Our Time
Mellers, Wilfrid: Bach and the Dance of God
Mellers, Wilfrid: Beethoven and the Voice of God
Mellers, Wilfrid: Caliban Reborn - Renewal in Twentieth Century Music

Music and Books published by Travis & Emery Music Bookshop:

Mellers, Wilfrid: Darker Shade of Pale, A Backdrop to Bob Dylan
Mellers, Wilfrid: François Couperin and the French Classical Tradition
Mellers, Wilfrid: Harmonious Meeting
Mellers, Wilfrid: Le Jardin Retrouvé, The Music of Frederic Mompou
Mellers, Wilfrid: Music and Society, England and the European Tradition
Mellers, Wilfrid: Music in a New Found Land: ... ... American Music
Mellers, Wilfrid: Romanticism and the Twentieth Century (from 1800)
Mellers, Wilfrid: The Masks of Orpheus: ...... the Story of European Music.
Mellers, Wilfrid: The Sonata Principle (from c. 1750)
Mellers, Wilfrid: Vaughan Williams and the Vision of Albion
Panchianio, Cattuffio: Rutzvanscad Il Giovine
Pearce, Charles: Sims Reeves, Fifty Years of Music in England.
Playford, John: An Introduction to the Skill of Musick.
Purcell, Henry et al: Harmonia Sacra ... The First Book, (1726)
Purcell, Henry et al: Harmonia Sacra ... Book II (1726)
Quantz, Johann: Versuch einer Anweisung die Flöte trave   rsiere zu spielen.
Rameau, Jean-Philippe: Code de Musique Pratique, ou Methodes.
Rastall, Richard: The Notation of Western Music.
Rimbault, Edward: The Pianoforte, Its Origins, Progress, and Construction.
Rousseau, Jean Jacques: Dictionnaire de Musique
Rubinstein, Anton : Guide to the proper use of the Pianoforte Pedals.
Sainsbury, John S.: Dictionary of Musicians. (1825). 2 vols.
Serré de Rieux, Jean de : Les dons des Enfans de Latone
Simpson, Christopher: A Compendium of Practical Musick in Five Parts
Spohr, Louis: Autobiography
Spohr, Louis: Grand Violin School
Tans'ur, William: A New Musical Grammar; or The Harmonical Spectator
Terry, Charles Sanford: Bach's Chorals – Parts 1, 2 and 3.
Terry, Charles Sanford: John Christian Bach
Terry, Charles Sanford: J.S. Bach's Original Hymn-Tunes for Congregational Use.
Terry, Charles Sanford: Four-Part Chorals of J.S. Bach. (German & English)
Terry, Charles Sanford: Joh. Seb. Bach, Cantata Texts, Sacred and Secular.
Terry, Charles Sanford: The Origins of the Family of Bach Musicians.
Tosi, Pierfrancesco: Opinioni de' Cantori Antichi, e Moderni
Tosi, Pierfrancesco: Observations on the Florid Song.
Van der Straeten, Edmund: History of the Violoncello, The Viol da Gamba ...
Van der Straeten, Edmund: History of the Violin, Its Ancestors... (2 vols.)
Walther, J. G. [Waltern]: Musicalisches Lexikon [Musikalisches Lexicon]
Zwirn, Gerald: Stranded Stories From The Operas

Travis & Emery Music Bookshop
17 Cecil Court, London, WC2N 4EZ, United Kingdom.
Tel. (+44) 20 7240 2129

© Travis & Emery 2010

Discographies by Travis & Emery:

Discographies by John Hunt.

1987: 978-1-906857-14-1: From Adam to Webern: the Recordings of von Karajan.
1991: 978-0-951026-83-0: 3 Italian Conductors and 7 Viennese Sopranos: 10 Discographies: Arturo Toscanini, Guido Cantelli, Carlo Maria Giulini, Elisabeth Schwarzkopf, Irmgard Seefried, Elisabeth Gruemmer, Sena Jurinac, Hilde Gueden, Lisa Della Casa, Rita Streich.
1992: 978-0-951026-85-4: Mid-Century Conductors and More Viennese Singers: 10 Discographies: Karl Boehm, Victor De Sabata, Hans Knappertsbusch, Tullio Serafin, Clemens Krauss, Anton Dermota, Leonie Rysanek, Eberhard Waechter, Maria Reining, Erich Kunz.
1993: 978-0-951026-87-8: More 20th Century Conductors: 7 Discographies: Eugen Jochum, Ferenc Fricsay, Carl Schuricht, Felix Weingartner, Josef Krips, Otto Klemperer, Erich Kleiber.
1994: 978-0-951026-88-5: Giants of the Keyboard: 6 Discographies: Wilhelm Kempff, Walter Gieseking, Edwin Fischer, Clara Haskil, Wilhelm Backhaus, Artur Schnabel.
1994: 978-0-951026-89-2: Six Wagnerian Sopranos: 6 Discographies: Frieda Leider, Kirsten Flagstad, Astrid Varnay, Martha Moedl, Birgit Nilsson, Gwyneth Jones.
1995: 978-0-952582-70-0: Musical Knights: 6 Discographies: Henry Wood, Thomas Beecham, Adrian Boult, John Barbirolli, Reginald Goodall, Malcolm Sargent.
1995: 978-0-952582-71-7: A Notable Quartet: 4 Discographies: Gundula Janowitz, Christa Ludwig, Nicolai Gedda, Dietrich Fischer-Dieskau.
1996: 978-0-952582-75-5: Leopold Stokowski (1882-1977): Discography and Concert Register
1996: 978-0-952582-76-2: Makers of the Philharmonia: 11 Discographies: Alceo Galliera, Walter Susskind, Paul Kletzki, Nicolai Malko, Issay Dobrowen, Lovro Von Matacic, Efrem Kurtz, Otto Ackermann, Anatole Fistoulari, George Weldon, Robert Irving.
1996: 978-0-952582-72-4: The Post-War German Tradition: 5 Discographies: Rudolf Kempe, Joseph Keilberth, Wolfgang Sawallisch, Rafael Kubelik, Andre Cluytens.
1996: 978-0-952582-73-1: Teachers and Pupils: 7 Discographies: Elisabeth Schwarzkopf, Maria Ivoguen, Maria Cebotari, Meta Seinemeyer, Ljuba Welitsch, Rita Streich, Erna Berger.
1996: 978-0-952582-75-5: Leopold Stokowski: Discography and Concert Listing.
1996: 978-0-952582-76-2: Makers of the Philharmonia: 11 Discographies Alceo Galliera, Walter Susskind, Paul Kletzki, Nicolai Malko, Issay Dobrowen, Lovro Von Matacic, Efrem Kurtz, Otto Ackermann, Anatole Fistoulari, George Weldon, Robert Irving.
1996: 978-0-952582-77-9: Tenors in a Lyric Tradition: 3 Discographies: Peter Anders, Walther Ludwig, Fritz Wunderlich.
1997: 978-0-952582-78-6: The Lyric Baritone: 5 Discographies: Hans Reinmar, Gerhard Huesch, Josef Metternich, Hermann Uhde, Eberhard Waechter.
1997: 978-0-952582-79-3: Hungarians in Exile: 3 Discographies: Fritz Reiner, Antal Dorati, George Szell.
1997: 978-1-901395-00-6: The Art of the Diva: 3 Discographies: Claudia Muzio, Maria Callas, Magda Olivero.
1997: 978-1-901395-01-3: Metropolitan Sopranos: 4 Discographies: Rosa Ponselle, Eleanor Steber, Zinka Milanov, Leontyne Price.
1997: 978-1-901395-02-0: Back From The Shadows: 4 Discographies: Willem Mengelberg, Dimitri Mitropoulos, Hermann Abendroth, Eduard Van Beinum.
1997: 978-1-901395-03-7: More Musical Knights: 4 Discographies: Hamilton Harty, Charles Mackerras, Simon Rattle, John Pritchard.
1998: 978-1-901395-95-2: More Giants of the Keyboard: 5 Discographies: Claudio Arrau, Gyorgy Cziffra, Vladimir Horowitz, Dinu Lipatti, Artur Rubinstein.

Back matter

1998: 978-1-901395-94-5: Conductors On The Yellow Label: 8 Discographies: Fritz Lehmann, Ferdinand Leitner, Ferenc Fricsay, Eugen Jochum, Leopold Ludwig, Artur Rother, Franz Konwitschny, Igor Markevitch.
1998: 978-1-901395-96-9: Mezzo and Contraltos: 5 Discographies: Janet Baker, Margarete Klose, Kathleen Ferrier, Giulietta Simionato, Elisabeth Hoengen.
1999: 978-1-901395-97-6: The Furtwaengler Sound Sixth Edition: Discography and Concert Listing.
1999: 978-1-901395-98-3: The Great Dictators: 3 Discographies: Evgeny Mravinsky, Artur Rodzinski, Sergiu Celibidache.
1999: 978-1-901395-99-0: Sviatoslav Richter: Pianist of the Century: Discography.
2000: 978-1-901395-04-4: Philharmonic Autocrat 1: Discography of: Herbert Von Karajan [Third Edition].
2000: 978-1-901395-05-1: Wiener Philharmoniker 1 - Vienna Philharmonic and Vienna State Opera Orchestras: Discography Part 1 1905-1954.
2000: 978-1-901395-06-8: Wiener Philharmoniker 2 - Vienna Philharmonic and Vienna State Opera Orchestras: Discography Part 2 1954-1989.
2001: 978-1-901395-07-5: Gramophone Stalwarts: 3 Separate Discographies: Bruno Walter, Erich Leinsdorf, Georg Solti.
2001: 978-1-901395-08-2: Singers of the Third Reich: 5 Discographies: Helge Roswaenge, Tiana Lemnitz, Franz Voelker, Maria Mueller, Max Lorenz.
2001: 978-1-901395-09-9: Philharmonic Autocrat 2: Concert Register of Herbert Von Karajan Second Edition.
2002: 978-1-901395-10-5: Sächsische Staatskapelle Dresden: Complete Discography.
2002: 978-1-901395-11-2: Carlo Maria Giulini: Discography and Concert Register.
2002: 978-1-901395-12-9: Pianists For The Connoisseur: 6 Discographies: Arturo Benedetti Michelangeli, Alfred Cortot, Alexis Weissenberg, Clifford Curzon, Solomon, Elly Ney.
2003: 978-1-901395-14-3: Singers on the Yellow Label: 7 Discographies: Maria Stader, Elfriede Troetschel, Annelies Kupper, Wolfgang Windgassen, Ernst Haefliger, Josef Greindl, Kim Borg.
2003: 978-1-901395-15-0: A Gallic Trio: 3 Discographies: Charles Muench, Paul Paray, Pierre Monteux.
2004: 978-1-901395-16-7: Antal Dorati 1906-1988: Discography and Concert Register.
2004: 978-1-901395-17-4: Columbia 33CX Label Discography.
2004: 978-1-901395-18-1: Great Violinists: 3 Discographies: David Oistrakh, Wolfgang Schneiderhan, Arthur Grumiaux.
2006: 978-1-901395-19-8: Leopold Stokowski: Second Edition of the Discography.
2006: 978-1-901395-20-4: Wagner Im Festspielhaus: Discography of the Bayreuth Festival.
2006: 978-1-901395-21-1: Her Master's Voice: Concert Register and Discography of Dame Elisabeth Schwarzkopf [Third Edition].
2007: 978-1-901395-22-8: Hans Knappertsbusch: Kna: Concert Register and Discography of Hans Knappertsbusch, 1888-1965. Second Edition.
2008: 978-1-901395-23-5: Philips Minigroove: Second Extended Version of the European Discography.
2009: 978-1-901395-24-2: American Classics: The Discographies of Leonard Bernstein and Eugene Ormandy.
2010: 978-1-901395-25-9: Dirigenten der DDR: Conductors of the German Democratic Republic

Discography by Stephen J. Pettitt, edited by John Hunt:
1987: 978-1-906857-16-5: Philharmonia Orchestra: Complete Discography 1945-1987

Available from: Travis & Emery at 17 Cecil Court, London, UK.
(+44) 20 7 240 2129. email on sales@travis-and-emery.com .

© Travis & Emery 2010

www.ingramcontent.com/pod-product-compliance
Lightning Source LLC
Chambersburg PA
CBHW071642160426
43195CB00012B/1329